Information Compliance

Information Compliance
Fundamental Concepts and Best Practices

William Saffady

ROWMAN & LITTLEFIELD
Lanham • Boulder • New York • London

Published by Rowman & Littlefield
An imprint of The Rowman & Littlefield Publishing Group, Inc.
4501 Forbes Boulevard, Suite 200, Lanham, Maryland 20706
www.rowman.com

86-90 Paul Street, London EC2A 4NE

British Library Cataloguing in Publication Information Available

Library of Congress Cataloging-in-Publication Data Available

ISBN: 978-1-5381-6766-3 (cloth)
ISBN: 978-1-5381-6767-0 (pbk.)
ISBN: 978-1-5381-6768-7 (electronic)

Contents

Preface

Compliance is one the components of the so-called GRC framework, which integrates three widely discussed elements of organizational strategy, the other two being governance and risk. The GRC abbreviation was introduced in a 2004 white paper by PricewaterhouseCoopers, an international accounting and consulting firm. Titled *Integrity-Driven Performance: A New Strategy for Success through Integrated Governance, Risk, and Compliance Management,* the white paper advocated a business strategy based on integrity, ethics, and values to meet the accountability and transparency demands and expectations of an organization's investors, regulators, customers, employees, and other stakeholders. Since that time, the GRC approach to principled performance has gained increasing attention and acceptance by both business executives and academic researchers. In late 2022, a Google search for the phrase "governance, risk, and compliance" combined with the abbreviation "GRC" retrieved 2.68 million items. The same search in Google Scholar retrieved over 2,460 citations, one-fifth of them published since 2020.

The GRC framework encompasses all aspects of organizational strategy and operations, including those that involve the creation, collection, retention, and use of information by companies, government agencies, and nonprofit entities. Information governance, information risk, and information compliance have closely aligned objectives. Information governance develops strategies, policies, and initiatives to maximize the value of an organization's information assets. Since the early 2000s, information governance has gained increasing recognition as an integral component of organizational governance. Information risk management is responsible for identifying, analyzing, and controlling threats to those assets. The author examined information risk, an important component of enterprise risk management, in a book titled *Managing Information Risks: Threats, Vulnerabilities, and Responses*, which was published by Rowman & Littlefield in 2020. Information compliance seeks to align an organization's information-related policies and practices with applicable legal and nonlegal requirements.

Compliance in general is discussed in many books, journal articles, conference papers, websites, and other sources. In late 2022, a Google Scholar search retrieved over 189,000 publications that include the word "compliance" in the title; but few publications consider compliance requirements that are specific to information, and those that do are generally limited to legal and regulatory mandates. This book takes a broader approach that recognizes the complexity of information compliance. It identifies compliance requirements that are specified in laws, regulations, contracts, standards, industry norms, and an organization's code of conduct and other internal policies. It also considers compliance with social and environmental concerns that are impacted by an organization's information-related policies and practices.

The book is intended for compliance officers, information governance specialists, risk managers, attorneys, records managers, information technology managers, and other decision-makers and analysts who need to understand and comply with legal and nonlegal requirements that apply to an organization's information assets. It can also be used as a textbook by colleges and universities that offer courses in compliance, risk management, information governance, or related topics at the graduate or advanced undergraduate level. In particular, the book may be useful for a curriculum that combines compliance with information governance, information risk, records management, information science, health informatics, and other information-related subjects.

Just as identification of threats and vulnerabilities is a precondition for effective risk management, identification of applicable requirements is critical for ensuring compliance. This book is organized into seven chapters that categorize and provide examples of legal and nonlegal compliance requirements for creation, collection, storage, retention, retrieval, disclosure, protection, and ownership of information:

- Chapter 1 provides an overview of legal and nonlegal aspects of compliance that will be surveyed in detail in subsequent chapters. It also discusses the major components of a compliance management program, the relationship of information compliance to information governance, and the interaction of compliance with information governance stakeholders, including risk management.
- Chapter 2 examines legal, contractual, and other compliance requirements for the creation and collection of data, documents, images, and other information, including restrictions imposed by data protection legislation, industry norms for collection of information for business or research purposes, and legal and ethical prohibitions on creation of misinformation.
- Chapter 3 surveys compliance requirements for retention and disposition of information, including laws, regulations, and contractual obligations that specify how long certain information must be kept. The discussion also encompasses recommended retention practices included in standards and industry norms, as well as ethical issues associated with destruction of information and the environmental impact of long retention periods.
- Chapter 4 discusses compliance requirements for storage and preservation of information, including laws, regulations, and contractual obligations

that specify how and where information must be stored and standards related to long-term usability and permanent preservation of information.

- Chapter 5 reviews laws, regulations, contractual obligations, industry norms, and internal policies that mandate or prohibit access to and disclosure of personal and business information maintained by government agencies, companies, and nonprofit organizations. The chapter also discusses compliance frameworks developed by concerned industry representatives and environmental groups for disclosure of information related to the societal impact of investments.
- Chapter 6 reviews compliance requirements for information security and protection, including laws and regulations related to data breaches, contractual obligations for the protection of information, and standards and organizational mandates that specify security requirements. The discussion also considers the adverse impact of security lapses on the well-being of individuals and society as a whole.
- Chapter 7 reviews compliance requirements related to ownership of information, including intellectual property, personal information, government records, medical records, and client records. The chapter includes a discussion of societal concerns about the relationship between information ownership and the public welfare.

Each chapter includes endnotes that reference legal and nonlegal requirements cited in the text and provide suggestions for further reading about specific matters. Links are provided to the full text of cited publications where available or to a digital object identifier (DOI) or other persistent identifier for the publication. All links were operational at the time the book was written, but the author has no control over the continued accessibility of nonpersistent links.

1

Information Compliance

TERMS AND CONCEPTS

Dictionary definitions equate compliance with adherence and obedience. According to the *Cambridge Dictionary*, for example, *compliance* is "the act of obeying an order, rule, or request." The *Merriam-Webster Dictionary* defines *compliance* as "the act or process of complying to a desire, demand, proposal or regimen." In the *Collins Dictionary*, *compliance* is "the act of conforming, acquiescing, or yielding." For the *Britannica Dictionary*, *compliance* is simply the "the act or process of doing what you have been asked or ordered to do." Adding a legal component, the *Macmillan Dictionary* defines *compliance* as "the practice of obeying a law, rule or request." In defining *compliance* as "the practice of obeying rules or requests made by people in authority," the *Oxford Learner's Dictionaries* suggests that the rule or request comes from a source with power or, at least, influence. Citing examples of usage from the seventeenth century, the *Oxford English Dictionary* (*OED*) defines *compliance* as "consenting to act in conformity with" a "desire, request, condition, direction, etc." Usage examples for *noncompliance*, which the *OED* defines as "failure or refusal to comply," date from the same period.[1]

Compliance is often modified by an adjective that provides context for the order, rule, or request that requires adherence. Some possibilities, each with its own issues and concerns, include taxpayer compliance, which relates to voluntary and timely payment of taxes owed to revenue authorities[2]; business process compliance, which is concerned with alignment of regulatory requirements with an organization's operational policies and procedures[3]; environmental compliance, which relates to conformity with environmental regulations and policies[4]; and therapeutic compliance, which refers to a patient's adherence to a recommended course of medical treatment.[5]

Information compliance seeks to align an organization's information-related policies and practices with applicable compliance requirements. As discussed in subsequent chapters, information compliance is concerned with legal and nonlegal requirements for all aspects of information processing and management: creation and collection of information, retention and disposition of information, storage and preservation of information, access to and disclosure of information, security and protection of information, and ownership of information. This chapter provide an overview of the legal and nonlegal aspects of information compliance. It also discusses compliance programs, organization placement of the compliance function, the relationship between information governance and the compliance function, and the interaction of compliance with other information governance stakeholders in companies, government agencies, and nonprofit organizations.

ASPECTS OF INFORMATION COMPLIANCE

Academic researchers, legal commentators, and management specialists have traditionally viewed compliance as a legal concern, but compliance is a multifaceted concept. While adherence to legal and regulatory requirements is widely acknowledged as a critical component of compliance initiatives, it is not the only one. An organization's information-related policies and practices must be legally compliant, but they must also be compatible with obligations specified in contracts and agreements; required and advisable practices presented in standards and industry norms; rules and requirements associated with an organization's internal control systems, code of conduct, and other internal mandates; and requirements that address societal issues and concerns.

LEGAL AND REGULATORY COMPLIANCE

Legal and regulatory compliance, the most widely publicized of the compliance requirements discussed in this book and the principal concern for many organizations, involves adherence to laws and regulations that apply to an organization's activities and business operations. All countries have laws and government regulations that specify how information can or cannot be acquired, maintained, controlled, and used by its owners and others, but specific compliance requirements vary from country to country. Laws and regulations that include information compliance requirements are numerous, particularly in industrialized countries. In the United States, where businesses have been regulated since the nineteenth century, there have been repeated attempts to minimize regulatory requirements in response to complaints that their burdensome costs outweigh their benefits.[6] Nonetheless, the information-related practices associated with specific business operations and industries remain subject to many federal, state, and local regulations.

Worldwide, at least ten thousand laws and regulations specify compliance requirements for some aspect of information processing. Some of these requirements apply to commonly encountered business operations and activities in all organizations; others are sector-specific, meaning that they apply to specialized operations in particular industries. While a comprehensive global survey of laws and regulations that specify information compliance requirements is beyond the scope of this book, subsequent chapters cite examples in the following categories:

- Laws and regulations that mandate the creation or collection of information that must be submitted to regulatory authorities
- Laws and regulations that prohibit or restrict the creation or collection of information about specific matters or in specific circumstances
- Laws and regulations that specify minimum and maximum retention periods for information related to particular matters
- Laws and regulations that prohibit destruction of information that is relevant for imminent or ongoing litigation, government investigations, or other legal proceedings
- Laws and regulations that specify destruction requirements for confidential or sensitive information
- Laws and regulations that require permanent preservation of government records and, in some countries, the records of companies and nongovernmental organizations
- Laws and regulations that specify file format and media requirements for information storage
- Laws and regulations that specify or restrict the locations or governmental jurisdictions where information can be stored
- Laws and regulations that require the creation of backup copies of certain information
- Laws and regulations that mandate access to information maintained by government agencies and other public bodies
- Laws and regulations that give individuals access to information that government agencies and nongovernmental entities maintain about them
- Laws and regulations that give shareholders the right to access certain nonpublic information about a corporation
- Laws and regulations that mandate proactive disclosure of information in the public interest
- Laws and regulations that prohibit the disclosure of nonpublic personal and business information
- Laws and regulations that require the disclosure of information in response to a court order
- Laws and regulations that prohibit the disclosure of information that a person shares with certain professionals
- Laws and regulations that mandate security measures to protect nonpublic information
- Laws and regulations that criminalize unauthorized access to or use of nonpublic information
- Laws and regulations that require organizations to report unauthorized access to or disclosure of nonpublic information

- Laws and regulations that govern the ownership and exploitation of intellectual property
- Laws and regulations that protect proprietary business information
- Laws and regulations related to ownership of government records
- Laws and regulations related to ownership of medical records

Organizations must comply with legal and regulatory requirements in every political jurisdiction where they create, maintain, or use information. United Nations membership is comprised of 193 sovereign nations, but that number excludes Taiwan, Kosovo, Northern Cyprus, and other entities that are recognized by at least one UN member. It also excludes semi-autonomous dependent territories such as Bermuda, the Cayman Islands, Gibraltar, Guernsey, Hong Kong, the Isle of Man, Jersey, and Macau, which have their own information compliance laws and regulations.

Most countries and all dependent territories are unitary states with a centralized government that issues laws, regulations, ordinances, directives, and other legal instruments that apply to the entire country. The authority of subnational jurisdictions, where they exist, is limited to administrative matters that do not impact information compliance. In federated countries, by contrast, the national government shares power with subnational jurisdictions—such as states, provinces, territories, and localities that are partially autonomous and may pass laws that specify information compliance requirements for matters that come within the scope of their authority. Of the 192 sovereign nations in the world, about two dozen are federated countries. In the United States, certain information compliance requirements are addressed in federal laws and regulations, but others may be specified in the laws and regulations of the fifty states, the District of Columbia, and the five inhabited U.S. dependent territories (Puerto Rico, the U.S. Virgin Islands, Guam, the Northern Mariana Islands, and American Samoa). Information compliance requirements may also be specified in municipal laws and ordinances. In Canada and Australia, information compliance requirements may be specified in federal, state, or territorial laws and regulations. The same is true in India, the most populous federated country.

Determining applicable legal and regulatory requirements in all jurisdictions where an organization creates, maintains, processes, or uses information requires time-consuming and often difficult research. Most national laws and regulations are online through one or more websites, but they are not equally easy to use and the ability to search in a country's official language is often required. In some countries, government-operated web sites provide convenient online access to databases that are comprehensive, up-to-date resources for national laws and regulations. In others, multiple resources of varying completeness, including some operated by nongovernmental organizations, must be consulted to identify applicable compliance requirements; even then, some laws and regulations may be overlooked, and there is no assurance that all amendments, consolidations, and recensions are accounted for. Online coverage of subnational legislation in federated countries is inconsistent. The latest versions of laws and regulations of U.S. and Canadian states, provinces, and territories are readily available in comprehensive online collections, but that is not the case with all of India's states and union provinces.

Identifying applicable laws and regulations can be especially challenging for multinational or transnational organizations. Multinational organizations are headquartered in one country but have branches or subsidiaries in other countries. Transnational organizations have distinct, autonomous operations in multiple countries. While multinational and transnational operations are closely associated with corporations and other businesses, many universities, scientific and medical research organizations, foundations, scholarly and professional associations, cultural institutions, philanthropic organizations, charities, religious groups, and other not-for-profit entities maintain information in multiple countries.

Noncompliance with legal and regulatory compliance requirements exposes an organization to fines, which can be substantial. Some examples are cited in subsequent chapters. Serious violations can lead to criminal prosecution, which may be punishable by imprisonment. Egregious offenses also carry reputational risks. For corporations, limited liability companies, partnerships, and other for-profit entities, widely publicized noncompliance can result in loss of customers and investor confidence.

CONTRACTUAL COMPLIANCE

A contract is an agreement between two parties. In the context of information compliance, the parties are a client organization, which may be a government agency, company, or nonprofit entity, and a contractor, which may be a consultant, accounting firm, cloud computing service, or another provider of information-related services. A contract's terms and conditions specify the parties' rights and obligations. The objective of contractual compliance is to ensure that both parties adhere to a contract's terms and conditions. While oral contracts are honored in some jurisdictions, written contracts are almost invariably used for information-related services.

Most contracts include requirements for information that a contractor creates, maintains, and uses in the course of its work for a client organization. Because contracts are legally binding agreements, contractual compliance is a form of legal compliance, although a contract may encompass requirements that are not specified in statutes and regulations. The following examples of terms and conditions related to a contractor's handling of a client's information will be discussed more fully in subsequent chapters:

- Most contracts require a contractor to comply with all applicable legal and regulatory requirements for creation, collection, retention, and use of the client's information. A contract may include a noninclusive list of laws and regulations that are relevant for the work to be performed.
- Depending on the nature of the work, a contractor's obligations may include nonlegal information compliance requirements, such as adherence to specific international standards or industry norms.
- Contracts and agreements for professional services typically specify the types of information a contractor must collect and the types of reports, manuals, and other written products a contractor must create. A contract may also prohibit collection of information by illegal, unethical, or deceptive means.
- Many contracts and agreements specify requirements for retention and disposition of information that a contractor creates, collects, receives, processes, or maintains in the course of its work.
- Many contracts and agreements specify locations, facility characteristics, formats, and other requirements for storage and preservation of information that a contractor maintains on a client's behalf.
- Contractors are typically required to protect a client's information against unauthorized access and disclosure. Contractor personnel are typically subject to the same data protection and privacy laws, regulations, and restrictions as the client's own employees.
- Many contracts and agreements include clauses that specify a contractor's security and protection obligations for nonpublic personal and business information that the contractor processes and stores for a client.
- Most contracts and agreements include clauses that address ownership issues and property rights for information that a client provides to contractors and that contractors may create or collect in the course of their work for the client.

While legal and regulatory compliance requirements are enforced by government authorities, contractual compliance is determined by the contracting parties. Some contracts require the contractor to monitor and maintain compliance with a contract's terms and conditions. Ultimately, however, the client organization is responsible for evaluating a contractor's performance, investigating suspected deficiencies, and dealing with violations. Typically, the client and contractor will cooperate to address compliance issues and correct violations to ensure the work is performed correctly and its progress is not impeded.

When cooperative measures fail, remedies for noncompliance are usually specified in the contract itself. Possibilities include withholding payments until the deficiency is corrected, refusing payment for work deemed noncompliant, suspending further work on specific tasks until compliance is attained, or—

where these corrective actions do not achieve the desired objective—suspending or terminating the entire contract.[7] Depending on the nature of the violation, a client organization may seek redress for noncompliance through arbitration, mediation, or—when other solutions fail—civil litigation for breach of contract, which can be time-consuming and costly for both the client and the contractor.

STANDARDS AND INDUSTRY NORMS

Broadly defined, a standard establishes requirements and recommended practices for a specific activity, process, system, product, or service. Standards may be proprietary or nonproprietary. Proprietary standards are developed for an organization for its own business processes and operations or to guide the development, production, and use of its own products and services. Some proprietary standards have been so widely adopted by an industry or consumers that they are characterized as de facto standards, but they were not developed by public consensus or with the customer or other end user in mind. This view is reflected in the often-quoted statement by Steve Jobs that Apple built the first Macintosh computer "for ourselves."[8]

Nonproprietary standards, by contrast, are intended for a wider community of producers and users. Nonproprietary standards are developed by government agencies, private organizations, and other standardization groups in many countries. Examples of national standardization organizations include the American National Standards Institute, CSA Group (formerly, the Canadian Standards Association), BSI Group (formerly, the British Standards Institution), Deutsches Institut fur Normung, Association Francaise de Normalisation, Japan Industrial Standards Committee, and Standards Australia. The nonproprietary standards discussed in this book are developed and issued by global standardization organizations—in particular, the International Standardization Organization (ISO) and the International Electrotechnical Commission (IEC). Those global standards are typically compatible with national standards. The following chapters cite standards that include pertinent information compliance requirements. For some topics, like information storage and preservation, a number of standards are cited; for others, few or no standards are applicable.

The standards discussed in this book do not have the force of law. They are only legally binding when compliance is mandated by a law or regulation, which is rare, or when a specific standard is referenced in contractual terms and conditions. Otherwise, compliance is voluntary, and there is no penalty for noncompliance. However, compliance is usually advisable for operational reasons, given that national and international standards are developed by subject matter experts and typically represent a consensus of best practices for information creation, collection, retention, security, access, disclosure, and related matters.[9] In the United States, the National Technology Transfer and Advancement Act directs federal agencies to adopt voluntary consensus standards whenever possible, thereby avoiding the need to develop unique government standards.[10]

Information compliance requirements are also specified in industry norms, which establish rules of proper behavior and ethical conduct for particular professions and business activities. Compliance requirements for collection and use of information have been developed by professional associations that serve a broad range of practitioners, including accountants, financial planners, market and opinion researchers, private investigators, journalists, engineers, and operators of nuclear power plants and commercial record centers. In the United States, bar association rules provide guidance about ownership, retention, and use of an attorney's client records. Professional associations in medicine, psychology, social work, speech pathology, and other health-care fields have played an important role in defining ethical practices for collection, retention, and disclosure of confidential information about patients and clients in full compliance with applicable privacy and data protection legislation. They have also established guidelines for collection, processing, and security of personal information collected for scientific and biomedical research involving human subjects.

INTERNAL MANDATES

Most organizations have a code of conduct or other policy that summarizes its mission, core values, and ethical expectations and presents internal standards and rules that employees and other workforce members are expected to acknowledge and follow. Issued by an organization's highest executive officer and (ideally) reinforced by the exemplary behavior of senior management, a code of conduct is a key component in building an organizational culture of compliance. As defined in ISO 37301:2021, *Compliance Management Systems—Requirements with Guidance for Use*, a culture of compliance means the "values, ethics, beliefs and conduct that exist throughout an organization and interact with the organization's structures and control systems [to] produce behavioral norms that are conducive to compliance." A culture of compliance is achieved when compliance with internal and external rules and requirements is embedded and accorded a high priority at every level of the organization.[11]

Organizational codes of conduct and similar internal policies typically include compliance mandates related to ownership, creation, collection, retention, storage, disclosure, protection, and use of information.[12] These mandates apply to all workforce members, including full- and part-time employees, temporary workers, leased employees, and unpaid interns and volunteers. They may also apply to an organization's consultants and contractors. Examples of information compliance mandates that may be incorporated into codes of conduct or other internal policies include the following:

- Workforce members must comply fully with all applicable laws and regulations in the locations where they are employed.
- Workforce members must avoid creating unnecessary information and limit collection of personal data to the minimum amount needed for legitimate business purposes.

- Workforce members must comply with retention and disposal policies for information in their custody or under their supervisory control.
- Workforce members must store information in approved locations.
- Workforce members must protect information from unauthorized access and disclosure.
- Workforce members must comply with security measures that safeguard the organization's information.
- Workforce members must protect the organization's intellectual property rights, and they must respect the intellectual property rights of others.

Additional examples of internal information compliance mandates will be discussed in subsequent chapters. Depending on the circumstances of the violation, noncompliance with internal mandates may be punishable by an informal warning, a written warning, an adverse performance evaluation, or, for the most serious infractions, demotion or termination of employment.

SOCIETAL COMPLIANCE

In recent years, environmental, social, and governance (ESG) factors have gained increased attention and influence as nonfinancial screening criteria for socially conscious investments.[13] ESG factors have proved especially important to institutional investors, particularly large pension, endowment, and sovereign wealth funds. The Principles for Responsible Investment, which were developed by an international group of institutional investors, emphasize the role of ESG analysis in investment decisions and call for companies to address ESG concerns in their codes of conduct and include ESG disclosures in their annual financial reports.[14] In response to investors' increased ESG awareness, some companies have incorporated ESG goals and metrics into their strategic plans and have implemented policies and practices to responsibly manage the social and environmental impact of their business operations. ESG concerns are not limited to companies. Motivated by their duty to act in the public interest and responding to the demands of citizens and taxpayers, government agencies at all levels have adopted ESG policies and incorporated ESG considerations into their plans and decisions. Academic institutions and nonprofit organizations, which have a long history of social responsibility, have likewise formalized their ESG policies and practices and integrated ESG principles into their investment decisions, in part to address the expectations of donors committed to environmental and social concerns.[15]

Governance aspects of ESG policies and practices are outside the scope of this book, but environmental and social considerations have an impact on all information-related operations and activities. For the most part, these considerations relate to ethical and sustainability issues. Examples, which will be discussed more fully in subsequent chapters, include the following:

- Ethical compliance requirements prohibit the intentional creation or collection of information that is verifiably false, biased, misleading, harmful, or appropriated from others without permission or acknowledgment.
- The creation, retention, and disposal of large quantities of data and documents raises sustainability concerns.
- Retention decisions also raise concerns related to unethical destruction of information.
- The energy required for long-term preservation of databases, digital documents, video recordings, and other electronic information endangers environmental sustainability.
- Failure to protect the confidentiality, integrity, and availability of nonpublic information can adversely affect an individual's well-being and have negative consequences for society as whole.
- Security requirements may be used as a justification to suppress information that is essential to the well-being of a nation's citizens, an organization's employees, a corporation's shareholders, a physician's patients, or others who have a legitimate interest in the information.
- Intellectual property laws protect the work of authors, artists, and inventors but impede the free flow of information to an extent that may harm rather than help society.
- From a moral perspective, individual ownership of personal information is a fundamental human right that is not recognized by intellectual property laws.

COMPLIANCE PROGRAMS

Broadly defined, a compliance program is responsible for ensuring that an organization adheres to applicable compliance requirements. There is general agreement that an effective compliance program provides an indispensable framework for an organizational culture of compliance, but many compliance programs began with a more limited scope. Historically, compliance programs have emphasized adherence to legal and regulatory requirements, especially financial and sector-specific regulations that mandate the periodic submission of reports, financial statements, tax filings, and other documents.[16] In the United States, the Foreign Corrupt Practices Act of 1977, which was passed in response to widespread acknowledgment that hundreds of companies were making illegal payments to foreign officials, raised awareness about corporate corruption, bribery, misuse of assets, fraud, kickbacks, price-fixing, diversion of assets, and other financial misconduct.[17] In the late 1980s, an investigation of defense contractors by the Federal Bureau of Investigation exposed illegal procurement practices and led to the conviction of high-level corporate executives and military officials. Within months, Congress passed the Procurement Integrity Act, which prohibited disclosure or obtaining contractors' bids and related information and imposed post-employment restrictions on government officials.[18]

In response to these scandals, some corporations initiated compliance programs that targeted specific areas of legal risk, such as bribery, fraud, and violations of antitrust law. In 1988, the Insider Trading and Securities Fraud Enforcement Act imposed an affirmative duty on investment advisors and broker-dealers to have written compliance programs.[19] Throughout the 1980s, many U.S. corporations introduced codes of conduct as self-regulatory mechanisms to curb financial malfeasance, although early examples were little more than aspirational statements of corporate values.[20] True corporate compliance programs came to prominence the early 1990s, when the U.S. Sentencing Commission's guidelines for organizations provided an incentive for companies to adopt an effective compliance and ethics program to detect and ultimately eliminate criminal conduct.[21]

Three decades later, fear of criminal liability for financial malfeasance, corruption, misuse of assets, fraud, kickbacks, price-fixing, and other illegal acts by an organization's employees remains a strong motive for implementing and enforcing a corporate compliance program. Apparently, these concerns are justified: A 2020 survey of three thousand employees in thirty-three countries found that one-third of junior employees and board members believe that unethical behavior is tolerated in their companies if the people involved are senior executives or high performers, and one-third of respondents indicated that they would be prepared to act unethically to improve their own remuneration or carrier progression.[22] In the latest edition of its compliance manual, the Society of Corporate Compliance and Ethics (SCCE) references the federal sentencing guidelines and the U.S. Department of Justice's guidance to prosecutors for evaluating corporate compliance programs.[23] Other countries have adopted similar laws, modeled in part on the U.S. sentencing guidelines, that diminish corporate culpability for illegal acts of employs if a compliance program has been implemented.[24] Good Practice Guidance on Internal Controls, Ethics, and Compliance issued by the OECD focuses on corporate programs for preventing and detecting bribery of foreign officials.[25]

Various laws and regulations require organizations to develop, implement, and enforce a compliance program to deter misconduct by an organization's officers, employees, and agents. In health care, for example, mandatory compliance programs are principally intended to detect inappropriate payments and prevent fraud. In the United States, the Affordable Care Act, Sec. 6401, requires health-care providers to establish a compliance program with core elements prescribed by the Department of Health and Human Services as a condition of enrollment in Medicare, Medicaid, or the Children's Health Insurance Program.[26] The Centers for Medicare & Medicaid Services (CMS) requires long-term care facilities to implement and enforce a compliance and ethics program with written policies and high-level oversight to prevent violations of the Social Security Act.[27] According to CMS regulations, states must include compliance program requirements in their medical assistance contracts with managed care organizations,[28] and some state laws include similar requirements. In New York, for example, Medicaid providers must implement a compliance program to detect and correct billing mistakes and fraud.[29]

Among examples of compliance program requirements in other regulated industries, financial institutions supervised by the Federal Deposit Insurance Corporation must develop a program to ensure and monitor compliance with the Bank Secrecy Act.[30] The Financial Industry Regulatory Authority requires broker/dealers to develop, implement, and test an anti-money laundering compliance program.[31] The Federal Reserve System requires banks to develop a program to ensure compliance with prohibitions and restrictions on proprietary trading.[32] Entities regulated by the Federal Housing Finance Agency must establish a program to ensure compliance with applicable laws, rules, and regulations.[33]

The Ethics & Compliance Initiative, a nonprofit membership association and research institution that is concerned with organizational integrity, characterizes compliance programs that focus on alignment of organizational practices with legal and regulatory requirements as meeting a minimum standard.[34] In recent years, some organizations have broadened the scope of their compliance programs to encompass violations of internal codes of conduct, international standards, industry norms, and other nonlegal requirements where noncompliance may result in civil litigation, reputational harm, or other adverse consequences.[35] Even legal and regulatory requirements have broadened from their original focus on financial malfeasance to encompass compliance with privacy, data protection, environmental, and antidiscrimination mandates. These are important considerations for nonprofit entities as well as corporations, although charities and other nonprofit organizations are not free of concerns about financial misconduct.[36] For both businesses and nonprofit entities, a compliance culture can help an organization attract and retain customers, investors, donors, and employees.

PROGRAM COMPONENTS

An organization's compliance program is responsible for encouraging and ensuring compliance with all applicable legal and nonlegal requirements, including industry norms and internal codes of conduct. The program must also enable an organization to identify compliance requirements, prevent noncompliance, detect it as soon as possible when it occurs, and correct it expeditiously to limit negative consequences. Compliance guidelines issued by regulatory agencies and other authorities cite the following program components as essential to accomplish these objectives:[37]

- For corporations and nonprofit entities, compliance is a critical governance issue. It is widely accepted that an organization's governing body has a duty to oversee the behavior of management.[38] An organization's compliance program must be formally authorized by its board of directors or other governing body, but the board's involvement with compliance does not end there. The program's initiatives and effectiveness must be subject to ongoing board review and supervision. The board may establish a compliance committee for the purpose. Alternatively, oversight of the compliance program may be delegated to the board's audit committee, which presumably monitors compliance with financial regulations and investigation of suspected financial misconduct.

- Top management plays an indispensable role in establishing and maintaining an organizational culture of compliance. An effective compliance program requires an explicit commitment, strong support, and visible encouragement from the organization's senior management, which must model proper behavior for subordinates. Middle management must be committed to and accountable for implementation of requirements and policies established by the organization's compliance program and provided with the resources necessary to do so.
- The compliance program must he headed by a senior official with appropriate knowledge and experience, as well as sufficient stature within the organization to enforce compliance requirements. The head of the compliance program must have access to key decision-makers and the authority and autonomy to deal with alleged misconduct at any level of the organization. As discussed in the next section, some organizations have designated a chief compliance officer with enterprise-wide compliance authority. In large organizations, deputy compliance officers may be appointed for individual divisions or departments. The compliance program may also have an advisory committee with membership consisting of key stakeholders. The compliance program must have an appropriately qualified professional and administrative staff and sufficient resources to accomplish its objectives. The program's staff must receive continuing education to maintain their knowledge and skills.
- A compliance program must develop and communicate written policies that clearly explain an organization's standards of behavior for workforce members and other applicable parties, such as board members, contractors, consultants, suppliers, agents, and business partners. Compliance policies must be written in plain language at an appropriate reading level. They must be compatible with applicable laws, regulation, standards, and industry norms, as well as with the organization's own mission statement and code of conduct. In some organizations, the compliance program is also responsible for the confidentiality policy, privacy and data protection policy, conflict of interest policy, policy on gifts and gratuities, and other relevant policies. These policies may be integrated into an all-encompassing compliance manual.
- A compliance program must develop and implement internal controls, methods, and written procedures to detect compliance violations, and

it must provide a trusted and confidential method with appropriate whistleblower protection to encourage workforce members to report suspected noncompliance by their superiors without fear of retaliation. The compliance program must clearly and unequivocally communicate the organization's position about the consequences of misconduct by workforce members and others. Alleged compliance violations must be investigated promptly and thoroughly, and the findings documented in sufficient detail for tracking, follow-up investigation, reporting, and analysis to identify patterns of misconduct. Noncompliance must be corrected and those responsible subjected to appropriate disciplinary action. Procedural fairness and impartiality are necessary to maintain the program's creditability and acceptance of discipline.

- The compliance program must work with human resources and other departments to incorporate compliance awareness and organizational standards of behavior into onboarding sessions for newly hired workforce members, as well as for an organization's consultants, contractors, agents, and business partners. The compliance program must work with human resources to ensure that departing employees are aware of any continuing compliance obligations involving personal data, trade secrets, or other confidential information.
- The compliance program must work with contracting and procurement departments to monitor the business practices and ethical behavior of suppliers, distributors, and other third-party relationships. Autonomous and semi-autonomous subsidiaries and acquired entities must adopt the parent organization's code of conduct and comply with all applicable legal and nonlegal compliance mandates.
- The compliance program must develop and implement an enterprise-wide training plan. Compulsory training must be provided to all stakeholders to enable them to understand the importance of compliance and internalize the organization's legal requirements and compliance policies. Legal and regulatory requirements must be explained at an appropriate level of detail. Training content must be evaluated regularly for relevance and updated as necessary to reflect changes in legal and nonlegal compliance mandates. Training must be repeated at scheduled intervals, typically annually or more frequently if warranted by incidents of noncompliance.
- Existing training curricula for all organizational operations and activities must be modified to include applicable compliance requirements. Training must include a testing component to determine that the content was understood. Department managers must be responsible for ensuring that all workforce members and other eligible parties receive required training and for documenting their participation.
- Training must be tailored to different audiences, depending on their duties and compliance responsibilities. Of particular relevance for topics

discussed in this book, the compliance program must provide training for IT personnel, record custodians, and any other workforce members who are involved in the creation, collection, storage, retention, disclosure, and use of information. Where appropriate, compliance obligations should be included in job descriptions and a compliance appraisal should be included in workforce members' performance reviews.

- An organization's compliance program must be evaluated by periodic audits and inspections performed by an impartial internal or external authority. These evaluations must consider the effectiveness of the program's structure, leadership, staffing, resources, written policies, internal controls, and procedures to detect, investigate, and correct compliance violations. Any deficiencies noted must be addressed promptly.
- The compliance program's training initiatives must be assessed periodically to determine whether they are reaching all stakeholders and whether the training content, delivery method, and participation level are compatible with the program's objectives. As part of the assessment process, workforce members should be surveyed to confirm that compliance training is useful and sufficient.

CHIEF COMPLIANCE OFFICER

Reflecting its historical emphasis on alignment of an organization's practices with applicable laws and regulations, a compliance program may be based in a legal department or, less commonly, a finance or audit unit. With such organizational placements, compliance is one of several functions within a larger department. On the department's organization chart, the employee in charge of the compliance program is one or more levels below a department head and reports directly or indirectly to the organization's general counsel, chief financial officer, or director of internal audit. In some organizations, compliance is integrated into a risk management department that is headed by a chief risk officer. A case can be made for any of these organizational placements. Compliance involves adherence to laws and regulations, for which the general counsel provides the requisite knowledge and experience. Compliance violations often involve fiscal malfeasance, which the chief financial officer is well-positioned to detect and evaluate. The internal audit department investigates misconduct by workforce members. Because noncompliance exposes an organization to significant risk, compliance requirements are an important concern for the chief risk officer.

As their principal shortcoming, none of the organizational placements described above deals with all facets of compliance, and none are charged with building an organizational culture of compliance. Taking an integrated approach, an increasing number of organizations have established separate compliance departments headed by a chief compliance officer (CCO), who has enterprise-wide responsibilities for all legal and nonlegal compliance requirements.[39] The chief compliance officer is a high-level executive and a key member of the organization's top management team, on par with the general counsel, chief financial officer, chief operating officer, and other senior executives. The CCO is responsible for developing, communicating, and operationalizing an organization's compliance policies; detecting, investigating, and correcting compliance violations; planning and implementing training initiatives; and other operations and activities associated with the compliance program components discussed in the preceding section.

A chief compliance officer's responsibilities complement rather than supplement or overlap with those of other members of the senior management team. The CCO must work closely with the general counsel when interpretation of compliance laws is required or when noncompliance leads to civil litigation and criminal prosecution, but the CCO does not provide legal advice or negotiate legal transactions and may not even have legal training. The compliance function is responsible for identifying and evaluating adherence to applicable laws and regulations, but it addresses nonlegal compliance mandates as well. The CCO must work closely with the chief financial officer to ensure compliance with laws and regulations that prohibit fiscal misconduct, but the CCO is not concerned with accounting and other financial operations that do not involve compliance mandates. Similarly, the CCO needs cooperation from the director of internal audit for noncompliance investigations and from the chief risk officer when assessing the possible consequences of compliance violations, but there are many aspects of internal audit and risk management that do not involve compliance.

In most organizations, the chief compliance officer reports to the chief executive officer. To maintain the independence and objectivity of compliance reviews, a CCO may report directly to the organization's board of directors or the board's compliance or audit committee in cases involving suspected misconduct by senior officials. An independent compliance department headed by a high-level executive is prescribed by the Department of Health and Human Services' Office of Inspector General[40] and by the previously cited federal sentencing guidelines. Having its own branch in the top tier of the organization chart raises the status and visibility of the compliance function, and it recognizes compliance as a distinct discipline with its own knowledge base and scope rather than a subsidiary aspect of law, finance, audit, or risk management. According to the Basil Committee on Banking Supervision, which establishes global standards for regulation of banks, a formally established, independent compliance program headed by a senior executive is necessary to ensure the program's effectiveness when working with the management and staff of individual business units.[41]

In some cases, the appointment of an independent chief compliance officer is required by law. In the United States, for example, the Dodd-Frank Wall Street Reform and Consumer Protection Act requires swap dealers and certain swap participants to designate a chief compliance officer who reports to the board of directors or the company's senior officer.[42] Similarly, the Securities and Exchange Commission requires investment advisors to appoint a chief compliance officer.[43] The SEC also views the appointment of "an officer with ownership of corporate compliance and ethics issues" as necessary to satisfy the corporate responsibility mandate specified in Title III of the Sarbanes-Oxley Act.[44] The Federal Energy Regulatory Commission requires public utilities that transmit energy in interstate commerce to appoint a chief compliance officer who will be responsible for compliance with FERC standards of conduct.[45] The Department of Health and Human Services requires a long-term care facility to designate a high-level employee who will be responsible for the facility's compliance and ethics program.[46]

While "chief compliance officer" is a relatively new title, the idea that legal compliance and ethical business practices are high-priority concerns that merit high-level attention has a long history. In the early 1970s, some companies designated a corporate responsibility officer to assuage growing concerns about the societal impact of business operations.[47] An early use of the phrase "corporate compliance officer" characterized the position as "a kind of social responsibility ombudsman" who receives and responds to complaints from employees and the public about unacceptable business policies and practices,[48] unlike the modern CCO, who plays a proactive role in preventing illegal and unethical behavior. While the specific responsibilities of a chief compliance officer vary with the industry and, within a given industry, from one organization to another, the CCO's mission is to prevent misconduct. A CCO does not define compliance requirements; he or she identifies them and assists an organization's workforce members and the organization's contractors, consultants, suppliers, and other external parties in satisfying them. When compliance violations are suspected, the CCO must investigate them and, if necessary, take corrective action to avoid or minimize adverse consequences to the organization and others.

In a multinational organization, a chief compliance officer at the headquarters location may have global authority to define compliance expectations, issue compliance policies, and initiate training programs that apply in all locations. While employee behavior in individual countries is presumably subject to an enterprise-wide code of conduct and ethical requirements, the global CCO must work with the organization's local legal department to identify and interpret national and subnational laws and regulations that include compliance mandates.[49] To support the CCO's global authority, deputy compliance officers may be appointed for each country or region where an organization operates. These local compliance officers, who take direction from the global CCO and also report to country management, handle inquiries from workforce members about compliance requirements, monitor participation in training initiatives, investigate alleged misconduct, and work with the CCO and country management to determine appropriate corrective actions. Alternatively, individual country or regional operations may have autonomous compliance officers who are familiar with national legal and regulatory requirements and are empowered to develop compliance policies, advise workforce members about appropriate behavior, implement and monitor compliance training, and investigate suspected compliance violations.

COMPLIANCE AND INFORMATION GOVERNANCE

As noted in the preface to this book, compliance is part of the GRC framework, which also includes risk and governance. The *Oxford English Dictionary*, citing references that date from the fourteenth century, defines *governance* as the "action or manner of governing," in the sense of directing and controlling with the authority of a superior.[50] As a noun, *governance*, like *compliance*, is often modified by an adjective that indicates the activity being governed or the context in which governance occurs, the most common example being corporate governance. According to the *Report of the Committee on the Financial Aspects of Corporate Governance*—popularly known as the Cadbury Report—corporate governance is the system by which companies are directed and controlled.[51] The concept of corporate governance is not limited to for-profit businesses; it also applies to educational and cultural institutions, scientific and technical research organizations, professional associations, philanthropic foundations, community-based organizations, religious groups, and other nonprofit entities. Reflecting this broad usage, ISO 37000:2021, *Governance of Organizations—Guidance* defines *governance* as the human-based system by which an organization is directed, overseen, and held accountable for achieving its defined purpose.

Information governance is a focused aspect of organizational governance that determines how information-related initiatives will be conducted and aligned with the organization's mission. ISO 24143:2022, *Information and Documentation—Information Governance—Concepts and Principles* defines *information governance* as a strategic, organization-wide framework for governing information assets to achieve business outcomes and manage risks to the organization's operational capabilities and integrity.[52] Effective governance ensures that an organization will act diligently and prudently when making decisions about the acquisition, maintenance, use, and disposition of assets. Information governance enables organizational governance to fulfill its responsibility for stewardship of its highly valued information assets. For many organizations, strategic plans, financial data, product formulations, technical specifications, customer lists, supplier data, trade secrets, and other information contained in databases, documents, and other records are more valuable than equipment, inventory, and physical assets.[53]

Information governance's principal stakeholders are the business functions responsible for information-related operations or information-dependent activities. Compliance is one of those stakeholders. The *G20/OECD Principles of Corporate Governance* cites compliance with legal requirements and ethical principles as an essential characteristic of good corporate governance,[54] and compliance programs play a key role in information governance as well. Other information governance stakeholders include information technology, information security, the legal department, risk management, records management, and archival administration. Information governance has a multidisciplinary perspective that facilitates collaboration and cooperation among these stakeholders to support an organization's information-related initiatives and operations. It encourages dialogue, synergies, and consensus-building to identify potential problems, minimize disagreements, resolve conflicts, and enhance organizational effectiveness. The compliance function must work with other information governance stakeholders to ensure adherence to internal and external mandates related to the disclosure, use, retention, and protection of information.

COMPLIANCE AND INFORMATION TECHNOLOGY

Information technology is the generic name for the business function that develops and maintains an organization's computing and networking infrastructure, including computer and communications hardware, software, and networking components and services. As an information governance stakeholder, the information technology function plays an enabling role. It provides the technological resources, expertise, and support required to process, store, retrieve, and transmit an organization's data, digital documents, images, and other electronic information.

In most organizations, information technology is involved with virtually every business function. It serves all information governance stakeholders and consults with them about decisions, initiatives, business processes, and other matters related to the implementation and use of technological resources. The information technology function operates the servers and software thatprocess an organization's information, and it manages the networking resources that support data transmission. In some organizations, it also arranges and supervises relationships with cloud-based services and other external providers. While new paper documents are still being created and many older paper files remain in storage, the compliance requirements discussed in this book are increasingly satisfied by electronic recordkeeping. This has made information technology an indispensable collaborator for compliance initiatives.

Given the importance of digital information for audits, investigations, and regulatory submissions, information technology's responsibilities have a direct impact on an organization's ability to satisfy compliance mandates. Compliance and information technology must work together to ensure that computing and networking policies, practices, resources, and services are consistent with internal and external requirements. This is the case with technologies and processes for continued accessibility and reliability of digital information, controls to prevent unauthorized access to digital information, processes to identify and delete obsolete digital information, and backup protection and disaster recovery initiatives. In certain industries, such as banking and pharmaceuticals, an organization's information technology operations and capabilities may be subject to inspection by regulatory authorities. In the United States, for example, the Consumer Financial Protection Bureau examines the technology controls of the entities it regulates to confirm compliance with federal laws related to consumer finance.[55] Similarly, the U.S. Food and Drug Administration requires validation of computer systems that store electronic records that are relevant for regulatory submissions.[56]

To address regulatory concerns, information technology policies must be subject to review by the compliance function, and compliance must be consulted about the acquisition or implementation of computing and networking components, operations, or services to avoid noncompliant practices—the use of an out-of-country cloud-based service, for example, to store information that national regulations specify must be retained in the country or to transfer personal information to a country that lacks acceptable data protection. For its part, compliance must consult with information technology when investigating possible violations of internal or external mandates that involve digital information or when assembling information from digital sources for submission to regulatory authorities.

COMPLIANCE AND INFORMATION SECURITY

As defined in ISO/IEC 27000:2018, *Information Technology—Security Techniques—Information Security Management Systems—Overview and Vocabulary, Information Security* is responsible for the "preservation of confidentiality, integrity and availability of information." As discussed in subsequent chapters, many compliance requirements involve protection of information from unauthorized use, disclosure, alteration, or destruction. Data breaches, internal control failures, and other information security lapses expose an organization to risk of regulatory violations, civil litigation, and reputational damage. Depending on the organization, information security responsibilities may be handled by an independent department, possibly headed by a chief information security officer; alternatively, the information security function may be assigned to an information technology or a corporate security department with broad responsibilities for safeguarding personnel and property.[57]

Regardless of organizational placement, information security requirements apply to virtually all business functions. Although it is often discussed in the context of storage, retrieval, and transmission of digital data, document theft and other information security threats predate the computerization of business operations by centuries. With the rise of cybersecurity concerns and the increased demands of data protection legislation,[58] senior management is increasingly aware of the importance of effective information security measures. As a result, the information security function has gained visibility and support as organizations upgrade their security policies and precautionary measures to protect confidential and mission-critical business and personal information.

Information security and the compliance function must work together to align an organization's security policies and practices with internal and external requirements for access to and disclosure of information. Information security must consult with the compliance function when developing policies to prevent security lapses or when investigating data breaches and other events that may violate laws and regulations. Information security must also consult with the compliance function to identify content, such as customer data or protected health information, that requires special security arrangements, for clarification or interpretation of regulatory requirements for secure destruction of obsolete information, and for advice or opinions about equipment, software, and services to protect information that is subject to internal or external compliance mandates.

COMPLIANCE AND THE LEGAL DEPARTMENT

Depending on the organization, the legal department may be known as the legal affairs department, law department, or legal services department. The department head is typically an organization's general counsel or comparably titled high-level official. As an organization's legal advisor and authority, the legal department drafts, reviews, and approves contracts, agreements, and other legal documents; prepares legal filings; deals with labor relations issues and personnel problems; interprets laws and regulations; handles intellectual property matters; initiates and responds to inquiries and complaints with legal implications; and provides legal opinions and advice about organizational strategies and operations.

An organization's legal department interacts with other information governance stakeholders and most business units. Among its many duties, the legal department is responsible for aligning information-related policies, procedures, and practices with legal obligations and requirements, including contractual obligations as well as statutory and regulatory mandates. As discussed in a preceding section, the legal and compliance functions are closely associated, perhaps more so than other information governance stakeholders. Both functions are concerned with adherence to legal and regulatory mandates, but their perspectives differ, and their authority does not overlap. Compliance is a business function, not a branch of legal affairs. The chief compliance officer or other compliance official is responsible for administering an organization's compliance program and preventing compliance violations. Even if the chief compliance officer is an attorney, an organization's legal department is solely empowered to provide official interpretations of legal requirements and advise management about legal aspects of compliance matters.

In some organizations, as previously discussed, the compliance function is based in a legal department, and the head of compliance reports to the general counsel or other chief legal officer. This arrangement, which is encountered in small- and medium-size companies and nonprofit entities, can simplify the coordination of legal and compliance duties and promote a consistent approach to both functions.[59] Where compliance is an independent organizational unit reporting directly to the chief executive officer, as it increasingly is in many large companies, support and cooperation from the legal department is indispensable for effective implementation and enforcement of compliance requirements. The chief compliance officer must consult with the legal department for advice, clarifications, interpretations, and opinions about the legal implications of internal and external mandates that deal with information-related policies, processes, initiatives, and activities. The legal department must also be consulted about inquiries and investigations into possible compliance violations that may lead to civil litigation or criminal prosecution as well as submissions, inquiries, and other interactions with regulatory authorities.

COMPLIANCE AND RISK MANAGEMENT

Risk is a combination of threats, vulnerabilities, and consequences related to a particular event or course of action. Risk is a characteristic of all organizational initiatives, including information-related operations and activities.[60] ISO Guide 73:2009, *Risk Management—Vocabulary* defines *risk management* as "coordinated activities to direct and control an organization with regard to risk." An organization's risk management function is responsible for the identification of threats and vulnerabilities, assessment of their impact, and mitigation of any negative consequences. In some large companies and nonprofit entities, an Enterprise Risk Management (ERM) program provides a coherent, organization-wide approach that treats risk management as a component of organizational governance and business strategy. It assigns risk management authority, defines risk responsibilities, formulates risk management policies, and allocates resources required for the development and implementation of risk management initiatives. Risks associated with specific business processes, operations, and initiatives are evaluated, prioritized, and addressed based on agreed-upon criteria. An ERM program may be headed by a chief risk officer (CRO) who is responsible for coordinating, directing, and monitoring risk management processes.[61] Alternatively, risk management responsibility may be assigned to an organization's general counsel, chief financial officer, or another senior executive.

As it relates to information governance, risk may be associated with internal factors, such as an organization's information-related policies and practices, or external events, such as financial, regulatory, technological, geopolitical, or environmental developments that can affect an organization's information-related objectives or operations. The compliance and risk management functions have closely aligned responsibilities. Compliance is concerned with an organization's adherence to legal and nonlegal mandates. Risk is concerned with the adverse consequences of noncompliance. As discussed in subsequent chapters, compliance violations expose an organization to the risk of fines, penalties, and other disciplinary actions that are costly and disrupt specific business operations.

Noncompliance with legal and regulatory mandates can also lead to increased scrutiny by government authorities and, in extreme cases, criminal prosecution.

Compliance and risk management must work together to prevent this from occurring. Compliance must inform risk management about legal and regulatory developments, clarifications, interpretations, inquiries, or interactions with regulatory authorities that may impact the organization's risk profile. Compliance must consult with risk management when reviewing and monitoring an organization's policies and practices to ensure consistency with internal and external mandates. It must also consult with risk management when investigating possible compliance violations. The compliance function identifies possible violations; risk management assesses their impact.

COMPLIANCE AND RECORDS MANAGEMENT

As defined in ISO 15489-1:2016, *Information and Documentation—Records Management—Part 1: Concepts and Principles*, *records management* is responsible for "the efficient and systematic control . . . of information about business activities and transactions in the form of records." As an information governance stakeholder, records management is responsible for life cycle management of recorded information in electronic and physical formats. It develops policies, rules, and guidelines that specify how long and in what form and location computer data, paper documents, photographs, video recordings, audio recordings, and other information-bearing objects must be kept to satisfy an organization's legal, regulatory, fiscal, and operational requirements.

With its enterprise-wide scope, records management affects and is affected by the responsibilities, interests, and activities of other information governance stakeholders. Compliance and records management must collaborate to align life cycle management policies and retention guidance with legal and nonlegal requirements. Records management must consult with compliance to identify internal requirements and external mandates that affect or may be affected by information life cycle policies and rule, including laws and regulations that specify how long information pertaining to specific matters must be kept, the acceptability of specific storage formats and media, and disaster recovery requirements, as well as in-country retention requirements, limitations on cross-border information transfer, and other restrictions on the locations where information is stored. Compliance must consult with records management when investigating recordkeeping practices that may violate internal or external mandates—a department's failure to comply with the organization's retention schedule or with regulatory requirements for information in its custody, for example. Compliance may also seek records management's help when assembling information for submission to regulatory authorities. When requested by records management, compliance will contact regulatory authorities for opinions about or approval of an organization's recordkeeping practices

COMPLIANCE AND ARCHIVAL ADMINISTRATION

The information governance stakeholders discussed above are principally concerned with information that supports an organization's business initiatives and operations. Archival administration, by contrast, deals with information that is no longer needed for business purposes but that has continuing value for cultural or scholarly research purposes. Such information is termed "archival," a description that reflects both its significance and its age. Archival administration is typically involved with the end stage of the information life cycle. Archival information is often characterized as "historical," but historians are just one group of researchers that utilize archival records. Others include social scientists, political scientists, public policy analysts, urban planners, educators, journalists, economists, literary scholars, filmmakers, and genealogists.

Archival programs are well established in national and local government, where they are often required by law, and in many not-for-profit organizations, including universities, medical centers, professional societies, charities, foundations, religious groups, and cultural institutions. Some for-profit entities have established archives to preserve historical information about their founders, business operations, innovations, brands, products, and services. Archival administration must be informed about compliance requirements that apply to its initiatives and activities. Archival collections may include information that is subject to legal and regulatory compliance mandates. Archival records may contain personally identifiable information, protected health information, or other confidential information. While archival records do not deal with current matters, they are still subject to internal codes of conduct and possibly contractual obligations that protect sensitive information. The compliance function must consult with archival administration to ensure that policies and processes for access to such information are compatible with internal and external mandates.

SUMMARY OF MAJOR POINTS

- Information compliance seeks to align an organization's information-related policies and practices with applicable compliance requirements. Information compliance is concerned with all aspects of information governance and management: creation and collection, retention and disposition, storage and preservation, access and disclosure, security and protection, and ownership of information.
- An organization's information-related policies and practices must comply with applicable laws and regulations, but they must also be compatible with obligations specified in contracts and agreements, required and advisable practices presented in standards and industry norms, rules and requirements associated with an organization's code of conduct, and societal issues and concerns.

- Organizations must comply with legal and regulatory requirements in every political jurisdiction where they create, maintain, or use information. Globally, at least ten thousand laws and regulations specify compliance requirements for some aspect of information processing. Some of these requirements apply to commonly encountered business operations and activities in all organizations; others are sector-specific, meaning they apply to specialized operations in particular industries.
- Most contracts include requirements for information a contractor creates, maintains, and uses in the course of his or her work for a client organization. The objective of contractual compliance is to ensure that both parties adhere to a contract's terms and conditions related to information.
- Standards and industry norms represent a consensus of best practices for information creation, collection, retention, security, access, disclosure, and related activities. Standards are developed by government agencies, private organizations, and standardization bodies in many countries. Industry norms establish rules of proper behavior and ethical conduct for particular professions and business activities.
- Organizational codes of conduct and similar internal policies typically include compliance mandates related to ownership, creation, collection, retention, storage, disclosure, protection, and use of information. These mandates regulate the behavior of employees and other workforce members. They may also apply to an organization's consultants and contractors.
- Environmental and social considerations have an impact on all information-related operations and activities. For the most part, these considerations address ethical and sustainability issues related to the creation, collection, retention, use, and ownership of information.
- An effective compliance program provides an indispensable framework for an organizational culture of compliance. The program must enable an organization to identify compliance requirements, prevent noncompliance, detect it as soon as possible when it occurs, and correct it expeditiously to limit negative consequences. Historically, compliance programs have emphasized adherence legal and regulatory requirement, but some organizations have broadened their programs to encompass nonlegal compliance requirements.
- An increasing number of organizations have established separate compliance departments headed by a chief compliance officer (CCO), a senior executive who is responsible for developing, communicating, and operationalizing an organization's compliance policies; detecting, investigating, and correcting compliance violations; and planning and implementing training initiatives.
- Information governance is a focused aspect of organizational governance that determines how information-related initiatives will be conducted and

aligned with the organization's mission. An organization's compliance program plays a key role in information governance initiatives. The compliance function must work with other information governance stakeholders to ensure adherence to internal and external mandates related to disclosure, use, retention, and protection of information.

NOTES

1. *Cambridge Dictionary*, https://dictionary.cambridge.org/us/dictionary/english/compliance; *Merriam-Webster Dictionary*, https://www.merriam-webster.com/dictionary/compliance; *Collins Dictionary*, https://www.collinsdictionary.com/us/dictionary/english/compliance; *Britannica Dictionary*, https://www.britannica.com/dictionary/compliance; *Macmillan Dictionary*, https://www.macmillandictionary.com/us/dictionary/american/compliance; *Oxford Advanced Learner's Dictionary*, https://www.oxfordlearnersdictionaries.com/us/definition/english/compliance?q=compliance; *OED* Online, https://www.oed.com/view/Entry/37698?redirectedFrom=compliance-eid; *OED* Online, https://www.oed.com/view/Entry/127852?redirectedFrom=noncompliance-eid.
2. E. Marandu et al., "Determinants of tax compliance: a review of factors and conceptualizations," *International Journal of Economics and Finance* 7 (9), 207-18 (2015), https://doi.org/10.5539/ijef.v7n9p207; V. Trivedi et al., "Impact of personal and situational factors on taxpayer compliance: an experimental analysis," *Journal of Business Ethics* 47 (3), 175-97 (2003), https://doi.org/10.1023/A:1026294332606; Y. Rahaya et al., "The role of taxpayer awareness, tax regulation, and understanding in taxpayer compliance," *Journal of Accounting and Taxation* 9 (10), 139-46 (2017), https://doi.org/10.5897/JAT2017.0267.
3. M. Hashmi et al., "Are we done with business process compliance: state of the art and challenges ahead," *Knowledge and Information Systems* 57 (1), 79-133 (2018), https://doi.org/10.1007/s10115-017-1142-1; M. Fellman and A. Zasada, "State-of-the-art of business process compliance approaches—a survey," *EMISA Forum* 36 (2), 45-48 (2016), https://dl.gi.de/bitstream/handle/20.500.12116/36858/EMISA_36_2_6.pdf?sequence=1&isAllowed=y; C. Corea and P. Delfmann, "A taxonomy of business rule organizing approaches in regard to business process compliance," *Enterprise Modelling and Information Systems Architectures* 15 (4), 1-28 (2020), https://doi.org/10.18417/emisa.15.4.
4. H. Gabel and B. Sinclair-Desgagne, "Managerial incentives and environmental compliance," *Journal of Environmental Economics and Management* 24 (3), 229-40 (1993), https://doi.org/10.1006/jeem.1993.1015; J. Wu, "Environmental compliance: the good, the bad, and the super green," *Journal of Environmental Management* 90 (11), 3363-81 (2009), https://doi.org/10.1016/j.jenvman.2009.05.017; V. Bhat, "Does environmental compliance pay?" *Ecotoxicology* 7 (4), 221-25 (1998), https://doi.org/10.1023/A:1008938811813; J. Singh, "Making business sense of environmental compliance," *Sloan Management Review* 41 (3), 91-100 (2000), https://sloanreview.mit.edu/article/making-business-sense-of-environmental-compliance/.
5. M. Linden, "Definition of compliance," *International Journal of Clinical Pharmacology, Therapy, and Toxicology* 19 (2)k 86-90 (1981), https://europepmc.org/article

/med/7216556; M. Nichol et al., "A critical evaluation of the methodology of the literature on mediation compliance," *Annals of Pharmacotherapy* 33 (5), 531–40 (1999), https://doi.org/10.1345/aph.18233; C. De las Cuevas, "Towards a clarification of terminology in medicine taking behavior: compliance, adherence and concordance are related although different terms with different uses," *Current Clinical Pharmacology* 6 (2), 74–77 (2011), https://doi.org/10.2174/157488411796151110; J. Aronson, "Compliance, concordance, adherence," *British Journal of Clinical Pharmacology* 63 (4), 383–84 (2007), https:/doi.org/ 10.1111/j.1365-2125.2007.02893.x; P. Czobor and P. Skilnick, "The secrets of a successful clinical trial: compliance, compliance, and compliance," *Molecular Interventions* 11 (2), 107–10 (2011), https://doi.org/ 10.1124 /mi.11.2.8.

6. See, for example, Jimmy Carter, Executive Order 12044—Improving Government Regulations, https://www.presidency.ucsb.edu/documents /executive-order-12044-improving-government-regulations; Ronald Reagan, 12291—Federal Regulation, https://www.presidency.ucsb.edu/documents /executive-order-12291-federal-regulation; William J. Clinton, Executive Order 12866—Regulatory Planning and Review, https://www.archives.gov/files/federal-register/executive-orders/pdf/12866.pdf; Donald J. Trump, Executive Order 13771—Reducing Regulation and Controlling Regulatory Costs, https://www .federalregister.gov/documents/2017/02/03/2017-02451/reducing-regulation-and-controlling-regulatory-costs.
7. See, for example, 2 CFR 200.339, which specifies remedies for noncompliance by federal government contractors, https://www.law.cornell.edu/cfr/text/2/200.339; also, 45 C.F.R. 75.371, https://www.law.cornell.edu/cfr/text/45/75.371.
8. The statement was made in an interview in the February 1985 issue of *Playboy*; see https://allaboutstevejobs.com/verbatim/interviews/playboy_1985.
9. On the development and importance of international standards, see C. Murphy and J. Yates, *The International Organization for Standardization (ISO): Global Governance through Voluntary Consensus* (London: Routledge, 2009); T. Buthe, "Engineering uncontestedness? The origins and institutional development of the International Electrotechnical Commission (IEC)," *Business and Politics* 12 (3), 1–62 (2010), https:// doi.org/10.2202/1469-3569.1338; T. Buthe and W. Mattli, "International standards and standard-setting bodies," in D. Coen et al., eds., *The Oxford Handbook of Business and Government* (Oxford: Oxford University Press, 2010), 440–71, https://doi. org/10.1093/oxfordhb/9780199214273.003.0020; G. Swann, *OECD Trade Policy Papers No. 97, International Standards and Trade: a Review of the Empirical Literature* (Paris: OECD Publishing, 2010), https://doi.org/10.1787/18166873; W. Mattli and T. Buthe, "Setting international standards: technological rationality or primacy of power?" *World Politics* 56 (1), 1–42 (2003), https://doi.org/10.1353/wp.2004.0006.
10. Public Law 104-113, The National Technology Transfer and Advancement Act of 1995, https://www.govinfo.gov/content/pkg/PLAW-104publ113/pdf/PLAW-104publ113. pdf.
11. Examples of the many publications on the concept of a culture of compliance include D. Jenkinson, "Compliance culture," *Journal of Financial Regulation and Compliance* 4 (1), 41–46 (1996), https://doi.org/10.1108/eb024866; L. Interligi, "Compliance culture: a conceptual framework," *Journal of Management & Organization* 16 (1), 235–49 (2010), https://doi.org/10.5172/jmo.16.2.235; C. Rossi, "Compliance: an over-looked business strategy," *International Journal of Social Economics* 37 (10), 816–31 (2010), http

s://doi.org/10.1108/03068291011070471; I. Andreisova, "Building and maintaining an effective compliance program," *International Journal of Organizational Leadership* 5 (1), 24–39 (2016), https://doi.org/10.33844/ijol.2016.60259; S. Killingsworth, "Modeling the message: communicating compliance through organizational values and culture," *Georgetown Journal of Legal Ethics* 25 (3), 961–87 (2012), https://cclg.rutgers.edu/wp-content/uploads/25GeoJLegalEthics961.pdf; M. DeStefano, "Creating a culture of compliance: why departmentalization may not be the answer," *Hastings Business Journal* 10 (1), 71–179 (2013), https://papers.ssrn.com/sol3/papers.cfm?abstract_id=2391434.

12. A. Sharbatoghlie et al., "Exploring tends in the codes of ethics of the Fortune 100 and Global 100 corporations," *Journal of Management Development* 32 (7), 675–89 (2013), https://doi.org/10.1108/JMD-04-2011-0044; S. Singh, "A comparison of the contents of the codes of ethics of Canada's largest corporations in 1992 and 2003," *Journal of Business Ethics* 64 (1), 17–29 (2006), https://doi.org/10.1007/s10551-005-2408-1; J. Singh et al, "A longitudinal and cross-cultural study of the contents of codes of ethics of Australian, Canadian and Swedish corporations," *Business Ethics: a European Review* 20 (1), 103–19 (2011), https://doi.org/10.1111/j.1467-8608.2010.01612.x; C. Stohl et al., "A new generation of corporate codes of ethics," *Journal of Business Ethics* 90 (4), 607–22 (2009), https://doi.org/10.1007/s10551-009-0064-6; A. Popescu, "In brief: pros and cons of corporate codes of conduct," *Journal of Public Administration, Finance and Law* (9), 125–30 (2016), https://www.jopafl.com/uploads/issue9/PROS_AND_CONS_OF_CORPORATE_CODES_OF_CONDUCT.pdf.
13. Surveys of the large and growing literature on ESG factors in investment decisions include D. Daugaard, "Emerging new themes in environmental, social and governance investing: a systematic literature review," *Accounting & Finance* 60 (2), 1501–30 (2019), https://doi.org/10.1111/acfi.12479; P. Matos, *ESG and Responsible Institutional Investing around the World: A Critical Review* (Charlottesville, VA: CFA Institute Research Foundation, 2020), https://www.cfainstitute.org/en/research/foundation/2020/esg-and-responsible-institutional-investing; L. Widyawati, "A systematic literature review of socially responsible investment and environmental social governance metrics," *Business Strategy and the Environment* 29 (2), 619–37 (2019), https://doi.org/10.1002/bse.2393; M. Camillera, "The market for socially responsible investing: a review of the developments," *Social Responsibility Journal* 17 (3), 412–28 (2021), https://doi.org/10.1108/SRJ-06-2019-0194.
14. For an explanation of the six Principles of Responsible Investment, see https://www.unpri.org/about-us/what-are-the-principles-for-responsible-investment. See also A. Majoch et al., "Sources of stakeholder salience in the responsible investment movement: why do investors sign the Principles for Responsible Investment?" *Journal of Business Ethics* 140 (4), 723–41 (2017), https://doi.org/10.1007/s10551-016-3057-2; J. Gond and V. Piani, "Enabling institutional investors' collective action: the role of the principles for responsible investment initiative," *Business & Society* 52 (1), 64–104 (2012), https://doi.org/10.1177/0007650312460012; G. Capelle-Blancard and S. Monjon, "Trends in the literature on socially responsible investment: looking for the keys under the lamppost," *Business Ethics: a European Review* 21 (3), 239–50 (2012), https://doi.org/10.1111/j.1467-8608.2012.01658.x.

15. S. Gary, "Values and value: university endowments, fiduciary duties, and ESG investing," *Journal of College and University Law* 42 (2), 248-312 (2016), https://www.nacua.org/docs/default-source/jcul-articles/volume-42/42_jcul_247.pdf?sfvrsn=250b66be_10; M. Schanzenbach and R. Sitkoff, "Reconciling fiduciary duty and social conscience: the law and economics of ESG investing by a trustee," *Stanford Law Review* 72 (2), 384-454 (2020), https://review.law.stanford.edu/wp-content/uploads/sites/3/2020/02/Schanzenbach-Sitkoff-72-Stan.-L.-Rev.-381.pdf.
16. See, for example, G. Adams, "What is compliance?" *Journal of Financial Regulation and Compliance* 2 (4), 278-85 (1994), https://doi.org/10.1108/eb024816), which equates compliance with management of regulatory risk.
17. Anti-bribery and Books & Records Provisions of the Foreign Corrupt Practices Act, https://www.justice.gov/sites/default/files/criminal-fraud/legacy/2012/11/14/fcpa-english.pdf. See also M. Koehler, "The Foreign Corrupt Practices Act in the ultimate year of its decade of resurgence," *Indiana Law Review* 43 (2), 398-421 (2010), https://mckinneylaw.iu.edu/ilr/pdf/vol43p389.pdf; M. Diamant et al., "FCPA enforcement against U.S. and non-U.S. companies," *Michigan Business and Entrepreneurial Law Review* 8 (2), 353-79 (2019), https://repository.law.umich.edu/mbelr/vol8/iss2/5; M. Koehler, "The facade of FCPA enforcement," *Georgetown Journal of International Law* 41 (4), 907-1010 (2009), https://papers.ssrn.com/sol3/papers.cfm?abstract_id=1705517.
18. 41 U.S.C. §§ 2101 et seq., https://www.law.cornell.edu/uscode/text/41/subtitle-I/division-B/chapter-21. See P. Lansing and K. Burkard, "Ethics and the defense procurement system," *Journal of Business Ethics* 10 (5), 357-64 (1991), https://doi.org/10.1007/BF00383237; R. Burguet and Y. Che, "Competitive procurement with corruption," *RAND Journal of Economics* 35 (1), 50-68 (2004), https://doi.org/10.2307/1593729; E. Dietrich, "The potential for criminal liability in government: a closer look at the Procurement Integrity Act," *Public Contract Law Journal* 34 (3), 521-38 (2005), https://www.jstor.org/stable/25755328; T. Cox, "Is the Procurement Integrity Act 'important' enough for the mandatory disclosure rule? A case for inclusion," *Public Contract Law Journal* 40 (2), 347-92 (2011), https://www.jstor.org/stable/23057946.
19. Public Law 100-704, https://www.congress.gov/bill/100th-congress/house-bill/5133/text. For a discussion, see M. Steinberg and J. Fletcher, "Compliance programs for insider trading," *SMU Law Review* 47 (5), 1784-835 (1994), https://scholar.smu.edu/cgi/viewcontent.cgi?referer=&httpsredir=1&article=2384&context=smulr.
20. For an historical overview of the development of corporate compliance programs, see E. Soltes, "Evaluating the effectiveness of corporate compliance programs: establishing a model for prosecutors, courts, and firms," *New York University Journal of Law & Business* 14 (3), 966-1011 (2018), https://www.hbs.edu/faculty/Pages/item.aspx?num=55233; D. Hess, "Ethical infrastructures and evidence-based corporate compliance and ethics programs: policy implications from the empirical evidence," *New York University Journal of Law & Business* 12 (2), 318-68 (2016), https://www.nyujlb.org/_files/ugd/716e9c_3df84d0e1846479cab753cc1afe1f31a.pdf. On the development of corporate codes of conduct in the 1980s and 1990s, see M. Baker, "Private codes of corporate conduct: Should the fox guard the henhouse?" *University of Miami*

Inter-American Law Review 24 (3), 399–433 (1993), http://repository.law.miami.edu/umialr/vol24/iss3/2; M. Schwartz, "The nature of the relationship between corporate codes of ethics and behavior," *Journal of Business Ethics* 32 (3), 247–62 (2001), http://www.jstor.org/stable/25074572.
21. United States Sentencing Commission, Organizational Sentencing Guidelines, chapter 8, https://www.ussc.gov/guidelines/2021-guidelines-manual/annotated-2021-chapter-8. See also K. Huff, "The role of corporate compliance programs in determining corporate criminal liability: a suggested approach," *Columbia Law Review* 96 (5), 1252–98 (1996), https://doi.org/10.2307/1123405; O. Ferrell et al., "The federal sentencing guidelines for organizations: a framework for ethical compliance," *Journal of Business Ethics* 17 (4), 353–63 (1998), https://www.jstor.org/stable/25073086; D. Murphy, "The federal sentencing guidelines for organizations: a decade of promoting compliance and ethics," *Iowa Law Review* 87 (3), 698–719 (2002), https://www.ussc.gov/sites/default/files/pdf/training/organizational-guidelines/selected-articles/Murphy1.pdf; J. Arlen, "The failure of the organizational sentencing guidelines," *University of Miami Law Review* 66 (2), 321–62 (2012), https://repository.law.miami.edu/umlr/vol66/iss2/2.
22. EY Global Integrity Report 2020, https://assets.ey.com/content/dam/ey-sites/ey-com/en_gl/topics/assurance/assurance-pdfs/ey-is-this-the-moment-of-truth-for-corporate-integrity.pdf.
23. *The Complete Compliance and Ethics Manual* (Eden Prairie, MN: Society of Corporate Compliance and Ethics, 2022), https://www.corporatecompliance.org/publications/books/complete-compliance-ethics-manual.
24. See, for example, the Italian Decreto Legislativo 231/01, which incentives companies to strengthen their self-regulatory measure to prevent misconduct, https://www.gazzettaufficiale.it/eli/id/2001/06/19/001G0293/sg.
25. Annex II of Recommendation of the Council for Further Combating Bribery of Public Officials in International Business Transactions, https://www.oecd.org/corruption/anti-bribery/OECD-Anti-Bribery-Recommendation-ENG.pdf.
26. Public Law 111-148, https://www.govinfo.gov/content/pkg/PLAW-111publ148/pdf/PLAW-111publ148.pdf.
27. 42 CFR 483.85, https://www.law.cornell.edu/cfr/text/42/483.85.
28. 42 CFR 438.608, https://www.law.cornell.edu/cfr/text/42/438.608.
29. New York State Social Services Law, 363-d, https://codes.findlaw.com/ny/social-services-law/sos-sect-363-d.html.
30. 2 CFR 326.8, https://www.law.cornell.edu/cfr/text/12/326.8.
31. FINRA Rule 3310, https://www.finra.org/rules-guidance/rulebooks/finra-rules/3310.
32. 12 CFR 248.20, https://www.law.cornell.edu/cfr/text/12/248.20.
33. 12 CFR 1239.12, https://www.law.cornell.edu/cfr/text/12/1239.12.
34. *Measuring the Impact of Ethics & Compliance Programs: Global Business Ethics Survey* (Vienna, VA: Ethics & Compliance Initiative, 2018), https://www.ethics.org/document/measuring-the-impact-of-ethics-and-compliance-programs/.
35. J. Weber and D. Wasieleski, "Corporate ethics and compliance programs: a report, analysis and critique," *Journal of Business Ethics* 112 (4), 609–26 (2013), https://doi.org/10.1007/s10551-012-1561-6.

36. See, for example, M. LeClair, "Reported instances of nonprofit corruption: Do donors respond to scandals in the charitable sector?" *Corporate Reputation Review* 22 (1), 39–47 (2019), https://doi.org/10.1057/s41299-018-0056-5; M. LeClair, "Malfeasance in the charitable sector: determinants of 'soft' corruption at nonprofit organizations," *Public Integrity* 21 (1), 54–68 (2019), https://doi.org/10.1080/10999922.2017.1422310; P. Smith et al., "Nonprofit employees' Machiavellian properties," *Financial Accountability & Management* 25 (3), 335–52 (2009), https://doi.org/10.1111/j.1468-0408.2009.00480.x; M. Gallagher and V. Radcliffe, "Internal controls in nonprofit organizations: the case of the American Cancer Society, Ohio Division," *Nonprofit Management and Leadership* 12 (3), 313–25 (2003), https://doi.org/10.1002/nml.12307.
37. See, for example, U.S. Department of Justice, Evaluation of Corporate Compliance Programs, https://www.justice.gov/criminal-fraud/page/file/937501/download; HCCA-OIG Compliance Effectiveness Roundtable, Measuring Compliance Effectiveness—a Resource Guide, https://oig.hhs.gov/documents/toolkits/928/HCCA-OIG-Resource-Guide.pdf; Medicare Advantage and Prescription Drug Compliance Program Effectiveness Self-Assessment Questionnaire, https://www.cms.gov/Medicare/Compliance-and-Audits/Part-C-and-Part-D-Compliance-and-Audits/Downloads/Compliance-Program-Effectiveness-Self-Assessment-Questionnaire.pdf; U.S. Department of Labor, Federal Contract Compliance Manual, https://www.dol.gov/agencies/ofccp/manual/fccm/table-of-contents. Examples of the many publications that discuss the characteristics of effective compliance programs from different perspectives include M. Stucke, "In search of effective ethics & compliance programs," *Journal of Corporate Law* 39 (4), 770–832 (2014), https://cclg.rutgers.edu/wp-content/uploads/39JCorpL769.pdf; R. Walker, "International corporate compliance programmes," *International Journal of Disclosure and Governance* 3 (1), 70–81 (2006), https://doi.org/10.1057/palgrave.jdg.2040066; T. Stober et al., "Design matters: on the impact of compliance program design on corporate ethics," *Business Research* 12 (2), 383–424 (2019), https://doi.org/10.1007/s40685-018-0075-1; L. Andreisova, "Building and maintaining an effective compliance program," *International Journal of Organizational Leadership* 5 (1), 24–39 (2016), https://doi.org/10.33844/ijol.2016.60259; M.Baer, "Governing corporate compliance," *Boston College Law Review* 50 (4), 949-1019 (2009), https://lira.bc.edu/work/ns/551da541-9c8c-4ea3-8142-f9a5a7e0f2b3; D. Webb and S. Molo, "Some practical considerations in developing effective compliance programs: a framework for meeting the requirements of the sentencing guidelines," *Washington University Law Quarterly* 71 (2), 375–96 (1993), https://openscholarship.wustl.edu/law_lawreview/vol71/iss2/7.
38. J. Fanto, "The governing authority's responsibilities in compliance and risk management, as seen in the American Law Institute's Draft Principles of Compliance, Risk Management, and Enforcement," *Temple Law Review* 90 (4), 699–726 (2018), https://www.templelawreview.org/lawreview/assets/uploads/2018/08/Fanto_90-Temp.-L.-Rev.-699.pdf; E. Veasey and R. Holland, "Caremark at the quarter-century watershed: modern-day compliance realities frame corporate directors' duty of good faith oversight, providing new dynamics for respecting Chancellor Allen's 1996 Caremark landmark," *Busi-*

ness Lawyer 76 (1), 2-29 (2020), https://www.gfmlaw.com/sites/default/files/pdfs/NV Caremark Publication in Business Lawyer.PDF.
39. Examples of the many publications on the duties and challenges of an organization's chief compliance officer include D. DeMott, "The crucial but (potentially) precarious position of the chief compliance officer," *Brooklyn Journal of Corporate, Financial, & Commercial Law* 8 (1), 56-79 (2013), https://scholarship.law.duke.edu/faculty_scholarship/3170/; Sobol, "Conversations at the top: the tone of the independent chief compliance officer," *Journal of Investment Compliance* 10 (4), 1-15 (2009), https://doi.org/10.1108/15285810911007336; P. Gnazzo, "The chief ethics and compliance officer: a test of endurance," *Business and Society Review* 116 (4), 533-53 (2011), https://doi.org/10.1111/j.1467-8594.2011.00396.x; L. Trompeter, "Summary narrative of Chief Compliance Officer liability," *American University Business Law Review* 6 (2), 341-54 (2017), http://digitalcommons.wcl.american.edu/aublr/vol6/iss2/3; S. Martin, "Compliance officers: more jobs, more responsibility, more liability," *Notre Dame Journal of Law, Ethics & Public Policy* 29 (1), 170-98 (2015), https://scholarship.law.nd.edu/cgi/viewcontent.cgi?article=1743&context=ndjlepp.
40. Department of Health and Human Services, Office of the Inspector General, Publication of the OIG Compliance Program Guidance for Hospitals, Federal Register, 8987, note 35, https://www.govinfo.gov/content/pkg/FR-1998-02-23/pdf/98-4399.pdf.
41. Basil Committee on Banking Supervision, *Compliance and the Compliance Function in Banks* (Basel: Bank for International Settlements, 2005), https://www.bis.org/publ/bcbs113.pdf.
42. 7 U.S.C. 6s, https://www.law.cornell.edu/uscode/text/7/6s, also 17 C.F.R. 37.1501, https://www.law.cornell.edu/cfr/text/17/37.1501.
43. 17 C.F.R. 275.206-7, https://www.law.cornell.edu/cfr/text/17/275.206(4)-7.
44. Speech by SEC Commissioner: Sarbanes-Oxley and the Idea of "Good" Governance, September 27, 2002, https://www.sec.gov/news/speech/spch586.htm.
45. 18 C.F.R. 358.8, https://www.law.cornell.edu/cfr/text/18/358.8.
46. 42 C.F.R. 483.85, https://www.law.cornell.edu/cfr/text/42/483.85.
47. M. Baer, "Compliance elites," *Fordham Law Review* 88 (5), 1599-630 (2020), https://brooklynworks.brooklaw.edu/faculty/1135/; H. Eilbirt and I. Parket, "The corporate responsibility officer: a new position on the organization chart," *Business Horizons* 16 (1), 45-51 (1973), https://doi.org/10.1016/0007-6813(73)90060-8; H. Eilbirt and I. Parket, "The practice of business: the current status of corporate social responsibility," *Business Horizons* 16 (4), 5-14 (1973), https://doi.org/10.1016/0007-6813(73)90043-8; A. Carroll, "Corporate social responsibility: its managerial impact and implications," *Journal of Business Research* 2 (1), 75-88 (1974), https://doi.org/10.1016/S0148-2963(74)80008-1; S. Holmes, "Adding corporate structure for social responsiveness," *California Management Review* 21 (1), 47-54 (1978), https://doi.org/10.2307/41165294; B. Lowes and C. Pass, "Corporate social objectives," *Managerial Finance* 4 (1), 80-90 (1978), https://doi.org/10.1108/eb013415; A. Acquier et al., "Corporate social responsibility as an organizational and managerial challenge: the forgotten legacy of the corporate social responsiveness movement," *Management* 14 (4), 221-50 (2011), https://www.sco-

pus.com/record/display.uri?eid=2-s2.0-84858419562&origin=inward&txGid=d34a556336c4255f7f5d8bc033229082.

48. H. Manne, "Shareholder social proposals viewed by an opponent," *Stanford Law Review* 24 (3), 481-506 (1972), https://doi.org/10.2307/1227949.
49. On compliance issues in multinational companies, see J. Mean, "The implementation of compliance programmes in multinational organizations," in B. Fryzel and P. Dembinski, eds., *The Role of Large Enterprises in Democracy and Society* (London: Palgrave Macmillan, 2010), 119-37, https://doi.org/10.1057/9780230283138_10; S. Delia and E. Gurgu, "Ethics and integrity in multinational companies," *Review of Comparative Management* 10 (1), 113-20 (2009), https://www.rmci.ase.ro/ro/no10vol1/Vol10_No1_Article10.pdf; C. Basri, "International corporate compliance programs," in C. Campbell and D. Dowling, eds., *International Employment Law: the Multinational Employer and the Global Workforce* (Ardsley, NY: Transnational Publishers 1999), 155-61, https://doi.org/10.1163/9789004480605_017.
50. This is the definition from the second edition of the *OED*, which was published in 1989, https://www.oed.com/oed2/00097297. The third edition, which was initially published in 2015, defines *governance* as "the action or fact of governing" or "the manner in which something is governed or regulated," https://www.oed.com/view/Entry/80307?redirectedFrom=governance-eid.
51. *Report of the Committee on the Financial Aspects of Corporate Governance* (London: Gee and Co., LTD, 1992), https://ecgi.global/sites/default/files//codes/documents/cadbury.pdf. The Committee was chaired by Sir Adrian Cadbury, then-chairman of the well-known confectionary company. See also "The Report of the Cadbury Committee on the Financial Aspects of Corporate Governance: the Code of Best Practice," *Corporate Governance: an International Review* 1 (3), 124-27 (1993), https://doi.org/10.1111/j.1467-8683.1993.tb00025.x; P. Stiles and B. Taylor, "Benchmarking corporate governance: the impact of the Cadbury Code," *Long Range Planning* 26 (5), 61-71 (1993), https://doi.org/10.1016/0024-6301(93)90078-T; A. Belcher, "The Cadbury Code compliance report," *Journal of Financial Regulation and Compliance* 4 (1), 82-89 (1996), https://doi.org/10.1108/eb024869; M. Conyon and C. Mallin, "A review of compliance with Cadbury," *Journal of General Management* 22 (3), 24-37 (1997), https://doi.org/10.1177/030630709702200303; C. Jordan, "Cadbury Twenty Years On," *Villanova Law Review* 58 (1), 1-24 (2013), https://digitalcommons.law.villanova.edu/cgi/viewcontent.cgi?referer=&httpsredir=1&article=3169&context=vlr; E. Dedman, "The Cadbury Committee recommendations on corporate governance—a review of compliance and performance impacts," *International Journal of Management Reviews* 4 (4), 335-52 (2003), https://doi.org/10.1111/1468-2370.00091.
52. Similar definitions are presented in ISO 13972:2022, *Health informatics—Clinical information models—Characteristics, structures and requirements*; ISO/TS 14441:2013, *Health informatics—Security and privacy requirements of HER systems for use in conformity assessment*; ISO/TS 22287:2019, *Health informatics—Workforce roles and capabilities for terminology and terminology services in healthcare (term workforce)*; and ARMA TR 22-2016, *Glossary of Records and Information Management Terms.*
53. Hawley Committee, *Information as an Asset: The Board Agenda—a Consultative Report* (London: KPMG IMPACT Programme, 1995); C. Oppenheim et al., "Studies

on information as an asset I: definitions," *Journal of Information Science* 29, no. 3 (2003), 159-66, https://doi.org/10.1177/016555150302930003; R. Wilson and J. Stenson, "Valuation of information assets on the balance sheet: the recognition and approaches to the valuation of intangible assets," *Business Information Review* 25, no. 3 (2008), 167-82, https://doi.org/10.1177/0266382108095039; S. Ward and D. Carter, "Information as an asset—today's board agenda: the value of rediscovering gold," *Business Information Review* 36, no. 2 (2019), 53-59, https://doi.org/10.1177/0266382119844639. According to the 2018 revision of the Conceptual Framework for Financial Reporting, issued by the International Accounting Standards Board, information is properly considered an asset: It is controlled by the organization that owns it and is capable of producing economic benefits through sale or use, https://www.ifrs.org/issued-standards/list-of-standards/conceptual-framework/.

54. *G20/OECD Principles of Corporate Governance* (Paris: OECD, 2015), https://www.oecd-ilibrary.org/governance/g20-oecd-principles-of-corporate-governance-2015_9789264236882-en.
55. CFPB Examination Procedures, Compliance Management Review—Information Technology, CMR-IT, https://www.consumerfinance.gov/compliance/supervision-examinations/compliance-management-review-information-technology-examination-procedures/.
56. 21 CFR Part 11, https://www.accessdata.fda.gov/scripts/cdrh/cfdocs/cfcfr/CFRSearch.cfm?CFRPart=11.
57. E. Karanja and M. Rosso, "The Chief Information Security Officer: an exploratory study," *Journal of International Technology and Information Management* 26 (2), 23-47 (2017), https://scholarworks.lib.csusb.edu/jitim/vol26/iss2/2; D. Whitten, "The Chief Information Security Officer: an analysis of the skills required for success," *Journal of Computer Information Systems* 48 (3), 15-19 (2008), https://dooi/10.1080/08874417.2008.11646017; S. Solms, "Information security governance—compliance management vs. operational management," *Computers & Security* 24 (6), 443-47, https://doi.org/10.1016/j.cose.2005.07.003; A. Dutta and K. McCrohan, "Management's role in information security in a cyber economy," *California Management Review* 45 (1), 67-87 (2002), https://doi.org/10.2307/41166154; T. Fitzgerald, "Clarifying the roles of information security: 13 questions the CEO, CIO, and CISO must ask each other," *Information Systems Security* 16 (5), 257-63 (2007), https://doi.org/10.1080/10658980701746577.
58. On the relationship of information security and cybersecurity, see R. Solms and J. Niekerk, "From information security to cybersecurity," *Computers & Security* 38 (1), 97-102 (2013), https://doi.org/10.1016/j.cose.2013.04.004; B. Solms and R. Solms, "Cybersecurity and information security—what goes where," *Information and Computer Security* 26 (1), 2-9 (2018), https://doi.org/10.1108/ICS-04-2017-0025.
59. On the relationship between an organization's legal department and compliance function, see J. McNeece, "The ethical conflicts of the hybrid General Counsel and Chief Compliance Officer," *Georgetown Journal of Legal Ethics* 25 (3), 677-94 (2012), https://articleworks.cadmus.com/geolaw/zs000312.

html; J. Pacella, "The regulation of lawyers in compliance," *Washington Law Review* 95 (2), 947-95 (2020), https://digitalcommons.law.uw.edu/wlr/vol95/iss2/11; D. Ruffi, "Attorney-client privilege in corporate administration: a new approach," *Brooklyn Journal of Corporate, Financial & Commercial Law* 9 (2), 640-60 (2015), https://brooklynworks.brooklaw.edu/bjcfcl/vol9/iss2/7.

60. For a more complete discussion, see W. Saffady, *Managing Information Risks: Threats, Vulnerabilities, and Responses* (Lanham, MD: Rowman & Littlefield, 2020).
61. On Enterprise Risk Management and chief risk officers, see B. Nocco and R, Stulz, "Enterprise risk management: theory and practice," *Journal of Applied Corporate Finance* 18, no. 4 (2006), 8-20, https://doi.org/10.1111/j.1745-6622.2006.00106.x; R. Baxter et al., "Enterprise risk management program quality: determinants, value relevance, and the financial crisis," *Contemporary Accounting Research* 30, no. 4 (2013), 1264-95, https://doi.org/10.1111/j.1911-3846.2012.01194.x; R. Hoyt and A. Liebenberg, "The value of enterprise risk management," *Journal of Risk and Insurance* 78, no. 4 (2011), 795-822, https://doi.org/10.1111/j.1539-6975.2011.01413.x; J. Lam and B. Kawamoto, "Emergence of the chief risk officer," *Risk Management* 44, no. 9 (1997), 30-35, https://search.proquest.com/openview/538524217dc9d9e07539341a615b5cbf/1?pq-origsite=gscholar&cbl=47271; T. Aabo et al., "The rise and evolution of the chief risk officer: enterprise risk management at Hydro One," *Journal of Applied Corporate Finance* 17, no. 3 (2005), 62-75, https://doi.org/10.1111/j.1745-6622.2005.00045.x; E. Karanja and M. Rosso, "The chief risk officer: a study of roles and responsibilities," *Risk Management* 19, no. 2 (2017), 103-30, https://link.springer.com/article/10.1057/s41283-017-0014-z; D. Pagach and R. Warr, "The characteristics of firms that hire chief risk officers," *Journal of Risk and Insurance* 78, no. 1 (2011), 185-211, https://doi.org/10.1111/j.1539-6975.2010.01378.x; E. Karanja, "Does the hiring of chief risk officers align with the COSO/ISO enterprise risk management frameworks?" *International Journal of Accounting & Information Management* 25, no. 3 (2017), 274-95, https://doi.org/10.1108/IJAIM-04-2016-0037.

2

Information Creation and Collection

This chapter identifies and discusses compliance requirements for the creation and collection of data, documents, images, or other information by companies, government agencies, and not-for-profit organizations. The most widely publicized compliance requirements are contained in laws and regulations that mandate or prohibit the creation or collection of information related to specific business operations, activities, or functions. An organization may also need to create or collect specific information to comply with contractual obligations. Industry norms and organizational codes of conduct provide guidelines for creation and collection of information in specific situations. The chapter closes with a discussion of ethical and environmental considerations that relate to the creation and collection of information.

LEGAL AND REGULATORY COMPLIANCE

All countries have laws and regulations that mandate the creation or collection of certain information about business operations and activities that are subject to government oversight. These legal and regulatory compliance requirements support the preparation of reports or data compilations that regulated entities must submit to government agencies. They also ensure that government authorities will have the information needed for inspections, audits, investigations, and policymaking related to regulated operations and activities. A smaller but no less important group of laws and regulations prohibits or restricts the creation or collection of information about specific matters or in specific circumstances.

Some laws and regulations that require or prohibit the creation or collection of information apply to all organizations that have offices, factories, retail outlets, laboratories, or other business operations in a given country, state, province, dependent territory, or other political jurisdiction. Others are limited to the creation and collection of information associated with specific industries, organizations, or activities.

Laws and regulations that mandate or limit the creation or collection of information are more numerous than those related to other compliance requirements discussed in this chapter. Failure to comply exposes an organization to fines or other penalties, but in the absence of an authoritative global compilation or even a comprehensive reference source for a single country, it can be difficult for compliance officers and other stakeholders to identify all applicable regulatory requirements. This is particularly the case with organizations that operate in multiple political jurisdictions.

The legal and regulatory mandates discussed in this chapter are sometimes described as *data collection* requirements, but they are not limited to computer-processible data. Depending on the circumstances, they may apply to paper records, databases, digital documents, images, audio content, or other types of information. Until the late twentieth century, laws and regulations typically assumed that information would be created or collected in paper form, and that is still the case in some countries. In the United States and other industrialized nations, however, most regulations are now media neutral. If a specific format is required, it is more likely to be electronic than paper. Among the many examples that might be cited, the U.S. Department of Health and Human Services requires hospitals to collect information about their standard charges in machine-readable form and publish it online.[1] Similarly, the U.S. Office of the Comptroller of the Currency requires banks that are subject to the Community Reinvestment Act to collect and maintain loan information in machine-readable form, although exceptions are made for small banks.[2] Regulatory agencies in the United States, Canada, Australia, and some other countries require pharmaceutical companies to file new drug applications, amendments, reports, and other submissions electronically in a prescribed format.[3] National and subnational regulations increasingly require electronic submission of tax filings.[4]

The following discussion is limited to laws and regulations that compel organizations to create or collect certain information. It does not include voluntary collection of information requested by government agencies, but that exclusion does not denigrate the importance of data that is collected and submitted voluntarily. As an example, the Mortality in Correctional Institutions program operated by the U.S. Bureau of Justice Statistics collects information about the deaths of inmates in state prisons and local jails. Participation is currently voluntary. Collection about deaths of incarcerated persons was previously mandatory under the Deaths in Custody Reporting Act of 2000, which expired in 2006.[5]

GENERAL REQUIREMENTS

All countries have laws or regulations that specify requirements for the creation or collection of information associated with commonly encountered business functions, operations, and activities. Examples that apply to a broad range of organizations include the following:

- Most countries have accounting laws, commercial codes, or other laws and regulations that require the creation of accounting ledgers, journals, and registers as well as lists of assets and liabilities, income and expense statements, fiscal audit reports, inventory lists, and other records that accurately represent an organization's financial position and tax obligations. These laws and regulations generally apply to for-profit companies and other taxpaying entities, but some countries have similar compliance requirements for nonprofit organizations.[6]
- Most countries have laws and regulations that require companies and other organizations engaged in international trade to create and collect information related to import and export of merchandise to and from their customs territories. The required information may be included in import and export authorizations, invoices, cargo manifests, bills of lading, packing lists, customs certificates, transport documents, customs declarations, customs clearances, or other customs documentation.[7]
- Many countries have business laws and regulations that require registered corporations and limited liability companies to create minutes of meetings of their governing bodies and committees thereof. In the United States, compliance requirements for meeting minutes are covered by state laws. In Delaware, a state in which many businesses choose to incorporate, one of the officers of a corporation "shall have the duty to record the proceedings of the meetings of the stockholders and directors in a book to be kept for that purpose."[8] In Canada, corporate minutes are required by both federal and provincial laws.[9] In Australia and New Zealand, minutes must record proceedings and resolutions of company meetings and director's meetings.[10] In some jurisdictions, the information to be collected includes supplementary materials that are distributed in advance of a meeting and incorporated into the minutes by reference.
- Many countries have laws and regulations that require corporations to create and collect information about their shareholders. The information, which is usually obtained from the shareholders themselves and recorded in lists or registers, must identify individual shareholders and indicate the extent of their ownership. In the United States, these information creation and collection requirements are contained in state laws and regulations. Many states have adopted the Model Business Corporation Act (MBCA), which requires corporations to maintain a record of their current shareholders in alphabetical order by class of shares showing the address of and the number and class or series of shares held by each shareholder.[11] In some jurisdictions, the information must include a shareholder's occupation and the price paid for shares. The Canada Business Corporations Act contains similar requirements for collection of shareholder information and creation of shareholder lists, as do the Companies Act 2006 in the United Kingdom, the Swiss Code of Obligations, and the comparable legislation of other

countries.[12] Similar requirements for information creation and collection apply to owners of limited liability companies.

- Most countries have labor codes or other employment laws and regulations that require companies, government agencies, and not-for-profit organizations to collect information from or about their employees. Typical examples of such information include the employee's name, address, date of birth, gender, citizenship, job title or description of duties, educational level, qualifications or certifications, hours worked, work location, leave taken, remuneration and wages paid, starting date, and termination date. In some countries, organizations must also collect information about an employee's marital status, children, and, for minors, the name and address of the parent or legal guardian. Depending on the jurisdiction, employers may be required to compile this information in one or more registers, logs, or ledgers.[13]
- Many countries and subnational jurisdictions have laws and regulations that require companies, government agencies, and not-for-profit organizations to create, collect, and report information about occupational health and safety incidents. Employers must create investigative reports and statistical compilations about workplace injuries and illnesses that have occurred within a specified time frame.[14] Certain types of incidents—workplace deaths, for example—must be reported immediately or within a short time after occurrence. In the United States, work-related deaths must be reported to the Occupational Safety and Health Administration within eight hours; injuries resulting in hospitalization, amputation, or the loss of an eye must be reported within twenty-four hours.[15] In Canada, employers must report serious workplace injuries to the provincial workers' compensation board as soon as possible.[16]
- Many countries have laws and regulations that require companies, government agencies, and not-for-profit organizations to collect information about inspection and maintenance of elevators, heating, air-conditioning, fire alarms, and industrial equipment in factories, offices, places of public assembly, construction sites, and other locations. Laws and regulations also require organizations to collect information about hazardous substances in the workplace and possible exposures to such substances.[17]

The information creation and collection requirements summarized above are so broadly applicable that no organization is entirely exempt, but compliance rarely imposes burdensome obligations. For the most part, compliance requirements correspond to administrative operations that an organization would need to perform in the absence of legal and regulatory mandates. Companies, government agencies, and not-for-profit organizations need reliable accounting information to support decision-making, budget preparation, and day-to-day completion of financial transactions and tasks. Corporations need to keep a written record of topics discussed and decisions made at meetings. Organizations involved in international trade must create and collect customs information for their own purposes. Corporations need accurate information about their shareholders and a record of decisions and actions taken at meetings of their governing bodies. Responsible organizations inspect their industrial equipment regularly to minimize downtime that has an adverse impact on productivity and revenue. Most organizations investigate the causes and consequences of workplace accidents to determine their legal liability and to prevent future occurrences.

SECTOR-SPECIFIC REQUIREMENTS

Thousands of sector-specific laws and regulations require the creation or collection of information by companies and other organizations in specific economic sectors or industries that are subject to government oversight. The following examples indicate the wide variety of industries and business operations that are subject to sector-specific regulatory requirements in the United States and elsewhere:

- Collection of customer information is a key component of anti-money laundering (AML) recommendations issued by the Financial Action Task Force (FATF), an intergovernmental body that develops and promotes policies to protect the global financial system. The FATF has thirty-seven member countries. Its recommendations are embodied in national laws and regulations that require banks, savings associations, credit unions, broker-dealers, and other providers of financial and investment services to collect sufficient information to establish a customer's true identity with reasonable certainty at the time an account is opened. These compliance requirements are collectively described as Know Your Customer (KYC) rules. Subject to national variations, the information to be collected includes the customer's name, date of birth, address, a taxpayer identification number or other numeric identifier, and the type, identifying number, and other descriptions of the documents that were examined to verify a customer's identity. Similar due diligence regulations apply to customer information collected by stockbrokers and investment advisors.[18]
- In the United States, banks, savings associations, credit unions, and other mortgage lenders subject to the Home Mortgage Disclosure Act must collect certain information about each loan that they originate, including the location and value of the property, the loan's terms and conditions, and the age, gender, race, ethnicity, and annual income of the applicant or borrower.[19] Regulatory authorities in other countries have similar requirements. In Canada, for example, banks and other deposit-taking institutions must report information about their mortgage lending activity to the Office of the Superintendent of Financial Institutions. In Australia, deposit-taking institutions must make similar reports to the Australian Prudential Regulation Authority.

- Unlike many other developed countries, the United States does not have a national accounting law, but federal and state level regulations specify requirements for creation and collection of accounting information in certain industries, including banks, credit unions, insurance companies, public utilities, railroads, motor carriers, air carriers, and educational institutions that receive federal student aid.[20]
- Companies that develop, manufacture, and market medicines and medical devices must collect certain information about the safety of drugs and medical devices during product development and clinical testing. Collection requirements in countries that regulate the pharmaceutical industry encompass information about serious adverse events, unscheduled hospitalizations, nonserious adverse events for which sufficient safety data was not previously collected, and nonserious adverse events that lead to dosage modifications, drug discontinuation, or withdrawal from a clinical trial. To satisfy pharmacovigilance regulations after a drug or medical device is approved for use, safety data may be collected from physicians or from hospitalized patients.[21]
- In the United States, health-care credentialing laws and regulations specify the types of information that hospitals must collect to assess and verify the qualifications of their medical staff. Some states have adopted the Health Care Professional Credentialing Verification Model Law issued by the National Association of Insurance Commissioners. Other states have developed their own laws with similar provisions. Examples of information to be collected include education and postgraduate training, licensing history, board certifications, professional practice history, and malpractice history.[22] Other countries have similar regulatory requirements.
- Environmental regulations include information collection requirements related to testing and measurement of pollutants. In the United States, industrial, municipal, and other facilities that are licensed to discharge pollutants into water must collect information about the date, time, location, and amount of discharge activity as specified in regulations for the Clean Water Act. Similarly, facilities subject to the Clean Air Act must collect information about the date, time, duration, and magnitude of emissions in excess of applicable limits. Operators of certain facilities must also collect data about greenhouse gas emissions.[23] Under the Canadian Environmental Protection Act, the minister of the environment can mandate collection of information about water or air pollutants for purposes of assessing whether and how to control a substance.[24]
- Many countries have safety regulations that restrict the working hours of commercial drivers. In the United States, trucks, buses, and other vehicles operated by commercial motor carriers must be equipped with electronic logging devices that automatically collect information about a driver's hours of service. According to EU regulations, commercial vehicles that

transport passengers or goods must have similar devices that collect information about drivers' working hours.[25]

- In the United States, air carriers, motor carriers, railroads, and other industries that are subject to transportation regulations must collect information about drug and alcohol testing of employees with safety-sensitive duties. Such information collection requirements are less common in other countries.[26]
- Under the Animal Welfare Act, U.S. research facilities that uses live animals in tests or experiments must collect the name, address, and other information about the person from whom a dog or cat was acquired as well as descriptive information about the animal, including the species, breed, type, sex, date of birth or approximate age, color, and distinctive markings.[27] In Canada, research facilities in Ontario must collect similar information about every dog or cat subject to the Animals for Research Act.[28] Some other countries have similar regulations. Research facilities in EU member states must create an individual history file with relevant reproductive, veterinary, and social information for each dog, cat, or non-human primate.[29]
- In the United States, organizations must collect information about noise levels in workplaces where employees are subject to sound exceeding a specified minimum level. EU regulations similarly require employers to collect information about the level, type, and duration of exposure to noise.[30]
- In the United States, recipients of federal funds must collect certain information to confirm compliance with civil rights laws and regulations. As an example, state, local, tribal, and territorial governments that receive assistance from the Federal Emergency Management Agency must collect data about the populations they serve, including the geographic distribution of individuals by age, disability status, race, color, and national origin. Similarly, public school districts and other educational entities that receive federal funding have a legal obligation to collect certain data about students, including enrollment and educational programs and services disaggregated by ethnicity, gender, English proficiency, and disability.[31]

These sector-specific information collection requirements pose significant compliance challenges. In some industries, laws and regulations are so numerous that they can be difficult to comprehensively identify. Some provisions can be difficult to interpret. Unlike the general requirements discussed in the preceding section, sector-specific regulations are widely criticized for imposing burdensome recordkeeping operations that an organization would not otherwise perform and that increase the complexity and cost of doing business.[32] In particular, some sector-specific laws and regulations mandate the collection of large quantities of information about transactions, events, data subjects, and other matters at a high degree of granularity that is unrelated to, and possibly at odds with, an organization's business objectives.

DATA PROTECTION AND PRIVACY LAWS

More than 120 countries and dependent territories have data protection and privacy laws and regulations that restrict or prohibit the collection of personal information about an organization's customers, clients, employees, suppliers, and other data subjects. These laws and regulations define personal information to include any information that can be used to distinguish or trace an individual's identity, either by itself or in combination with other information. Names and unique numeric identifiers are obvious examples of information that directly identifies a data subject. Other possibilities include an individual's mailing address, email address, telephone number, date of birth, job title, distinctive physical characteristics, and information about personally owned property, such as vehicle registration numbers.

The most widely publicized example of data protection and privacy legislation is the General Data Protection Regulation (GDPR), which applies to all member states of the European Union.[33] The GDPR limits the collection of personal information about EU citizens regardless of their place of residence, EU residents who are not EU citizens, and visitors to the EU to the extent that they obtain products or services that are provided in the EU. Many countries outside the European Union have adopted data protection and privacy laws and regulations that are based on the GDPR's predecessor, Directive 95/46/EC of the European Parliament. Some countries have recently revised such legislation to align it more closely with the GDPR.[34]

National data protection and privacy requirements are based on the principles of informed consent and data minimization. These principles prohibit indiscriminate or excessive collection of personal information:

- Data subjects must be informed about the purpose for which their personal information is being collected and explicitly agree to the collection process. Information collection must be transparent, but the principle of informed consent has limits. It does not allow a data subject to withhold information that is needed for a valid purpose, such as national security, public safety, or enforcement of a civil claim.
- Collection of personal information must be limited to the minimum amount necessary for specific, explicit, and legitimate purposes. This data minimization principle applies to personal information that is collected directly from a data subject or obtained from other sources. Further restrictions may apply to specific types of personal information. The GDPR, for example, prohibits the collection of information about an individual's racial or ethnic origin, political opinions, religious or philosophical beliefs, health, sex life, sexual orientation, or trade union membership unless the data subject gives explicit consent to such collection or the information is

necessary for legal or medical reasons, to protect the vital interests of the data subject, or the public interest. The same restrictions apply to genetic data and biometric data that uniquely identifies an individual.[35]

Even countries without comprehensive data protection and privacy legislation prohibit the collection of personal information in some circumstances. In some countries, labor laws and regulations prohibit excessive collection of personal information about employees, including information about their political or religious affiliations. The ILO Code of Practice on Protection of Workers' Personal Data, issued by the International Labour Office, prohibits collection of personal data concerning an employee's sex life, medical history, criminal convictions, or political or religious beliefs unless it is directly relevant for an employment decision and in conformity with national legislation.[36] While it does not have the force of law, the ILO Code is intended for inclusion in collective agreements, work rules, and employment policies at the enterprise level.

In the United States, which does not have comprehensive data protection or privacy laws, limited collection of personal information is one of the Fair Information Practice Principles (FIPPS) adopted by federal government agencies. According to those principles, personal information collected by federal agencies must be relevant and necessary for a legally authorized purpose. The Fair Information Practice Principles were initially proposed by a federal advisory committee in 1973 as the Code of Fair Information Practice, which formed the basis for the Privacy Act of 1974, which will be discussed in a subsequent chapter. The principles were subsequently expanded for inclusion in the *OECD Guidelines on the Protection of Privacy and Transborder Flows of Personal Data*, which were issued by the Organization for Economic Cooperation and Development in 1980.[37] In keeping with FIPPS, the USA FREEDOM Act, the successor to the USA PATRIOT Act, limited the National Security Agency's authority to collect information about private telephone calls, a practice that was revealed in 2013 by Edward J. Snowden, a former intelligence contractor.[38]

Some federal laws restrict the collection of personal information by nongovernmental entities. The Children's Online Privacy Protection Act (COPPA), for example, requires operators of commercial websites and online services to obtain verifiable parental consent before collecting personal information from a child under the age of thirteen. Financial institutions subject to the Financial Services Modernization Act of 1999 must comply with the Financial Privacy Rule, which requires periodic notification about the categories of nonpublic personal information collected from customers. Among state laws, the California Consumer Privacy Act of 2018 requires certain businesses to inform consumers about the categories of personal information to be collected from them and prohibits the collection of additional categories unless the consumer is notified. Other states have laws that limit the collection of personal information in specific situations.

Organizations must comply with data protection and privacy laws and regulations in all political jurisdictions where they create or collect personal information. Initially, this required modification of some organizations' information collection practices, but data protection compliance requirements are now well established, reasonably well understood, and widely incorporated into organizational policies. Most data protection and privacy laws regulate the collection of personal information within a single country and, in some cases, its dependent territories. The GDPR is a notable exception. It applies to organizations that are established within an EU member state, whether or not the actual collection of personal information occurs in the European Union. It also applies to organizations established elsewhere that provide goods and services to EU data subjects.

This broad territorial scope has made the GDPR a *de facto* global privacy standard that poses significant compliance challenges.[39] Multinational and transnational organizations established outside of the European Union have modified their information collection procedures to comply with informed consent requirements and reduce the amount of personal information they collect to comply with the data minimization principles. As a particular concern, the GDPR's data minimization requirements are incompatible with "big data" initiatives, which create and analyze large datasets that may contain personal information about EU citizens or residents.[40]

SURVEILLANCE LAWS

Broadly defined, surveillance involves visual or audio observation of people or property. Depending on the circumstances, surveillance may collect information about an organization's customers, employees, visitors, or other data subjects. Surveillance may also collect information about accidents, criminal activity, violations of organizational policies, or other exceptional occurrences. The following discussion is limited to surveillance operations that use visual or audio recording to create or collect information. Real-time video or audio surveillance without recording is omitted because no information is created or collected by such activities.

In many countries, surveillance devices are widely installed in parks, streets, airports, bus stations, office building lobbies, and other publicly accessible locations. Because these devices capture images, voices, and other personally identifiable information indiscriminately and without the explicit consent of data subjects, they raise significant privacy concerns. Laws that restrict the collection of information by photographic, video, audio, or other surveillance technologies address these concerns, although the restrictions they impose are not necessarily limited to collection of personal information.[41]

Compared to other information creation and collection requirements discussed in this chapter, visual and audio surveillance laws pose fewer compliance challenges:

- Most countries permit nonconsensual photographic or video surveillance in situations where there is no reasonable expectation of privacy. The resulting data protection and privacy concerns are addressed by limiting the amount of time that surveillance recordings are retained rather than by prohibiting surveillance outright. In the United States, for example, collection of information via photographic or video surveillance is permitted unless it constitutes a warrantless search, which is generally prohibited by the Fourth Amendment to the Constitution. This principle applies to surveillance of people and property, including aerial surveillance via drones or other aircraft.[42]
- In some countries, nonconsensual photographic or video surveillance is expressly prohibited in public or private spaces, including offices or other work areas, unless public notice is conspicuously posted on the premises or the presence of photographic or video surveillance devices is immediately obvious. Otherwise, all persons subject to surveillance must be notified and their explicit consent must be obtained. Even then, photographic or video surveillance is typically prohibited in publicly accessible spaces, such as bathrooms or changing rooms, where privacy is customary. In the United Kingdom where video surveillance is pervasive in public spaces, a Code of Practice issued by the Home Office presents guiding principles and defines acceptable surveillance operations.[43]
- Many countries restrict audio recording of telephone calls or other private communications. In the United States, most states require the consent of at least one participant and some require all parties to agree to recording. Some states permit the use of eavesdropping devices for business or security purposes on an organization's own property provided that notice is given to the public.[44] In Canada, the criminal code requires the consent of one party for audio recording of private communications but eavesdropping by nonparticipants is prohibited.[45] In EU member states, the principles outlined article 6 of the GDPR requires consent of a data subject for audio recording, subject to some exceptions.
- Information collection via other surveillance technologies and methodologies is lightly regulated. In the United States, the Computer Fraud and Abuse Act prohibits unauthorized access to someone's computer to collect information, but workplace surveillance of employees' computer use without notification or consent is commonplace and generally legal.[46] Some other countries restrict monitoring of employees' use of computer applications, email system, internet connection, and other computing facilities. Unless an employer prohibits nonbusiness use of such facilities, national data protection laws may prohibit unauthorized access to personal information that an email message or other computer data may contain. Finnish law, for example, specifies limited circumstances in which an employer can open an employee's email.[47] The same prohibition applies to surveillance of an

employee's telephone calls where personal use of workplace telephones is permitted. Some countries also limit surveillance of employee's access to social media accounts, shopping websites, or other nonbusiness content during working hours.[48]

- Laws and regulations do not prohibit the use of GPS devices to collect information about the locations of company vehicles when used by employees who are away from the office during business hours. An employer's business interest in protecting its property generally outweighs any privacy concerns raised by GPS tracking.[49]

MISINFORMATION LAWS

Misinformation is false or misleading content that is communicated to others. Misinformation may be spoken, incorporated into business documents or data, included in publications or web pages, or posted on social media sites. Depending on the circumstances, misinformation may be attributable to misunderstanding or misinterpretation of facts, lack of knowledge, poor judgment, gullibility, inadequate research, unreliable sources, or other factors. In addition to false statements, misinformation may include unjustified assumptions, inadequately documented or exaggerated claims, speculation presented as fact, and quotes taken out of context. Misinformation is not limited to textual content; photographs, video recordings, voice recordings, and other visual or audio media may be altered, incorrectly identified, or presented out of context.

Some sources characterize false or misleading content as disinformation rather than misinformation. A widely cited report prepared for the Council of Europe defines disinformation as false content that is knowingly shared to cause harm.[50] Disinformation may be an outright fabrication, or it may be partially factual with crucial content withheld or distorted to cause confusion or dissention. Misinformation, by contrast, is false content that is shared without malicious intent, although it may have harmful effects on individuals or organizations. As an example, content that is created or collected by a marketing department for a sales presentation may include inaccurate information about a competitor's products, services, business practices, or financial position. If the inaccurate content was knowingly included for deceptive purposes, it is considered disinformation. If the inaccuracy resulted from inadequate research or reliance on unreliable sources, it is considered misinformation. According to the Council of Europe report, disinformation and misinformation are varieties of information disorder. A third variety, malinformation, consists of true content that is shared with harmful intent, as when nonpublic content about the private life of an individual or a previously undisclosed action of an organization is publicized, for example.

Terminology aside, the creation of misinformation raises societal concerns that are discussed later in this chapter. Creation of misinformation may also be illegal. Some countries have laws and regulations that criminalize the creation of false or misleading content with intent to deceive. In the United States, for example, it is a federal crime to knowingly convey false or misleading information about terrorism, explosives, nuclear, biological, or chemical weapons, or other threats under circumstances where such information may reasonably be believed.[51] Some states have false reporting statutes based on the Modern Penal Code developed by the American Law Institute.[52] New York's false reporting law, one of the broadest, criminalizes the creation and circulation of false or baseless information about a crime, catastrophe, or emergency under circumstances that will result in public alarm.[53]

In China, it is a crime to fabricate information with intent to disrupt the economic or social order.[54] Kenya imposes penalties of fine or imprisonment for knowingly creating false information with intent to deceive.[55] In Singapore, it is illegal to create false statements of fact that are likely to have an adverse impact on national security, public safety, public health, public tranquility, public finances, or public confidence in government.[56] Countries that criminalize the creation of misinformation intended to disrupt the political process include Belarus, Burkina Faso, Cambodia, Cameroon, France, and Malaysia.[57] In other countries, people have been arrested by government authorities and fined or imprisoned for creating false news stories, doctored photographs, and other misinformation. Some journalists have noted that these laws can be used improperly to suppress dissent or freedom of the press, but compliance is nonetheless mandatory.[58] Creation of misinformation is only illegal, however, if it is done knowingly with the intention to deceive. Regulatory compliance requirements do not apply to unintentional creation of false or misleading information.

False advertising, a widely publicized and pervasive form of misrepresentation, involves intentionally inaccurate or misleading claims about the purpose, quality, effectiveness, cost, or other aspect of a product or service. While it does not cause political or social disruption, false advertising is generally illegal. In the United States, federal law prohibits unfair or deceptive advertising of food, drugs, devices, services, or cosmetics.[59] Many states have similar laws and regulations that prohibit deceptive trade practices as do Canada, the United Kingdom, Australia, EU member states, and other countries.[60]

Some government agencies have used false advertising laws to prohibit misinformation and misrepresentation in various forms. In 2019, for example, New York State successfully prosecuted a company that created and sold fake social media followers, including names and profile images of real people, to unsuspecting customers. The company also sold endorsements from social media influencers without disclosing that they paid for the endorsements. The prosecution was based on violations of New York laws that prohibit misrepresentation, deceptive practices, false advertising, and false impersonation. The company was also investigated for violation of a Florida law prohibiting deceptive trade practices.[61]

CONTRACTUAL COMPLIANCE

Many organizations outsource the creation or collection of information associated with specific business operations or activities. In such situations, contracts and other legally binding agreements typically include compliance requirements or restrictions for creation and collection of information.[62] For example:

- Contracts for consulting, auditing, due diligence investigations, property appraisals, graphic design, marketing, or other services typically specify the scope, format, or other characteristics of reports, data compilations, images, or other information that the contractor must create. Where a contract is won through a competitive bidding process, the information to be created or collected is usually stipulated in a request for proposals or other solicitation that preceded the contract award.
- Contracts for engineering and construction projects typically require the contractor to create drawings, technical specifications, project plans and timetables, progress reports, and supporting documentation while a project is ongoing. Engineering and construction contracts also specify the drawings, manuals, and other documentation that is to be delivered to the client when a project terminates.
- Contracts for market research, opinion polls, and similar surveys require collection of information from targeted audiences about specific topics or products. These contracts may specify the method of data collection—one-on-one interviews, focus groups, or online surveys, for example—and the desired number and demographic characteristics of respondents. In some cases, the contracts require that data collection process exclude information that would permit personal identification of the respondents.
- Contracts for intelligence gathering require collection of information about a company's competitors or prospective acquisitions. In some cases, these contracts specify the specific data elements to be collected about each competitor.
- Contracts with executive search firms require collection of information about candidates for high-level jobs. In some cases, these contracts specify the minimum number of candidates to be investigated and the sources to be used in the investigation.

In most cases, these contractual compliance requirements include completion dates for creation or collection of information. Failure to comply with contractual obligations may result in delayed payments, penalties, contract termination, or civil litigation.

Contractual compliance requirements may limit or prohibit the creation or collection of specific information to avoid risks associated with problematic practices. As noted in chapter 1, most contracts include a general provision that contracting parties must comply with applicable laws and regulations. Rather than allowing the contracting parties to determine the relevance of specific laws and regulations, a contract may cite those for which compliance is mandated. As an example, collection of personal information is often limited by contractual provisions that mandate compliance with applicable privacy and data protection laws, which require explicit consent to information collection by data subjects and prohibit collection of unnecessary information about identifiable individuals.

A contract may expressly prohibit collection of information by illegal, unethical, or deceptive means. A competitive analysis or benchmarking contract, for example, may prohibit the collection of trade secrets or other confidential information by theft, by bribing a knowledgeable employee of a competitor, by cyber intrusion, or by other forms of industrial espionage. Similarly, a market research contract may prohibit fictitious sponsor identification, false promises of compensation, misleading descriptions of the purpose of the research, or other deceptive practices to collect information from unwitting consumers. A contract may prohibit a private investigator from impersonating a journalist or otherwise using a false identity to collect information. In a widely publicized incident in 2006, private investigators working under contract to Hewlett-Packard impersonated journalists and the company's board members to obtain their telephone records in order to identify the source of an information leak. Hewlett-Packard ultimately paid $14.5 million to settle civil claims related to the investigation. The impersonation, described as "pretexting," has been used by the consumer finance units of automobile companies and other businesses to obtain customers' phone and financial records.[63]

STANDARDS AND INDUSTRY NORMS

There is no all-encompassing standard that defines compliance requirements or best practices for creation or collection of information. Hundreds of standards mention data collection as an aspect of specific business or technical operations or tasks, but they do not specify compliance requirements. Some standards address information collection requirements and methods in the context of specific topics or issues, such as auditing, fire safety, acoustics, reliability of nuclear power plants, health care, environmental management, IT project performance benchmarking, and occupational safety. As an example, the *ASCE Standard Guideline for Recording and Exchanging Utility Infrastructure Data*, issued by the American Society of Civil Engineers, specifies requirements for collection of information about the locations and characteristics of underground and above-ground utility infrastructure.[64]

Among international standards that deal with information creation requirements in specific situations, ISO 45001:2018, *Occupational health and safety management system* lists the types operational, technical, legal, and other "documented information" that an organization must create.[65] International standards that specify requirements for collection of information include ISO/TS 17755-1:2020, *Fire safety—Statistical data collection—Part 2: Vocabulary*; ISO/TS 12913-2:2018, *Acoustics—soundscape—Part 2: Data collection and reporting requirements*; ISO 21378:2019, *Audit data collection*; ISO/IEC 29155-4:2016, *Systems and software engineering—Information technology project benchmarking framework—Part 4: Guidance for data collection and maintenance*; ISO 7385:1983, *Nuclear power plants—Guidelines to ensure quality of collected data on reliability*; ISO/TS 17975, *Health informatics—Principles and data requirements for consent in the collection, use or disclosure of personal health information;* and ISO 14031:2013, *Environmental management—Environmental performance evaluation—guidelines.*

A more broadly applicable group of international standards defines practices for collection of personal information. Those standards incorporate data minimization principles, limitations on information collection, informed consent, voluntary participation in the information collection process, respect for the privacy rights of data subjects, and other compliance requirements specified in the data protection laws and regulations discussed in preceding sections. Examples include ISO/IEC 29100:2011, *Information technology—Security techniques—Privacy framework*; ISO/IEC 29101:2018, *Information technology—Security techniques—Privacy architecture framework;* ISO/IEC 29134:2017, *Information technology—Security techniques—Guidelines for privacy impact assessment*; ISO/IEC 15944-12:2020, *Information technology—Business operational view—Part 12: Privacy Protection Requirements (PPR) on Information Life Cycle Management (ILCM) and EDI of Personal Information (PI)*; ISO/IEC 27018:2019, *Information technology—Security techniques—Code of practice for protection of Personally Identifiable Information (PII) in public clouds acting as PII processors;* and ISO/IEC 27701:2019, *Security techniques—Extension to ISO/IEC 27001 and ISO/IEC 27002 for privacy information management—Requirements and guidelines.*

Principles and compliance requirements related to data minimization, informed consent, and voluntary participation of data subjects are also reflected in information collection norms for specific activities, industries, and professions. For example:

- The Belmont Report, which was issued in 1979 by the National Commission for the Protection of Human Subjects of Biomedical and Behavioral Research, identifies self-determination and informed consent as preconditions for ethical collection of personal information about participants in biomedical and scientific research projects.[66] Prospective participant must understand the purpose of the research, the manner in which information collected from or about them will be used, and any risks associated with the information collection process. These same principles apply to collection of personal information for nonresearch purposes, such as delivery of health-care services or development of public health programs.

- The Belmont Report established the moral principles for conduct of scientific and biomedical research involving human subjects. Its information collection requirements are incorporated into regulations for government-sponsored research and enforced by institutional review boards. They are also reflected in the European Code of Conduct for Research Integrity, which is a reference document for EU-funded research projects,[67] and in norms issued by professional organizations in a nonmedical fields, including the American Educational Research Association,[68] the Association for Information Systems,[69] the American Sociological Association,[70] and the Academy of Criminal Justice Sciences.[71]
- The American Health Information Management Association, American Medical Informatics Association, American Academy of Family Physicians, and other health-care organizations have developed guidelines for a core data set for medical records that includes information to be collected directly from a patient. Examples include basic identification information (name, address, date of birth, gender), lifestyle information, prior medical history, and family history.[72]
- According to IAEA Nuclear Safety Standards, the operator of a nuclear power plant must have all essential information relating to a plant's systems and components. To satisfy this requirement, it must collect testing, operating, inspection, and maintenance history data for all systems and components.[73]
- According to the Market Research Society (MRS) Code of Conduct, members must ensure that there is a lawful basis for collection of personal information. The MRS Code was introduced in 1954. The latest revision incorporates requirements for compliance with data protection laws and regulations. Data subjects must be aware of the purpose for which their information is collected. They must participate voluntarily and have the right to withdraw at any time. They must be told about recording, monitoring, or observation of the information collection process, including such surveillance activities as video monitoring and mystery shopping. Informed consent of a responsible adult is required prior to collecting information from children. All MRS members are required to comply with the Code's provisions and restrictions.[74]
- ESOMAR, a not-for-profit membership organization for opinion and market researchers, distinguishes between active and passive collection of information. Active collection involves asking and answering questions via interviews or questionnaires. It requires informed consent and voluntary participation of respondents who are aware of purpose of data collection. Passive collection of information may involve human observers, video surveillance, data collected by websites via cookies or other mechanisms, and data collected as by-product of other activities, such as use of mobile phones or credit cards. Informed consent or voluntary participation may

not be possible in such situations, but passive information collection must be legally permissible. For both active and passive information collection, the ICC/ESOMAR International Code on Market, Opinion, and Social Research and Data Analytics, which was developed jointly with the International Chamber of Commerce, emphasizes data minimization.[75] Researchers must behave ethically and avoid any harm to data subjects. Compliance with the Code is compulsory for ESOMAR members. Noncompliance may result in a disciplinary investigation.

- The ICC/ESOMAR code is closely aligned with the Member Code of Conduct issued by the Advertising Research Foundation (ARF), a not-for-profit organization that supports the scientific practice of advertising and marketing research.[76] ARF member companies must ensure that personal information is collected with the informed consent and voluntary participation of research subjects. Members must comply with laws that limit the collection of information from children and other vulnerable populations. ARF member companies must designate one person who will be responsible for compliance with the Code and submit annual statements affirming compliance.
- Similar compliance requirements are specified in the IA Code of Standards and Ethics for Marketing Research and Data Analytics, developed by the Insights Association, which establishes standards and best practices for companies in the market research industry. The IA Code emphasizes the principles of transparency, notice, and choice when collecting personal information for research projects and nonresearch activities, such as advertising and marketing. A data subject's participation must be voluntary and based on a clear understanding of the purpose for which the information is collected. The data subject must be able to terminate participation at any time or refuse requests for additional interviews or other forms of participation.[77] Whenever possible, a data subject's consent must be obtained for passive collection of information through observation. If this not possible, passive information collection must be legally permissible. Compliance with the IA Code is compulsory for all members. The Insights Association Standards Committee, which is responsible for enforcement, investigates complaints and imposes warnings, reprimands, or other sanctions, up to and including expulsion, for members judged to be guilty of violations.
- The Codes of Ethics issued by the Council of International Investigators requires compliance with applicable laws and, in particular, prohibits wiretapping in any form in countries where it is unlawful.[78] The Code of Ethics of the National Association of Legal Investigators prohibits any violation of the rights or privileges of individual citizens.[79]
- The Code of Ethics issued by Strategic & Competitive Intelligence Professionals (SCIP), a global association of intelligence strategists, requires members to accurately disclose their identities prior to interviews

to collect information. Impersonation or other misrepresentation is prohibited. Members who violate this rule will be terminated.[80]

- The Code of Ethics of the Society of Professional Journalists (SPG), the Ethics Guidelines of the Canadian Association of Journalists (CAJ), and the Global Charter of Ethics of the International Federation of Journalists (IFJ) emphasize accuracy and transparency in information collection. Journalists must gather up-to-date and accurate information throughout the life of a news story, identify nonconfidential sources, and avoid undercover or surreptitious methods unless information vital to the public cannot be obtained by traditional methods.[81]
- News organizations have their own ethical codes that limit information collection. The *New York Times*, for example, prohibits wiretapping, computer hacking, and other illegal forms of electronic eavesdropping.[82] The Radio Television Digital News Association (RTDNA) similarly prohibits undisclosed recording and other deception in newsgathering.[83] The RTDNA has developed a set of coverage guidelines to assist journalists, newsroom managers, and station managers ethical issues that may arise pertaining to specific situations.[84]

INTERNAL MANDATES

Data minimization principles and their associated compliance mandates are key elements of privacy policies issued by companies, government agencies, and not-for-profit organizations. These privacy policies, which are typically posted on an organization's website, specify acceptable practices and limitations for the collection of personal information about current or prospective customers, clients, vendors, visitors, and other data subjects with whom the organization may interact.[85] The policies define self-imposed requirements and restrictions that obligate an organization's employees. The requirements and restrictions may also apply to an organization's contractors, consultants, and business partners who collect personal information on the organization's behalf.

Most privacy policies include a general affirmation of compliance with applicable laws and regulations, including those that require or restrict information collection. Since 2018, many companies, government agencies, and not-for-profit entities have revised their privacy policies to reflect GDPR compliance requirements, which apply to all organizations that offer goods or services to data subjects located in the European Union. Such policies restrict collection to personal information that is relevant and necessary for a stated purpose—to provide or improve specific services, to communicate with a data subject after a service is provided, or for research and development, for example. Most privacy policies further limit collection to personal information that is obtained voluntarily from a data subject when an account is established, when a service is requested, when transactions occur, through customer satisfaction surveys, or in the course of other interactions.

Additional information about a data subject's computer system, network connection, location, search activity, content downloads, and other matters may be collected automatically during online interactions, but some privacy policies allow data subjects to prevent or limit the automatic collection of such information. Privacy policies may specify the types of personal information that an organization is restricted or prohibited from collecting. Examples include certain information about children, which cannot be collected without parental consent, or information about a data subject's political opinions, religious beliefs, ethnicity, or sexual orientation unless it is required by law or provided voluntarily and directly related to a service the data subject requests.

Like privacy policies, organizational codes of conduct typically limit collection of personal information to the minimum amount needed for legitimate business purposes. Some codes of conduct also emphasize the collection of accurate information to maintain the trust of customers, investors, and business partners. Several codes of conduct advise employees to use good judgment and avoid creating unnecessary information. One company's code of conduct instructs employees to "think before writing and decide whether it is necessary to create a record."[86] As with other organizational policies, compliance with these information creation and collection requirements is a condition of employment. Noncompliance can result in a negative performance evaluation, formal warning, disciplinary action, or, for the worst offenses, termination of employment. Compliance requirements may also apply to contractors, business partners, and others who provide services to or act on behalf of an organization.

SOCIETAL COMPLIANCE

Societal compliance requirements for information creation and collection are intended to address ethical and sustainability concerns. Ethical compliance requirements relate to the content of data or documents an organization creates. They prohibit the intentional creation or collection of content that is verifiably false, biased, misleading, harmful, or appropriated from others without permission or acknowledgment. Sustainability compliance is concerned with the environmental impact of creating and collecting information without regard to its content.

ETHICAL ISSUES

As discussed above, internal codes of conduct and similar organizational policies prohibit falsification of business records, but that prohibition principally relates to information about an organization's financial condition. Professional journalism codes of ethics similarly mandate accuracy in reporting and other writing. They prohibit false claims, inaccurate quotes, and manipulated images, as well as composite characters, fictional names, and other fabrications in news stories.[87] These egregious practices are not ubiquitous, but they do occur.

Plagiarism, a more common problem, is the creation of content that incorporates the work of others without appropriate attribution. Plagiarism may be complete or partial. It may be intentional or inadvertent.[88] A plagiarist may copy another person's work exactly or paraphrase it. The plagiarized content may be text, quantitative data, images, or music. The most widely discussed incidents of plagiarism are associated with academic misconduct where students or even faculty are suspected of passing off previously written content as their own, but appropriation of the work of others may occur in any situation where information is created.[89] Plagiarism is an acknowledged problem in journalism, songwriting, screenwriting, graphic arts, politics, and other fields.[90] Plagiarism detected after publication is one of the most common reasons articles are retracted from medical journals.[91] Popular historians and other well-known scholars have been involved in widely publicized plagiarism cases.[92] In business settings, plagiarism may be encountered in reports, brochures, press releases, speeches, presentations, blogs, and social media posts.

From a business perspective, the intentional creation or collection of data, documents, or communications with false, misleading, or plagiarized content is inadvisable. If detected, as it sometimes is, false or misleading information will damage a company's competitive position and reputation, undermine investors' confidence, erode goodwill, and cause customer defections.[93] Ethical compliance requirements address these matters as a societal problem that has an adverse impact on the public good. Ethical compliance requirements for the creation and collection of information are based on religious and philosophical precepts that prohibit lying with intent to harm.[94] To ensure ethical compliance, organizations must rigorously fact-check all marketing communications, media releases, executive presentations, annual reports, blogs, social media posts, and other public statements to detect and eliminate false or misleading content.

Legal compliance becomes an issue when a plagiarized work is protected by copyright or trademark registration, which will be discussed in chapter 7. Otherwise, plagiarism is not illegal, but it does violate ethical norms, which view it as a form of lying at best and theft at worst.[95] Organizations must clearly define and prohibit plagiarism, emphasize the importance of original work, and instruct creators of information to credit sources when using content created by others, but compliance is not easy to achieve. Plagiarism is difficult to detect. In widely publicized cases, it has typically been discovered long after the plagiarized content was created. Plagiarism-detection software, which is principally intended for checking term papers and other academic assignments, may detect problematic content in research reports, blogs, marketing presentations, websites, and social media posts, but it is less useful for general business documents.[96]

SUSTAINABILITY ISSUES

United Nations Sustainable Development Goal 12 addresses responsible consumption of natural resources, reduction of an organization's global material footprint, and minimization of nonrecyclable waste. Sustainable Development Goal 13 is concerned with combatting climate change through the reduction of greenhouse gas emissions. Information creation and collection pose compliance challenges for these goals. These sustainability challenges apply to both paper and electronic records:

- Creation of paper documents by manual or automated methods consumes natural resources and generates environmental contaminants. Paper is produced from forest products. Paper manufacturing requires energy, consumes water, emits greenhouse gases, and generates industrial pollutants, including measurable levels of toxic chemicals.
- Computer printers and photocopiers, the two devices that generate most paper records, consume energy.[97] While the carbon footprint of a single page is small, the accumulated environmental impact of high-volume printing and photocopying activity can be significant.[98] Many paper copies, such as database reports printed for review or photocopies distributed at meetings, are discarded shortly after they are read. While some discarded office paper is recycled, much of it is deposited as solid waste in landfills where it will decompose after several decades, emitting methane, a greenhouse gas, in the process.[99] As an additional environmental concern, decomposing papers contain toxic inks and dyes that can contaminate soil and groundwater.
- The energy footprint of information technology operations has decreased in recent years as newer servers have replaced older mainframes and mobile computing devices have replaced desktop models, but computer manufacturing and use remain significant consumers of energy. While computing activity has increased significantly since the early 2000s, energy consumption has remained stable.[100] According to recent estimates, data centers account for just 1 percent of total energy use worldwide; still, a large data center can consume more electricity than some countries. Annual emissions associated with energy-intensive computing operations like cryptocurrency mining are comparable to those of a medium-size city. One study found that bitcoin mining's annual emissions of greenhouse gases are equivalent to those of Kansas City. According to the Cambridge Bitcoin Electricity Consumption Index, bitcoin mining consumes more electricity annually than Sweden.[101]
- The broad spectrum of information and communications technology, including mobile phones and televisions as well as computers, accounts for about the same share of global emissions as the airline industry.[102] Even the software industry requires energy for product development, testing, delivery, use, and maintenance.[103]
- Commonplace computing operations can have significant environmental impacts. An email's carbon footprint is derived from the energy that powers the devices that compose, transmit, store, and read it. While an average email has about one-sixtieth the carbon footprint of a letter, the quantity of email messages that an organization's employees receive in a given day vastly exceeds the volume of incoming correspondence. A widely

publicized estimate found that the carbon footprint of a typical annual accumulation of incoming business email is about the same as driving an average car two hundred miles.[104]

Creating and collecting less information is the key to compliance with sustainability requirements. To support this objective, organizations can reduce the number of printers and photocopiers installed in the workplace and place them in locations that discourage casual use. Employees should be instructed to limit printing and photocopying to the minimum number of paper copies needed for a given purpose. Routine printing of reference copies, drafts, notes, and other documents of transitory value should be avoided to the extent possible. Where paper copies are needed for reference or distribution, recycled paper and double-side printing should be used where practical.

Because most documents originate in digital form, on-screen viewing and distribution is the preferred alternative to paper copies. The estimated carbon footprint of a business process involving the creation and delivery of paper invoices is 21 grams of CO_2 per invoice; by contrast, the carbon footprint of an incoming electronic invoice is 75 percent smaller.[105] Word processing uses more electricity than typewriters, but on-screen editing eliminates the need to print drafts for manual markup, which reduces paper consumption and waste. It also allows users to work faster, possibly reducing office lighting and utility costs.[106] To reduce energy consumption, the creation of unnecessary emails, such as messages that merely thank someone for previously sending an email, should be avoided, and the size of necessary messages and attachments should be reduced. A 2019 study by OVO Energy, the United Kingdom's leading independent energy provider, calculated that sixty-four million unnecessary emails are sent in the UK every day and that sending one less "thank you" email a day would save over 16,430 tons of carbon annually—the equivalent of over eighty-one thousand flights from London to Madrid.[107]

These sustainability measures are easier to discuss than to put into effect. Their implementation requires a strong management commitment and employee cooperation.

SUMMARY OF MAJOR POINTS

- All countries have laws and regulations that mandate the creation or collection of information about business operations and activities that are subject to government oversight. These legal and regulatory compliance requirements support the preparation of reports or data compilations that regulated entities must submit to government agencies. They also ensure that government authorities will have the information needed for inspections, audits, investigations, and policymaking related to regulated operations and activities.

- Some laws and regulations that mandate the creation or collection of information apply to commonly encountered business functions, such as accounting and human resources. Others apply to companies and other organizations in specific economic sectors or regulated industries. Unlike the general requirements, sector-specific regulations are widely criticized for imposing burdensome recordkeeping operations that an organization would not otherwise perform and that increase the complexity and cost of doing business.
- Many countries and dependent territories have data protection and privacy laws and regulations that restrict or prohibit the collection of personal information about an organization's customers, clients, employees, suppliers, and other data subjects. In particular, collection of personal information must be limited to the minimum amount necessary for specific, explicit, and legitimate purposes.
- Some countries have laws that restrict the collection of information by photographic, video, audio, or other surveillance technologies.
- Some countries have laws and regulations that criminalize the creation of misinformation with the intent to deceive.
- Contracts and other legally binding agreements often include compliance requirements for creation and collection of information. A contract may also prohibit collection of information by illegal, unethical, or deceptive means.
- There is no all-encompassing standard that defines compliance requirements or best practices for creation or collection of information, but some international standards address information collection requirements and methods in the context of specific topics or issues.
- A more broadly applicable group of industry norms and professional codes of conduct define requirements for collection of personal information based on data minimization principles, limitations on information collection, informed consent, voluntary participation in the information collection process, and respect for the privacy rights of data subjects.
- Internal codes of conduct and similar policies specify requirements for creation and collection of information by an organization's employees, contractors, and business partners.
- Ethical compliance requirements prohibit the intentional creation or collection of content that is verifiably false, biased, misleading, harmful, or appropriated from others without permission or acknowledgment.
- Sustainability compliance is concerned with the environmental impact of creating and collecting information. Creating and collecting less information is the key to compliance with sustainability requirements.

NOTES

1. 45 C.F.R. § 180.50, https://www.law.cornell.edu/cfr/text/45/180.50.
2. 12 C.F.R. § 228.42.

3. U.S. Food and Drug Administration, eCTD submission requirements: what you need to know, https://www.fda.gov/files/drugs/published/eCTD-Submission-Requirements—What-You-Need-to-Know.PDF; Guidance document: Health Canada, Guidance docment, filing submissions electronically, https://www.canada.ca/en/health-canada/services/drugs-health-products/drug-products/applications-submissions/guidance-documents/filing-submissions-electronically.html; Australian Therapeutic Goods Administration, electronic submissions, https://www.tga.gov.au/electronic-submissions.
4. See, for example, 26 U.S.C. § 6011 (e), https://www.law.cornell.edu/uscode/text/26/6011.
5. See Z. Zeng, *Assessing Inmate Cause of Death: Deaths in Custody Reporting Program and National Death Index* (Washington, DC: Bureau of Justice Statistics, U.S. Department of Justice, 2016), https://www.prisonlegalnews.org/media/publications/Assessing_Inmate_Cause_of_Death_DOJ_2016.pdf.
6. For compliance requirements in specific countries, see W. Saffady, *Retention of Accounting Records: a Global Survey of Laws and Regulations* (Pittsburgh, PA: ARMA International Educational Foundation, 2019), http://armaedfoundation.org.
7. For a detailed discussion of customs-related information, see D. Bade, *Export/Import Procedures and Documentation, Fifth Edition* (New York: AMACOM, 2015).
8. Del. Code tit. 8, § 142, https://delcode.delaware.gov/title8/title8.pdf.
9. See, for example, Ontario Business Corporations Act, R.S.O. 1990, Ch. B.16, § 140, https://www.ontario.ca/laws/statute/90b16.
10. Australian Corporations Act 2001, https://www.legislation.gov.au/Details/C2017C00129; New Zealand Companies Act 1993, https://legislation.govt.nz/act/public/1993/0105/188.0/DLM323510.html.
11. *Model Business Corporation Act Annotated, Fifth Edition* (Chicago: American Bar Association, 2020). The model act is online at https://www.americanbar.org/content/dam/aba/administrative/business_law/corplaws/2020_mbca.pdf. Examples of the many publications about the model act include R. Garrett, "History, purpose, and summary of the Model Business Corporation Act," *Business Lawyer* 6 (1), 1-7 (1950), https://www.jstor.org/stable/40682994; M. Dooley and M. Goldman, "Some comparisons between the Model Business Corporation Act and the Delaware General Corporation Law," *Business Lawyer* 56 (2), 737-66 (2001), https://www.jstor.org/stable/40687993; and J. Gorris et al., "Delaware corporate law and the Model Business Corporation Act: a study in symbiosis," *Law and Contemporary Problems* 74 (1), 107-20 (2011), https://www.jstor.org/stable/25800698.
12. Canada Business Corporations Act, https://laws-lois.justice.gc.ca/eng/acts/C-44/page-4.html-h-108627; Companies Act 2006, https://www.legislation.gov.uk/ukpga/2006/46/contents; Swiss Code of Obligations, https://www.fedlex.admin.ch/eli/cc/27/317_321_377/en.
13. For compliance requirements in specific countries, see W. Saffady, *Global Requirements for Personnel Records: a Survey of Laws and Regulations* (Pittsburgh, PA: ARMA International Educational Foundation, 2021), http://armaedfoundation.org.
14. See, for example, 29 C.F.R. § 1904.41, which requires certain employers to collect injury and illness information for electronic submission to the Occupational Safety and Health Administration annually, https://www.law.cornell.edu/cfr/text/29/1904.41.

15. 29 C.F.R. § 1904.39, https://www.osha.gov/laws-regs/regulations/standardnumber/1904/1904.39.
16. Canadian Centre for Occupational Health and Safety, OH&S Legislation in Canada—Injury Reporting, https://www.ccohs.ca/oshanswers/legisl/injury_reporting.html.
17. On the role of information collection requirements in occupational safety, see E. Tansey, "Regulatory recordkeeping, worker safety, and United States extractive industries," *Extractive Industries and Society* 7 (1), 209-16 (2020), https://doi.org/10.1016/j.exis.2020.01.010.
18. On global requirements for anti-money laundering regulations, see *International Standards on Combating Money Laundering and the Financing of Terrorism & Proliferation* (Paris: Financial Action Task Force, 2020), http://www.fatf-gafi.org/publications/fatfrecommendations/documents/fatf-recommendations.html; K. Alexander, "The international anti-money-laundering regime: the role of the Financial Action Task Force," *Journal of Money Laundering Control* 4 (3), 231-48 (2001), https://doi.org/10.1108/eb027276; J. Johnson and Y. Desmond Lim, "Money laundering: has the Financial Action Task Force made a difference?" *Journal of Financial Crime* 10 (1), 7-22 (2002), https://doi.org/10.1108/13590790310808556; and E. Mekpor et al., "The determinants of anti-money laundering compliance among the Financial Action Task Force (FATF) member states," *Journal of Financial Regulation and Compliance* 26 (3), 442-59 (2018), https://doi.org/10.1108/JFRC-11-2017-0103. On KYC requirements, see D. Mulligan, "Know your customer regulations and the international banking system: towards a general self-regulatory regime," *Fordham International Law Journal* 22 (5), 2324-72 (1998), https://ir.lawnet.fordham.edu/cgi/viewcontent.cgi?article=1647&context=ilj.; M. Gill and G. Taylor, "Preventing money laundering or obstructing business? Financial Companies' perspectives on 'know your customer' procedures," *British Journal of Criminology* 44 (4), 582-94 (2004), https://doi.org/10.1093/bjc/azh019; E. Gouvin, "Bringing out the big guns: the USA PATRIOT Act, money laundering, and the war on terrorism," *Baylor Law Review* 55 (3), 955-90 (2003), https://digitalcommons.law.wne.edu/cgi/viewcontent.cgi?article=1075&context=facschol; D. Sahr and D. Morales, "U.S. anti-money laundering legislation," *Law and Business Review of the Americas* 8 (4), 583-602 (2002), https://scholar.smu.edu/lbra/vol8/iss4/5/.
19. 12 CFR 1003.4, https://www.law.cornell.edu/cfr/text/12/1003.4. On the rationale for information collection and the value of the data, see G. Canner, "Home Mortgage Disclosure Act: expanded data on residential lending," *Federal Reserve Bulletin* 77 (11), 859-81 (1991), https://fraser.stlouisfed.org/title/federal-reserve-bulletin-62/november-1991-20834/home-mortgage-disclosure-act-expanded-data-residential-lending-77975; R. Avery et al., "Opportunities and issues in using HMDA data," *Journal of Real Estate Research* 29 (4), 351-80 (2007), https://doi.org/10.1080/10835547.2007.12091206; and P. McCoy, "The Home Mortgage Disclosure Act: a synopsis and recent legislative history," *Journal of Real Estate Research* 29 (4), 381-98 (2007), https://doi.org/10.1080/10835547.2007.12091207.
20. For examples of sector-specific accounting regulations, see W. Saffady, *U.S. Record Retention Requirements: a Guide to 100 Commonly Encountered Record Series* (Prairie Village, KS: ARMA International, 2018).
21. On global requirements for pharmacovigilance, see M. Hans and S. Gupta, "Comparative evaluation of pharmacovigilance regulation of the United States,

United Kingdom, Canada, India and the need for global harmonized practices," *Perspectives in Clinical Research* 9 (4), 170–74 (2008), https://doi.org/10.4103/picr.PICR_89_17; C. Curran and C. Engle, "An index of United States federal regulations and guidelines which cover safety surveillance of drugs," *Drug Information Journal* 31 (3), 833–41 (1997), https://doi.org/10.1177/009286159703100323; J. Borg et al., "European Union pharmacovigilance capabilities: potential for the new legislation," *Therapeutic Advances in Drug Safety* 6 (4), 120–40 (2015), https://doi.org/doi: 10.1177/2042098615591802; T. Vial, "French pharmacovigilance: missions, organization and perspectives," *Therapies* 71 (2), 143–50 (2016), https://doi.org/10.1016/j.therap.2016.02.029; E. Hoffman et al., "Pharmacovigilance regulatory requirements in Latin America," *Pharmaceutical Medicine* 26 (3), 153–64 (2012), https://doi.org/10.1007/BF03262389; T. Alshammari et al., "Pharmacovigilance systems in Arab countries: overview of 22 Arab countries," *Drug Safety* 42 (7), 849–68 (2019), https://doi.org/10.1007/s40264-019-00807-4; S. Olsson et al., "Pharmacovigilance activities in 55 low- and middle-income countries," *Drug Safety* 33 (8), 689–703 (2010), https://link.springer.com/article/10.2165/11536390-000000000-00000.

22. Health Care Professional Credentialing Verification Model Law, https://content.naic.org/sites/default/files/inline-files/MDL-070.pdf. On noncompliance with health-care credentialing requirements, see W. Foster, "Health law—negligent credentialing and you: what happens when hospitals fail to monitor physicians," *University of Arkansas at Littler Rock Law Review* 31 (2), 321–49 (2009), https://lawrepository.ualr.edu/cgi/viewcontent.cgi?article=1115&context=lawreview.
23. 40 CFR 122.41, https://www.law.cornell.edu/cfr/text/40/122.41; 40 CFR 60.7, https://www.law.cornell.edu/cfr/text/40/60.7; 40 CFR 98.3, https://www.law.cornell.edu/cfr/text/40/98.3. See also E. Morss, "Clean Air Act implementation: an industry perspective," *Pace Environmental Law Review* 14 (1), 63–68 (1996), https://digitalcommons.pace.edu/pelr/vol14/iss1/7.
24. Canadian Environmental Protection Act, 1999, Part 3: Information Gathering, Objectives, Guidelines, and Codes of Practice, https://www.canada.ca/en/environment-climate-change/services/canadian-environmental-protection-act-registry/publications/canadian-environmental-protection-act-1999/part-3.html.
25. Commercial Motor Vehicle Safety Enhancement Act, 49 CFR Subpart B, https://www.law.cornell.edu/cfr/text/40/60.7. Regulation (EC) No. 561/2006 on harmonization of certain social legislation relating to road transport, https://eur-lex.europa.eu/legal-content/EN/TXT/HTML/?uri=CELEX:32006R0561&from=EN; Regulation (EU) No. 165/2014 on tachographs in road transport, https://eur-lex.europa.eu/legal-content/EN/TXT/?uri=uriserv%3AOJ.L_.2014.060.01.0001.01.ENG&toc=OJ%3AL%3A2014%3A060%3ATOC.
26. 49 CFR Part 40, https://www.law.cornell.edu/cfr/text/49/part-40. A. Pierce, "Regulatory aspects of workplace drug testing in Europe," *Drug Testing and Analysis* 4 (2), 62–65 (2012), https://doi.org/10.1002/dta.1326.
27. 9 CFR 2.35, https://www.law.cornell.edu/cfr/text/9/2.35. See A. Cardon et al., "The Animal Welfare Act: from Enactment to Enforcement," *Journal of the American Association for Laboratory Animal Science* 51 (3): 301–05 (2012), https://www.ingentaconnect.com/content/aalas/jaalas/2012/00000051/00000003/art00004; J. Marceau, "How the Animal Welfare Act harms animals," *Hastings*

Law Journal 69 (3), 925-59, https://www.hastingslawjournal.org/wp-content/uploads/Marceau-69.3.pdf.

28. RRO 1990, Regulation 24: Research Facilities and Supply Facilities, https://www.ontario.ca/laws/regulation/900024.
29. Directive 2010/63/EU on the Protection of Animals Used for Scientific Purposes, https://eur-lex.europa.eu/LexUriServ/LexUriServ.do?uri=OJ:L:2010:276:0033:0079:en:PDF. See S. Pinto da Silva et al., "Protecting animals and enabling research in the European Union: an overview of development and implementation of Directive 2010/63/EU," *ILAR Journal* 57 (3), 347-57 (2016), https://doi.org/10.1093 ilar/ilw029. Some countries have regulations that mandate the collection of information about other types of animals in specific situations. In Wales, for example, anyone who transports or markets poultry must collect information about the date and place where the poultry were obtained, their species and description, the name and address of the person from whom they were obtained, and the date and manner of disposal. See The Diseases of Poultry (Wales) Order 2003, https://www.legislation.gov.uk/wsi/2003/1079/contents.
30. 29 CFR 1910.95, https://www.osha.gov/laws-regs/regulations/standardnumber/1910/1910.95; EU Directive 2003/10/EC, https://eur-lex.europa.eu/legal-content/EN/TXT/?uri=CELEX:02003L0010-20190726.
31. See FEMA Advisory: Civil Rights Data Collection, https://www.fema.gov/sites/default/files/documents/fema_civil-rights-data-collection_advisory_02-06-2021.pdf; R. Kim, "Under the law: civil rights enforcement in education, the federal role," *Phi Delta Kappan* 102 (3), 64-65 (2020), https://doi.org/10.1177/0031721720970707.
32. See, for example, D. Skupsky, "Recordkeeping requirements to promote public interests—a balance between government needs and burdens," *ARMA Records Management Quarterly* 27 (4), 36, 40 (1993), https://search.proquest.com/openview/40a945b0c445ac8d14d6211508f89841/1?pq-origsite=gscholar&cbl=47365; S. Weaver, "Modern day money laundering: does the solution exist in an expansive system of monitoring and recordkeeping regulations?" *Annual Review of Banking & Financial Law* 24, 443-65 (2005), https://heinonline.org/HOL/LandingPage?handle=hein.journals/annrbfl24&div=8&id=&page=; P. Klamert, "Complying with changes in OSHA's recordkeeping requirements," *AAOHN Journal* 50 (7), 324-33 (2002), https://journals.sagepub.com/doi/pdf/10.1177/216507990205000710.
33. For the official text of the GDPR and its recitals, which provide additional details about specific requirements, see https://gdpr-info.eu. Examples of the many publications about the GDPR and its provisions for collection of personal information include M. Krzysztofek, *GDPR: Personal Data Protection in the European Union* (Alphen aan den Rijn, Netherlands: Wolters Kluwer Law International, 2021); D. Solove and P. Schwartz, *EU Data Protection and the GDPR* (New York: Wolters Kluwer, 2021); A. Calder, *EU GDPR* (Ely, United Kingdom: IGTP, 2020); A. Denley et al., *GDPR: How to Achieve and Maintain Compliance* (London: Routledge, 2019); A. Kolah, *GDPR Handbook: a Guide to Implementing the Eu General Data Protection Regulation* (London: Kogan Page, 2018); D. Basin et al., "On purpose and by necessity: compliance under the GDPR," in S. Meiklejohn and K. Sako, eds., *Financial Cryptography and Data Security* (Berlin: Springer, 2018), 20-37, https://doi.org/10.1007/978-3-662-58387

-6_2; https://doi.org/10.1177/0759106321995709; M. Brodin, "A framework for GDPR compliance for small- and medium-sized enterprises," *European Journal for Security Research* 4 (2), 243-64 (2019), https://doi.org/10.1007/s41125-019-00042-z; S. Mendoza, "GDPR compliance—it takes a village," *Seattle University Law Review* 42 (3), 1155-62 (2019), https://digitalcommons.law.seattleu.edu/sulr/vol42/iss3/8/.

34. While Directive 95/46/EC has been rescinded, it remains available at https://eur-lex.europa.eu/legal-content/EN/TXT/?uri=celex%3A31995L0046. Publications that survey national privacy and data protection laws include W. Leichter and D. Berman, *Global Guide to Data Protection Laws: Understanding Privacy and Compliance Requirements in More Than 80 Countries* (San Jose, CA: CipherCloud, 2018); G. Greenleaf, *Global Privacy Laws 017: 120 National Data Privacy Laws, Including Indonesia and Turkey* (Sydney, Australia: University of New South Wales Research Series, 2017), https://papers.ssrn.com/sol3/papers.cfm?abstract_id=2993035; G. Greenleaf, *Asian Data Privacy Laws: Trade & Human Rights Perspectives* (Oxford: Oxford University Press, 2014); L.A. Bygrave, *Data Privacy Law: an International Perspective* (Oxford: Oxford University Press, 2014); D. Banisar and S. Davies, "Global Trends In Privacy Protection: an International Survey of Privacy, Data Protection, and Surveillance Laws and Developments," *John Marshall Journal of Information Technology & Privacy Law*, vol. 18, no. 1; 1-111 (Fall 1999), https://repository.jmls.edu/cgi/viewcontent.cgi?article=1174&context=jitpl.
35. On the data minimization principle, which predates the GDPR, see A. Biega et al., "Operationalizing the legal principle of data minimization for personalization," in *SIGR '20: Proceedings of the Forth-Third International ACM SIGIR Conference on Research and Development in Information Retrieval* (New York: Association for Computing Machinery, 2020), 399-408, https://doi.org/10.1145/3397271.3401034; K. Borcea Pfitzmann et al., "Privacy 3.0:=data minimization+user control+contextual integrity," *Information Technology* 53 (1), 34-40 (2011), http://doi.org/10.1524/itit.2011.0622.
36. *Protection of Workers' Personal Data: an ILO Code of Practice* (Geneva: International Labour Office, 1997), https://www.ilo.org/wcmsp5/groups/public/—-ed_protect/—-protrav/—-safework/documents/normativeinstrument/wcms_107797.pdf. See also S. Wallach, "Whose info is it anyway? Employees' rights to privacy and protection of personal data in the workplace," *International Journal of Comparative Labour Law and Industrial Relations* 23 (2), 195-226 (2007), https://kluwerlawonline.com/journalarticle/International+Journal+of+Comparative+Labour+Law+and+Industrial+Relations/23.2/IJCL2007010.
37. *OECD Guidelines on the Protection of Privacy and Transborder Flows of Personal Data*, https://www.oecd.org/internet/ieconomy/oecdguidelinesontheprotectionofprivacyandtransborderflowsofpersonaldata.htm.
38. See *Transparency Report: The USA FREEDOM Act Business Records FISA Implementation* issued by the NSA Civil Liberties and Privacy Office in January 2016, https://www.nsa.gov/Portals/70/documents/about/civil-liberties/reports/UFA_Civil_Liberties_and_Privacy_Report.pdf.
39. J. Blume, "A contextual extraterritoriality analysis of the DPIE and DPO provisions of the GDPR," *Georgetown Journal of International Law* 49 (4), 1427-60 (2018), https://www.law.georgetown.edu/international-law-journal/wp-content

/uploads/sites/21/2019/10/GT-GJIL190005.pdf; A. Azzi, "The challenges faced by the extraterritorial scope of the General Data Protection Regulation," *Journal of Intellectual Property, Information Technology and Electronic Commerce Law* 9 (2), 126–37 (2018), https://www.jipitec.eu/issues/jipitec-9-2-2018/4723; M. Klar, "Binding effects of the European General Data Protection Regulation (GDPR) on U.S. companies," *Hastings Science and Technology Law Journal* 11 (2), 102–54 (2020), https://repository.uchastings.edu/cgi/viewcontent.cgi?article=1095&context=hastings_science_technology_law_journal; A. Makulilo, "The long arm of GDPR in Africa: reflection on data privacy law reform and practice in Mauritius," *International Journal of Human Rights* 25 (1), 117–46 (2020), https://doi.org/10.1080/13642987.2020.1783532; B. Greze, "The extra-territorial enforcement of the GDPR: a genuine issue and the quest for alternatives," *International Data Privacy Law* 9 (2), 109–28 (2019), https://doi.org/10.1093/idpl/ipz003.

40. Examples of the large and growing literature on GDPR's impact on big data initiatives include T. Zarsky, "Incompatible: the GDPR in the age of big data," *Seton Hall Law Review* 47 (4), 995–1020, https://scholarship.shu.edu/cgi/viewcontent.cgi?article=1606&context=shlr; N. Forgo et al., "The principle of purpose limitation and big data," in M. Corrales et al., eds., *New Technology, Big Data and the Law* (Singapore: Springer Nature, 2017), 17–42, https://doi.org/10.1007/978-981-10-5038-1_2; N. Clarke et al., "GDPR: an impediment to research?" *Irish Journal of Medical Science* 188 (4), 1129–35(2019), https://doi.org/10.1007/s11845-019-01980-2; S. Duchesne and M. Ferry, "Is time on the side of change? Incorporating the GDPR in (some of) our research practices," *Bulletin of Sociological Methodology* 150 (1), 106–24 (2021), https://doi.org/10.1177/0759106321995709; S. Ziegler et al., "The impact of the European General Data Protection Regulation (GDPR) on future data business models: toward a new paradigm and business opportunities," in A. Aagaard, ed., *Digital Business Models* (Cham, Switzerland: Palgrave Macmillan, 2019), 201–26, https://doi.org/10.1007/978-3-319-96902-2_8; V. Mayer-Schonberger and Y. Padova, "Regime change? Enabling big data through Europe's new data protection regulation," *Columbia Science & Technology Law Review* 17 (2), 315–30 (2016), https://doi.org/10.7916/stlr.v17i2.4007; U. Pagalio, "The legal challenges of big data: putting secondary rules first in the field of EU data protection," *European Data Protection Law Review* 3 (1), 36–46 (2017), https://doi.org/10.21552/edpl/2017/1/7; M. Gal and O. Aviv, "The competitive effects of the GDPR," *Journal of Competition Law & Economics* 16 (3), 349–91 (2020), https://doi.org/10.1093/joclec/nhaa012.
41. On the relationship between surveillance and privacy, see J. Andres and M. Baker, "The General Data Protection Regulation in the age of surveillance capitalism," *Journal of Business Ethics* 168 (3), 565–78 (2021), https://doi.org/10.1007/s10551-019-04239-z; Q. Rajpoot and C. Jensen, "Video surveillance: privacy issues and legal compliance," in V. Kumar and J. Svensson,eds., *Promoting Social Change and Democracy through Information Technology* (Hershey, PA: IGI Global, 2015), 69–92, https://doi.org/10.4018/978-1-4666-8502-4.ch004; J. Granick, *American Spies: Modern Surveillance, Why You Should Care, and What To Do About It* (Cambridge: Cambridge University Press, 2017).
42. See, for example, *Dow Chemical Co. v. United States*, 476 U.S. 227 (1986) on the lawfulness of aerial photography to observe a chemical plant after the plant's operator

refused a request by the Environmental Protection Agency for onsite inspection. The Supreme Court ruled that aerial photography in public navigable airspace without a warrant did not constitute a search (https://supreme.justia.com/cases/federal/us/476/227/). S. Winkler et al., "Privacy and civilian drone use: the need for further regulation," *IEEE Security & Privacy* 16 (5), 72-80 (2018), https://doi.org/10.1109/MSP.2018.3761721; A. Zwickle et al., "Comparing public concern and support for drone regulation to the current legal framework," *Behavioral Sciences & the Law* 37 (1), 109-24 (2019), https://doi.org/10.1002/bsl.2357; C. Lin et al., "Security and privacy for the Internet of drones: challenges and solutions," *IEEE Communications Magazine* 56 (1), 64-69 (2018), https://doi.org/10.1109/MCOM.2017.1700390.

43. On the regulation of photographic and video surveillance, see D. Gray and S. Henderson, eds., *The Cambridge Handbook of Surveillance Law* (Cambridge: Cambridge University Press, 2017); J. Brown, "Pan, tilt, zoom: regulating the use of video surveillance of public places," *Berkeley Technology Law Journal* 23 (1), 755-81 (2008), https://www.jstor.org/stable/24118339; UK Home Office, Surveillance Camera Code of Practice, 2022 update, https://www.gov.uk/government/publications/update-to-surveillance-camera-code.
44. On the technology of audio surveillance, see M. Crocco et al., "Audio surveillance: a systematic review," *ACM Computing Surveys* 48 (4), article 52, 46 pages (2016), https://doi.org/10.1145/2871183; K. Greenawalt, "The consent problem in wiretapping & eavesdropping: surreptitious monitoring with the consent of a participant in a conversation," *Columbia Law Review* 68 (2), 189-240 (1968), https://doi.org/10.2307/1120882.
45. Criminal Code, R.S.C., 1985, c. C-46, Section 184 (2), https://laws-lois.justice.gc.ca/eng/acts/c-46/section-184.html.
46. On the Computer Fraud and Abuse Act, see *Prosecuting Compute Crimes,* issued by the Office of Legal Education, Executive Office for United States Attorneys, https://www.justice.gov/sites/default/files/criminal-ccips/legacy/2015/01/14/ccmanual.pdf; K. Field, "Agency, code, or contract: determining employees' authorization under the Computer Fraud and Abuse Act," *Michigan Law Review* 107 (5), 819-52 (2009), https://repository.law.umich.edu/mlr/vol107/iss5/3/.
47. Law 759/2004, Act on the Protection of Privacy in Working Life, Sections 18-20, https://finlex.fi/fi/laki/kaannokset/2004/en20040759.pdf; C. Eklund, "Monitoring employees' email correspondence and Internet use—a Finnish perspective," *European Law Journal* 10 (2), 116-33 (2019), https://doi.org/10.1177/2031952519852110; T. Jaatinen and E. Rautanen, "Finland: accessing employees' email in the workplace—a Gordian knot," *European Data Protection Law Review* 2 (3), 384-90 (2016), https://doi.org/10.21552/EDPL/2016/3/15; L. Mitrou and M. Karyda, "Employees' privacy vs. employers' security: can they be balanced?" *Telematics and Informatics* 23 (3), 164-78 (2006), https://doi.org/10.1016/j.tele.2005.07.003; K. Ball et al., "Dimensions of employee privacy: an empirical study," *Information Technology & People* 25 (4), 376-94 (2012), https://doi.org/10.1108/09593841211278785; A. Townsend and J. Bennett, "Privacy, technology, and conflict: emerging issues and action in workplace privacy," *Journal of Labor Research* 24 (2), 195-205 (2003), https://doi.org/10.1007/BF02701789; S. Cox et al., "Workplace surveillance and employee privacy: implementing an effective computer use policy," *Communications of the IIMA* 5 (2), 57-65 (2005),

https://scholarworks.lib.csusb.edu/cgi/viewcontent.cgi?article=1263&context=ciima; C. Cohen and M. Cohen, "On-duty and off-duty: employee right to privacy and employer's right to control in the private sector," *Employee Responsibilities and Rights Journal* 19 (2), 235–46 (2007), https://doi.org/10.1007/s10672-007-9050-2; C. Frayer, "Employee privacy and Internet monitoring: balancing workers' rights and dignity with legitimate management interests," *Business Lawyer* 57 (2), 857–74 (2002), https://www.jstor.org/stable/40688047; L. Evans, "Monitoring technology in the American workplace: would adopting English privacy standards better balance employee privacy and productivity?" *California Law Review* 95 (4), 1115–49 (2007), https://doi.org/10.2307/20439120; W. Smith, "Can we borrow your phone? Employee privacy in the BYOD era," *Journal of Information, Communication and Ethics in Society* 15 (4), 397–411 (2017), https://doi.org/10.1108/JICES-09-2015-0027.

48. B. Mund, "Social media searches and the reasonable expectation of privacy," *Yale Journal of Law & Technology* 19 (1), 239–71 (2017), https://digitalcommons.law.yale.edu/cgi/viewcontent.cgi?article=1129&context=yjolt; C. Garden, "Labor organizing in the age of surveillance," *Saint Louis University Law Journal* 63 (1), 55–68 (2018), https://scholarship.law.slu.edu/lj/vol63/iss1/5/; O. Kerr, "Internet surveillance law after the USA Patriot Act: the big brother that isn't," *Northwestern University Law Review* 97 (2), 607–73 (2003), https://papers.ssrn.com/sol3/papers.cfm?abstract_id=317501; C. Ciocchetti, "The eavesdropping employer: a twenty-first century framework for employee monitoring," *American Business Law Journal* 48 (2), 285–369 (2011), https://doi.org/10.1111/j.1744-1714.2011.01116.x; L. Determann and R. Sprague, "Intrusive monitoring: employee privacy expectations are reasonable in Europe, destroyed in the United States," *Berkeley Technology Law Journal* 26 (2), 979–1036 (2011), https://www.jstor.org/stable/24118681; T. Traylor-Notaro, "Workplace privacy in the age of social media," *Global Business Law Review* 7 (1), 133–55 (2018), https://engagedscholarship.csuohio.edu/cgi/viewcontent.cgi?article=1064&context=gblr.
49. K. Rosenberg, "Location surveillance by GPS: balancing an employer's business interest with employee privacy," *Washington Journal of Law, Technology & Arts* 6 (2), 144–54 (2010), https://digitalcommons.law.uw.edu/cgi/viewcontent.cgi?article=1108&context=wjlta; D. Towns and L. Cobb, "Notes on GPS technology: employee monitoring enters a new era," *Labor Law Journal* 63 (3), 203–08 (2012), https://search.proquest.com/openview/faa68c4906175719b9cdf8cddb219ce6/1?pq-origsite=gscholar&cbl=41326; A. McNichol, "Privacy in the age of smartphones: a better standard for GPS tracking," *Arizona State Law Journal* 45 (3), 1277–96 (2013), https://arizonastatelawjournal.org/wp-content/uploads/2014/04/45-Ariz.-St.-L.J.-1277-2013.pdf.
50. C. Wardle and H. Derakhshan, *Information Disorder: Toward an Interdisciplinary Framework for Research and Policymaking* (Brussels: Council of Europe, 2017), https://rm.coe.int/information-disorder-report-version-august-2018/16808c9c77. See also D. Fallis, "What is disinformation?" *Library Trends* 63 (3), 401–26 (2015), https://doi.org/10.1353/lib.2015.0014; L. Turcilo and M. Obrenovic, *Misinformation, Disinformation, Malinformation: Causes, Trends, and Their Influence on Democracy* (Berlin: Heinrich Boll Foundation, 2020), https://www.boell.de/sites/default/files/2020-08/200825_E-Paper3_ENG.pdf.

51. 18 U.S. Code 1038, https://www.law.cornell.edu/uscode/text/18/1038.
52. H. Wechsler, "Codification of criminal law in the United States: the Model Penal Code," *Columbia Law Review* 68 (8), 1425–56 (1968), https://doi.org/10.2307/1121103.
53. New York Penal Law 240.50, Falsely reporting an incident in the third degree, https://codes.findlaw.com/ny/penal-law/pen-sect-240-50.html. This law also applies to false reports of child abuse and maltreatment.
54. Cybersecurity Law of the People's Republic of China, adopted November 7, 2016, https://perma.cc/3HAP-D6MZ.
55. Computer and Cybercrimes Bill, 2017, which was signed into law in May 2018, http://kenyalaw.org/kl/fileadmin/pdfdownloads/bills/2017/ComputerandCybercrimesBill_2017.pdf.
56. Protection from Online Falsehoods and Manipulation Act 2019, https://sso.agc.gov.sg/Acts-Supp/18-2019.
57. Belarus: https://news.tut.by/society/595733.html; Burkina Faso: https://cpj.org/2019/07/burkina-faso-parliament-passes-legal-revisions-cri/; France: https://www.assemblee-nationale.fr/dyn/15/textes/l15t0190_texte-adopte-provisoire.pdf; Cambodia: https://www.article19.org/data/files/medialibrary/37516/Draft-Law-On-CyberCrime_Englishv1.pdf; Cameroon: https://www.minpostel.gov.cm/index.php/en/les-textes/telecoms-tic/lois-telecoms-tic/179-law-no-2010-012-of-21-december-2010-on-cybersecurity-and-cybercrime-in-cameroon; Malaysia: https://asset.mkn.gov.my/web/wp-content/uploads/sites/3/2021/03/Ordinan-Anti-Berita-Tidak-Benar-20211.pdf.
58. For a variety of journalistic viewpoints about misinformation, see H. Tumber and S. Waisbord, eds., *The Routledge Companion to Media Disinformation and Populism* (New York: Routledge, 2021).
59. The Fair Trade Commission Act, 15 U.S.C. §§ 52 et seq. https://www.law.cornell.edu/uscode/text/15/chapter-2/subchapter-I. See I. Millstein, "The Federal Trade Commission and false advertising," *Columbia Law Review* 64 (3), 439–99 (1964), https://doi.org/10.2307/1120732; G. Klass, "False advertising law," in A. Gold et al., eds., *The Oxford Handbook of the New Private Law* (New York: Oxford University Press, 2021), 391–408.
60. Examples include the Canadian Competition Act, R.S.C., 1985, c. C-34, especially Part VII.1, https://laws.justice.gc.ca/eng/acts/C-34/index.html; the United Kingdom Consumer Protection from Unfair Trading Regulations 2008, https://www.legislation.gov.uk/uksi/2008/1277/contents/made; and Business Protection from Misleading Marketing Regulations 2008, https://www.legislation.gov.uk/uksi/2008/1276/pdfs/uksi_20081276_en.pdf; the Australian Competition and Consumer Act 2010, https://www.legislation.gov.au/Details/C2021C00289; and Directive 2006/114 EC concerning misleading and comparative advertising, https://eur-lex.europa.eu/legal-content/EN/TXT/?uri=celex%3A32006L0114.
61. T. Quach, "In groundbreaking settlements, Attorneys General find fake social media engagement illegal," *National Law Review*, April 1, 2019, https://www.natlawreview.com/article/groundbreaking-settlements-attorneys-general-find-fake-social-media-engagement; N. Confessore et al., "The follower factory," *New York Times*, January 27, 2018, https://www.nytimes.com/interactive/2018/01/27/technology

/social-media-bots.html; A. Anand et al., *Influencer Marketing with Fake Followers*, IIM Bangalore Research Paper No. 580 (Bengaluru, India: Indian Institute of Management Bangalore, 2020), https://papers.ssrn.com/sol3/papers.cfm?abstract_id=3306088.

62. As an example, see chapter 1825 of the National Institutes of Health Policy Manual, which specifies compliance requirements for collection of information from the public by NIH contractors. https://policymanual.nih.gov/1825. Examples of the few publications that deal with outsourcing of information collection include T. Schoenherr et al., "A note on the use of survey research firms to enable empirical data collection," *Journal of Business Logistics* 36 (3), 288-300, https://doi.org/10.1111/jbl.12092, and K. Ahlstrom-Vij, "Is there a problem with cognitive outsourcing?" *Philosophical Issues* 26 (1), 7-24 (2016), https://doi.org/10.1111/phis.12072.
63. D. Kaplan, "Suspicions and spies in Silicon Valley," *Newsweek*, September 17, 2006, https://www.newsweek.com/suspicions-and-spies-silicon-valley-109827; M. Baer, "Corporate policing and corporate governance: what can we learn from Hewlett Packard's pretexting scandal," *University of Cincinnati Law Review* 77 (4), 524-83, https://core.ac.uk/download/pdf/228610556.pdf; J. Emshwiller, "Old Trick: Hewlett-Packard was far from first to try 'pretexting'—but long-used device to gain personal data now faces stiffer federal prohibition—new reality for auto lenders," *Wall Street Journal*, December 16, 2006, A1, http://osint.pbworks.com/f/pretexting nothing new.pdf; S. Bennett, "Ethics of pretexting in a cyber world," *McGeorge Law Review* 41 (2), 271-79 (2010), https://scholarlycommons.pacific.edu/cgi/viewcontent.cgi?article=1234&context=mlr.
64. *ASCE Standard Guideline for Recording and Exchanging Utility Infrastructure Data*, https://ascelibrary.org/doi/abs/10.1061/9780784415924.
65. C. Campailla et al., "ISO 45001," in M. Sartor and G. Orzes, eds., *Quality Management: Tools, Methods, and Standards* (Bingley, England: Emerald Publishing, 2019), 217-34, https://doi.org/10.1108/978-1-78769-801-720191014; N. Sadiq, *Establishing an Occupational Health & Safety Management System Based on ISO 45001* (Ely, Cambridgeshire, UK: IT Governance Publishing, 2019).
66. National Commission for the Protection of Human Subjects of Biomedical and Behavioral Research, *The Belmont Report: Ethical Principles and Guidelines for the Protection of Human Subjects of Research* (Washington, D.C.: Department of Health, Education, and Welfare, 1979), https://www.hhs.gov/ohrp/regulations-and-policy/belmont-report. Examples of the many articles on the Belmont Report's impact on bioethics and continuing relevance include E. Adashi et al., "The Belmont Report at 40: Reckoning with time," *American Journal of Public Health* 108 (10), 1345-48 (2018), https://doi.org/10.2105/AJPH.2018.304580; J. Childress et al., eds., *Belmont Revisited: Ethical Principles for Research with Human Subjects* (Washington, DC: Georgetown University Press, 2005); A. Paxton, "The Belmont Report in the age of big data: Ethics at the intersection of psychological science and data science," in S. Woo et al., eds., *Big Data in Psychological Research* (Washington, DC: American Psychological Association, 2020), https://doi.org/10.1037/0000193-016; and K. Brothers et al., "Belmont Reboot: Building a normative foundation for human research in the twenty-first century," *Journal of Law, Medicine & Ethics* 47 (1), 165-72 (2019), https://doi.org/10.1177/1073110519840497.

67. https://allea.org/code-of-conduct/.
68. https://cdn.ymaws.com/wera.site-ym.com/resource/resmgr/a_general/aera.pdf.
69. https://aisnet.org/page/MemberCodeOfConduct. On information requirements for IT professionals, see E. Oz, "Ethical standards for computer professionals: a comparative analysis of four major codes," *Journal of Business Ethics* 12, 709–26 (1993), https://doi.org/10.1007/BF00881385.
70. https://www.asanet.org/sites/default/files/savvy/images/asa/docs/pdf/Ethics Code.pdf.
71. https://www.acjs.org/page/Code_Of_Ethics.
72. B. Tran and P. Gonzales, "Standards and guidelines for personal health records in the United States: finding consensus in a rapidly evolving and divided environment," *Journal of Health and Medical Informatics* S6:001 (2012), open access journal, https://doi.org/10.4172/2157-7420.S6-001.
73. *Safety of Nuclear Power Plants: Commissioning and Operation*, No. SSR-2/2. Vienna: International Atomic Energy Agency, 2016, https://www.iaea.org/publications/10886/safety-of-nuclear-power-plants-commissioning-and-operation; *Ageing Management and Development of a Programme for Long Term Operation of Nuclear Power Plants*, No. SSG-48 (Vienna: International Atomic Energy Agency, 2018), https://www.iaea.org/publications/12240/ageing-management-and-development-of-a-programme-for-long-term-operation-of-nuclear-power-plants; A. Rashdan and S. St. Germain, "Methods of data collection in nuclear power plants," *Nuclear Technology* 205 (8), 1062–74 (2019), https://doi.org/10.1080/00295450.2019.1610637.
74. https://www.mrs.org.uk/pdf/MRS-Code-of-Conduct-2019.pdf. Publications that discuss the MRS Code and ethical marketing codes in general include A. Yallop and S. Mowat, "Investigating marketing research ethics: an empirical study of codes of ethics in practice and their effect on ethical behaviour," *International Journal of Market Research* 58 (3), 381–400 (2016), https://doi.org/10.2501/IJMR-2016-011; R. Giacobbe and M. Segal, "Comparative analysis of ethical perceptions in marketing research: *U.S.A. vs. Canada*," *Journal of Business Ethics* 27 (2), 229–45 (2000), https://doi.org/10.1023/A:1006121122073; S. Robson, "Ethics: informed consent of misinformed compliance," *International Journal of Market Research* 33 (1), 1–12 (1991), https://doi.org/10.1177/147078539103300103; J. Dawson and J. Hiller, "Competitor mystery shopping: methodological considerations and implications for the MRS code of conduct," *International Journal of Market Research* 37 (4), 1–10 (1995), https://doi.org/10.1177/147078539503700406.
75. https://www.esomar.org/uploads/public/knowledge-and-standards/codes-and-guidelines/ICCESOMAR_Code_English_.pdf. The same principles are presented in the ESOMAR/GRBN Guideline for Researchers and Clients Involved in Primary Data Collection, which was developed jointly with the Global Research Business Network, https://www.esomar.org/what-we-do/code-guidelines/primary-data-collection-guideline. On the ICC/ESOMAR code and ethical aspects of information collection, see K. Joe et al., "The ethical issues of survey and market research," in C. Wolf et al., eds., *The Sage Handbook of Survey Methodology* (Los Angeles: Sage Reference, 2016), 77–86; M. Kirkup and M. Carrigan, "Video surveillance research in retailing: ethical issues," *International Journal of Retail & Distribution Manage-*

ment 28 (11), 470-80 (2000), https://doi.org/10.1108/09590550010356831; D. Nunan and M. Di Domenico, "Market research and the ethics of big data," *International Journal of Market Research* 55 (4), 505-20 (2013), https://doi.org/10.2501/IJMR-2013-015; M. Couper and E. Singer, "Informed consent for web paradata use," *Survey Research Methods* 7 (1), 57-67 (2013), https://www.ncbi.nlm.nih.gov/pmc/articles/PMC3790572/-R24.

76. Advertising Research Foundation, Member Code of Conduct, https://thearf.org/wp-content/uploads/2019/03/ARF-Code-of-Conduct-2019.pdf.
77. https://www.insightsassociation.org/issues-policies/insights-association-code-standards-and-ethics-market-research-and-data-analytics-0.
78. Council of International Investigators, Code of Ethics, https://www.cii2.org/code-of-ethics; https://nalionline.org/become-a-member/code-of-ethics/. See also A. Aubry, "Ethics for investigators," 53 (2), 269-71 (1962), https://scholarlycommons.law.northwestern.edu/cgi/viewcontent.cgi?article=5097&context=jclc; S. Miller and I. Gordon, *Investigative Ethics: Ethics for Police Detectives and Criminal Investigators* (Chichester, West Sussex: Wiley Blackwell, 2014).
79. National Association of Legal Investigators, Code of Ethics, https://nalionline.org/become-a-member/code-of-ethics/.
80. Strategic & Competitive Intelligence Professionals, Code of Ethics, https://www.scip.org/page/Ethical-Intelligence. Examples of the many articles on the ethics of business intelligence and information collection include N. Schultz et al., "The ethics of business intelligence," *Journal of Business Ethics* 13 (4), 305-14 (1994), https://www.jstor.org/stable/25072534; Lal. Collins and N. Schultz, "A review of ethics for competitive intelligence activities," *Competitive Intelligence Review* 7 (2), 56-66 (1996), https://doi.org/10.1002/cir.3880070209; Paine, "Corporate policy and the ethics of competitor intelligence gathering," *Journal of Business Ethics* 10 (6), 423-36 (1991), https://www.jstor.org/stable/25072169; L. Trevino and G. Weaver, "Ethical issues in competitive intelligence practice: consensus, conflicts, and challenges," *Competitive Intelligence Review* 8 (1), 61-72 (2006), https://doi.org/10.1002/cir.3880080111.
81. Society of Professional Journalists, SPJ Code of Ethics, https://www.spj.org/ethicscode.asp; Canadian Association of Journalists, Ethics Guidelines, https://caj.ca/ethics/; and IFJ Global Charter of Ethics for Journalists, https://www.ifj.org/who/rules-and-policy/global-charter-of-ethics-for-journalists.html. For additional discussion, see R. Herrscher, "A universal code of journalism ethics: problems, limitations, and proposals," *Journal of Mass Media Ethics* 17 (4), 277-89 (2002), https://doi.org/10.1207/S15327728JMME1704_03; S. Ward, "Philosophical foundations for global journalism ethics," *Journal of Mass Media Ethics* 20 (1), 3-21 (2010), https://doi.org/10.1207/s15327728jmme2001_2; K. Hafez, "Journalism ethics revisited: a comparison of ethics codes in Europe, North Africa, the Middle East, and Muslim Asia," *Political Communication* 19 (2), 225-50 (2010), https://doi.org/10.1080/10584600252907461.
82. *Ethical Journalism: a Handbook of Values and Practices for the News and Opinion Departments*, https://www.nytimes.com/editorial-standards/ethical-journalism.html.
83. RTDNA Code of Ethics, https://www.rtdna.org/content/rtdna_code_of_ethics.
84. RTDNA coverage guidelines, https://www.rtdna.org/content/coverage_guidelines.

85. C. Liu and K. Arnett, "An examination of privacy policies in Fortune 500 web sites," *American Journal of Business* 17 (1), 13-22 (2002), https://doi.org/10.1108/19355181200200001; R. Zaeem and K. Barber, "A study of web privacy policies across industries," *Journal of Information Privacy and Security* 13 (4), 169-85 (2017), https://doi.org/10.1080/15536548.2017.1394064.
86. The Roche Group Code of Conduct, https://code-of-conduct.roche.com/en/records-information-management.html.
87. See, for example, the Associated Press New Values and Principles, https://www.ap.org/about/news-values-and-principles/; the NPR Ethics Handbook, https://www.npr.org/ethics; and the *Los Angeles Times* Ethics Guidelines, https://latimesblogs.latimes.com/readers/2011/02/la-times-ethics-guidelines.html.
88. On plagiarism resulting from carelessness, see N. Perrin, "How I became a plagiarist," *American Scholar* 61 (2), 257-59 (1992), https://www.jstor.org/stable/41212011.
89. For an excellent overview, see J. Geraldi, "Plagiarism in project studies," *Project Management Journal* 52 (1), 3-10 (2021), https://doi.org/10.1177/8756972820982443. Also R. Posner, *The Little Book of Plagiarism* (New York: Pantheon, 2007); J. Snapper, "The matter of plagiarism: what, why, and if," in K. Himma and H. Tavani, eds., *The Handbook of Information and Computer Ethics* (Hoboken, NJ: Wiley, 2008), 533-52, https://www.cems.uwe.ac.uk/~pchatter/2011/pepi/The_Handbook_of_Information_and_Computer_Ethics.pdf-page=568.
90. T. Tudoroiu, "No prime minister: PhD plagiarism of high level public officials," *European Review* 25 (4), 623-41 (2017), https://doi.org/10.1017/S1062798717000229.
91. See, for example, S. Stretton et al., "Publication misconduct and plagiarism retractions: a systematic, retrospective study," *Current Medical Research and Opinion*, 28 (10): 1575-83 (2012), https://doi.org/10.1185/03007995.2012.728131; J. Wang et al., "Retraction of neurosurgical publications: a systematic review," *World Neurosurgery* 103, 809-14 (2017), https://doi.org/10.1016/j.wneu.2017.04.014; L. Chambers et al, "Plagiarism and data falsification are the most common reasons for retracted publications in obstetrics and gynaecology," *BJOG* 126, 1134-40 (2019), https://obgyn.onlinelibrary.wiley.com/doi/pdf/10.1111/1471-0528.15689; T. Wang et al., "Retracted publications in the biomedical literature from open access journals," *Science and Engineering Ethics* 25 (3), 855-68 (2019), https://doi.org/10.1007/s11948-018-0040-6; K. Amos, "The ethics of scholarly publishing: exploring differences in plagiarism and duplicate publication across nations," *Journal of the Medical Library Association* 102(2), 87-91 (2014), https://doi.org / 10.3163/1536-5050.102.2.005.
92. P. Hoffer, *Past Imperfect: Facts, Fictions, Fraud—American History from Bancroft and Parkman to Ambrose, Bellesiles, Ellis, and Goodwin* (New York: Public Affairs, 2004); R. Robin, *Scandals and Scoundrels: Seven Cases That Shook the Academy* (Berkeley: University of California Press, 2004).
93. On the prevalence and impact of corporate disinformation, see A. Scott, "Blinded by a culture of disinformation," *Skeptical Inquirer* 34 (4), 39-44 (2010), https://skepticalinquirer.org/wp-content/uploads/sites/29/2010/07/p39.pdf. P. Dishman and P. Nitse, "Disinformation usage in corporate communications: CI'ers beware," *Competitive Intelligence Review* 10 (4), 20-29 (1999), https://doi.org/10.1002/(SICI)1520-6386(199934)10:4<20::AID-CIR5>3.0.CO;2-L; E. Kane, "Continuing dangers of disinformation in corporate accounting reports," *Review of Financial*

Economics 13 (1-2), 149-64 (2004), https://doi.org/10.1016/j.rfe.2003.09.007; W. Laufer, "Social accountability and corporate greenwashing," *Journal of Business Ethics* 43 (3), 253-61 (2003), https://doi.org/10.1023/A:1022962719299; S. Kolmes, "Climate change: a disinformation campaign," *Environment: Science and Policy for Sustainable Development* 53 (4), 33-37 (2011), https://www.tandfonline.com/doi/full/10.1080/00139157.2011.588553; K. Mulvey et al., *The Climate Deception Dossiers: Internal Fossil Fuel Industry Memos Reveal Decades of Corporate Disinformation* (Cambridge, MA: Union of Concerned Scientists, 2015), https://www.ucsusa.org/resources/climate-deception-dossiers?s_src=socnet&s_subscr=twitter&utm_campaign=tw&utm_medium=tw&utm_source=tw-ucs-report-downloads; B. Rockwood, "Corporate disinformation & business social responsibility: the case of climate change denial," in J. Belloit, ed., *NABET Proceedings 2007* (Clarion, PA: Northeastern Association of Business, Economics, and Technology, 2007), 330-40, http://www.nabet.us/Archives/2007/NABET 2007 Proceedings.pdf-page=339; T. Lyon and M. Maxwell, "Greenwash: corporate environmental disclosure under threat of audit," *Journal of Economics & Management Strategy* 20 (1), 3-41 (2011), https://doi.org/10.1111/j.1530-9134.2010.00282.x; L. Edwards, "Organized lying and professional legitimacy: public relations' accountability in the disinformation debate," *European Journal of Communication* (December 2020, online only), https://doi.org/10.1177/0267323120966851.

94. C. Sunstein, *On the Wrongness of Lies*, Harvard Public Law Working Paper No. 21-05 (May 6, 2020), https://papers.ssrn.com/sol3/papers.cfm?abstract_id=3594420; C. Sunstein, *Liars: Falsehood and Free Speech in an Age of Deception* (New York: Oxford University Press, 2021).
95. R. Howard, "The ethics of plagiarism," in M. Pemberton, eds., *The Ethics of Writing Instruction: Issues in Theory and Practice* (Stamford, CT: Ablex Publishing, 2000), 79-89; D. Jameson, "The ethics of plagiarism: how genre affects writers' use of source materials," *Bulletin of the Association for Business Communication* 56 (2): 18-28 (1993), https://doi.org/10.1177/108056999305600204; B. Martin, "Plagiarism: a misplaced emphasis," *Journal of Information Ethics* 3 (2), 36-47 (1994), https://www.bmartin.cc/pubs/94jie.html; B. Martin, "Plagiarism, misrepresentation, and exploitation by established professionals," in T. Bretag, ed., *Handbook of Academic Integrity* (Singapore: Springer, 2016), 913-27, https://www.bmartin.cc/pubs/16hai/Martin.html.
96. T. Foltynek et al., "Academic plagiarism detection: a systematic literature review," *ACM Computer Surveys* 52 (6), 1-42 (2020), https://doi.org/10.1145/3345317.
97. W. Biswas, "Carbon footprint and embodied energy consumption assessment of building construction works in Western Australia," *International Journal of Sustainable Built Environment* 3 (2), 179-86 (2014), https://doi.org/10.1016/j.ijsbe.2014.11.004, found that printers account for a small percentage of an office building's total energy consumption, but A. Mezes et al., "Estimating the energy consumption and power demand of small power equipment in office buildings," *Energy and Buildings* 75, 199-209 (2014), https://doi.org/10.1016/j.enbuild.2014.02.011, concluded that printers, photocopiers, and other small power devices collectively account for substantial energy use and internal heat gains in office buildings. When operating, laser printers use more energy than personal computers. Some models even use more energy than personal computers in the standby mode. Ink jet printers use a smaller but not negligible amount

of energy when compared to laser models. See G. Katarzyna and T. Tomasz, "Life cycle assessment of an inkjet printer," *Policy Journal of Environmental Studies* 21 (5A), 95–105 (2012), https://www.researchgate.net/profile/Katarzyna-Grzesik-2/publication/276385268_Life_cycle_assessment_of_an_inkjet_printer/links/5840a77408ae2d21755f3b9d/Life-cycle-assessment-of-an-inkjet-printer.pdf; W. Kerr and C. Ryan, "Eco-efficiency gains from remanufacturing: a case study of photocopier remanufacturing at Fuji Xerox Australia," *Journal of Cleaner Produc tion* 9 (1), 75–81 (2001), https://doi.org/10.1016/S0959-6526(00)00032-9.

98. Estimates of the carbon footprint of one sheet of A4-size office paper from its origin to delivery to the consumer ranges from 4.29 to 4.72 CO_2 equivalent, according to A. Dias and L. Arroja, "Comparison of methodologies for estimating the carbon footprint: case study of office paper," *Journal of Cleaner Production* 24, 30–35 (2012), https://doi.org/10.1016/j.jclepro.2011.11.005. On the environmental impact of knowledge-based activities, see N. Cambaz et al., "Life cycle assessment of an office: carbon footprint of an office staff," *Environmental Research and Technology* 1 (4), 34–39 (2018), https://dergipark.org.tr/en/pub/ert/issue/39504/428798; T. Tjandra et al., "Framework and method to quantify carbon footprint based on an office environment in Singapore," *Journal of Cleaner Production* 112 (5), 4183–95 (2016), https://doi.org/10.1016/j.jclepro.2015.06.067.
99. Studies suggest that paper products deposited in landfills will decompose within twenty years. See, for example, X. Wang et al., "Decomposition and carbon storage of selected paper products in laboratory-scale landfills," *Science of the Total Environment* 532, 70–79 (2015), https://doi.org/10.1016/j.scitotenv.2015.05.132; X. Wang et al., "Decomposition of forest products buried in landfills," *Waste Management* 33 (11), 2267–76 (2013), https://doi.org/10.1016/j.wasman.2013.07.009; J. Micales and K. Skog, "The decomposition of forest products in landfills," *International Biodeterioration & Biodegradation* 39 (2-3), 145–58 (1997), https://doi.org/10.1016/S0964-8305(97)83389-6; M. Barlaz, "Forest products decomposition in municipal solid waste landfills," *Waste Management* 26 (4), 321–33 (2006), https://doi.org/10.1016/j.wasman.2005.11.002; T. Counsell and J. Allwood, "Reducing climate change gas emissions by cutting out stages in the life cycle of office paper," *Resources, Conservation and Recycling* 49 (4), 340–52 (2007), https://doi.org/10.1016/j.resconrec.2006.03.018.
100. E. Masanet et al., "Recalibrating global data center energy-use estimates," *Science* 367 (6481), 984–86, https://doi.org/10.1126/science.aba3758; J. Malmodin and D. Lunden, "The energy and carbon footprint of the global ICT and E&M sectors 2010–2015," *Sustainability* 10 (9), 3027 (2018), https://doi.org/10.3390/su10093027; A. Shehabi et al., *United States Data Center Energy Usage Report* (Berkeley, CA: Lawrence Berkeley National Laboratory, 2016), https://www.osti.gov/servlets/purl/1372902.
101. C. Stoll et al., "The carbon footprint of bitcoin," *Joule* 3 (7), 1647–61, https://doi.org/10.1016/j.joule.2019.05.012; Cambridge Bitcoin Electricity Consumption Index, https://cbeci.org/cbeci/comparisons.
102. N. Jones, "How to stop data centres from gobbling up the world's electricity," *Nature* 561, 163–66 (2018), https://doi.org/10.1038/d41586-018-06610-y.

103. J. Taina, "How green is your software?" in P. Tyrvainen et al., eds., *Software Business: ICSOB 2010—Lecture Notes in Business Information Processing, Vol. 51* (Berlin: Springer, 2010), https://doi.org/10.1007/978-3-642-13633-7_13; S. Agarwal et al., "Sustainable approaches and good practices in green software engineering," *International Journal of Research and Reviews in Computer Science* 3 (1), 1425-28, https://www.researchgate.net/profile/Asoke-Nath-4/publication/266052297_Sustainable_Approaches_and_Good_Practices_in_Green_Software_Engineering/links/5516ce390cf2f7d80a39add8/Sustainable-Approaches-and-Good-Practices-in-Green-Software-Engineering.pdf.
104. M. Berners-Lee, *How Bad are Bananas?: The Carbon Footprint of Everything.* (Vancouver: Greystone Books, 2011), but a 2020 revision of the book downplays the significance of email's carbon footprint.
105. J. Recker et al., "Measuring the carbon footprint of business processes," in M. zur Muehlen and J. Su, eds., *Business Process Management Workshops, BPM 2010: Lecture Notes in Business Information Processing* (Berlin: Springer, 2011), 511-20, https://doi.org/10.1007/978-3-642-20511-8_47; M. Tenhunen and E. Penttinen, "Assessing the carbon footprint of paper vs. electronic invoicing," *ACIS 2010 Proceedings*, 95, https://aisel.aisnet.org/cgi/viewcontent.cgi?article=1012&context=acis2010.
106. A. Huang, "A model for environmentally sustainable information system development," *Journal of Computer Information Systems* 49 (4), 114-21 (2009), https://www.tandfonline.com/doi/abs/10.1080/08874417.2009.11645346. On the other hand, G. Song et al., "Carbon footprint of a scientific publication," *Ecological Indicators* 60, 275-82 (2016), https://doi.org/10.1016/j.ecolind.2015.06.044, found that the adverse environmental impact of reading from a printed copy can be lower than reading online in some circumstances. G. Chowdhury, "How digital information services can reduce greenhouse gas emissions," *Online Information Review* 36 (4), 489-506 (2012), https://doi.org/10.1108/14684521211254022, advocates digitization to replace printed content in libraries.
107. OVO Energy press release, November 26, 2019, https://www.ovoenergy.com/ovo-newsroom/press-releases/2019/november/think-before-you-thank-if-every-brit-sent-one-less-thank-you-email-a-day-we-would-save-16433-tonnes-of-carbon-a-year-the-same-as-81152-flights-to-madrid.

3

Information Retention and Disposition

Policies and procedures for the retention and disposition of information are developed by records managers and information governance specialists who work with an organization's legal department, compliance officers, risk managers, department heads, and other interested parties to ensure that all stakeholders' interests, business requirements, and external mandates are addressed. In this context, retention refers to the period of time that information must be kept, while disposition refers to the actions to be taken when the retention period elapses. Compliant retention and disposition practices are an essential component of an organization's information governance framework.

Legal and regulatory requirements for retention and disposition of information are the most widely discussed compliance concerns, but they are not the only ones. An organization may be contractually obligated to keep, destroy, or transfer information in specific situations. Standards and norms provide retention and disposition guidelines for information maintained by certain industries and professions. In many organizations, codes of conduct mandate compliance with internal policies for retention and disposition of information. Such policies may be guided by ethical norms and sustainability objectives in addition to business objectives.

This chapter is principally concerned with retention and disposition requirements for nonpermanent records maintained by companies, government agencies, and nonprofit organizations. Compliance requirements for information that warrants permanent preservation are discussed in the next chapter.

LEGAL AND REGULATORY COMPLIANCE

Legal requirements for the retention and disposition of information are more numerous than those associated with other topics discussed in this book. Globally, thousands of laws, regulations, rules, ordinances, directives, and other legal instruments specify retention and disposition mandates for information related to business operations and activities that are subject to government oversight. These legal and regulatory compliance requirements can be divided into four broad groups:

- Laws, regulations, and related legal instruments that specify minimum retention periods for information. In the twentieth century, records retention programs emphasized the destruction of obsolete information to reduce recordkeeping costs. Over the last several decades, the focus has shifted to ensuring that information is retained long enough to satisfy legal and regulatory mandates. This is the largest category of compliance requirements discussed in this book. Laws and regulations affect the information retention and disposition practices of every organization in every location where it operates, but the pervasiveness of such legal requirements varies from one political jurisdiction to another.
- Laws, regulations, and related legal instruments that mandate the destruction of information, that specify maximum retention periods for information, or that allow external parties to specify a maximum retention period for certain information. This category of laws and regulations was once limited to a narrow range of information, but the widespread adoption of privacy and data protection legislation has broadened its applicability.
- Laws and regulations that prescribe destruction methods for information. These requirements principally apply to confidential or sensitive information that requires secure destruction.
- Laws that mandate retention of information that is deemed relevant for litigation, government investigations, or other legal proceedings. Failure to comply with requirements to preserve such information can have significant adverse consequences.

The legal and regulatory compliance requirements discussed in the following sections apply to a subset of an organization's recorded information, but that subset can be large, and compliance can be difficult to achieve. Accurate identification and interpretation of applicable requirements in all political jurisdictions where an organization has business operations is a challenging and time-consuming task. In the absence of a comprehensive global index to retention and disposition mandates, each country's laws and regulations must be researched individually. In federated countries, laws and regulations issued by states, provinces, and other subnational jurisdictions must be considered. In the United States, for example, many business operations and activities are regulated at the state level, and some municipalities or other local governmental entities have laws and regulations that specify retention or disposition requirements for particular types of information.

MINIMUM RETENTION PERIODS

In some countries, the information retention and disposition practices of government agencies are more heavily regulated than those of non-governmental entities. In the United States, legislation gives archival agencies the authority to define retention requirements for public records. At the federal level, laws and regulations authorize the archivist of the United States to identify government records that warrant permanent preservation and specify retention periods and disposition dates for nonpermanent records.[1] Based on that authority, the National Archives and Records Administration (NARA) has issued a set of general retention schedules that cover data, documents, and other information maintained by several or all federal agencies. These general retention schedules cover information associated with common functions, such as accounting, procurement, human resources, and facilities management. Federal agencies must adopt the general schedules and develop additional retention guidance for information that is not covered by them. The general retention schedules specify actual rather than minimum retention periods, but longer retention is permitted if there is a demonstrable business need. For some information, the general schedules specify a range of acceptable retention periods—from four to seven years, for example. Laws and regulations authorize NARA to inspect the records management practices of federal agencies for compliance with the general schedules.

The retention authority of state archives generally follows the federal model. Most state archives specify retention and disposition requirements for information maintained by state government agencies, county and municipal governments, public school districts, and public institutions of higher education, as well as public benefit corporations, authorities, boards, commissions, public utilities, and other quasi-government entities, subject to exception and exclusions. This authority is based on archival legislation. In a few states, however, the Archives' authority is limited information that warrants permanent preservation; retention requirements for nonpermanent information are defined by a nonarchival agency, such as a Secretary of State. Unified court systems, in states where they exist, typically establish their own retention rules. Some larger municipalities may have independent retention authority; in New York City, for example, the municipal archival agency has issued a retention schedule that supplements the New York State Archives' retention guidance and supplants it for certain records.

While their scope and completeness vary from state to state, the retention schedules prepared by archival agencies and other authorities cover a broad range of information related to general and specialized government operations. The most comprehensive examples are detailed and incorporate federal legal and regulatory retention and disposition requirements that apply to state and local government. Some archival agencies issue separate schedules for different types of state and local government entities; state government departments, counties, municipalities, school districts, and public benefit corporations may each have their own schedules, for example. For the most part, these schedules specify minimum retention requirements for information maintained by state and local government agencies. Individual agencies may retain records longer than the prescribed time period based on their business needs.

Archival agencies in other countries are similarly empowered to regulate the information retention and disposition practices of governmental entities at the national or subnational level. In some Asian and Eastern European countries, the minimum retention periods specified in schedules issued by archival authorities apply to selected data or documents maintained by companies and nonprofit organizations. The Archives Law of the People's Republic of China, for example, applies to all private enterprises, as do retention requirements specified in Order No. 10 of the State Archives Administration.[2] Similarly, Order No. 236 issued by Rosarkhiv, the Russian Federation's state archival agency, specifies retention requirements for information maintained by nongovernmental organizations.[3]

More commonly, however, retention requirements for information maintained by nongovernmental entities are specified in laws and regulations associated with particular business operations or industries. Retention periods specified by such laws and regulations are collectively described as recordkeeping requirements. Their purpose is to ensure that information related to regulated business operations or activities will be available when requested by government officials for audits, inspections, investigations, or enforcement actions. Recordkeeping laws and regulations apply to information of all types in all formats unless a particular type or format is specified.

All countries have recordkeeping laws or regulations that specify minimum retention requirements for certain information associated with commonly encountered business functions, operations, and activities. Examples include the following:

- Business formation and company registration laws specify retention periods ranging from three years to permanent for minutes and supporting documentation related to meetings of shareholders and governing bodies for corporations, limited liability companies, and other entities that operate in a given political jurisdiction. In some countries, these retention requirements also apply to resolutions that may be approved without a formal meeting and to information about a company's shareholders, partners, or other owners.
- Most countries have laws and regulations that specify retention requirements for information related to tax assessment and collection. Even countries without an income tax require retention of information related to sales taxes, excise taxes, and other revenue sources. In the United States, tax returns and supporting documentation must be retained as long as they are subject to audit, which is three years after the original due date of a tax return or the date the tax return was filed, whichever is later, although the audit period may be extended to six years or longer in some situations.[4] Tax laws in other countries specify minimum retention periods ranging from three to ten years from the end of the tax year to which the records pertain. These requirements apply to all organizations that are subject to tax laws in a given jurisdiction, even if no tax is owed. In the United States, charities, philanthropic foundations, and other tax-exempt entities must file tax returns and retain information that confirms their exempt status.

- National accounting laws, commercial codes, and other laws and regulations specify retention requirements for accounting databases, ledgers, financial reports, and other records that document an organization's business transactions and disclose its financial position. Minimum retention periods range from three to ten years, which may begin on the date when accounting information was created or, more commonly, the end of the calendar year, end of the fiscal year, or conclusion of the accounting transactions to which the information relates. In most countries, these minimum retention requirements are intended for for-profit companies, but they may also to apply to nonprofit organizations. The United States is one of the few countries without a national accounting law, but various federal and state regulations specify minimum retention periods for accounting records in certain industries, such as banking, insurance, transportation, and utilities. Regulations that specify record retention requirements also apply to accounting records maintained by federal contractors and any organization that receives federal grants.[5]
- Customs laws and regulations specify minimum retention periods ranging from several months to five or more years for certificates of origin, invoices, packing lists, shipping manifests, correspondence, and other information related to import or export of merchandise from the customs territory of one country to another.
- Most countries have laws and regulations that specify minimum retention periods for information related to an organization's employees, including names, job titles, duties, eligibility to work, wage rates, and the dates that employment began and ended. This information may be included in personnel files, human resources information systems, or other records. Typical retention requirements for employee information range from two to six years from the date the information was created or, in some cases, from termination of employment. Special retention requirements may apply to information about foreign workers, child labor, or workers in dangerous occupations.[6] Some countries also have laws and regulations that specify minimum retention periods for information related to unsuccessful job applicants. In the United States, federal and state laws specify minimum retention periods for information needed to confirm that an organization's hiring practices are not discriminatory. As with other retention regulations, an organization can keep information about employees or unsuccessful job applicants longer than the prescribed minimum period based on business needs. As discussed later in this chapter, however, privacy and data protection laws prohibit excessive retention of personal information.
- National laws and regulations specify minimum retention periods ranging from one to six years for payroll information, including regular and overtime hours worked by individual employees in each pay period, total wages per pay period, and deductions from wages paid.

- In most countries, employers must retain information about employment benefits, including details of retirement and welfare benefit plans and amendments, enrollment records, beneficiary designations, contributions made by the employer or individual employees, and records of benefits paid or due. In some countries, participants' information must be retained as long as benefits are payable, which may be a decade or longer following termination of employment. Following an employee's death, certain benefits may be payable to beneficiaries, which further extends the retention period.
- Occupational safety and health laws and regulations specify minimum retention periods for information related to workplace accidents, injuries, and illnesses. Special retention requirements apply to information about employees' exposure to hazardous substances. In some countries, such information must be retained for decades. In the United States, for example, employee medical records related to toxic exposure must be retained for thirty years following termination of employment. In EU member states, records of an employee's exposure to hazardous biological agents must be kept for forty years if an infection may arise in the future.

The recordkeeping requirements discussed above apply to commonly encountered information that is maintained by many types of organizations. A more numerous and varied group of retention requirements applies to specialized information maintained by industries and business operations that are regulated by one or more government agencies. Examples of such industries and business operations include banking, food processing, health care, insurance, investment services, petroleum manufacturing, pharmaceuticals, public accountancy, real estate, telecommunications, transportation, utilities, and waste management.

Among the thousands of industry-specific federal regulations that might be cited, banks must retain most records for a minimum of five years[7]; accounting firms must retain workpapers related to audits performed for public companies for seven years[8]; broker-dealers must retain customers' account information for a minimum of six years from the date an account is closed or the information was updated or replaced[9]; hospitals that participate in Medicare or Medicaid must retain patients' medical records for a minimum of five years from the date of discharge[10]; pharmaceutical manufacturers must retain production, control, or distribution information related to a batch of a drug for one year after the batch's expiration date[11]; pharmacies must retain records of transactions involving controlled substances for a minimum of two years[12]; operators of nuclear power plants must retain information related to special nuclear material for three years after transfer or disposal of the material[13]; and aircraft owners and operators must retain maintenance records for one year.[14] Industries and business operations that are regulated at the state level are subject to additional retention requirements.

As the foregoing examples suggest, sector-specific retention laws and regulations are so diverse that even a high-level survey is beyond the scope of this chapter, which can only provide an overview of the types of requirements with which an organization must comply. Minimum retention requirements vary from industry to industry, from country to country, and—for federated countries—from one state, province, or territory to another. Some sector-specific requirements for retention of information have been widely adopted. This is the case, for example, with anti-money laundering laws, which specify minimum retention requirements for customer and transaction records maintained by banks, credit unions, securities and commodities brokers and dealers, investment companies, life insurance companies, loan companies, currency exchange companies, casino operators, and other financial institutions and providers of financial services.[15] Such laws apply in more than one hundred countries.

For other industries, the more industrialized a country is, the greater the likelihood that it will have a well-established regulatory framework that includes information retention requirements. As an example, strict pharmaceutical regulations and their associated retention requirements for information related to testing, manufacturing, and marketing of drugs and medical devices have been adopted by about three dozen industrialized countries. By contrast, countries with limited or no oversight of the pharmaceutical industry have few, if any, regulatory requirements for retention of such information. Similarly, the telecommunications industry and its associated information retention practices are subject to laws and regulations in about three dozen countries and lightly regulated or unregulated elsewhere.

Compliance with minimum legal and regulatory retention requirements is not negotiable. Noncompliance may be detected during a routine regulatory audit, in the course of an investigation of suspected violations of the laws or regulations to which the information pertains, during the discovery phase of legal proceedings, or in other circumstances. Some laws require regulated entities to explain any premature destruction of information. Public utilities and licensees regulated by the Federal Energy Regulatory Commission, for example, must file a certified statement with the Commission listing the information that was destroyed and describing the circumstances of the destruction within ninety days of the date that the destruction was discovered.[16]

More commonly, noncompliance exposes an organization to fines, administrative penalties, increased regulatory scrutiny, and, in rare cases, criminal prosecution. Fines for willful or negligent noncompliance can be substantial. In the United States, for example, the Financial Crimes Enforcement Network (FINCEN), a unit of the Department of the Treasury that collects and analyzes information about financial transactions, imposes fines exceeding $212,000 for willful violations of the Bank Secrecy Act's recordkeeping requirements. The fine for a single negligent violation is $1,146, but the fine for a pattern of negligent activity exceeds $89,000.[17] Willful noncompliance involves intentional destruction of information before minimum retention requirements elapse. Negligent noncompliance involves unintentional but preventable destruction of information—accidental deletion of information that has not been backed up, for example.

Given the large number of laws and regulations that specify minimum retention requirements, inadvertent noncompliance is possible, even likely, in some situations. While an organization may be familiar with the most widely publicized retention requirements related to its business operations, laws and regulations that apply in a limited range of circumstances that occur infrequently may be overlooked. As an example, New York City prohibits the use of a job applicant's credit history in hiring decisions unless an exemption applies, but exemptions are strictly limited. In rare cases where an exemption is needed, an employer must retain records related to the exemption for five years from the date the exemption is used. Violations are subject to penalties up to $125,000. Penalties up to $250,000 apply to willful violations.[18]

MANDATORY DESTRUCTION OF INFORMATION

Laws and regulations that specify minimum retention periods establish baseline requirements that most organizations can satisfy with little or no disruption of their business operations. Many information custodians favor long retention of data or documents on the off-chance that they may be needed in the future. While unintentional or purposeful destruction of information before the minimum retention periods elapse is a possibility, data and documents are often allowed to accumulate after legal and regulatory requirements are satisfied. Large quantities of obsolete paper files must be removed from office areas when space is needed for other purposes, but housekeeping procedures to remove obsolete information from shared drives or personal computing devices are a low priority in many organizations. Obsolete email may only be deleted when an employee's mailbox reaches its capacity limit. Laws and regulations that specify minimum retention periods do not prohibit longer retention of information with continuing operational or scholarly value, and they do not mandate the destruction of information when its retention period elapses. From the perspective of some information custodians, retention beyond the required minimum time period eliminates the risk of noncompliance while satisfying an organization's future business needs, however poorly defined they may be.

By contrast, laws and regulations that limit or specify maximum retention periods mandate destruction of information when its retention period elapses. Data protection and privacy laws and regulations are the most widely encountered examples of legislation that limits retention of information. As noted in chapter 2, more than 120 countries and dependent territories have some form of data protection or privacy legislation, but their provisions related to retention and disposition of information are open to interpretation and dispute. All data protection and privacy laws and regulations mandate the prompt destruction of personal information when no longer needed for the purpose for which it was originally created or collected. Some data protection and privacy laws specify a time frame for this to occur. In the Russian Federation, for example, personal information must be destroyed within thirty days after it is no longer needed,[19] but prompt destruction is undefined in most countries. The European Union's General Data Protection Regulation, which was discussed in chapter 2, merely states that retention should be "limited to a strict minimum" and advises that "time limits should be established . . . for erasure or periodic review."[20] No time period is specified.

As a complication for compliance, interpretation is necessary to determine the point when personal information is no longer needed. As an example, many organizations retain information about former employees for three to ten years following termination of employment. Legal considerations account for a portion of that retention period, but operational needs also play a role. Personal information about a former employee may be useful if the employee wants to return to the organization, as is common in industries such as retail or hospitality with seasonal employment patterns, but facilitation of re-employment may not be one of the reasons that such information was originally collected. Even if it were, the accuracy and value of information about a former employee diminishes as time passes. Information about former employees may be useful for a few years to fulfill requests for verification of recent prior employment when authorized by a former employee or to simplify onboarding if the employee wants to return, but the legality and appropriateness of retaining inactive personnel files or database records for half a decade or longer is questionable.

Some countries have laws and regulations that specify short retention periods followed by mandatory destruction of images captured by video surveillance devices installed in publicly accessible spaces. In Macau, for example, surveillance recordings must not be retained longer than sixty days or thirty days after completion of any legal proceedings for which a recording is relevant.[21] In Albania, the maximum retention period for surveillance recordings is two months after a recording's purpose is fulfilled.[22] The United States is a notable exception. Retention of surveillance recordings is not regulated at the national level. Some state laws and regulations establish minimum rather than maximum retention periods for video surveillance recordings. In Nevada, for example, surveillance recordings from casinos must be retained for a minimum of thirty days if security interviews, detentions, or medical evaluations are depicted or for a minimum of seven days otherwise.[23] In New York State, surveillance recordings at ATM facilities must be retained for a minimum of forty-five days.[24]

Short retention of surveillance recordings is intended to protect the personal privacy and civil liberties of individuals depicted in the recordings. In EU member states, national video surveillance laws have been supplanted by the General Data Protection Regulation, which requires the timely destruction of surveillance recordings that depict recognizable persons if they are not needed as evidence in legal proceedings, but the GDPR does not specify a maximum retention period for surveillance recordings.[25] Some non-EU countries similarly interpret their data protection laws to encompass surveillance recordings without specifying a maximum retention period. Principle 6 of the Surveillance Camera Code of Practice, issued in the United Kingdom by the Home Office, is typical. It states that surveillance recordings should be deleted when their purposes are fulfilled, but a maximum retention period cannot be specified because purposes vary.[26] In Ontario, guidelines issued by the Information and Privacy Commissioner limit the retention of surveillance recordings by government institutions to the amount of time that is reasonably necessary to discover incidents that occurred in the area under surveillance. Any unused recordings should be discarded promptly thereafter, usually within seventy-two hours, but surveillance recordings that are used for law enforcement or other purposes must be retained for a minimum of one year to give individuals a reasonable opportunity to access personal information that the recordings may contain about them.[27]

Data protection laws and retention requirements for surveillance recordings apply to many types of organizations. In addition to public spaces, video surveillance devices are widely installed in banks, office building lobbies, stores, shopping malls, and other commercial locations. Other laws and regulations that specify maximum retention periods or mandate destruction of information when certain conditions are met are sector-specific:

- Some countries mandate the destruction of information maintained by social services agencies about unsubstantiated child abuse investigations, either immediately or after a specified period of time. In the United States, state social services agencies must have provisions and procedures for destruction of such information in place as a precondition for grants under the Child Abuse Prevention and Treatment Act.[28]
- Rules adopted by the United Nations General Assembly call for sealing of criminal case records of juvenile offenders followed by expungement after an appropriate period of time.[29] In many countries, criminal case information related to juvenile offenders is sealed when court proceedings are completed. National laws provide for court-ordered destruction of the information when the offender attains a specified age or after certain conditions are met. This may be done automatically or in response to a petition by the offender.[30]
- In some countries, adults convicted of certain criminal offenses can petition to have their court records destroyed after a specified period of time.[31] In many jurisdictions, destruction of criminal records is mandatory upon petition for cases terminated in favor of the accused.[32]
- In the United States, public school districts must destroy personally identifiable information about special education students at a parent's request when the information is no longer needed to provide educational

services to the child, but significant limitations apply. A school is allowed to retain a permanent record of a special education student's name, address, phone number, attendance, courses, grades, highest grade level completed, and year completed.[33]

- The "right to be forgotten," which is codified in article 17 of the GDPR, is the best known example of a legal provision that gives data subjects control over retention of personal information that is no longer necessary for the purpose for which it was originally collected. Upon request by the data subject, such information must be deleted or destroyed without delay; but, as noted above, an organization's continuing need for specific types of personal information is open to interpretation.
- Less ambiguously, data protection legislation mandates destruction or deletion of personal information if the data subject withdraws consent for processing it, if the retention period consented to has expired, if the data subject objects to the processing of personal data for a given purpose, or if the personal data has not been lawfully processed. Exclusions are provided for reasons related to national security, national defense, public safety, prosecution of criminal offenses, and avoidance of ethical breaches by regulated professions.[34]
- Destruction of information may be mandated by laws and regulations that apply in a limited range of circumstances and are not widely known to all organizations that must comply with them. According to the New York State Security Guard Act, for example, a security guard company or organization that employs its own registered security guards must destroy a security guard's records one year after termination of employment. This requirement applies to the security guard's registration card, photograph, and training records, as well as to the employer's proof of due diligence for verification information contained in a security guard's file.[35]

As with minimum retention requirements, violations of the laws and regulations described above expose an organization to fines and penalties. Civil actions by data subjects for over-retention of personal information are also possible. Sanctions for GDPR infractions, in particular, have been widely publicized. Administrative fines imposed by national data protection authorities in EU member states vary with the nature, gravity, and duration of the violation. A reprimand or small fine may be imposed for minor violations. According to GDPR article 83, however, fines can be as much as twenty million euros or up to four percent of an offending organization's worldwide annual profit for the preceding financial year, whichever is higher. Significant fines have been imposed to date. In addition, data subjects have the right to seek judicial remedies leading to a compensation award.[36]

DESTRUCTION METHODS

Some laws and regulations prescribe a destruction method for information. In the United States, the much publicized HIPAA Security Rule (Security Standards for the Protection of Electronic Protected Health Information) instructs covered entities to implement policies and procedures for final disposition of electronic protected health information and the hardware or media on which such information is stored. The covered entities are health-care providers, health plans, electronic health-care clearinghouses, and their business associates. The HIPAA Security Rule, which implements provisions of the Health Insurance Portability and Accountability Act, applies to individually identifiable health information that is transmitted or maintained by covered entities. The Security Rule does not list acceptable disposal methods, and it does not prohibit recycling or redeployment of electronic media that contain protected health information, provided that the information is removed prior to reuse.[37] New York State's CyberSecurity Regulation similarly requires secure disposal of nonpublic information maintained by financial service companies but it does not identify acceptable disposal methods.[38]

Some laws and regulations that require secure destruction of information do cite examples of compliant disposal methods. As an example, the Fair and Accurate Credit Transactions Act (FACTA) Disposal Rule, lists burning, pulverizing, or shredding paper records and destruction or irreversible erasure of electronic media as reasonable measures to prevent unauthorized access to consumers' personal information in connection with its disposal.[39] In California, businesses must take reasonable steps to dispose of customer records by shredding, erasing, or otherwise rendering personal information in the records unreadable or indecipherable by any means.[40] The Vermont Document Safe Destruction Act contains the same provisions.[41] In Massachusetts, records that contain personal information must be redacted, burned, pulverized, or shredded to prevent reading or reconstruction of their contents.[42] In Delaware, employers must dispose of personnel records by shredding, erasing, or other secure methods.[43] Other states have data disposal laws with similar requirements,[44] as do other countries. Regulations issued by the Saudi Arabian Monetary Authority (SAMA) require secure disposal of sensitive information maintained by banks and other financial service companies. The regulations list irreversible erasure, incineration, and double crosscut shredding as examples of acceptable disposal methods. If a third-party service provider is used for secure disposal, it must be periodically evaluated for compliance with approved destruction methods.[45]

Failure to comply with data disposal laws exposes an organization to fines, penalties, and other sanctions. Penalties for noncompliance with the HIPAA Security Rule depend on the extent to which a covered entity is aware of the violation. Fines begin at $100 per incident for a HIPAA-covered entity that is unaware of the violation up to a maximum of $25,000 per year. Fines for willful violations begin at $50,000 per incident up to a maximum of $1.5 million per year. The New York State Department of Financial Services has imposed fines exceeding one million dollars for violations of its Cybersecurity Regulations. Penalties for FACTA noncompliance can range up to $2,500 per violation. Those fines can add up quickly if many data subjects are involved. In 2008, the Federal Trade Commission imposed a fine of $50,000 for a mortgage company's failure to properly dispose of documents containing personal information about consumers. In 2012, the Federal Trade Commission fined a payday loan company over $100,00 for violation of FACTA disposal requirements. State laws impose fines for each data subject that is affected by improper destruction of personal information. In Massachusetts, for example, the penalty is $100 per data subject up to a total of $50,000 per instance of improper disposal.

MANDATORY RETENTION OF EVIDENCE

In the United States, rules of evidence for civil and criminal trials allow the opposing parties to request information during the discovery phase of legal proceedings to help them build their claims or defenses. Organizations involved in litigation, government investigations, arbitrations, or other legal proceedings have a common law duty to retain information that may be relevant as evidence.[46] This obligation also applies, subject to national variations, in other common law countries, such as Australia, Canada, Ireland, New Zealand, Singapore, and the United Kingdom (England, Wales, and Northern Ireland). The duty to preserve evidence applies to information in all forms, including but not limited to data, documents, video recordings, audio recordings, web pages, and social media posts. The obligation takes effect when legal proceedings are pending, threatened, or reasonably anticipated and remains in effect until legal actions are resolved or no longer a threat. Relevance for future litigation or government investigations is always a possibility for information associated with certain industries or business operations. Examples include data and documents related to product manufacturing and testing, contracts or other agreements related to work to be performed, insurance coverage and claims, health-care information related to a patient's diagnosis and treatment, and information related to promotion, demotion, or dismissal of employees.

The requirement to preserve information that is relevant as evidence may also arise from a statute or regulation. In the United States, for example, federal regulations require retention of information related to federal contracts or grants until final resolution of any litigation or audit involving the information.[47] Among similar requirements that might be cited, a research facility must retain animal welfare records while an investigation is pending[48]; a bank must retain records related to electronic funds transfers upon notice of an investigation or enforcement proceeding[49]; and an employer must preserve all employment records related to a charge of discrimination or an action brought by the Equal Employment Opportunity Commission or the U.S. Attorney General until final disposition of the charge or action.[50]

When relevant information is identified, it must be protected from destruction until litigation is no longer likely or, once legal proceedings begin, until they are completed. A well-managed legal hold process is essential to attain compliance with this requirement:

- A legal hold temporarily suspends destruction of data, documents, or other information that may be relevant for legal proceedings.[51] To comply with the duty to preserve evidence, an organization must initiate a legal hold process as soon as it receives a summons or complaint, when it is first on notice regarding possible legal proceedings, or when a prelitigation dispute or repeated inquiries about a specific matter suggests that legal proceedings can be reasonably anticipated.
- Routine retention policies and practices must be temporarily and immediately suspended for information that comes within the scope of a legal hold. Such information will not be destroyed until the legal matters to which they relate are fully resolved and the legal hold is rescinded, even if the information's retention period elapses in the interim.
- A legal hold may be issued by an organization's in-house law department or by external legal counsel. Attorneys responsible for legal proceedings must become familiar with their organization's information systems and recordkeeping processes at a level sufficient to identify data, documents, and other information that needs to be kept.
- Attorneys responsible for legal proceedings must communicate retention requirements in writing to every custodian of information that is subject to a legal hold. This must be done promptly to avoid inadvertent noncompliance. In a 2018 case, a long delay in communicating a legal hold notice led to the destruction of 750,000 email messages and attachments, which were purged on a regular schedule.[52]
- The need to preserve information must be clearly stated. In a 2017 case, employees reportedly interpreted an announcement of an impending legal hold notice as a suggestion to destroy potentially incriminating documents before the hold notice took effect.[53] The responsible attorneys must oversee the continued retention of information and addressing any problems or issues that may arise.
- A high level of oversight must remain in effect until legal proceedings are completed. Compliance must be closely monitored to ensure that a legal hold is understood and enforced by employees who have relevant information in their custody or under their supervisory control. The attorneys responsible for a legal hold must also work with an organization's information technology unit to ensure preservation of electronic records saved on network servers that they manage or by cloud-based systems that they supervise or interact with.

Failure to comply with the duty to preserve evidence can have serious consequences. If the intentional or negligent destruction of information that is relevant for pending or reasonably foreseeable legal proceedings is suspected, a court may award impose monetary penalties or issue an adverse inference instruction, in which a jury is allowed to infer that the destroyed information was harmful to the party that destroyed it. Less commonly, a court may issue a default judgment that ends the litigation in favor of the opposing party. Extreme cases may lead to criminal charges for obstruction of justice.[54] The opposing party may also be able to initiate a negligence claim for monetary damages for destruction of evidence that significantly harms its case.

These sanctions are well documented in decades of U.S. case law. Among widely cited examples, a federal court issued a default judgement in 1984 against an aircraft manufacturer for intentionally destroying documents that might be harmful in product liability litigation.[55] In 1987, a court issued a default judgement for willful and flagrant destruction of documents by a corporate officer who lied about the destruction during his testimony.[56] in a widely cited employment discrimination case heard between 2003 and 2005, a court issued an adverse inference instruction for an employer's deliberate destruction of relevant information contained in emails and backup tapes.[57] In a 2003 securities fraud case, a celebrity defendant was found to have altered the electronic text of a message to conceal illegal stock trading activity, which led to a prison sentence.[58] In the most widely publicized case involving failure to preserve evidence, Arthur Andersen LLP, a public accounting firm, was found guilty of obstructing justice in 2002 for destroying large quantities of paper and electronic records related to its audits of Enron Corporation, a utility and services provider engaged in fraudulent accounting practices,[59] although the criminal conviction was later reversed.

Noncompliance with the duty to preserve evidence can occur for several reasons. An organization may have faulty processes for disseminating and enforcing legal holds. A legal hold order may be too narrow to preserve all relevant information. An organization may wait too long to initiate the preservation process, thereby allowing relevant data and documents to be discarded in the meantime. An organization's information repositories may be poorly organized, making it difficult to identify relevant information. Such information may be stored in databases, on shared drives, on desktop computers or mobile devices, in paper files, by cloud-based services, or in other repositories that are scattered throughout an organization, possibly in multiple geographic locations.

Legal commentators have long acknowledged the possibility, even the likelihood, of undetected destruction of information that an opposing litigant may find useful.[60] Given the huge quantity of paper and electronic information that an organization creates and maintains and the many locations where information is kept, the chances of someone being caught destroying or concealing relevant information during litigation or a government investigation appears to be less than

100 percent, but how much less cannot be determined. Violations have typically involved witness testimony about destruction of information or inadvertent discovery of undisclosed copies on backup media. Even then, the most severe penalties are typically reserved for flagrant noncompliance where destruction of relevant information is attributable to bad faith rather than ignorance or negligence.

CONTRACTUAL COMPLIANCE

Many organizations rely on contractors to provide services that involve the maintenance and retention of data, documents, or other information. As an example, a municipal or county social services agency may contract with community-based organizations, charities, or other nongovernmental entities to provide preventive or foster care services. The contractor will be expected to create and maintain case files and other records for families and children who receive such services. A company's legal department may contract with outside counsel to handle litigation, intellectual property protection, or other matters for which the department lacks the required time or specialized knowledge. Outside counsel is expected to maintain all necessary information for the matters it handles. The company's legal department may receive reference copies of selected documents, but outside counsel's files are complete and authoritative. An insurance company may contract with a third-party administrator (TPA) to process claims for employee benefit plans. The TPA will be expected to create and maintain records for such claims. Similarly, many companies, government agencies, and nongovernmental organizations use third-party administrators to manage their workers compensation claims, in which case the TPA is expected to create and maintain injury reports, applications for compensation, medical reports, and other case records.

In some circumstances, a contractor may be hired specifically and exclusively for recordkeeping. Broker-dealers, for example, may contract with third-party services to prepare or maintain information that is required by government regulators. Small organizations may contract with accounting firms to prepare and maintain their ledgers, journals, tax returns, and financial reports. Many organizations contract with commercial record centers and cloud-based services for offsite storage of physical and electronic records that are transferred from the organization's offices or in-house computer systems.

Many contracts and agreements specify requirements for retention and disposition of information that a contractor creates, collects, receives, processes, or maintains in the course of its work. A contract or agreement may state that the contracting party is the owner of all information that a contractor creates, collects, or maintains on its behalf, in which case the information is subject to the contracting party's retention and disposition policies. With clinical research contracts, for example, information that is created or collected in the course of a research study is typically considered the property of the sponsoring organization, which may be a pharmaceutical company or an academic institution.[61] The information is to be retained in accordance with the sponsoring organization's policies and practices. Similarly, contracts routinely specify that any confidential or proprietary information that an organization discloses to a contractor remains the exclusive property of the disclosing party and is subject to that party's retention instructions.

If ownership of information is not addressed, a contract may specify retention requirements that a contractor must satisfy:

- A contract may mandate the immediate destruction or deletion of all or selected information in a contractor's possession or control upon termination of the contract, receipt of final payment, or—for contracts of long duration—when designated events, such as completion of specific tasks or other contractual milestones, occur. Mandatory destruction applies to all copies in the contractor's possession, including backup copies. It also applies to any copies distributed to subcontractors, business partners, agents, or other third parties. This requirement can pose compliance problems for contractors. Backup copies may exist on multiple media that are stored in multiple locations. A contractor may not have a comprehensive list of all information it has distributed to third parties and not have control over the storage locations of those copies.
- Alternatively, a contractor may be required to return all copies of specific information to the contracting organization when a contract terminates or when specific work is completed. Nondisclosure agreements typically include similar provisions. An exception may be made where the contractor's continued retention of specific information is required by a law or regulation or where the contractor's legal counsel advises that the information may be needed for legal proceedings involving the contractor.
- A contractor may be required to transfer all or selected information in its possession to a designated third party in an agreed-upon format when a contract terminates or at another specified time.
- A contractor may be required to retain specific information for a minimum period of time following termination of the contract. The purpose of such contractual obligations is to ensure that information will be available for audits, inspections, investigations, or other examination. According to Federal Acquisition Regulations, for example, U.S. government contractors must retain most records for six years after final payment.[62] Other contracts may specify shorter periods. With some contracts, the contractor must destroy the information when the specified retention period elapses. Alternatively, a contractor may be allowed to retain certain records longer than the minimum period based on its own operational requirements.
- A contract may specify the method of disposal for information held by the contractor. One or more acceptable or unacceptable disposal methods may be specified. Secure destruction methods that prevent the recovery

or reconstruction of information, such as cross-cut shredding or pulping of paper records, may be required. For electronic information saved on hard drives or other erasable media, disposal requirements may be satisfied by overwriting the information, but a contract may require physical destruction rather than overwriting of electronic media that contains confidential or sensitive data, including personal information. Recycling of electronic storage devices that contain confidential or sensitive information may be prohibited. A contract may require the contractor to certify that all information has been destroyed in the specified manner or allow the contracting organization to witness the destruction of information.

Noncompliance with these retention and disposition obligations exposes a contractor to early termination of the contract, civil litigation for breach of contract, or other adverse consequences. While the amount of any financial award from contract-related litigation is determined by the damages resulting from the violation, both parties may incur significant costs to litigate such matters.

In a variation of contractual compliance, a contractor may state its intended retention and disposition practices for information that it will create, process, or maintain on behalf of the contracting organization. This is often the case with cloud storage providers, file sharing services, and social media sites. According to the terms and conditions of their subscriber contracts, most cloud storage providers and file sharing services give customers complete control over retention and deletion of their own information as long as an account is active and in good standing. Depending on the service, an organization may be able to retain information indefinitely or for a specified number of days from the date it was created or last modified. Some services allow customers to specify complex retention rules for individual files based on elapsed time or specific events. For inactive accounts, however, cloud storage and file sharing services will delete customer information without further notice after a specified period of time—30 to 180 days or even longer after an account is closed or in default. The delay allows an organization to extract its data before it is permanently deleted.

Even where customers control the retention and disposition of information, a cloud storage provider or file sharing service may not remove deleted information from its computer systems immediately. Information deleted by a customer may remain on a provider's servers or backup media for a brief period of time—several days or longer—for technical reasons. According to their terms and conditions, cloud storage and file sharing services further reserve the right to retain a customer's information to resolve disputes or enforce their agreements, thereby overriding the customer's own retention and disposition policies and practices.

Social media companies have retention rules for content that organizations post to their sites. For active accounts, the organization that posts the information determines how long the information will be retained on a given site in most circumstances, but some social media platforms reserve the right to delete content that violates their terms and conditions of service. Examples of such content include defamatory statements, misinformation, and information that infringes intellectual property rights. Most social media sites delete information from closed or delinquent accounts after a relatively short period of time, although they may retain certain information for legal reasons. A social media site may also retain copies of information that was deleted for violating the site's terms and conditions of service. This is done to prevent repeated violations.[63]

STANDARDS AND INDUSTRY NORMS

There are no omnibus national or international standards for retention of information. Some standards specify retention requirements for information associated with specialized business or technical operations. According to ISO 13485:2016, *Medical Devices—Quality Management Systems—Requirements for Regulatory Purposes,* for example, records related to medical devices must be retained for the lifetime of the device but not less than two years from the date the device was released for medical use. ISO 10407-2:2008, *Petroleum and Natural Gas Industries—Rotary Drilling Equipment—Part 2: Inspection and Classification of Used Drill Stem Elements* specifies a minimum retention period of one year for inspection records. According to ISO 14313:2007, *Petroleum and Natural Gas Industries—Pipeline Transportation Systems—Pipeline Valves,* manufacturer must retain design documents, specifications, and testing records for a minimum of ten years from the manufacturing date.

These examples are the exception. Most standards that address retention of information do so in a general way that acknowledges its importance without compliance mandates. ISO 15489-1:2016, *Information and Documentation—Records Management—Part 1: Concepts and Principles* includes retention of information as a core component of a records management program, but it does not specify retention requirements for specific types of information. According to ISO 9001:2015, *Quality Management Systems—Requirements*, an organization must retain documented information to the extent necessary to have confidence that its processes are being carried out as planned, but determination of appropriate retention periods is left to the organization that creates and maintains the information.[64] Other standards that discuss retention of information without prescribing retention periods include ISO 13008:2012, *Information and Documentation—Digital Records Conversion and Migration Process;* ISO/TR 21965:2019, *Information and Documentation—Records Management in Enterprise Architecture;* ISO 13680:2020, *Petroleum and Natural Gas Industries—Corrosion-Resistant Alloy Seamless Tubular Products for Use as Casing, Tubing, Coupling Stock and Accessory Material—Technical Delivery Conditions;* ISO 16696-1:2019, *Timber Structures—Cross Laminated Timber—Part 1: Component Performance, Production Requirements and Certification Scheme;* ISO 11960:2020, *Petroleum and Natural Gas Industries—Steel Pipes for Use as Casing or Tubing for Wells;* and ISO 27789:2013, *Health Informatics—Audit Trails for Electronic Health Records.*

Standards provide more informative guidance for destruction of information. Secure destruction methods for information recorded on various media are covered by ISO/IEC 21964-1:2018, *Information Technology—Destruction of Data Carriers—Part 1: Principles and Definitions;* ISO/IEC 21964-2:2018, *Information Technology—Destruction of Data Carriers—Part 2: Requirements for Equipment for Destruction of Data Carriers;* and ISO/IEC 21964-3:2018, *Information Technology—Destruction of Data Carriers—Part 3: Process of Destruction of Data Carriers.* While it is not an international standard, NIST SP 800-88, *Guidelines for Media Sanitization* issued by the National Institute of Standards and Technology provides guidelines for secure destruction of information recorded on paper or electronic media.[65]

Requirements and guidelines for retention and disposition of information are addressed at differing levels of specificity in various professional and industry norms. Examples include the following:

- ABA Informal Opinion 1384, issued by the American Bar Association, instructs attorneys to retain records of client funds and all client property for a minimum of five years following termination of representation. Records related to receipt and disbursement of trust funds should be retained indefinitely. Various state bar associations have adopted this retention rule. Otherwise, Informal Opinion 1384 allows attorneys discretion in determining retention periods for information related to a client's legal matters, but it cautions attorneys to avoid destroying or discarding information that a client may need, that is not otherwise readily available to the client, and that a client might reasonably expect an attorney to preserve.[66]
- According to a model regulation issued by the National Association of Insurance Commissioners, insurance companies must keep policy record files for three years after a policy is no longer in force. Insurance claim information must be retained for three years following the end of the year in which a claim is closed. Declined underwriting files must be retained for the current year plus three years. Records that certify compliance with cybersecurity requirements must be retained for five years.[67]
- Actuarial Standards of Practice (ASOPs) issued by the Actuarial Standards Board do not specify retention periods for actuarial information but they do provide some retention guidance. ASOP 23 recommends that an actuary review current data for consistency with prior analysis, which implies that the prior analysis must be retained. According to ASOP 36, an actuary should retain the most recent prior opinion for comparison with current assumptions. According to ASOP 41, an actuary should

retain supporting information that was not included in an actuarial report as well as information for any recurring projects.[68]

- According to the American Psychological Association's Ethics Code, psychologists must retain the records of former clients for a sufficient period of time in order to facilitate the provision of services later by them or by other professionals. Ethical codes of other mental health professionals contain similar provisions.[69] In many countries, however, laws and regulations specify minimum retention requirements for such information. In the absence of a legal mandate, the American Psychological Association recommends retaining the records of adult clients for seven years after the last date of service and the records of minors for seven years or three years after the client attains the age of majority, whichever is later.[70]
- According to a practice brief issued by the American Health Information Management Association (AHIMA), health-care providers should retain medical records for adult patients for ten years after the most recent encounter, which is longer than the minimum retention periods specified by most federal and state laws and regulations.[71]
- Guidelines issued by International Cemetery, Cremation and Funeral Association (ICCFA) identify records that member organizations should retain permanently.[72]
- The Payment Card Industry Security Standards Council, which represents payment industry stakeholders, advises merchants, payment card processors, payment card issuers, and service providers to limit retention of cardholder information to the minimum time period necessary for legal, regulatory, or business reasons and securely delete the information when it is no longer needed.[73]
- According to the Auditing Standards Board of the American Institute of Certified Public Accountants, an auditor should assemble a final audit file within sixty days of release of an audit report and retain the file for a minimum of five years.[74]
- The Uniform Accountancy Act Model Rules issued by the National Association of State Boards of Accountancy specify a five-year retention period for attest documentation, which is the principal record of procedures, information obtained, and findings for a particular auditing engagement.[75]
- Standard V(C) issued by the CFA Institute, a global association of investment professionals, advises members to retain records that support investment recommendations, actions, and communications with clients and prospective clients. Such records should be retained for a minimum of seven years.[76]
- The National Society of Professional Engineers (NSPE) and American Council of Engineering Companies (ACEC) advises design and engineering firms to retain professional service agreements, studies, reports, calcula-

tions, notes, and construction documentation for a minimum of three years after expiration of applicable statutes of repose, which define the time limit for legal action in a particular locality.[77]

For the most part, the professional standards and industry norms cited above present information retention and disposition guidelines rather than requirements. They do not specify disciplinary rules or penalties for infractions, and they do not have legal effect unless then are incorporated into a contract. The principal negative consequence of noncompliance is damaged reputation. For clients or others who may be adversely affected by noncompliance, it is not clear whether violations rise to the level of professional misconduct or an actionable offense.

INTERNAL MANDATES

An organization's information retention and disposition practices are usually specified in a record retention schedule and in any supplemental policies and procedures that the organization may issue. Retention schedules are not limited to legal and regulatory compliance. They also consider the operational and scholarly value of information. Operational retention decisions focus on information that is needed for administrative continuity, management planning and decision-making, transaction processing, customer service, marketing, and other day-to-day activities. In organizations with archival programs, a retention schedule identifies information that warrants permanent preservation to support historical, scientific, genealogical, or other research.

As previously discussed, government agencies must comply with retention requirements specified by archival agencies or other authorities that are empowered by law to determine how long public records must be kept. This legal obligation applies to federal, state, and local government agencies as well as to public benefit corporations and other quasi-governmental entities. It encompasses retention periods that are based on operational and scholarly criteria as well as legal and regulatory mandates. Nongovernmental organizations have no comparable legal obligation. Retention periods based on operational or scholarly considerations are not legally enforceable, but many companies and nonprofit entities have codes of conduct that mandate compliance with their approved policies and practices for retention and disposition of information.

These internal mandates apply to an organization's employees, directors, officers, and business associates, as well as consultants, interns, and others that may have custody or control of the organization's information. The mandates are not limited to legal and regulatory requirements. They encompass retention and disposition rules that are based on operational needs or permanent preservation of information of scholarly value. Compliance with information retention and disposition requirements may be explicitly addressed in a code of conduct through a brief statement that retention and disposition are guided by legal mandates and organizational policy, including the organization's record retention schedule. Alternatively, a code of conduct may mandate compliance with all organizational policies, in which case compliance with policies that specifically address retention and disposition of Information is implied.

Noncompliance with retention and disposition instructions based on operational or scholarly criteria is a matter of concern in many organizations. The principal infractions involve continued retention of information with elapsed retention periods. Such noncompliance may be unintentional. Some information custodians may be unaware of their organization's retention and disposition policies, which is a particular problem in large organizations that operate in multiple countries. Retention schedules and their associated policies can be lengthy, complicated, and difficult to understand.[78] In the absence of appropriate training, information custodians may interpret retention policies incorrectly. Even where training is provided, retention and disposition requirements and procedures are easily forgotten if they are not applied regularly.

Noncompliance may be rooted in uncertainty about retention guidance. In theory, retention rules are developed with the cooperation and agreement of knowledgeable employees who use information to fulfill their assigned work responsibilities, but employees may be reluctant to discard information, fearing that it will be needed for some unforeseen future purpose and that they will be blamed if it is not available. Even if the information is acknowledged to be obsolete, time-consuming purging of data and documents with elapsed retention periods is not an urgent priority for busy employees. This is particularly the case with electronic records, which are stored inexpensively on digital media with ever-increasing capacity.

To facilitate compliance with internal mandates, some organizations designate annual or semi-annual review periods or cleanup days for destruction of records with elapsed retention periods. Enforcement may involve self-certification, audits, or a combination of both methods:

- With self-certification, designated employees must provide a written attestation that they understand and are in full compliance with retention and disposition policies and procedures for information in their custody or under their supervisory control. Full compliance means that information is being kept for the period of time specified in the organization's retention schedule and supplemental policies and that data, documents, or other information with elapsed retention periods have been purged from computer storage, office files, offsite storage facilities, or other repositories, with exceptions limited to information that is subject to a legal hold. The attestation may be made monthly, quarterly, or annually. Self-certification may be limited to managers or required of all information custodians, including unpaid interns and volunteers.

- Auditing focuses on compliance with disposition requirements for obsolete information. The auditor reviews an information storage repository and destruction practices to detect data, documents, or other information with elapsed retention periods. The repository may be a database, a shared drive, an email server, an enterprise content management system, a filing cabinet, an offsite storage facility, or another place where information is kept. The audit may be performed by a records manager, an internal auditing unit, an external auditing authority, or a consultant or contractor hired for that purpose. Deficiencies are discussed with information custodians and their supervisors to determine appropriate corrective action. Penalties are limited to willful or repeated violations. An audit's objective is to obtain the information custodian's compliance rather than to punish noncompliance.

SOCIETAL COMPLIANCE

Ethical norms and sustainability objectives can affect an organization's policies and practices for retention and disposition of information. In particular, retention decisions can raise concerns related to unethical destruction of information, while retention and disposition of information can have significant environmental impacts.

ETHICAL COMPLIANCE

Minimum and maximum retention requirements specified in laws and regulations are not negotiable and have limited scope for interpretation. Operational retention decisions, by contrast, are based on subjective determinations about the likely future need for information to support an organization's mission, objectives, and activities. Records management and archival codes of ethics do not specifically address retention and disposition of information,[79] but retention decisions based solely on the continuing business value of information may pose ethical challenges when the interests of all stakeholders are considered.[80] Consider the following hypothetical but realistic examples:

- To minimize off-site storage charges, a public school district wants to destroy individualized education programs, evaluations, and other records for special education students six years after graduation, which is the minimum retention period permitted by educational regulations in the state where the district is located, but a special education student may need the records in later life to verify a history of disability for social security or other benefits.
- To support its fund-raising campaigns, a charity wants to retain donor records for ten years after last giving activity, but that long retention period exposes donor information to data breaches or other unauthorized disclosures.

- To facilitate its relocation to smaller offices, a gastroenterology practice wants to discard records for patients that have not sought medical care for more than six years, which complies with minimum retention requirements for patient records in the state where the practice is located, but that action will result in destruction of records for periodic medical procedures, such as colonoscopies, that may be repeated at intervals longer than six years.
- To minimize its legal discovery costs and exposure to unreasonable litigation, a company wants to discard financial data and documents when the minimum period of time specified in applicable laws and regulations elapses, but some information that shareholders, financial analysts, and prospective investors need to assess the company's future financial viability may be destroyed in the process.

In the above examples, an organization's retention decision may have unintended adverse consequences that are unrelated to the business reason for the decision. The adverse consequences will be experienced by external stakeholders rather than the organization itself. The ethical issues in these situations are based on the principles of avoidance of harm and double effect.

According to the principle of avoidance of harm, individuals have a moral obligation to avoid decisions or actions that cause harm to others. This concept, which is well-established in religious and philosophical thought, is a core component of professional ethics, most notably in medicine and law. A physician takes an oath to do no harm to patients. An attorney has an overriding duty to avoid harm to a client's interests. The stakeholder theory of business ethics similarly argues that an organization's business actions must consider the needs of all interested parties, including employees, contractors, suppliers, customers, investors, and the general public.[81] While the competing interests of these stakeholders do not necessarily override those of the organization that maintains information, they must be considered when retention and disposition decisions are made.

According to the principle of double effect, an action that has a desirable result but causes unintended harm to a person or organization may be ethically acceptable if certain conditions apply. As a necessary precondition, the action that produces a desirable result must be legal. In the examples cited above, information must be retained for the minimum period required by laws and regulations. The desirable result must outweigh the harmful consequences. Cost savings resulting from a smaller medical office must be more significant than the potential harm to patients whose older records are essential for future care. The societal benefits of a charity's fund-raising activities must outweigh whatever harm might result from a breach of a donor's personal information. To the extent possible, unintended harm should be minimized by foregoing some benefits of the intended action. A school district that wants to destroy special education records might allow parents to obtain copies of their children's records prior to destruction. A charity might allow donors concerned about data breaches to opt out of long retention of their information.

Most importantly, the desirable result must not be produced by the unintended harm. In this respect, the most serious ethical concerns relate to preemptive destruction of information to reduce an organization's exposure to civil litigation or criminal investigations.[82] It is not illegal to destroy information that may be relevant for future legal proceedings about which an organization has no knowledge. The Modern Penal Code only prohibits destruction of data or documents with the intent to prevent their use in a legal proceeding if the destruction occurs at the time that the records are subpoenaed. Nonetheless, the principle of avoidance of harm still applies: It may make good business sense to discard unnecessary information to reduce the cost of storing the large quantities of records that would otherwise accumulate, but an organization may also benefit from destruction of information that a future plaintiff might need for litigation related to wrongful termination, employment discrimination, defective products, anticompetitive behavior, or other actionable matters. That benefit is only obtained by harming the future plaintiff. This ethical concern is particularly relevant for organizations that have previously been involved in such litigation. Ethics aside, however, preemptive destruction of data or documents may not be completely effective because copies may be overlooked or in the possession of third parties.

ENVIRONMENTAL COMPLIANCE

As discussed in chapter 2, United Nations Sustainable Development Goal 12 addresses responsible consumption of natural resources, reduction of an organization's global material footprint, and minimization of non-recyclable waste. Sustainable Development Goal 13 is concerned with combating climate change through reduction of greenhouse gas emissions. Certain information retention and disposition practices pose compliance challenges for these goals:

- Life cycle assessment (LCA) is the systematic analysis of the environmental impacts of products and services throughout their life cycles.[83] In the case of information, one aspect of life cycle assessment addresses the environmental impact of the media on which information is recorded. As discussed in chapter 2, data center operations are energy-intensive and a significant source of greenhouse gas emissions. Data storage on file servers, email servers, and web servers is estimated to account for 25 to 35 percent of a data center's power consumption.[84] While energy consumption per stored bit is miniscule, the total amount of energy consumed by an ever-increasing quantity of digital information is large and growing, even when the improved energy-efficiency of newer storage technologies is considered.[85]
- Because energy consumption varies with the amount of information stored, indefinite retention of digital information—a common practice in many

organizations—is incompatible with sustainability goals. Taking a "green archiving" approach, an organization can address this issue by retaining digital information for the shortest period of time that is compatible with legal and operational requirements and purging content with elapsed retention periods.[86] An exception should be made for digital information that warrants permanent preservation for scholarly or scientific research. Duplicate data should be purged as soon as possible when its purpose is fulfilled. Data compression can also be used to reduce storage requirements for a given amount of information.[87]

- The proliferation of digital information raises other environmental and public health concerns. Digital storage devices and media contribute to the so-called "e-waste" problem, which is concerned with disposal of computers, televisions, cell phones, and other electronic products. Electronic waste is one of the fastest growing waste streams. Hard drives, magnetic tapes, solid-state storage devices, and other electronic media contain heavy metals and other hazardous substances. Their improper disposal contributes to water, soil, and atmospheric pollution. Electronic contaminants discarded in landfills can infiltrate drinking water and the food chain. This can be avoided by reusing digital storage devices and media or recycling them if reuse is not possible. Unrecycled electronic waste is often shipped to developing countries where environmental health and safety laws are weak or nonexistent.[88] In some political jurisdictions, electronic storage devices and media cannot be deposited in solid-waste landfills; they must be collected and sent to an approved recycling facility.
- Waste management issues are not limited to digital information. Paper records with elapsed retention periods continue to be deposited in solid waste landfills, either before or after shredding. Paper buried in a landfill decomposes slowly. When decomposition does occur, the toxic chemicals in paper and inks can pollute soil and groundwater. Decomposing paper also emits methane gas, which is gradually released into the atmosphere.[89] Recycling of paper records, which eliminates landfill deposits, is the preferred approach for compliance with sustainability goals.[90] Studies have found, however, that compliance depends on the convenience of the recycling collection process.[91]

SUMMARY OF MAJOR POINTS

- Tens of thousands of laws, regulations, rules, ordinance, directives, and other legal instruments specify retention and disposition requirements for information related to business operations and activities that are subject to government oversight.
- All countries have laws or regulations that specify minimum retention requirements for certain information associated with commonly encountered business functions, operations, and activities.

- A large and varied group of retention requirements applies to specialized information maintained by financial services companies, health-care organizations, manufacturing companies, pharmaceutical companies, and other industries that are subject to government regulation.
- Some laws and regulations specify maximum retention periods or mandate destruction of information when certain conditions are met. Data protection and privacy laws and regulations are the most widely encountered examples of such legislation.
- Some laws and regulations specify methods for secure destruction of information when its retention period elapses.
- Organizations have a legal obligation to retain information that is relevant for litigation, government investigations, or other legal proceedings. This obligation takes effect when legal proceedings are pending, threatened, or reasonably anticipated, and it remains in effect until legal actions are resolved or no longer a threat.
- Noncompliance with laws and regulations that specify retention and disposition requirements exposes an organization to fines, penalties, and—in extreme cases—criminal prosecution.
- Many contracts and agreements specify requirements for retention and disposition of information that a contractor creates, collects, receives, processes, or maintains in the course of its work. Noncompliance exposes a contractor to early termination of the contract, civil litigation for breach of contract, or other adverse consequences.
- Requirements and guidelines retention and disposition of information is addressed at differing levels of specificity in various professional and industry norms. The principal negative consequence of noncompliance with these norms is damaged reputation.
- Many companies and nonprofit entities have codes of conduct that mandate compliance with their approved policies and practices for retention and disposition of information. Enforcement may involve self-certification, audits, or a combination of both methods.
- An organization's policies for retention and disposition of information may have unintended adverse consequences for external stakeholders. The ethical issues in these situations are based on the principles of avoidance of harm and double effect.
- To reduce energy consumption, an organization may limit retention of digital information to the shortest period of time that is compatible with legal and operational requirements.
- Improper disposal of digital information and paper records raises environmental and public health concerns.

NOTES

1. See 44 U.S.C. § 2905, https://www.law.cornell.edu/uscode/text/44/2905, and 36 C.F.R. § 1220.12, https://www.law.cornell.edu/cfr/text/36/1220.12. General Records

Schedules issued by the National Archives and Records Administration are online at https://www.archives.gov/records-mgmt/grs.html.

2. For an English translation of the Archives Law, see http://english.court.gov.cn/2016-04/15/content_24565261.htm. On National Archives Order No. 10, see http://www.lawinfochina.com/display.aspx?lib=law&id=11997. See also W. Moss, "The Archives Law of the People's Republic of China: a summary and commentary," *American Archivist* 54 (2), 216--19 (1991), https://www.jstor.org/stable/40293554; J. Nalen, "Private archives in China," *Libri* 52 (4), 241-62 (2002), https://doi.org/10.1515/LIBR.2002.241; W. Lan, "Managing records in private companies in China," *Records Management Journal* 13 (3), 123-29 (2003), https://doi.org/10.3917/eh.090.0145; Z. Zeng, "Company archives and business history in contemporary China," *Enterprises et Histoire* 90 (1), 145-48 (2018), https://doi.org/10.3917/eh.090.0145; M. Li et al., "A typology of Chinese 'archives'," *Archival Science* 21 (2), 173-92 (2020), https://doi.org/10.1007/s10502-020-09352-x.
3. Order of Rosarkhiv dated 20.12.2019 N 246. On approval of the list of standard administrative archival documents generated in the course of the activities of state bodies, local authorities and organizations, indicating the terms of their storage, http://www.consultant.ru/document/cons_doc_LAW_345020/.
4. 26 U.S.C. § 6501, https://www.law.cornell.edu/uscode/text/26/6501.
5. See W. Saffady, *Retention of Accounting Records: a Global Survey of Laws and Regulations* (Palmyra, NJ: ARMA International Educational Foundation, 2019), http://armaedfoundation.org/wp-content/uploads/2019/06/AIEF-Research-Paper-Retention-Global-Accounting.pdf.
6. See W. Saffady, *Global Requirements for Personnel Records: a Survey of Laws and Regulations* (Palmyra, NJ: ARMA International Educational Foundation, 2021), http://armaedfoundation.org/wp-content/uploads/2021/06/Global-Requirements-for-Personnel-Records_-A-Survey-of-Laws-and-Regulations.pdf.
7. BSA/AML Manual, Appendix P: BSA Record Retention Requirements, issued by the Federal Financial Institutions Examination Council, https://bsaaml.ffiec.gov/manual/Appendices/17.
8. Securities and Exchange Commission, Final Rule: Retention of Records Relevant to Audits and Reviews, https://www.sec.gov/rules/final/33-8180.htm. See also AS 1215: Audit Documentation issued by the Public Company Accounting Oversight Board, https://pcaobus.org/oversight/standards/auditing-standards/details/AS1215.
9. Securities and Exchange Commission, RIN 3235-AH04, Books and Records Requirements for Brokers and Dealers Under the Securities Exchange Act of 1934, https://www.sec.gov/rules/final/34-44992.htm; FINRA Rule 4511, issued by the Financial Industry Regulatory Authority, https://www.finra.org/rules-guidance/rulebooks/finra-rules/4511.
10. 42 C.F.R. § 482.24, https://www.law.cornell.edu/cfr/text/42/482.24.
11. 21 C.F.R. § 211.180, https://www.accessdata.fda.gov/scripts/cdrh/cfdocs/cfcfr/CFRSearch.cfm?fr=211.180.
12. 21 C.F.R. § 1306.15, https://www.law.cornell.edu/cfr/text/21/1306.15. See also M. Gabay, "Federal Controlled Substances Act: ordering and recordkeeping," *Hospital Pharmacy* 48 (11), 919-21 (2013), https://doi.org/10.1310/hpj4811-919.
13. 10 C.F.R. § 74.19, https://www.law.cornell.edu/cfr/text/10/74.19.

14. Federal Aviation Administration, Advisory Circular 43-9C, https://www.faa.gov/documentLibrary/media/Advisory_Circular/AC_43-9C_CHG_2.pdf.
15. In the United States, for example, the Bank Secrecy Act requires depository institutions to retain most information about deposits, withdrawals, loans, payments, funds transfers, and other transactions for a minimum of five years.
16. 18 C.F.R. § 125.2, https://www.law.cornell.edu/cfr/text/18/125.2.
17. *Federal Register* 84 (197), 54496 (October 10, 2019), https://www.govinfo.gov/content/pkg/FR-2019-10-10/pdf/2019-22094.pdf.
18. New York City Commission on Human Rights, Legal Enforcement Guidance on the Stop Credit Discrimination in Employment Act, https://www1.nyc.gov/assets/cchr/downloads/pdf/CreditHistory-InterpretiveGuide-LegalGuidance.pdf.
19. Federal Law of 27 July 2006 N 152-FZ on Personal Data, https://pd.rkn.gov.ru/authority/p146/p164/. For an overview, see D. Garrie and I. Byhovsky, "Privacy and data protection in Russia," *Journal of Law & CyberWarfare* 5 (2), 235–53 (2017), https://www.jstor.org/stable/26441276.
20. GDPR, recital 39, Principles of Data Processing. https://gdpr-info.eu/recitals/no-39/.
21. Macau Law No. 2/2012, Legal Framework for Video Surveillance in Public Spaces, https://translate.google.com/translate?hl=en&sl=pt&u=https://bo.io.gov.mo/bo/i/2012/12/lei02.asp&prev=search&pto=aue.
22. Article 4c of Instruction No. 13 of December 22, 2011, which amends Instruction No. 3 on Video Surveillance Systems in Buildings, https://www.idp.al/wp-content/uploads/2016/11/udhezim_nr_13_date_22_12_2011.pdf.
23. Nevada Gaming Commission, Surveillance Standards for Nonrestricted Licensees, https://gaming.nv.gov/modules/showdocument.aspx?documentid=2944.
24. ATM Safety Act, N.Y. Banking Law § 75-C, https://www.nysenate.gov/legislation/laws/BNK/75-C.
25. On video recordings and privacy law, see E. Barnoviciu et al., "GDPR compliance in video surveillance and video processing application," in *2019 International Conference on Speech Technology and Human Computer Dialogue* (New York: IEEE, 2019), 130–35, https://doi.org/10.1109/SPED.2019.8906553; C. Cliza et al., "Video surveillance: standpoint of the EU and national legislation on data protection," *Challenges of the Knowledge Society* 12, 465–71 (2018), https://doaj.org/article/41899219f1e346b295821a0c37d7ee46; A. Golland and J. Ohrtmann, "Video surveillance: the supervisory authorities' view and recent case law," in T. Kahler, ed., *Turning Point in Data Protection Law* (Baden-Baden, Germany: Nomos, 2020), 175–78, https://doi.org/10.5771/9783748921561-175; D. Krivokapic et al., "Comparative analysis of video surveillance regulation in data protection laws in the former Yugoslav states," *Journal of Regional Security* 16 (1), 5–16 (2021), https://doi.org/10.5937/jrs16-27170.
26. *Surveillance Camera Code of Practice* (London: Home Office, 2021), https://assets.publishing.service.gov.uk/government/uploads/system/uploads/attachment_data/file/1010815/Surveillance_Camera_Code_of_Practice__update_.pdf. As an exception, Article 89 of the North Macedonian Law on Personal Data Protection of February 16, 2020, specifies a maximum retention period of thirty days for surveillance recordings, https://dzlp.mk/mk/domasni_propisi.

27. *Guidelines for the Use of Video Surveillance* (Toronto: Information and Privacy Commissioner of Ontario, 2015), https://www.ipc.on.ca/wp-content/uploads/Resources/2015_Guidelines_Surveillance.pdf.
28. 42 U.S.C. § 5106a, https://www.law.cornell.edu/uscode/text/42/5106a. For individual state requirements, see Child Welfare Information Gateway, *Review and Expunction of Central Registries and Reporting Records* (Washington, DC: U.S. Department of Health and Human Services, Children's Bureau, 2019), https://www.childwelfare.gov/pubPDFs/registry.pdf. For an argument in favor of retaining records of unsubstantiated investigations, see K. Kugler et al., "The effect of substantiated and unsubstantiated investigations of child maltreatment and subsequent adolescent health," *Child Abuse & Neglect* 87 (1), 112–19 (2019), https://doi.org/10.1016/j.chiabu.2018.06.005.
29. United Nations Rules for the Protection of Juveniles Deprived of their Liberty, adopted by General Assembly resolution 45/113 of December 14, 1990, http://www.cidh.org/ninez/pdf files/UN Rules for the Protection of Juveniles Deprived of their Liberty.pdf.
30. As specified in Cal. Welf. & Inst. § 781, court records of juvenile offenders in California are destroyed five years after the records were ordered sealed, https://leginfo.legislature.ca.gov/faces/codes_displaySection.xhtml?sectionNum=781.&lawCode=WIC. On destruction of juvenile court records, see N. Stone, "Expunging juvenile criminal histories: towards a 'clean break'?" *Youth Justice* 16 (1), 71–81 (2016), https://doi.org/10.1177/1473225415623667.
31. Examples of the many publications on expungement of criminal records include B. Murray, "A new era for expungement law reform? Recent developments at the state and federal levels," *Harvard Law & Policy Review* 10 (2), 361–83 (2016), https://harvardlpr.com/wp-content/uploads/sites/20/2016/06/10.2_4_Murray.pdf; J. Prescott and S. Starr, "Expungement of criminal convictions: an empirical study," *Harvard Law Review* 133 (8), 2461-550 (2020), https://repository.law.umich.edu/cgi/viewcontent.cgi?article=3167&context=articles; M. Yee, "Expungement law: an extraordinary remedy for an extraordinary harm," *Georgetown Journal on Poverty Law and Policy* 25 (1), 169–93 (2017), https://articleworks.cadmus.com/geolaw/z5800118.html; E. Larrauri, "Conviction records in Spain: obstacles to reintegration of offenders?" *European Journal of Probation* 3 (1), 50–62 (2011), https://doi.org/10.1177/206622031100300105; A. Burton et al., "Beyond the eternal criminal record: public support for expungement," *Criminology & Public Policy* 20 (1), 123–51 (2021), https://doi.org/10.1111/1745-9133.12531; J. Mujuzi, "The expungement of criminal records in South Africa: the drafting history of the law, the unresolved issues, and how they could be resolved," *Statute Law Review* 35 (3), 278–303 (2014), https://doi.org/10.1093/slr/hmu022.
32. See, for example, Del Code tit. 11, § 4372. As specified in Del. Code tit. 11, § 4373, a court can order expungement of criminal case records after three years if the offender has no prior or subsequent convictions, https://delcode.delaware.gov/title11/c043/sc07/.
33. 34 C.F.R. § 300.573, https://www.govinfo.gov/content/pkg/CFR-2002-title34-vol2/xml/CFR-2002-title34-vol2-sec300-573.xml.
34. The right to be forgotten is discussed in many publications, including C. Bartolini and L. Siry, "The right to be forgotten in the light of consent of the data subject," *Computer Law & Security Review* 32, no. 2 (2016), 218–37, https://doi.org/10.1016/j.

clsr.2016.01.005; C. Rees and D. Heywood, "The 'right to be forgotten' or the 'principle that has been remembered'," *Computer Law & Security Review* 30, no. 5 (2014), 574–78, https://doi.org/10.1016/j.clsr.2014.07.002; A. Bunn, "The curious case of the right to be forgotten," *Computer Law & Security Review* 31, no. 5 (2015), 336–50, https://doi.org/10.1016/j.clsr.2015.03.006; K. Bryrum, "The European right to be forgotten: A challenge to the United States Constitution's First Amendment and to professional public relations ethics," *Public Relations Review* 43, no. 1 (2017), 102–11, https://doi.org/10.1016/j.pubrev.2016.10.010; M. Ambrose, "Speaking of forgetting: Analysis of possible non-EU responses to the right to be forgotten and speech exception," *Telecommunications Policy* 38, no. 8–9 (2014), 800–11, https://www.dhi.ac.uk/san/waysofbeing/data/citizenship-robson-ambrose-2014.pdf; J. Townend, "Data protection and the 'fight to be forgotten' in practice: a UK perspective," *International Journal of Legal Information* 45, no. 1 (2017), 28–33, https://www.cambridge.org/core/journals/international-journal-of-legal-information/article/data-protection-and-the-right-to-be-forgotten-in-practice-a-uk-perspective/CA6EF1DA15B5C39525DFF0142DF2D2D0; L. Bode and M. Jones, "Do Americans want a right to be forgotten? Estimating public support for digital erasure legislation," *Policy & Internet* 10, no. 3 (2018), 244–63, https://doi.org/10.1002/poi3.174; A. Vavra, "The right to be forgotten: an archival perspective," *American Archivist* 81, no. 1 (2018), 100–11, https://doi.org/10.17723/0360-9081-81.1.100; and P. Korenhof et al., "Timing the right to be forgotten: a study into 'time' as a factor in deciding about retention or erasure of data," in S. Gutwirth et al., eds., *Reforming European Data Protection Law*, Heidelberg: Spring, 2015, 171–201.

35. New York State General Business Law, article 7A, Section 89-g, https://www.nysenate.gov/legislation/laws/GBS/89-G.
36. For an explanation of GDPR sanctions, see *Handbook on European Data Protection Law* (Vienna: European Agency for Fundamental Rights, 2018), especially 243–48, https://doi.org/10.2811/343461, and Guidelines on the Application and Setting of Administrative Fines for the Purpose of the Regulation 2016/79, issued by the Working Party on the Protection of Individuals with Regard to the Processing of Personal Data, https://ec.europa.eu/newsroom/article29/items/611237/en. Other sources include P. Voigt and A. Bussche, *The EU General Data Protection Regulation (GDPR): a Practical Guide* (Cham, Switzerland: Springer, 2017), especially 201–17, https://doi.org/10.1007/978-3-319-57959-7_7; W. Presthus and K. Sonslien, "An analysis of violations and sanctions following the GDPR," *International Journal of Information Systems and Project Management* 9 (1), 38–53 (2021), https://aisel.aisnet.org/ijispm/vol9/iss1/3/?utm_source=aisel.aisnet.org%2Fijispm%2Fvol9%2Fiss1%2F3&utm_medium=PDF&utm_campaign=PDFCoverPages; J. Wolff and N. Atallah, "Early GDPR penalties: analysis of implementation and fines through May 2020," *Journal of Information Policy* 11 (1), 63–103 (2021), https://doi.org/10.5325/jinfopoli.11.2021.0063; for a regularly updated list of fines and penalties for GDPR infractions imposed by national authorities, see https://www.enforcementtracker.com/.
37. 45 C.F.R § 164.310, https://www.law.cornell.edu/cfr/text/45/164.310. For HIPAA definitions, see 45 C.F.R § 160.103, https://www.law.cornell.edu/cfr/text/45/160.103.

38. New York State Department of Financial Services Cyber Security Regulation, 23 NYCRR 500.13, https://govt.westlaw.com/nycrr/Document/I60c6444d0d5f11e79781d-30ba488e782?contextData=%28sc.Default%29&bhcp=1&transitionType=Default.
39. 16 C.F.R. § 682.3, https://www.law.cornell.edu/cfr/text/16/682.3.
40. California Civil Code § 1798.81, https://leginfo.legislature.ca.gov/faces/codes_displaySection.xhtml?lawCode=CIV&sectionNum=1798.81.
41. Vermont Statutes, Title 9, § 2445, https://law.justia.com/codes/vermont/2020/title-9/chapter-62/section-2445/.
42. Massachusetts General Laws, Part I, Title XV, Ch. 93L, Section 2, Mass. Gen. Laws Ch. 93I, § 2.
43. Delaware Code, Title 19, Ch. 7, § 736, https://delcode.delaware.gov/title19/c007/sc04/index.html.
44. For a list developed by the National Conference of State Legislatures, https://www.ncsl.org/research/telecommunications-and-information-technology/da-ta-disposal-laws.aspx.
45. Saudi Arabian Monetary Authority, Cybersecurity Framework, May 2017, https://www.sama.gov.sa/en-US/Laws/BankingRules/SAMA Cyber Security Framework.pdf.
46. The Sedona Conference, "Commentary on Legal Holds, Second Edition: the Trigger & the Process," *Sedona Conference Journal* 20 (1), 342–414 (2019), https://these-donaconference.org/node/8755.
47. 2 C.F.R. § 200.334, https://www.law.cornell.edu/cfr/text/2/200.334. Examples of other federal regulations with the same retention requirements include 14 C.F.R. § 1274.601, https://www.law.cornell.edu/cfr/text/14/1274.601; 45 C.F.R. § 75.361, https://www.law.cornell.edu/cfr/text/45/75.361; and 49 C.F.R. § 18.42, https://www.govinfo.gov/app/details/CFR-2012-title49-vol1/CFR-2012-title49-vol1-sec18-42.
48. 9 C.F.R. § 2.35, https://www.law.cornell.edu/cfr/text/9/2.35.
49. 12 C.F.R. § 1005.13, https://www.law.cornell.edu/cfr/text/12/1005.13.
50. 29 C.F.R. § 1602.14, https://www.law.cornell.edu/cfr/text/29/1602.14.
51. Examples of the many articles on legal holds include T. Winslow and J. Malone, "Don't hold back: when and how corporate counsel should implement a litigation hold," *Jurimetrics* 51 (3), 245–78 (2011), https://www.jstor.org/stable/41307129; J. Pace and J. Rue, "E-discovery 'worst practices': ten sure-fire ways to mismanage a litigation hold," *NY Business Law Journal* 13 (2), 48–53 (2009), https://www.jstor.org/stable/41307129; N. Crystal, "Ethical responsibility and legal liability of lawyers for failure to institute or monitor litigation holds," *Akron Law Review* 43 (3), 715-27, https://ideaexchange.uakron.edu/akronlawreview/vol43/iss3/4; M. Luoma and V. Luoma, "Litigation holds: past present and future directions," *Journal of Digital Forensics, Security, and Law* 10 (1), 57–68 (2015), https://doi.org/10.15394/jdfsl.2015.1198.
52. *EPAC Techs., Inc. v. HarperCollins Christian Publ'g, Inc.*, No. 3:12-cv-00463 (M.D. Tenn. Mar. 29, 2018), https://casetext.com/case/epac-techs-inc-v-harpercollins-christian-publg-inc.
53. *United States of America v. Volkswagen AG*, No 16-CR-20394 (E.D. Michigan), https://www.justice.gov/opa/press-release/file/924436/download.
54. Spoliation of evidence is explained and analyzed in hundreds of legal publications. Examples that treat various aspects of the topic include M. Koesel and T. Turnbull, *Spoliation of Evidence: Sanctions and Remedies for Destruction of Evidence in Civil*

Litigation, Third Edition (Chicago: American Bar Association, 2014); P. Oot, ed., *Spoliation* (Washington, DC: Electronic Discovery Institute, 2019); G. Joseph, *Sanctions: the Federal Law of Litigation Abuse, Fourth Edition* (Newark, NJ: LexisNexis, 2008); and J. Gorelik et al., *Destruction of Evidence* (New York: Aspen Publishers, 1989).

55. *Carlucci v. Piper Aircraft Corp.*, 102 F.R.D. 472 (S.D. Fla. 1984), https://casetext.com/case/carlucci-v-piper-aircraft-corporation.
56. *Telectron, Inc. v. Overhead Door Corp.*, 116 F.R.D. 107 (S.D. Fla. 1987), https://casetext.com/case/telectron.
57. *Zubulake v. UBS Warburg LLC*, 220 F.R.D. 212, 217 (S.D.N.Y. 2003), https://casetext.com/case/zubulake-v-ubs-warburg-llc-5.
58. *Securities and Exchange Commission v. Martha Stewart and Peter Bacanovic*, 03-CIV-4070 (NRB) (S.D.N.Y.), https://www.sec.gov/litigation/complaints/comp18169.htm.
59. *United States v. Arthur Andersen LLP*, 374 F.3d 281 (5th Cir. 2004), https://casetext.com/case/us-v-arthur-andersen-llp.
60. W. Brazil, "Civil discovery: lawyers' views of its effectiveness, principal problems and abuses," *American Bar Foundation Research Journal* 5, no. 4 (1980), 789–902, https://scholarship.law.berkeley.edu/cgi/viewcontent.cgi?referer=https://www.google.com/&httpsredir=1&article=1320&context=facpubs; C. Nesson, "Incentives tonspoliate evidence in civil litigation: the need for vigorous judicial action," *Cardozo Law Review* 13, no. 4 (1991), 793–805, https://heinonline.org/HOL/LandingPage?handle=hein.journals/cdozo13&div=42&id=&page=; D. Nance, "Hear no evil, see no evil: On Professor Nesson's claims about evidence suppression," *Cardozo Law Review* 13, no. 4, 809–15, https://scholarlycommons.law.case.edu/cgi/viewcontent.cgi?referer=https://www.google.com/&httpsredir=1&article=1287&context=faculty_publications; T. Spencer, "Do not fold, spindle or mutilate: the trend towards recognition of spoliation as a separate tort," *Idaho Law Review* 37, no. 1 (1993), 37–65; on the possibility of undetected destruction or alteration of medical records, see A. Casamassima, "Spoliation of evidence and medical malpractice," *Pace Law Review* 14, no. 1 (1994), 235–99, https://digitalcommons.pace.edu/cgi/viewcontent.cgi?article=1381&context=plr; A. Hoffman and S. Sanbar, "Spoliation: Record retention, destruction, and alteration," in American College of Legal Medicine, *Medical Malpractice Survival Handbook*, Philadelphia: Mosby, 2007, 45–54.
61. On the issue of ownership of clinical data, see A. Ballantyne, "How should we think about clinical data ownership," *Journal of Medical Ethics* 46 (2), 289–94 (2020), https://doi.org/10.1136/medethics-2018-105340.
62. 48 C.F.R. 4.805, https://www.law.cornell.edu/cfr/text/48/4.805. The retention period was increased from three to six years to conform to retention periods defined by the National Archives and Records Administration for contract files in the General Retention Schedule for Financial Management and Reporting Records. See https://www.federalregister.gov/documents/2015/12/04/2015-30460/federal-acquisition-regulation-retention-periods.
63. On deletion of content from social media sites, see E. Newland et al., *Account Deactivation and Content Removal: Guiding Principles and Practices for Companies and Users, Research Publication No 2011-09* (Cambridge, MA: Berkman Center for Internet & Society at Harvard University, 2011), https://papers.ssrn.com/sol3/papers.cfm?abstract_id=1940454; F. Stjernfelt and A. Lauritzen, *Your Post Has Been Removed* (Cham,

Switzerland: Springer, 2020), especially 115-37, https://doi.org/10.1007/978-3-030-25968-6_11.

64. C. Cochran, *ISO 9001:2015 in Plain English* (Chico, CA: Paton Professional, 2015); J. Wilson and L. Campbell, "Developing a knowledge management policy for ISO 9001:2015," *Journal of Knowledge Management* 20 (4), 829-44 (2016), https://doi.org/10.1108/JKM-11-2015-0472; J. Wilson and L. Campbell, "ISO 9001:2015: the evolution and convergence of quality management and knowledge management for competitive advantage," *Total Quality Management and Business Excellence* 31 (7-8), 761-76 (2020), https://doi.org/10.1080/14783363.2018.1445965; R. Ticker, *Iso 9001:2015 Audit Procedures, Fourth Edition* (London: Routledge, 2016), https://doi.org/10.4324/9781315774817.
65. R. Kissel et al., *Guidelines for Media Sanitization, NIST Special Publication 800-88, Rev. 1* (Gaithersburg, MD: National Institute of Standards and Technology, 2014), http://dx.doi.org/10.6028/NIST.SP.800-88r1.
66. See S. Butler and R. Paszkiet, eds., *The Lawyer's Guide to Buying, Selling, Merging, and Closing a Law Practice* (Chicago: American Bar Association, 2008), especially 23-24; American Bar Association, Model Rules of Professional Conduct, Rule 1.15, https://www.americanbar.org/groups/professional_responsibility/publications/model_rules_of_professional_conduct/model_rules_of_professional_conduct_table_of_contents/.
67. NAIC Market Conduct Record Retention and Production Model Regulation, https://content.naic.org/sites/default/files/model-law-910-market-conduct-record.pdf; NAIC Insurance Data Security Model Law, https://content.naic.org/sites/default/files/inline-files/MDL-668.pdf.
68. ASOP No. 23, Data Quality; ASOP No. 36, Statement of Actuarial Opinion Regarding Property/Casualty Loss and Loss Adjustment Expense Reserves; ASOP 41, Actuarial Communications, https://www.actuary.org/content/actuarial-standards-practice.
69. American Psychological Association, Ethical Principles of Psychologists and Code of Conduct, Section 6.01, https://www.apa.org/ethics/code/ethics-code-2017.pdf; American Counselling Association, Code of Ethics, Section B.6.h, https://www.counseling.org/Resources/aca-code-of-ethics.pdf; National Association of Social Workers, Code of Ethics, Section 3.04, https://www.socialworkers.org/About/Ethics/Code-of-Ethics/Code-of-Ethics-English. See also E. Luepker, *Record Keeping in Psychotherapy and Counseling, Second Edition* (New York: Routledge, 2012), esp. 135-44; E. Drogin et al., "The American Psychological Association's revised 'record keeping guidelines': implications for the practitioner," *Professional Psychology: Research and Practice* 41 (3), 236-43 (2010), https://doi.org/10.1037/a0019001; T. Bernister and K. Dobson, "An updated account of the ethical and legal considerations of recordkeeping," *Canadian Psychology /Psychologie Canadienne* 52 (4), 296-309 (2011), https://doi.org/10.1037/a0024052.
70. American Psychological Association, Record Keeping Guidelines, https://www.apa.org/practice/guidelines/record-keeping; also published in *American Psychologist* 62 (9), 993-1004 (2007), https://doi.org/10.1037/0003-066X.62.9.993. See also E. Drogin, "The American Psychological Association's revised record keeping guidelines: implications for the practitioner," *Professional Psychology: Research and Practice* 41 (3), 236-43 (2010), https://doi.org/10.1037/a0019001; T.

Bernister and K. Dobson, "An updated account of the ethical and legal considerations of record keeping," *Canadian Psychology* 52 (4), 296–309 (2011), https://psycnet.apa.org/record/2011-15456-001; J. Scaife and M. Pomerantz, "A survey of the record-keeping practices of clinical psychologists," *Clinical Psychology & Psychotherapy* 6 (3), 210–26 (1999), https://doi.org/10.1002/(SICI)1099-0879(199907)6:3<210::AID-CPP198>3.0.CO;2-E.

71. Retention and Destruction of Health Information, https://library.ahima.org/PB/RetentionDestruction-.YVN86i1h2ks. See also M. Dehnavi and M. Baghini, "National medical record retention," *Specialty Journal of Medical Research and Health Science* 4 (4): 35–48 (2019), https://sciarena.com/storage/models/article/vz-pNwbrVPY6ud4WWIvnhRBQfsVTjCSZU1PyVVTxYxIlnvo3mFKjK48fMQmfL/national-medical-record-retention-laws.pdf.
72. Recordkeeping requirements developed by the Government and Legal Affairs Task Force, https://iccfa.com/2017/03/21/record-keeping-requirements/.
73. Payment Card Industry Data Security Standard, Requirements and Security Assessment Procedures, Version 3.2.1, https://www.pcisecuritystandards.org/documents/PCI_DSS_v3-2-1.pdf?agreement=true&time=1632862791591.
74. Statements on Auditing Standards, AU-C Section 230.17, https://www.aicpa.org/content/dam/aicpa/research/standards/auditattest/downloadabledocuments/au-c-00230.pdf. See also QC Section 10.A59, Retention of Engagement Documentation, https://www.aicpa.org/content/dam/aicpa/research/standards/auditattest/downloadabledocuments/qc-00010.pdf.
75. Uniform Accountancy Act Model Rule 7-9, Attest Documentation and Retention, https://nasba.org/app/uploads/2019/11/October2019ModelRulesFINAL.pdf.
76. CFA Institute, Code of Ethics and Standards of Professional Conduct, https://www.cfainstitute.org/-/media/documents/code/code-ethics-standards/code-of-ethics-standards-professional-conduct.ashx. See also https://www.cfainstitute.org/en/research/multimedia/2018/professional-conduct-standard-VC-record-retention.
77. Document Retention Guidelines: A Risk Management White Paper prepared jointly by the ACEC Risk Management Committee and the NSPE Professional Liability Committee, 2016, https://www.nspe.org/sites/default/files/resources/pdfs/liability/White-Paper-110216DocumentRetentionDocument-Final.pdf.
78. On problems with retention schedules, see SRA International, *Report on Current Recordkeeping Practices within the Federal Government* (Arlington, VA: SRA International, 2001), https://www.archives.gov/files/records-mgmt/faqs/pdf/report-on-recordkeeping-practices.pdf; R. Kahn, "The risk-cost retention model: a new approach to records retention," *Information Management Journal* 40 (3), 47–50, 52–54 (2006); S. Cisco, "How to win the compliance battle using 'big buckets,'" *Information Management Journal* 42 (4), 30–38 (2008); S. Cisco, "Big buckets for simplifying records retention schedules," *Information Management Journal* 42(5), 3–6 (2008); F. Diers, "In search of an effective RIM or IG program," *Information Management* 50 (2), 34–37, 47 (2016); J. McDonald and V. Leveille, "Whither the retention schedule in the era of big data and open data?" *Records Management Journal* 24 (2), 99–121 (2014), https://doi.org/10.1108/RMJ-01-2014-0010.
79. Code of Ethics, Institute of Certified Records Managers, https://www.icrm.org/code-of-ethics; Code of Ethics, Certified Information Governance Professionals, https://www.arma.org/page/IGP_Ethics; Society of American Archivists

Core Values Statement and Code of Ethics, https://www2.archivists.org/statements/saa-core-values-statement-and-code-of-ethics-code_of_ethics; Code of Ethics, Archives and Records Association, https://www.archives.org.uk/images/ARA_Documents/ARA_Code_Of_Ethics.pdf; Code of Ethics, Australian Society of Archivists, https://www.archivists.org.au/about-us/code-of-ethics. For a survey of ethical codes, see M. Cook, "Professional ethics and practice in archives and records management in a human rights context," *Journal of the Society of Archivists* 27 (1), 1-15 (2006), https://doi.org/10.1080/00039810600691205; and M. Neazor, "Recordkeeping professional ethics and their application," *Archivaria* (64), 47-84 (2007), https://www.semanticscholar.org/paper/Recordkeeping-Professional-Ethics-and-their-Neazor/cc7ba3753615bde209fe036625df32cdce0751a2; J. Kim, "A comparative study on the codes of ethics by professional associations of libraries, archives and museums in foreign countries," *Journal of the Korean BIBLIA Society for Library and Information Science* 25 (4), 5-27 (2014), https://doi.org/10.14699/kbiblia.2014.25.4.005.

80. On the ethics and records management, see N. Mooradian, *Ethics for Records and Information Management* (Chicago: ALA Neal-Schuman, 2018); W. Koehler and J. Pemberton, "A search for core values: towards a model code of ethics for information professionals," *Journal of Information Ethics* 9 (1), 26-54 (2000), http://hdl.handle.net/10822/933631; W. Koehler, "Professional values and ethics as defined by the 'The LIS Discipline,'" *Journal of Education for Library and Information Science* 44 (2): 99-119 (2003), https://www.jstor.org/stable/40323926; P. Ngulube, "Professionalism and ethics in records management in the public sector in Zimbabwe," *Records Management Journal* 10 (3), 161-73 (2000), https://doi.org/10.1108/EUM0000000007262; M. Palmer, "Records management and accountability versus corruption, fraud, and maladministration," *Records Management Journal* 10 (2), 61-72 (2000), https://doi.org/10.1108/EUM0000000007256; J. Pemberton and L. Pendergraft, "Toward a Code of Ethics: social relevance and the professionalization of records management," *ARMA Records Management Quarterly* 32 (4), 51-57 (1998), https://www.proquest.com/openview/b4f764fa48922e7a5833fa29900c3216/1?pq-origsite=gscholar&cbl=47365.
81. Examples of the many publications on stakeholder theory include K. Gibson, "The moral basis of stakeholder theory," *Journal of Business Ethics* 26 (3), 245-57 (2000), https://www.jstor.org/stable/25074344; W. Cragg, "Business ethics and stakeholder theory," *Business Ethics Quarterly* 12 (2), 113-42 (2002), https://doi.org/10.2307/3857807; R. Philips, "Stakeholder theory and a principle of fairness," *Business Ethics Quarterly* 7 (1), 51-66 (1997), https://doi.org/10.2307/3857232; B. Parmar et al., "Stakeholder theory: the state of the art," *Academy of Management Annals* 4 (1), 403-45, https://doi.org/10.5465/19416520.2010.495581; E. Sternberg, "The defects of stakeholder theory," *Corporate Governance: an International Review* 5 (1), 3-10 (2002), https://doi.org/10.1111/1467-8683.00034; R. Freeman et al., *Stakeholder Theory: Concepts and Strategies* (Cambridge: Cambridge University Press, 2018); R. Freeman et al., *Stakeholder Theory: the State of the Art* (Cambridge: Cambridge University Press, 2010); M. Bonnafous-Boucher and J. Renddtorff, *Stakeholder Theory: A Model for Strategic Management* (Cham, Switzerland: Springer, 2016).

82. For an excellent discussion of preemptive destruction of information, see J. Ruhnka and S. Weller, "The ethical implications of corporate records management practices and some suggested ethical values for decisions," *Journal of Business Ethics* 9 (2), 81–92 (1990), https://www.jstor.org/stable/25072009. For a study of the ethical implications of destroying accounting statements not used by management to avoid spending resources answering questions from auditors, R. Goza, "The ethics of record destruction," *Journal of Management Policy and Practice* 14(6), 107–15 (2013), case study of unnamed charity, http://www.na-businesspress.com/jmpp/gozar_web14_6_.pdf. Some celebrities, public figures, and intellectuals have preemptively destroyed documents to keep them out of the hands of biographers and to better control their own life stories. See, for example, P. Gay, *Freud: A Life for Our Time* (New York: W.W. Norton, 2006), xv.
83. Relevant international standards are ISO 14040:2006, *Environmental Management—Life Cycle Assessment—Principles and Framework*; ISO 14044:2006, *Environmental Management—Life Cycle Assessment—Requirements and Guidelines*; ISO/TS 14071:2014, *Environmental Management—Life Cycle Assessment—Critical Review Processes and Reviewer Competencies: Additional Requirements and Guidelines to ISO 14044:2006*; and ISO/TS 14072:2014, *Environmental Management—Life Cycle Assessment—Requirements and Guidelines for Organizational Life Cycle Assessment.*
84. E. Tomes and N. Altiparmak, "A comparative study of HDD and SSD RAIDs' impact on server energy consumption," *2017 IEEE International Conference on Cluster Computing* (Los Alamitos, CA: IEEE Computer Society, 2017), 625–26, https://par.nsf.gov/servlets/purl/10050305; A. Shehabi et al., *United States Data Center Energy Usage Report, LBNL-1005775* (Berkeley, CA: Lawrence Berkeley National Laboratory, 2016), https://www.osti.gov/servlets/purl/1372902; E. Masanet et al., "Recalibrating global data center energy-use estimates," *Science* 367 (6481), 984–86 (2020), https://doi.org/10.1126/science.aba3758; M. Koot, and F. Wijnhoven, "Usage impact on data center electricity needs: a system dynamic forecasting model," *Applied Energy* 291, article 116798 (2021), https://doi.org/10.1016/j.apenergy.2021.116798.
85. On energy consumption at the bit level, see L. Kish and C. Granqvist, "Does information have mass?" *Proceedings of the IEEE* 109 (9), 1895–99 (2013), https://arxiv.org/pdf/1309.7889.pdf; also W. Jiang, Energy to Store One Bit, submitted as coursework, Stanford University (2018), http://large.stanford.edu/courses/2018/ph240/jiang2/
86. As an unrelated usage, the phrase "green archiving" also refers to a form of open access self-archiving of journal articles, conference papers, and other scholarly publications in an institutional repository, thematic repository, or academic social network. See, for example, C. Morgan, "The role of the academic journal publisher and open access publishing models," *International Studies Perspectives* 13 (3), 228–34 (2012), https://doi.org/10.1111/j.1528-3585.2012.00495.x.
87. G. van Bussel et al., "Digital archiving, green IT and environment: deleting data to manage critical effects of the data deluge," *Electronic Journal of Information Systems Evaluation* 18 (2), 187–97 (2015), https://academic-publishing.org/index.php/ejise/article/view/181/144. On "Green IT" in general, see M. Singh and G. Sahu, "Towards adoption of Green IS: a literature review using classification methodology," *International Journal of Information Management* 54, article 102147, https://doi.org/10.1016/j.ijinfomgt.2020.102147.

88. The National Strategy for Electronics Stewardship, issued in 2011 by the Interagency Task Force on Electronics Stewardship, presents the federal government's plan to manage electronic waste, https://www.epa.gov/smm-electronics/national-strategy-electronics-stewardship.
89. Examples of the many publications on decomposition of paper under anaerobic conditions encountered in landfills include M. Barlaz, *Critical Review of Forest Products Decomposition in Municipal Decomposition in Municipal Solid Waste Landfills, Technical Bulletin No. 872* (Research Triangle Park, NC: National Council for Air and Stream Improvement, 2004), https://www.ncasi.org/wp-content/uploads/2019/02/tb872.pdf; M. Barlaz et al., "Anaerobic biodegradation of solid waste," in R. Mitchell and J. Gu, eds., *Environmental Microbiology* (Hoboken, NJ: Wiley, 2010), 259–77; X. Wang et al., "Decomposition of forest products buried in landfills," *Waste Management* 33 (11), 2267–76 (2013), https://doi.org/ 10.1016/j.wasman.2013.07.009; J. Micales and K. Skog, "The decomposition of forest products in landfills," *International Biodeterioration & Biodegradation* 39 (2–3), 145–58 (1997), https://doi.org/10.1016/S0964-8305(97)83389-6; J. Owens and D. Chynoweth, "Biochemical methane potential of municipal solid waste (MSW) components," *Water Science & Technology* 27 (2), 1–14 (1993), https://doi.org/10.2166/wst.1993.0065; W. Eleazer et al., "Biodegradability of municipal solid waste components in laboratory-scale landfills," *Environmental Science & Technology* 31 (3), 911–17 (1997), https://doi.org/10.1021/es9606788; J. Gonzalez-Estrella et al., "A review of anaerobic digestion of paper and paper board waste," *Reviews in Environmental Science and Bio/Technology* 16 (3), 569–90 (2017), https://doi.org/10.1007/s11157-017-9436-z.
90. T. Counsell and J. Allwood, "Reducing climate change gas emissions by cutting out stages in the life cycle of office paper," *Resources, Conservation and Recycling* 49 (4), 340–52 (2007), https://doi.org/10.1016/j.resconrec.2006.03.018; L. Wang et al., "A life cycle assessment (LCA) comparison of three management options for waste papers: bioethanol production, recycling and incineration with energy recovery," *Bioresource Technology* 120 (1), 89–98 (2012), https://doi.org/10.1016/j.biortech.2012.05.130; H. Merrild et al., "Assessing recycling versus incineration of key materials in municipal waste: the importance of efficient energy recovery and transport distances," *Waste Management* 32 (5), 100901018 (2012), https://doi.org/10.1016/j.wasman.2011.12.025; A. Villanueva and H. Wenzel, "Paper waste—recycling, incineration or landfilling? A review of existing life cycle assessments," *Waste Management* 27 (8), 529–46 (2007), https://doi.org/10.1016/j.wasman.2007.02.019.
91. K. Brothers et al., "Office paper recycling: a function of container proximity," *Journal of Applied Behavior Analysis* 27 (1), 153–60 (1994), https://doi.org/10.1016/j.resconrec.2006.03.018; T. Ludwig et al., "Increasing recycling in academic buildings: a systematic replication," *Journal of Applied Behavior Analysis* 31 (4), 683–86 (1998), https://doi.org/10.1901/jaba.1998.31-683; J. Counsell and J. Allwood, "Desktop paper recycling: a survey of novel technologies that might recycle office paper within the office," *Journal of Materials Processing Technology* 173 (1), 111–23 (2006), https://doi.org/10.1016/j.jmatprotec.2005.11.017; S. Oskamp et al., "Psychological factors affecting paper recycling by businesses," *Environment and Behavior* 26 (4), 477–503 (1994), https://doi.org/10.1177/001391659402600402; M. Kaisher et al., "Promoting recycling behavior in office environments," *Proceedings of the Human Factors and Ergonomics Society Annual Meeting* 37 (7), 484–88 (1993), https://doi

.org/10.1177/154193129303700703; A. Andrews, "Comparison of recycling outcomes in three types of recycling collection units," *Waste Management* 33 (3), 530–35 (2013), https://doi.org/10.1016/j.wasman.2012.08.018; R. Marans and Y. Lee, "Linking recycling behavior to waste management planning: a case study of office workers in Taiwan," *Landscape and Urban Planning* 26 (1–4), 203–14 (1993), https://doi.org/10.1016/0169-2046(93)90017-8; J. Vining and A. Ebreo, "What makes a recycler?: a comparison of recyclers and nonrecyclers," *Environment and Behavior* 22 (1), 55–73 (1990), https://doi.org/10.1177/0013916590221003.

4

Information Storage and Preservation

The preceding chapter identified compliance requirements that specify how long information must be retained. The compliance requirements discussed in this chapter specify where and how information must be stored until its retention period elapses. The chapter also identifies compliance requirements for records that require permanent preservation—that is, retention in perpetuity.[1] As with retention of information, compliance requirements for information storage and preservation are specified in laws and regulations, but they may also be included in contracts and other legally binding agreements. Information storage and preservation requirements are presented in a number of international standards and industry norms and in the internal policies of companies and nonprofit organizations. Societal compliance requirements address sustainability issues associated with energy-intensive information storage and preservation practices.

LEGAL AND REGULATORY COMPLIANCE

Four groups of laws and regulations specify compliance requirements for storage and preservation of information:

- Laws and regulations that empower archival agencies to identify public records that warrant permanent preservation. Archival regulations may also specify storage media, file format, and environmental conditions for permanent records.
- Laws and regulations that empower archival agencies to specify preservation requirements for the private archives of nongovernmental organizations.
- Laws and regulations that specify file format and media requirements for information storage, including compliance requirements for electronic records.
- Laws and regulations that specify or restrict the locations or governmental jurisdictions where information can be stored.
- Laws and regulations that specify compliance requirements for backup copies of information.

Compared to legislation that specifies minimum retention periods, legal and regulatory compliance requirements for information storage and preservation are less numerous, easier to identify, and applicable to a smaller subset of recorded information. In the United States and many other countries, preservation laws and regulations are limited to government records.

ARCHIVAL LEGISLATION

As with the information retention and disposition requirements discussed in chapter 3, the information storage and preservation practices of government agencies are more heavily regulated than those of nongovernmental entities. Many countries have archival laws that mandate preservation of government records with historical or other research value.[2] These laws, which emphasize the importance of preserving a country's documentary heritage, give archival officials the authority to designate documents, databases, or other records that are to be kept permanently and ultimately transferred to a national archives or another approved archival repository.[3]

In countries with a unitary system of government, archival legislation applies to permanent records of central government agencies, although a provision may also be made for a coordinated national system that includes local government records. In Sweden, for example, the National Archives is responsible for archival activities throughout the country.[4] In Slovakia, the system of archives includes the records of the central government, municipalities, and self-governing regions.[5] The French Heritage Code departs from this pattern; the Archives Nationales, which dates from the French Revolution, preserves the records of the national government, while provincial governments are responsible for their own archives.[6]

In federated countries, preservation of information maintained by government agencies is regulated by a combination of national and subnational legislation. Under U.S. law, the archivist of the United States has the authority to identify records of federal government agencies, the Congress, and the Supreme Court that have sufficient historical or other value to warrant transfer to the National Archives for continued preservation.[7] Such archival records may include, but are not limited to, paper documents, databases, digital documents, audio recordings, and photographic media, including microfilm. U.S. state laws and regulations give state archives and historical societies similar authority for identification and preservation of permanent records maintained by state and local government agencies.[8] Some larger U.S. cities have passed their own archival laws for identification and preservation of municipal records of historical value.

The authority of archival agencies in other federated countries is defined by a similar combination of national and subnational laws and regulations. The Library and Archives of Canada Act, for example, deals with identification and preservation of historically significant records of the federal government and ministerial agencies, while individual provinces and territories have their own legislation that empowers archival agencies to take custody of public records of permanent value.[9] Similarly, the Archives Act 1983 gives the National Archives of Australia authority to identify and preserve the Commonwealth's archival resources. Australian states and territories have passed legislation to establish their own archival agencies. In Switzerland, the Archiving Act gives the Federal Archives authority to identify and preserve records of the Federal Assembly, Federal Counsel, federal courts, and other federal bodies. Individual cantons have their own archival legislation.

In some countries, records that warrant preservation and transfer to archival custody are identified in retention schedules prepared or approved by archival authorities. In the United States, for example, retention schedules prepared by the National Archives and Records Administration list permanent records that federal agencies must transfer to the National Archives after a specified period of time, usually between fifteen and thirty years after the records were created or received. Retention schedules prepared by individual federal agencies must be reviewed by NARA to ensure that permanent records are properly identified.[10] Retention schedules prepared by U.S. state archives generally follow the NARA model: They identify permanent records that are to be transferred to archival custody. Retention schedules prepared by state or local government agencies themselves are subject to archival review to ensure that permanent records are identified. National archives in Trinidad and Tobago,[11] Cyprus,[12] and some other countries likewise use retention schedules to identify permanent records that must be transferred to archival custody.

Alternatively, legislation may specify that all records maintained by government agencies must be transferred to a designated archival repository after a specified period of time. The New Zealand Public Records Act 2005 is typical of that approach: Government records that are more than twenty-five years old must be transferred to an approved repository under the control of the chief archivist.[13] Presumably, records that have no continuing value will have been destroyed before that time. Among other examples that might be cited, the Croatian Law on Archival Material and Archives,[14] the Danish Archives Act,[15] the Icelandic Public Archives Act,[16] and the Taiwanese Archives Act[17] mandate transfer of government records to archival custody before they are thirty years old. In South Africa, government records must be transferred to an archival repository after twenty years unless it is determined that the records should remain in the custody of a governmental body.[18] Archival laws in other countries provide a similar exception for records that government agencies must have conveniently available for a longer period of time, but not indefinitely, to support their business operations.

In addition to identifying records of continuing value and mandating their transfer to archival custody, some archival laws and regulations specify requirements for recording media, file formats, and storage conditions for information that warrants permanent preservation:

- In the twentieth century, it was common for archival regulations to require paper or microfilm for storage and preservation of government records with long-term retention requirements, which was often defined as greater than ten years. Many archival agencies have rescinded that requirement. Recognizing that government operations are transitioning from paper to electronic recordkeeping and that some electronic records, such as databases, cannot be converted to paper or microfilm without compromising the integrity and usability of information, archival agencies increasingly accept permanent records in electronic form, subject to requirements and restrictions. For transfer of permanent records to the National Archives, for example, U.S. government agencies must use media that are "sound and free from defects." At the time of this writing, NARA would accept permanent electronic records on physical media, including magnetic tape, CD-ROMs, and DVDs. Electronic transfer via FTP protocol is also permitted, subject to NARA's approval.[19] NARA has also identified documentation requirements and preferred and acceptable file formats for permanent electronic records.[20]
- Some national and subnational archival regulations specify optimal and acceptable file formats for databases, word-processing files, spreadsheets, digital images, and other electronic records that are transferred to archival custody for permanent preservation. The goal of these regulations is to reduce the risk that electronic records will become unusable in the future. Archival regulations favor open source and nonproprietary file formats that are well documented and broadly compatible with available software, but widely adopted proprietary formats may be permitted. Thus, the Wisconsin Historical Society lists PDF/A and OpenDocument Text as optimal formats for word-processing documents for permanent records to be transferred to the State Archives, but the Microsoft Word document format and Rich Text Format are also acceptable.[21] Similarly, file formats recommended for transfer of permanent electronic records to the Library and Archives Canada include XML, HTML, SGML, and plain text, as well PDF/A, OpenDocument Text, and the Rich Text Format, but nonproprietary formats utilized by Microsoft Word and certain other applications are also acceptable for transfer.[22]
- A number of archival regulations specify environmental requirements for storage of permanent records in the custody of government agencies. According to federal regulations, U.S. government agencies must store permanent electronic records at 62 to 68 degrees Fahrenheit with relative humidity ranging from 35 to 45 percent. Magnetic tapes that contain permanent records must be inspected annually to identify and correct data loss, and the information must be copied onto new storage media at intervals of ten years or less.[23] Environmental requirements for storage of microfilm that contains permanent federal records are based on international standards discussed later in this chapter.[24] Master microforms must be inspected at prescribed intervals for signs of deterioration.[25] Less stringent environmental

conditions apply to storage of permanent paper records.[26] Some U.S. state archives have adopted these NARA requirements for permanent records maintained by state and local government agencies.[27]

PRIVATE ARCHIVES

The archival legislation discussed in preceding sections applies to the storage and preservation of recorded information maintained by government agencies and quasi-governmental entities, such as public benefit corporations, authorities, boards, and commissions. In most countries, archival legislation does not apply to information that is maintained by companies, charities, cultural institutions, professional associations, labor unions, and other nongovernmental entities. In the United States, Canada, the United Kingdom, Switzerland, and some other countries, privately owned information is not subject to legal and regulatory preservation mandates beyond the minimum retention periods discussed in the preceding chapter. Nongovernmental organizations are not obligated to preserve such information permanently. Some business formation laws require companies to preserve certain information about board meetings and shareholders, but that obligation ends when a company is dissolved.

In some countries, however, archival preservation regulations apply to certain nongovernmental records, which are characterized as private archives to distinguish them from the public archives maintained by government agencies. Nongovernmental organizations must comply with these regulations, which authorize archival agencies to identify privately owned information that warrants permanent preservation, the rationale being that such information is considered part of a nation's historical and cultural heritage. Private archives laws and regulations are a type of data sovereignty legislation, in which a sovereign nation asserts its authority over information that is created and maintained within its borders.

Compliance requirements for preservation of private archives vary from country to country. For example:

- In some countries, owners of private archives retain custody of them but must guarantee their preservation. In Italy, private information of public interest cannot be destroyed without archival authorization.[28] In Portugal, the designation of historically significant private archives does not affect property rights, but it does prohibit modification or destruction of culturally significant information without archival approval.[29] In Russia, owners of historically significant private archives are accountable for their storage and preservation. Failure to preserve private archives may lead to a court order for transfer of the archives to archival authorities.[30]
- In some countries, nongovernmental organizations must transfer historically significant information to archival custody for preservation when it is no longer needed for business purposes. This is the case, for example, In Hungary[31] and Latvia.[32]

- In some countries, archival authorities are empowered to acquire historically significant records from nongovernmental entities. In China, state archival officials have ultimate appraisal authority over private archives and can acquire them if they are not properly maintained by their owners or when certain other conditions apply.[33] In Taiwan, archival authorities can acquire private archives if is necessary to preserve them.[34]
- In some countries, archival authorities can identify private archives that contain information of historical or cultural significance, but they do not have unilateral authority to take privately owned information into archival custody. In France, for example, private archives may be designated as of historical interest by archival administration with or without the consent of the nongovernmental entity that owns them, but this does not imply transfer of ownership to the state.[35] In Finland, private archives can be transferred to the national or provincial archives by agreement with the owner of the information.[36]
- In some countries, an archival agency may be authorized to purchase or make copies of nongovernmental records if their owner intends to destroy, sell, or export them. In Slovenia, archival authorities can take custody of private archives that are in danger of damage or destruction for purposes of copying them. Archival authorities also have a preemptive right in the event of a sale of private archives.[37] In Denmark, the State Archives has the right to copy historically significant private archives before they leave the country.[38]

INFORMATION STORAGE LAWS

As noted above, archival legislation may specify format and media requirements for storage of government records. By contrast, nongovernmental entities can store information in any format on any medium they choose unless a particular format or medium is specified or prohibited by a law or regulation. Such laws and regulations are limited in both number and scope. In the Netherlands and Indonesia, for example, a company's balance sheet and profit-and-loss statements must be kept in paper form for the ten-year period mandated by law, but other accounting records can be stored in any format. In the Philippines, accounting information considered relevant for tax assessment must be stored in paper form for the first five years of the ten-year retention period required by law; any storage medium is acceptable thereafter. In Bangladesh, employees' service books must be kept as bound volumes; no format is prescribed for other personnel records.[39] In the United States, export administration regulations require storage and retention of original export control documents, contracts, correspondence, and other records unless reproductions comply with stringent requirements for legibility, integrity, and accessibility.[40] Importers must keep customs entry records in their original formats for 120 days and may use alternative storage method thereafter, subject to requirements for integrity, readability, security, inspection, labeling, filing, and indexing.[41] For these regulations, original records means records that are in the condition in which they were made or received.[42]

The requirements cited above are exceptional. Nongovernmental organizations are generally free to use any storage medium that meets their operational requirements. In the United States, many sections of the Code of Federal Regulations have been revised to accept electronic records to satisfy recordkeeping requirements. At the state level, the Uniform Electronic Transactions Act (UETA) contains virtually identical provisions. It has been adopted by forty-nine states, the District of Columbia, Puerto Rico, and the U.S. Virgin Islands (New York, the only nonadopting state, has its own statute pertaining to electronic transactions). According to the UETA, evidence of a record or signature may not be excluded solely because it is in electronic form. Similarly, Canadian provinces and territories, with the exception of the Northwest Territories, have adopted the Uniform Electronic Commerce Act, which establishes functional equivalency rules that allow electronic records to satisfy legal requirements for written communications and recordkeeping.

Many other countries have electronic transaction laws or electronic signature laws that affirm the legal status of information stored on electronic media. These laws, which describe electronic information as electronic documents or data messages, draw upon model laws developed by the United Nations Commission on International Trade Law (UNCITRAL). Information recorded on electronic media can satisfy recordkeeping requirements subject to certain compliance requirements, the most common being that the electronic storage medium must accurately preserve all content, the information must be retrievable and readable throughout its retention period, and printed copies must be provided when requested by government officials.[43] Computer equipment and software to support retrieval, display, and printing of electronic information must be available for as long as the records are retained.

These electronic transaction laws apply to information associated with business and government operations. They do not address the legal status of electronic records that deal with noncommercial or nongovernmental matters, including such personal matters as powers of attorney, health-care proxies, do-not-resuscitate orders, and noncommercial trusts. In the United States, the Uniform Electronic Transactions Act specifically excludes wills or other testamentary instruments, records associated with certain transactions covered by the Uniform Commercial Code, and any records that are required by other laws or regulations to be in non-electronic form. State-specific implementations of the UETA may include additional exceptions and exclusions. In some national and subnational jurisdictions, electronic transaction and electronic signature laws exclude recorded information related to adoptions, divorce, or family matters; pleadings, motions, and other official court documents; insurance cancelation notices; default notices associated with credit agreements;

foreclosure and eviction notices; documents that require notarization; and information related to transportation or handling of hazardous substances.

For most organizations, the exceptions and exclusions listed above will have little, if any, impact on business information, but compliance with electronic transaction laws is complicated by several factors that an organization must address:

- The life span of a given electronic storage medium—the period of time during which the medium will remain reliably readable—may be shorter than the retention period for the information that the medium contains. In the case of hard drives, the most widely used computer storage technology, the life span of recorded information is defined by the service life of a given device, which is subject to significant wear and tear over time. Few hard drives are engineered for a service life longer than ten years, and most devices will be replaced by newer equipment before that time period elapses.
- With removable electronic media, such as magnetic tapes and optical disks, the life span may be affected by physical damage to or chemical deterioration of the medium itself or by the unavailability of compatible reading equipment. While magnetic and optical recording media may remain physically and chemically stable for several decades, the device required to read a specific magnetic tape or optical disk may be taken out of service without a compatible replacement or discontinued by its manufacturer without a compatible successor. The history of electronic storage products indicates a reasonably high likelihood that this will occur within a ten-year time period.
- These complications are compounded by software-related dependencies. Electronic information is intended for retrieval or other processing by specific application programs that, in turn, operate in a specific systems software environment. Even more than electronic storage devices, computer software is subject to changes that can render previously recorded information unusable. Successor versions of a given program may not be able to read digital documents, data, photographs, or other electronic information recorded by earlier versions. While some backward compatibility is typically supported in new versions, it does not necessarily apply to all prior generations of a program.

Electronic storage media are broadly suitable for information that will be retained for ten years or less. Such information will likely remain usable until its retention period elapses, although the risk of unreadability increases after five years. Additional action is necessary to comply with requirements for continued usability of electronic information with longer retention periods. Specifically, the useful life of electronic information must be extended by copying it onto new storage media or converting it to a different file format. This process, which is termed "data migration," must be performed at predetermined intervals or whenever hardware or software replacement renders previously recorded information unreadable. Migration of electronic information to new storage media will maintain the readability of recorded information where the stable life span of a given storage medium is shorter than the retention period for information that the medium contains or where product modifications or discontinuations render a given storage medium unusable. Migration of electronic content to new file formats will maintain the readability of digital documents, databases, and other information when computer applications are upgraded or replaced. The longer the retention period, the greater the need for data migration to comply with readability requirements for electronic information.

To facilitate compliance, electronic information can be saved in a file format intended for long-term retention. This approach will lengthen the period of time between migration intervals. The best-known example of a preservation-oriented file format is PDF/Archival (PDF/A), a standardized subset of the Portable Document Format that is intentionally designed to avoid software dependencies and maintain the readability of digital documents over time. The various PDF/A standards are discussed later in this chapter. PDF/A is compatible with many computer platforms, has wide support in the digital preservation community, and is likely to remain in use for the foreseeable future. The benefits of PDF/A are limited to file format migration. Use of PDF/A will not affect the time interval for storage media migration.

Going beyond approval of electronic recordkeeping, some laws and regulations specify the types of electronic media that are acceptable for information storage and preservation. Various laws and regulations require that information be stored on a durable medium that provides reasonable assurance against degradation or unauthorized modification of the information recorded on it.[44] Some laws and regulations specify that information must be recorded on a storage medium with a life expectancy that is at least equal to the retention period for the information unless the information will be transferred from one medium to another without loss of data.[45]

As one of the most widely discussed media regulations, the U.S. Securities and Exchange Commission mandates the use of nonerasable or nonrewritable media for storage of certain information maintained by brokers, dealers, and members of a national securities exchange. This requirement applies to daily trade records, asset and liability ledgers, income ledgers, customer account ledgers, order tickets, trade confirmation records, communication with customers, and other records related to securities transactions. To comply, a medium may be inherently nonrewritable, such as a write-once optical disk, or it may use hardware and software controls to prevent erasure of media, such as hard drives, that are otherwise rewritable.[46] Some states specify similar requirements for nonerasable storage of information by banks, lenders, real estate companies, and other regulated industries.[47]

DATA LOCALIZATION LEGISLATION

As discussed above, archival legislation may prevent government agencies and owners of private archives from exporting historically significant information. Many countries have data localization laws and regulations that specify or restrict the locations or governmental jurisdictions where information can be stored. Sometimes described as data residency laws, data localization legislation mandates the storage of certain types of information within the territorial boundaries of a country or, less commonly, a state, province, or other subnational jurisdiction. Data localization laws and regulations principally apply to multinational and transnational organizations that create or collect information in one country but want to store it in a different country. They do not affect the storage of information in the country or other political jurisdiction where information is created or collected, and they have no impact on organizations with business operations in a single political jurisdiction.

As their principal purpose, data localization laws and regulations ensure that information will be readily available when requested by government officials for audits and investigations or for examination by authorized stakeholders, such as a company's shareholders or partners. In this respect, data localization legislation differs from national security and data protection laws that restrict cross-border transfer of information but do not necessarily require in-country storage of such information. Restrictions on cross-border information transfer will be discussed in a later chapter.

In the United States, some laws and regulations specify storage locations for certain types of information. Most states, for example, have business registration laws that require a corporation to keep its business registration documents, bylaws, amendments, meeting minutes, resolutions, annual financial statements, and other corporate records at an accessible location for examination by shareholders.[48] In most cases, that location is the corporation's principal place of business, but an alternate, comparably accessible location approved by the corporation's board of directors or other governing body may be acceptable in some states. A corporation must also keep a register containing the names, addresses, and holdings of its shareholders at the same location. Some state laws specify comparable storage requirements for business formation documents and ownership information maintained by limited liability companies and partnerships.[49]

U.S. federal laws do not specify data localization requirements, but various federal regulations require certain information to be stored in a readily accessible location for at least part of its retention period. Among the many examples that might be cited, organizations regulated under the Commodity Exchange Act must keep paper records in a readily accessible location for at least two years of a five-year retention period. Electronic information must be readily accessible for the entire five-year period.[50] A medical device manufacturer must maintain manufacturing and quality control records at its manufacturing establishment or at another location that is reasonably accessible to responsible officials of the manufacturer and to Food and Drug Administration inspectors.[51] A pharmacy must store paper prescriptions for controlled substances at its registered location. Electronic prescriptions for controlled substances may be stored elsewhere provided they are readily retrievable at the pharmacy's registered location.[52]

Some federal regulations define storage locations that are reasonably accessible in terms of the time required to retrieve information when needed. If a company regulated by the Federal Motor Carrier Safety Administration uses a service agent to store information about employees' alcohol and drug tests, for example, the information must be available at the employer's principal place of business within two business days when requested by a government inspector.[53] Owners and operators of municipal solid waste landfills must keep certain paper records or electronic information in a readily accessible on-site location for five years, although off-site storage is permitted if the information can be retrieved within four hours.[54] Farms may store records related to food for human consumption off-site if the records can be made available on-site within twenty-four hours.[55]

Canada does not have general data localization requirements at the federal level, but some sector-specific and provincial laws restrict the locations where information can be stored. As an example, the superintendent of financial institutions may direct a bank to maintain all copies of accounting and customer information in Canada if is determined that storage of the records outside Canada is incompatible with fulfillment of the superintendent's responsibilities.[56] Ontario law prohibits sending business records outside of the province, even to another part of Canada, for storage except in a narrow range of circumstances.[57] Quebec has a similar law.[58]

In recent years, international trade agreements have opposed data localization. Both the Comprehensive and Progressive Agreement for Trans-Pacific Partnership (CPTPP)—signed by Canada, Australia, Brunei, Chile, Japan, Malaysia, New Zealand, Mexico, Peru, Singapore, and Vietnam—and the United States-Mexico-Canada Agreement (USMCA) prohibit requirements for in-country use of computing facilities and restrictions on cross-border transfer of electronic information.[59] Nonetheless, national and subnational laws and regulations that prohibit out-of-country storage of information are common. A study by the Information Technology & Innovation Foundation found that national data localization requirements have increased significantly in recent years.[60] Over half of the world's sovereign nations and dependent territories have laws that mandate storage of accounting records at an organization's principal business location or another location within the country or dependent territory. This is done to ensure the availability of accounting records for tax audits and, in the case of for-profit companies, inspection by shareholders and government regulators. Even where in-country retention is not mandated, many countries require that sufficient accounting information be available in the country to accurately indicate an organization's financial position for a specified period time, such as the most recent quarter, six months, or fiscal year. In some countries and dependent territories, tax officials must approve out-of-country retention or in-country storage locations apart from an organization's registered office.

In several dozen countries, labor laws and regulations require employers to keep certain personnel records at a worker's place of employment or, if that is not practical, at the employer's domestic headquarters or other principal place of business in the country. This is done to make the records available for examination by labor inspectors during unannounced visits, which is a requirement of most labor laws and regulations.

Data localization legislation does not necessarily prohibit out-of-country storage of backup copies or other duplicate records, but they may limit or prohibit the centralization of information on network servers located at a regional center or headquarters site. In-country storage requirements have an impact on enterprise-wide implementations of database management systems, content management systems, records management application software, email archiving systems, and other systems that support consolidated storage of electronic information. They also affect the use of cloud-based information services and the transfer of physical records to commercial storage providers located in other countries. These data localization requirements limit the information storage options available to organizations based in small countries, which may lack such providers, or in border cities that are most conveniently served by providers located in adjacent countries.

BACKUP COPIES

Backup copies are created specifically for restoration of information following loss, damage, inadvertent deletion, or other adverse events that render original copies of information unusable. Laws and regulations specify few compliance requirements for storage of backup copies of information. Some sector-specific laws identify the types of information for which backup copies are required. For example:

- U.S. regulations for good manufacturing practices require pharmaceutical companies to make exact and complete backup copies of production and control records, but they do not specify an acceptable format, storage location, or environmental conditions for such copies.[61]
- The same is true of HIPAA security regulations that require covered entities and business associates to create a retrievable, exact backup copy of electronic protected health information.[62] No comparable backup requirements apply to health information that is not maintained electronically.

- In Bahrain, banks must store copies of vital electronic and nonelectronic records offsite as soon as possible after they are created, and the backup copies must be readily accessible when needed.[63]
- Banks in Israel must store backup copies at a location that is sufficiently distant from the original information so as not to be affected by the same disasters.[64]

The requirements cited above are exceptions, however. More commonly, laws and regulations mention backup copies as a mandatory component of a business continuity or data recovery plan but provide no details about the types of copies that are required or how they should be stored. This is the case, for example, with FINRA Rule 4370, issued by the Financial Industry Regulatory Authority.[65] It requires broker-dealers to have a data backup and recovery plan for all electronic and nonelectronic information that is needed to satisfy customer obligations, but no details are provided. Some legal compliance requirements for data recovery are even more vague. According to 23 NYCRR 500.3, cybersecurity policies developed by banks, financial services companies, and insurance companies that are licensed in New York State must include a business continuity and disaster recovery plan to permit restoration of normal operations.[66] Backup copies are presumably a component of such a plan, but they are not explicitly mentioned.

No laws or regulations require permanent preservation of backup copies. Often, backup copies are replaced by updated copies at regular and frequent intervals. In most cases, such copies can be discarded when they are no longer relevant for data recovery, although some sector-specific legislation specifies nonpermanent retention periods for backup copies of certain information. The Central Bank of Uruguay, for example, requires financial intermediation institutions to create at least two weekly full backup copies of accounting records and financial statements and retain them for a minimum of ten years. One of the copies must be stored in a separate building at a reasonable distance for the financial intermediation institution's data center.[67] In the United Arab Emirates, backup copies of lending and borrowing transactions involving securities must be kept to ten years,[68] while insurance companies, agents, and brokers must keep backup copies of their account books for seven years or until the end of the working relationship with the insured party.[69]

CONTRACTUAL COMPLIANCE

Contracts, purchase orders, memoranda of understanding, and similar agreements often specify requirements for storage and preservation of information that a contractor creates, processes, or maintains on an organization's behalf. Such requirements apply to service providers who are in possession of information that the contracting organization considers its property. Examples include third-party administrators who process claims for insurance companies, nonprofit agencies who provide family services under contract to county or municipal social services departments, law firms who handle litigation or other matters for companies, accounting firms that provide billing services, marketing firms that have access to their client's customer information, medical researchers who conduct clinical trials for pharmaceutical manufacturers, and facilities management companies that create and store maintenance and repair records for their clients' buildings. Contractual requirements also apply to commercial providers of physical and electronic information storage services, including cloud-based computing services and physical record storage services.

Possible contractual compliance requirements for information storage and preservation include the following:

- A contractor will typically be required to comply with all applicable laws and regulations for information storage, including data localization laws that limit the geographic locations where information can be kept.
- In the absence of data localization laws, a contract may specify the locations where information must be stored. Contracts with cloud-based computing services may prohibit storage of information on servers that are located in politically unstable countries or in countries that restrict the transfer of information across national borders. Contracts with physical record storage providers often require that records be kept in a location that is close enough to provide responsive service. A maximum acceptable distance may be specified. Contracts may also specify unacceptable storage locations, such as facilities that storage facilities in close proximity to airports, factories, or other perceived hazards.
- Government contractors may be required to comply with archival legislation for information storage. In the United States, federal contractors who maintain information for government use or that is under the legal control of federal agencies must comply with environmental, property, and fire safety requirements for storage facilities, as specified by NARA. Some federal agencies may impose additional compliance requirements for a contractor's storage facilities.[70]
- A contract or other legal agreement may mandate compliance with specific international standards or industry norms for information storage, which are discussed in the next section. Contracts and agreements often list applicable standards and industry norms, which are incorporated by reference.
- Safe, secure storage conditions are a minimum expectation, but a contract may require special environmental controls for some information. Vault storage with temperature and humidity in a specified range may be required for certain paper records, as well as for microfilm, computer tapes, video tapes, optical disks, and other electronic or photographic media that may be damaged by unregulated heat and humidity.

- When contracting for physical record storage services, some organizations require dedicated storage space to avoid comingling their records with those of other customers in an open warehouse. Similarly, an organization may require a dedicated server located in a single data center when contracting for cloud-based storage of digital content.
- A contract may specify that some or all information be stored in a particular format—the PDF format, for example, for digital documents to be kept less than ten years and PDF/A for documents requiring longer retention. A contract may also specify that certain documents be stored in paper form where required by law, although such legal requirements are increasingly uncommon.
- A contractor may be required to prepare and validate one or more backup copies of specific information at agreed-upon intervals for data recovery purposes. A contract may specify administrative and technical safeguards for such backup copies, including acceptable or prohibited storage formats, locations, environmental conditions, and fire protection at the storage site. A contract may mandate off-site storage of backup copies in a secure location that is reasonably accessible when information recovery is necessary but sufficiently distant from the original information so as not to be affected by the same adverse events. A contract may include requirements for disposition of backup copies when no longer needed for data recovery.
- Individuals and groups that donate their data, documents, or other information to archival institutions and research libraries may impose similar contractual restrictions and requirements related to storage locations, storage formats, environmental controls, vault storage, or other information storage practices, although donors' restrictions more often relate to access than to storage arrangements. Donors may also require an archival institution or other research repository to create and periodically validate backup copies and to perform data migrations and format conversions at specified intervals to preserve their information in usable form in perpetuity or at least as long as it is in the archival institution's custody. These contractual compliance issues must be negotiated before a deed of gift or deposit agreement is finalized and signed. Archives and research libraries will accept a donor's requirements to the extent that they are compatible with an institution's mission, responsibilities, and capabilities.[71]

STANDARDS AND INDUSTRY NORMS

International standards and industry norms play an important role in establishing compliance requirements for information storage and preservation. These standards are often the basis for storage and preservation requirements specified in contracts, purchase orders, requests for proposals, bid invitations, and other procurement documents and solicitations:

- ISO 11799:2015, *Information and documentation—Document storage requirements for archive and library materials* specifies desirable characteristics of repositories for storage of archival records and other research documents of long-term value. ISO/TR 19815:2018, *Information and documentation—Management of the environmental conditions for archive and library collections* includes recommendations for sustainability with examples of the practices of representative institutions.
- While there are no international standards for the organization and operation of storage facilities for business records that do not warrant permanent preservation, ARMA TR01-2011, *Record Center Operations,* issued by ARMA International's Standards Development Program, discusses in-house and commercial facilities that store physical records.[72] ARMA International's *Guideline for Evaluating Offsite Records Storage Facilities* focuses on criteria for selecting a commercial record storage provider.[73]
- NFPA 232, *Standard for Protection of Records,* issued by the National Fire Protection Association, is the authoritative source for fire protection requirements for facilities that store physical records in paper, photographic, and electronic formats.[74] *Standard for the Fire Protection of Information Technology Equipment* covers fire protection requirements for file servers and other online data storage devices.[75]
- Some archival agencies have developed standards for facilities that store government records. While some of those requirements have the force of law, they are included in this discussion of standards because their scope is limited to government agencies that are subject to archival authority. In the United States, the National Archives and Records Administration specifies minimum structural, environmental, property, pest control, and life safety standards for record storage facilities operated by federal agencies and federal contractors, as well as commercial storage facilities that will house federal records.[76] While intended specifically for records maintained by federal agencies, these requirements have influenced the policies of state archives, which have adopted them for offsite storage of records generated by state and local government agencies.[77] NARA's requirements have also had an indirect impact on offsite storage of nongovernmental records because many commercial providers have upgraded their facilities to comply with federal specifications.
- Not as well-known but nonetheless useful, NARA 1571, *Archival Storage Standards* is a policy directive for appropriate storage conditions in government-owned and leased facilities used by NARA itself to store archival records.[78] In Australia, standards for off-site storage of government records have been issued by the National Archives and by state archives.[79] They apply to paper, photographic, and electronic records stored in agency-operated facilities as well as those stored by commercial providers. Some archival authorities provide recommendations for evaluation of offsite

storage facilities for government records, but those recommendations do not rise to the level of requirements.[80]

- International standards that deal with the stability and longevity of photographic media[81] include ISO 18901:2010, *Imaging materials—Processed silver gelatin type black-and-white films—Specifications for stability*; ISO 18905:2002, *Imaging materials—Ammonia-processed diazo photographic film—Specifications for stability*; ISO 18912:2002, *Imaging materials—Processed vesicular photographic film—Specifications for stability; and ISO 18919:1999, Imaging materials—Thermally processed silver microfilm—Specifications for stability.*
- Standards that deal with the stability and longevity of paper records include ISO 9706:1994, *Information and documentation—Paper for documents—Requirements for permanence*; ISO 11108:1996, *Information and documentation—Archival paper—Requirements for permanence and durability*; ISO 20494:2017, *Paper—Requirements for stability for general graphic applications*; ISO 11789:1999, *Information and documentation—Permanence and durability of writing, printing and copying on paper—Requirements and test methods*; and ISO 18939:2013, *Imaging materials—Digital hard copy for medical imaging—Methods of measuring permanence.*
- Environmental storage and handling requirements for various information media are addressed in ISO 18911:2010, *Imaging materials—Processed safety photographic films—Storage practices*; ISO 18918:2000, *Imaging materials—Processed photographic plates—Storage practices; ISO 18923:2000, Imaging materials—Polyester base magnetic tape—Storage practices*; ISO 18925:2013, *Imaging materials—Optical disc media—Storage practices*; ISO 18928:2013, *Imaging materials—Unprocessed photographic films and papers—Storage practices*; ISO 18929:2012, *Imaging materials—Wet-processed silver-gelatin type black-and-white photographic reflection prints—Specifications for dark storage*; ISO 18933:2012, *Imaging materials—Magnetic tape—Care and handling practices for extended usage*; ISO 18934:2011, *Imaging materials—Multiple media archives—Storage environment*; ISO 16245:2009, *Information and documentation—Boxes, file covers, and other enclosures, made from cellulosic materials, for storage of paper and parchment documents*; and NISO TR01-1995, *Environmental guidelines for the storage of paper records.*[82]
- As discussed in a preceding section, the PDF/A format is intended for preservation of electronic information. It is a constrained version of the PDF format that omits certain features, such as encryption and font linking, that are incompatible with long-term usability of digital documents. The PDF format is standardized by ISO 19005-1:2005, *Document management—Electronic document file format for long-term preservation—Part 1: Use of PDF 1.4 (PDF/A-1)*; ISO 19005-2:2011, *Document management—Electronic document file format for long-term preservation—Part 2: Use of ISO 32000-1 (PDF/A-2)*; ISO 19005-3:2012, *Document management—Electronic document file format for long-term preservation—Part 3: Use of ISO 32000-1 with support for embedded files (PDF/A-3)*; and ISO 19005-4:2020, *Document manage-*

ment—Electronic document file format for long-term preservation—Part 4: Use of ISO 32000-2 (PDF/A-4).

- ISO 14721:2012, *Space data and information transfer systems—Open archival information system (OAIS)* provides a conceptual reference model for an archival system to preserve and provide access to digital content. It is intended for information that warrants long-term preservation, where long-term extends into the indefinite future. ISO 16363:2012, *Space data and information transfer systems—Audit and certification of trustworthy digital repositories* and ISO 16919:2014, *Space data and information transfer systems—Requirements for bodies providing audit and certification of candidate trustworthy digital repositories* present criteria to assess whether a given repository supports reliable long-term preservation of and access to digital content. These standards are principally intended for research institutions that maintain archival data repositories. Some digital preservation products and services advertise compliance with ISO 14721.
- ISO 14721 is also incorporated into maturity models for digital preservation, such as the Digital Preservation Capability Maturity Model (DPCMM), the Digital Preservation Coalition Rapid Assessment Model (DPC RAM), and the Levels of Digital Preservation (LoP) Matrix developed by the National Digital Stewardship Alliance (NDSA).[83] These maturity models, which define the desirable characteristics of digital preservation programs, have become influential industry norms that are widely referenced in archival publications and conference presentations. Developed by the digital preservation community, they support assessment, benchmarking, and gap analysis by defining a digital preservation program's organizational viability and service capabilities at varying levels of effectiveness.
- Data migration for long-term usability of electronic information is covered by ISO 13008:2012, *Information and documentation—Digital records conversion.*
- Codes of ethics issued by archival associations include guidance for preservation of information.[84] I-SIGMA, the trade association for commercial record storage and information destruction providers has developed a code of ethics for the data lifecycle management industry.[85]
- No international standard deals specifically and exclusively with storage and preservation of backup copies, but several standards cover data backup in the context of information security concepts and principles. Examples include ISO/IEC 27001:2015, *Information technology—Security techniques—Information security management systems—Requirements*; ISO/IEC 27002:2013, *Information technology—Security techniques—Code of practice for information security controls*; and ISO/IEC 27040:2015, *Information technology—Security techniques—Storage security*. NSIT SP 8-171, *Protecting Controlled Unclassified Information in Nonfederal Systems and Organizations*

emphasizes the need to protect the confidentiality of backup copies at storage locations.[86]

INTERNAL MANDATES

Internal policies may mandate specific offsite storage arrangements for inactive physical records, either at an in-house facility or through a commercial storage provider. Organizations that operate their own record storage facilities will typically have policies that specify the types of records that are eligible for storage, the types of physical media that are accepted, the storage containers that must be used, proper methods for identifying the records to be sent to storage, and timeframes and transportation arrangements for transfer of the records from their originating business units. Information that fails to comply with these policies will not be accepted for storage. Commercial storage facilities have their own policies that specify the storage containers to be used, the way in which records should be packed and identified, and transportation arrangements.

Word-processing files, spreadsheets, digital photographs, video recordings, and other digital documents are often saved on departmental shared drives, which tend to be poorly organized and largely ungoverned. Important information may be comingled with work in progress, drafts, superseded documents, duplicate records, personal files, material downloaded from websites, and other unrelated or transitory content that does not warrant continued retention. These obsolete and redundant items may remain on shared drives indefinitely. As an alternative, some organizations have implemented a controlled repository for digital documents using a content management or records management application. As with off-site storage of physical records, policies specify the types of information to be included in the repository, acceptable file formats, proper methods for organizing and identifying digital documents, and timeframes and procedures for transferring documents from their originating business units.

Storage of backup copies of electronic information is typically guided by policies and practices implemented by an organization's information technology or information security unit. Storage policies and practices for backup copies of nonelectronic information are usually the responsibility of an organization's records management unit. In either case, these policies and practices specify the number of backup copies to be created, the storage formats and locations for each copy, environmental conditions and fire protection at the storage site, security provisions and access controls, and other administrative and technical requirements. They usually require offsite storage for at least one of the backup copies.

Organizations with a professionally staffed archives unit may have policies for transfer to archival custody of data and documents that warrant permanent preservation for their historical or other scholarly value. This is most common in government agencies and in not-for-profit entities with an educational, cultural, scientific, or societal mission. Permanent records are typically identified in the organization's retention schedule, which the archives unit must approve. The policy may specify the timeframe for transfer of permanent records from business units to archival custody as well as record formats that the archives unit is prepared to accept. As an alternative to an in-house archives unit, an organization may transfer its permanent records to an external repository operated by a university or other research institution, in which case transfer and preservation policies will be developed jointly by the originating organization and the receiving repository.[87]

SOCIETAL COMPLIANCE

The archival profession views society's documentary heritage as a significant cultural asset and considers the preservation of information of long-term value as a societal imperative.[88] The Archivist's Code, issued by the U.S. National Archives in 1955 for its in-service training program, states that archivists have a "moral obligation to society to preserve evidence of how things actually happened."[89] This is widely accepted by users of archival collections, including academic scholars and students in a wide range of disciplines, independent writers and researchers, genealogists, journalists, political and social activists, environmentalists, and a variety of other specialists and nonspecialists with interests for which archival collections may be relevant.

Compliance with societal interests is mandated by the archival legislation discussed in preceding sections. Archival laws and regulations are designed to ensure the permanent preservation of information that protects the rights of citizens and serves the public interest. In the absence of laws related to private archives, no comparable preservation mandate exists for nongovernmental information, but many universities, museums, religious groups, charities, and other not-for-profit organizations have established archival programs that preserve information of broad societal significance in addition to documenting their own initiatives, activities, and accomplishments. While some for-profit entities have archival programs, most corporations, limited liability companies, and partnerships have no formal commitment to preservation of information once its business value has elapsed. The retention schedules of some companies avoid permanent preservation altogether, preferring instead to specify that significant information be kept until the dissolution of the enterprise or simply for ninety-nine years, a time period that has already elapsed for some well-known, long-established companies.

The societal benefits associated with archival preservation comes at a cost. Energy consumed by preservation activities impacts environmental sustainability. As discussed in other chapters, the United Nations' environmental sustainability goals call for responsible consumption of natural resources, reduction of an organization's global material footprint, and reduction of greenhouse gas emissions. Given the budgetary constraints within which archives and other research repositories must operate and the growing quantity of information to be preserved, most discussions of the sustainability of archival preservation initiatives are concerned with the continued availability of appropriate technological and professional resources. Those concerns are outside the scope of this discussion, although budgetary and technological issues have an obvious impact on compliance with U.N. sustainability goals. In particular, there is growing concern about the negative environmental impact of long-term preservation of databases, digital documents, video recordings, and other electronic information. This concern encompasses information that originates in digital form as well as paper and photographic records that are digitized for preservation.

With respect to budget, the cost of energy consumption will force digital preservation programs to limit their activities to remain economically viable. Over the last decade, archival literature has suggested various ways of reducing the environmental footprint to comply with sustainability objectives:

- Like all technology-based initiatives, digital preservation is energy-intensive. For compliance with sustainability objectives, an environmentally aware preservation program must prioritize energy-efficiency over performance. Attention should be given to electrical consumption when selecting servers, storage devices, personal workstations, and other computing components.
- Hard drives, the principal storage devices in most data centers, are major consumers of electrical power, but electrical consumption varies from product to product. Compared to higher-speed devices, slow-spinning hard drives have longer access times for reading and recording data, but they use less energy and generate less heat. Smaller hard drives consume less power than larger ones.
- Tiered storage configurations trade off fast access for lower energy consumption by combining online, nearline, and offline storage at different levels of performance and cost. Online storage can be received for information that is subject to high demand or that needs to be immediately available when requested. Nearline storage on slower devices can be used for information that does not require split-second availability. Information that has a limited audience or that will not be available for researcher until some future time can be stored on offline media, which requires fewer technological resources. To reduce storage and bandwidth requirements, archival repositories can create lower resolution copies of document images and video content for online access and store high-resolution preservation copies offline.
- Energy consumption can be reduced by limiting preservation actions for all or selected digital content, an approach that has been characterized as "more product, less process (MPLP)." The preservation maturity models discussed in a preceding section define requirements for preparing backup

copies, verifying the continued integrity of stored information, migrating information to new media and file formats, and other preservation actions. These actions can be simplified or curtailed. The number of backup copies can be reduced. Verification of stored information, which is a computationally intensive operation, can be performed less frequently. Data migration intervals can likewise be increased.

- Some digital preservation programs utilize cloud-based storage services rather than in-house data centers, but this merely shifts responsibility for environmental compliance to an external provider who is paid to accept the burden of implementing a sustainable preservation infrastructure or to take the blame for failure to do so. Nonetheless, some cloud-based storage providers have taken steps to address sustainability concerns to a greater degree than the typical digital preservation program can achieve in-house. A digital preservation program can work toward environmental compliance by utilizing one of the growing number of cloud-based data centers that have increased their reliance of renewable energy, but a survey by Greenpeace indicates that progress toward carbon-neutral cloud services varies from provider to provider and from country to country.[90]
- Organizations are long past the point where computerization is reserved for the most important business operations. Much digital content has little or no value beyond its moment of immediate usefulness. Information that is useful for business operations may lack research value. Storage demand and its associated energy consumption can be reduced by limiting the amount of information to be preserved. This requires rigorous appraisal of digital content to determine whether it truly merits preservation. Environmental impact must be factored into appraisal decisions. Long-term energy costs must be considered when deciding to preserve digital content, just as space availability is considered when appraising paper records. This emphasis on selective rather than indiscriminate preservation of digital content has been characterized as a paradigm shift, but it merely applies concepts that have been part of archival practice for more than a century.

To further reduce the amount of digital content that needs to be stored, some sources advise archives and libraries to restrict digitization of paper records to documents that are at preservation risk or that are requested for specific research projects or other purposes, but sustainability issues are not limited to digital preservation. Archives, libraries, and other storage repositories for physical records rely on energy from fossil fuels, which are sources of carbon emissions and greenhouse gasses. To achieve long life, paper documents and photographic media require temperature and humidity controls defined by international standards discussed in a preceding section. Microfilm, long a staple of archival preservation initiatives, requires a controlled storage environment that can only be achieved in a vault.

SUMMARY OF MAJOR POINTS

- Many countries have archival laws that mandate preservation of government records with historical or other research value. These laws, which emphasize the importance of preserving a country's documentary heritage, give archival officials the authority to designate documents, databases, or other records that are to be kept permanently and ultimately transferred to a national archives or another approved archival repository.
- In some countries, archival preservation regulations apply to certain nongovernmental records, which are characterized as private archives to distinguish them from the public archives maintained by government agencies. These laws and regulations are a type of data sovereignty legislation, in which a sovereign nation asserts its authority over information that is created and maintained within its borders.
- Nongovernmental entities can store information in any format on any medium they choose unless a particular format or medium is specified or prohibited by a law or regulation, but such laws and regulations are limited in both number and scope.
- Many countries have electronic transaction laws or electronic signature laws that affirm the legal status of information stored on electronic media provided that certain compliance requirements are satisfied.
- Data migration is necessary to comply with requirements for continued usability of electronic information with long retention periods. To facilitate compliance, electronic information can be saved in a file format, such as PDF/A, which is intended for long-term preservation.
- Many countries have data localization laws and regulations that specify or restrict the locations or governmental jurisdictions where information can be stored. As their principal purpose, these laws and regulations ensure that information will be readily available when requested by government officials for audits and investigations or for examination by authorized stakeholders, such as a company's shareholders or partners.
- Some sector-specific laws identify the types of information for which backup copies are required, but no laws or regulations require permanent preservation of backup copies.
- Contracts, purchase orders, and other legally binding agreements often specify requirements for storage and preservation of information that a contractor creates, processes, or maintains on an organization's behalf.
- International standards and industry norms play an important role in establishing compliance requirements for information storage and preservation. These standards and norms are often the basis for storage and preservation requirements specified in contracts and procurement documents.

- Internal policies may mandate storage requirements for an organization's information. Organizations with a professionally staffed archives unit may have policies for transfer to archival custody of data and documents that warrant permanent preservation for their historical or other scholarly value.
- Archival laws and regulations are designed to ensure the permanent preservation of information that protects the rights of citizens and serves the public interest, but the societal benefits associated with archival preservation comes at a cost, as the energy consumed by preservation activities impacts environmental sustainability.

NOTES

1. Some legislation uses the term differently. As an example, 8 NYCRR 126.11 specifies that schools must keep permanent student records for a minimum of twenty years after the student completes the program, https://govt.westlaw.com/nycrr/Document/I365b69a5c22211ddb29d8bee567fca9f?viewType=FullText&originationContext=documenttoc&transitionType=StatuteNavigator&contextData=%28sc.Default%29&bhcp=1.
2. For a global survey of national archival agencies, see P. Franks and A. Bernier, *The International Directory of National Archives* (Lanham, MD: Rowman & Littlefield Publishers, 2018).
3. Examples of the many publications on archival legislation include G. Peterson and T. Peterson, *Arcives & Manuscripts: Law* (Chicago: Society of American Archivists, 1985), http://www.archivists.org/publications/epubs/Archives&Mss-Law.pdf; H. Andresen, "On the internationalization and harmonization of archival law," *European Journal of Comparative Law and Governance* 7 (1), 64–88 (2019), https://brill.com/view/journals/ejcl/7/1/article-p64_64.xml; N. Mnjama, "Archival legislation and archival services in Africa," in P. Sebina et al., *Digital Access and E-Government Perspectives from Developing and Emerging Countries* (Hershey, PA: IGI Global, 2014), 27–48; S. Martinezx-Cardama and A. Pacios, "National archives' priorities: an international overview," *Archival Science*, 2021, Open Access, https://doi.org/10.1007/s10502-021-09367-y; M. Ngoepe & Saurombe, "Provisions for managing and preserving records created in networked environments in the archival legislative frameworks of selected member states of the Southern African Development Community," *Archives and Manuscripts* 44 (1), 24–41 (2016), https://doi.org/10.1080/01576895.2015.1136225.
4. Archive Act (1990: 782), https://lagen-nu.translate.goog/1990:782?_x_tr_sl=auto&_x_tr_tl=en&_x_tr_hl=en-US&_x_tr_pto=nui; Ordinance (2009:1593) with Instructions for the National Archives, https://lagen-nu.translate.goog/2009:1593?_x_tr_sl=auto&_x_tr_tl=en&_x_tr_hl=en-US&_x_tr_pto=nui.
5. Act No. 395 of 17 May 2002 on Archives and Registries, https://www.eui.eu/Projects/InternationalArtHeritageLaw/Documents/NationalLegislation/Slovakia/act395of2002archives.pdf.
6. Code du patrimoine, consolidated version, articles L.211-1 et seq., https://wipolex.wipo.int/en/legislation/details/18525.

7. 44 U.S.C. § 2107, https://www.archives.gov/about/laws/nara.html-accept; 36 C.F.R. §§ 1235 et seq.
8. On the historical development of subnational archival legislation in the United States, see A. Newsome, "Uniform state archival legislation," *American Archivist* 2 (1), 1-16 (1939), https://www.jstor.org/stable/40288138; M. Bryan, "Recent state archival legislation," *American Archivist* 19 (1), 63-67 (1956), https://www.jstor.org/stable/40289397; G. Bain, "State archival law: a content analysis," *American Archivist* 46 (2): 158-74, https://doi.org/10.17723/aarc.46.2.j707664h6778v1l1; E. Posner, *American State Archives* (Chicago: University of Chicago Press, 1964).
9. Library and Archives of Canada Act, S.C. 2004, c. 11, https://laws-lois.justice.gc.ca/eng/acts/l-7.7/fulltext.html; L. Thomas, "Provincial archives in Canada," *American Archivist* 18 (4), 343-47 (2955), https://www.jstor.org/stable/40289370; H. Taylor, "Canadian Archives: patterns from a federal perspective," *Archivaria* 1 (2), 3-19 (1976), https://www.archivaria.ca/index.php/archivaria/article/view/10431; M. Beyea, "Pennies from heaven: the history of public funding for Canadian archives," in C. Avery and M. Holmlund, eds., *Better Off Forgetting? Essays on Archives, Public Policy and Collective Memory* (Toronto: University of Toronto Press, 2010), 3-16, https://doi.org/10.3138/9781442689879.
10. According to 36 C.F.R. Part 1235, U.S. government agencies must transfer permanent records to the National Archives on a date specified in the agency's retention schedule or when the records are thirty years old, https://www.law.cornell.edu/cfr/text/36/part-1235. For descriptions of records that NARA commonly appraises as permanent, see https://www.archives.gov/records-mgmt/scheduling/perm-examples.
11. National Archives of Trinidad and Tobago, Procedure for Disposing of Public Records, http://natt.gov.tt/node/150.
12. State Archives Law, No. 208 of 1991, http://www.mjpo.gov.cy/mjpo/statearchive.nsf/D32FF04EF9495F3CC22579B200347DE8/$file/The State Archives Law 208 of 1991.pdf.
13. Public Records Act 2005, https://www.legislation.govt.nz/act/public/2005/0040/latest/whole.html-DLM346104.
14. Law on Archival Material and Archives, NN 61/2018, http://www.arhiv.hr/hr-hr/Arhivska-sluzba/Arhivski-propisi.
15. Danish Archives Act, No. 1050 of 17 December 2002, https://www.sa.dk/wp-content/uploads/2014/12/Danish-Archives-Act.pdf.
16. Public Archives Act, 2014 No. 77, 28 May, https://skjalasafn.is/files/docs/ThePublicArchivesAct-in-Iceland-No-77-2014.pdf.
17. Archives Act CH, https://law.moj.gov.tw/ENG/LawClass/LawAll.aspx?pcode=A0030134.
18. National Archives and Record Service of South Africa Act, No. 43 of 1996, https://www.gov.za/documents/national-archives-south-africa-act.
19. 36 C.F.R. §1235.46, https://www.law.cornell.edu/cfr/text/36/1235.46.
20. NARA Bulletin 2014-04 (Revised August 2018), Format Guidance for the Transfer of Permanent Electronic Records, https://www.archives.gov/records-mgmt/bulletins/2014/2014-04.html. On documentation requirements for electronic records transferred to the National Archives, see 36 C.F.R. § 1235.48, https://www.law.cornell.edu/cfr/text/36/1235.48.

21. Wisconsin Historical Society, Best Practices for the Selection of Electronic File Formats, https://www.wisconsinhistory.org/Records/Article/CS15427; see also Illinois Secretary of State, Sustainable File Formats for Electronic Records: a Guide for Government Agencies, https://www.ilsos.gov/publications/pdf_publications/ard156.pdf.
22. Library and Archives of Canada, File Format Guidelines for Preservation and Long-Term Access, http://www.councilofnsarchives.ca/sites/default/files/LAC File Format Guidelines for Preservation and Long-term v1_2010-12_0.pdf.
23. 36 C.F.R. §1236.28, https://www.law.cornell.edu/cfr/text/36/1236.28.
24. 36 C.F.R. §1238.20, https://www.law.cornell.edu/cfr/text/36/1238.20.
25. 36 C.F.R. §1238.22, https://www.law.cornell.edu/cfr/text/36/1238.22.
26. 36 C.F.R. §1234.14, https://www.law.cornell.edu/cfr/text/36/1234.14.
27. See, for example, Electronic Records Management Guidelines issued under the authority of Mass. Gen. Laws ch. 66, § 1, https://www.sec.state.ma.us/arc/arcpdf/Electronic_Records_Guidelines.pdf; Fla. Admin.Code R. 1B-26.0021 et seq., https://www.law.cornell.edu/regulations/florida/department-1/division-1B/chapter-1B-26; Standards for Permanent Records issued pursuant to A.R.S. § 39.101, https://azlibrary.gov/sites/default/files/arm-standard-for-permanent-records_april_23_2013_signed.pdf; N.J.A.C. § 15:3-6.1 et seq., https://www.law.cornell.edu/regulations/new-jersey/title-15/chapter-3/subchapter-6; OAR 166-017-0075, https://oregon.public.law/rules/oar_166-017-0075.
28. Legislative Decree No. 42 of 22 January 2004, Code of Cultural Heritage and Landscape, https://www-camera-it.translate.goog/parlam/leggi/deleghe/04042dl.htm?_x_tr_sl=auto&_x_tr_tl=en&_x_tr_hl=en-US&_x_tr_pto=nui,op.
29. Decree-Law No. 16/93, https://dre.pt/dre/legislacao-consolidada/decreto-lei/1993-72851445.
30. Federal Law of 22.10.2004, No. 125-FZ on Archival Affairs in the Russian Federation, https://archives.gov.ru/documents/fz/zakon-archivnoe-delo.shtml.
31. Act LXVI of 1995 on Public Records, Public Archives, and the Protection of Private Archives, https://www.legislationline.org/documents/id/6756.
32. Archives Law, https://likumi.lv/ta/id/205971-arhivu-likums.
33. Archives Law of the People's Republic of China, http://english.court.gov.cn/2016-04/15/content_24565261.htm; J. Nalen, "Private archives in China," *Libri* 52 (4), 241–62 (2002), https://doi.org/10.1515/LIBR.2002.241; X. An et al., "Reinventing the concept of the state archival fond in China," *Archives and Manuscripts* 42 (2), 146–50 (2014), https://doi.org/10.1080/01576895.2014.911673.
34. Archives Act CH, https://law.moj.gov.tw/ENG/LawClass/LawAll.aspx?pcode=A0030134.
35. Ordinance no. 2004-178 of 20 February 2004, ttps://www.legifrance.gouv.fr/jorf/id/JORFTEXT000000615405/.
36. Archives Act, No. 831 of 1994, https://www.legislationline.org/download/id/1244/file/d79f42a78c20ace1b22935d4971e.pdf.
37. Archives and Archival Institutions Act, https://www.legislationline.org/download/id/1295/file/c816408d90b376ac7190db615833.pdf.
38. Danish Archives Act, https://www.sa.dk/wp-content/uploads/2014/12/Danish-Archives-Act.pdf.

39. Labor Act, 2006 (No. XLII of 2006), articles 6-9, 17, 25, 78, 80, , 127, 132, 209-10, 319, 339, 344, http://www.dpp.gov.bd/upload_file/gazettes/14212_75510.pdf; Labor Rules, 2015, articles 19-24, 34, 101, 111, 363, Addendum Forms 6-10, Form 15(a), https://osmanlaw.files.wordpress.com/2016/11/bangladesh_labor_rules_2015_english_version_15-09-2015.pdf.
40. 15 C.F.R. § 762.4, https://www.law.cornell.edu/cfr/text/19/163.5.
41. 19 C.F.R. § 163.5, https://www.law.cornell.edu/cfr/text/19/163.5.
42. 19 C.F.R. § 163.1, https://www.law.cornell.edu/cfr/text/19/163.1.
43. See, for example, 49 C.F.R. § 40.333, which requires employers in the transportation industry to converted electronic drug testing records to printed documentation if they are not easily accessible, legible, and formatted and stored in an organized manner, https://www.law.cornell.edu/cfr/text/49/40.333.
44. See, for example, 11 NYCRR 243.1, which regulates the insurance industry, https://govt.westlaw.com/nycrr/Document/I500e4ff2cd1711dda432a117e6e0f345?viewType=FullText&originationContext=documenttoc&transitionType=CategoryPageItem&contextData=(sc.Default).
45. See the following examples of regulations that apply to information storage media used by public utilities: 18 C.F.R. § 125.2, https://www.law.cornell.edu/cfr/text/18/125.2; also 18 C.F.R. § 368.2, https://www.law.cornell.edu/cfr/text/18/368.2; 18 C.F.R. § 225.2, https://www.law.cornell.edu/cfr/text/18/225.2; 18 C.F.R. § 356.2, https://www.law.cornell.edu/cfr/text/18/356.2; and 7 C.F.R. § 1770.4, https://www.law.cornell.edu/cfr/text/7/1770.4.
46. 17 C.F.R. § 240.17a-4(f), https://www.law.cornell.edu/cfr/text/17/240.17a-4. See also https://www.sec.gov/rules/interp/34-47806.htm.
47. See, for example, New York State Banking Law § 36-b, https://codes.findlaw.com/ny/banking-law/bnk-sect-36-b.html; Ohio Admin. Code § 1301:8-8-03, https://www.law.cornell.edu/regulations/ohio/Ohio-Admin-Code-1301-8-8-03; Cal. Code Regs. tit. 10, § 2729.4, https://www.dre.ca.gov/files/pdf/relaw/2019/regs.pdf; OAR 863-015-0260, https://oregon.public.law/rules/oar_863-015-0260; Ill. Admin. Code tit. 86, § 3000.840, https://www.law.cornell.edu/regulations/illinois/IL-Admin-Code-86-3000-840.
48. This requirement is included in the Model Business Corporation Act (MBCA), which has been issued in successive editions by the Committee on Corporate Laws of the Section of Business Law of the American Bar Association, https://www.americanbar.org/content/dam/aba/administrative/business_law/corplaws/2016_mbca.authcheckdam.pdf. Examples of state laws and regulations that have adopted the MCBA requirement include Fla. Stat. § 607.1601, http://www.leg.state.fl.us/statutes/index.cfm?App_mode=Display_Statute&Search_String=&URL=0600-0699/0607/Sections/0607.1601.html; O.C.G.A § 14-2-1602, https://codes.findlaw.com/ga/title-14-corporations-partnerships-and-associations/ga-code-sect-14-2-1602.html; Iowa Code § 490.1601, https://www.legis.iowa.gov/docs/code/490.1601.pdf; Neb. Rev. Stat. § 21-2,221, https://nebraskalegislature.gov/laws/statutes.php?statute=21-2,222; Minn. Stat. § 302A.461, https://www.revisor.mn.gov/statutes/cite/302A.461; and Conn. Gen. Stat. § 33-945, https://codes.findlaw.com/ct/title-33-corporations/ct-gen-st-sect-33-945.html.

49. See, for example, Tex. Bus. Org. Code § 101.501, https://codes.findlaw.com/tx/business-organizations-code/bus-org-sect-101-501.html; 805 ILCS § 180/1-40, https://ilga.gov/legislation/ilcs/documents/080501800K1-40.htm; Mass. Gen. Laws ch. 156C, § 9, https://malegislature.gov/Laws/GeneralLaws/PartI/TitleXXII/Chapter156C/Section9.
50. 17 C.F.R. § 1.31, https://www.law.cornell.edu/cfr/text/17/1.31.
51. 21 C.F.R. § 820.180, https://www.law.cornell.edu/cfr/text/21/820.180.
52. 21 C.F.R. Part 1304, https://www.accessdata.fda.gov/scripts/cdrh/cfdocs/cfcfr/CFRSearch.cfm?CFRPart=1304&showFR=1'.
53. 49 C.F.R. § 40.333, https://www.law.cornell.edu/cfr/text/49/40.333.
54. 40 C.F.R. § 60.768, https://www.law.cornell.edu/cfr/text/40/60.768.
55. 21 C.F.R. § 112.162, https://www.law.cornell.edu/cfr/text/21/112.162.
56. Bank Act, S.C. 1991, c. 46, § 245, https://laws-lois.justice.gc.ca/eng/acts/b-1.01/page-26.html-docCont.
57. Business Records Protection Act, R.S.O. 1990, c. B.19, https://www.ontario.ca/laws/statute/90b19.
58. Business Concerns Records Act, CQLR c D-12, http://legisquebec.gouv.qc.ca/en/document/cs/d-12.
59. Consolidated CPTPP Text, § 14.13, https://www.international.gc.ca/trade-commerce/trade-agreements-accords-commerciaux/agr-acc/cptpp-ptpgp/text-texte/index.aspx?lang=eng; Agreement between the United States of America, the United Mexican States, and Canada, 7/1/20, § 19.11, https://ustr.gov/trade-agreements/free-trade-agreements/united-states-mexico-canada-agreement/agreement-between.
60. N. Cory and L. Dascoli, *How Barriers to Cross-Border Data Flows Are Spreading Globally, What they Cost, and How to Address Them* (Washington, DC: Information Technology & Innovation Foundation, 2021), https://itif.org/sites/default/files/2021-data-localization.pdf.
61. 21 C.F.R. 211.68, https://www.accessdata.fda.gov/scripts/cdrh/cfdocs/cfcfr/cfrsearch.cfm?fr=211.68.
62. 45 C.F.R. 164.308, https://www.law.cornell.edu/cfr/text/45/164.308.
63. Central Bank of Bahrain Rulebook, OM-4.7, https://cbben.thomsonreuters.com/entiresection/115911.
64. Bank of Israel Regulation on Proper Conduct of Banking Business No. 357, https://www.boi.org.il/en/BankingSupervision/SupervisorsDirectives/Pages/nihultakin.aspx.
65. Rule 4370, Business Continuity Plans and Emergency Contact Information, https://www.finra.org/rules-guidance/rulebooks/finra-rules/4370.
66. Cybersecurity Requirements for Financial Services Companies, https://www.governor.ny.gov/sites/default/files/atoms/files/Cybersecurity_Requirements_Financial_Services_23NYCRR500.pdf.
67. Ultima Circular No, 2077 of 2011, https://www.bcu.gub.uy/Acerca-de-BCU/Normativa/Documents/Recopilacion-de-Normas/Instituciones Financieras/libro05.pdf.
68. SCA Board Decision No. 47, Concerning the Regulations as to Lending and Borrowing Securities, https://studylib.net/doc/10118755/the-sca-board-decision-no.—47—of-2012-concerning-the.

69. Board of Directors Decision of 2011 on Instructions Pertinent to the Principles of Organizing Account Books and Records of Each Company's Agents and Brokers and Determine Data to be Inserted in these Books and Records, https://ia.gov.ae /en/Documents/Takaful Accounting Book Principles.pdf.
70. See https://www.archives.gov/records-mgmt/storage-standards-toolkit and https://www.archives.gov/records-mgmt/policy/records-mgmt-language. For an example of contractual provision referencing NARA requirements, see the CMS General Information, Eligibility, and Entitlement Manual, chapter 7—Contract Administrative Requirements, Section 30.80, issued by the Centers for Medicare and Medicaid Services, https://www.cms.gov/Regulations-and-Guidance/Guidance /Manuals/downloads/ge101c07.pdf.
71. On archival deeds of gift, see *A Guide to Deeds of Gift* (Chicago: Society of American Archivists, 1998); T. Peterson, "The gift and the deed," *American Archivist* 42 (1), 61-6 (1979), https://www.jstor.org/stable/40292155.
72. https://www.arma.org/store/ViewProduct.aspx?id=10515234.
73. https://www.arma.org/store/ViewProduct.aspx?id=10512042.
74. https://www.nfpa.org/codes-and-standards/all-codes-and-standards/list-of-codes-and-standards/detail?code=232.
75. https://www.nfpa.org/codes-and-standards/all-codes-and-standards/list-of-codes-and-standards/detail?code=75.
76. 36 C.F.R. Part 1234, https://www.law.cornell.edu/cfr/text/36/part-1234. While it does not deal with information storage directly, Government Paper Specification Standards (Washington, DC: U.S. Government Printing Office, 2019) addresses environmental, longevity, and workplace requirements for writing and copy papers to be used by federal agencies, https://www.gpo.gov/docs/default-source/forms -and-standards-files-for-vendors/vol_13.pdf.
77. See, for example, Texas Local Government Code 7.164 et seq., which specifies minimum and optional enhanced storage conditions for permanent records, https:// www.tsl.texas.gov/slrm/pubs/bulletinf. Among institutional standards, see the University of Virginia's storage standard covers cabinets, shelving, and containers for office, on-site, and off-site storage of highly sensitive records, internal use records, and public information, https://recordsmanagement.virginia.edu/physical-records-storage.
78. https://www.archives.gov/foia/directives/nara1571.
79. Standard for the Physical Storage of Commonwealth Records, National Archives of Australia, https://www.naa.gov.au/sites/default/files/2019-09/standard-for-the-physical-storage-of-commonwealth-records_1.pdf; Australia PROS 20/2 Storage Standard, issued by the Public Record Office Victoria, https://prov.vic.gov.au/sites/default/files/files/documents/2002v1.0.pdf ;and its accompanying Record Storage Guideline, https://prov.vic.gov.au/recordkeeping-government /document-library/pros-1101-g5-records-storage-guideline; Queensland State Archives, Recommended Record Storage Housing and Environmental Storage Conditions, https://www.forgov.qld.gov.au/__data/assets/pdf_file/0020/182603 /recommended-storage-environmental-conditions.pdf.
80. See, for example, the U.K. National Archives, Identifying and Specifying Requirements for Offsite Storage of Physical Records, https://cdn.nationalarchives.gov.

uk/documents/information-management/considerations-for-developing-an-off-site-store.pdf.
81. For definitions related to stability and longevity of information storage media, see ISO 18913:2021, Imaging materials—Permanence—Vocabulary.
82. http://www.niso.org/publications/niso-tr01-1995-environmental-guidelines-storage-paper-records.
83. E. Maemura et al., "Organizational assessment frameworks for digital preservation: a literature review and mapping," *Journal of the Association for Information Science and Technology* 68 (7), 1619–37 (2017), https://doi.org/10.1002/asi.23807; M. Phillips et al., "The NSDA levels of digital preservation: explanation and uses," *Archiving 2013 Final Program and Proceedings* (Springfield, VA: Society for Imaging Science and Technology, 2013), 216–22, https://www.ingentaconnect.com/content/ist/ac/2013/00002013/00000001/art00047; L. Ashley and M. Misic, "Digital Preservation Capability Maturity Model (DPCMM): genesis and practical use." In S. Katuu, ed., *Diverse Applications and Transferability of Maturity Model* (Hershey, PA: IGI-Global, 2019), 152–67, https://doi.org/10.4018/978-1-5225-7080-6.ch006; C. Dollar and L. Ashley, "Ensuring long-term access to digital assets using a capability maturity model," *Journal of Digital Media Management* 4 (4), 202–17 (2016), https://www.ingentaconnect.com/content/hsp/jdmm/2016/00000004/00000003/art00002-expand/collapse.
84. See, for example, the International Council on Archives Code of Ethics, https://www.ica.org/sites/default/files/ICA_1996-09-06_code of ethics_EN.pdf.
85. https://isigmaonline.org/about/code-of-ethics/.
86. https://csrc.nist.gov/publications/detail/sp/800-171/rev-2/final.
87. As an example, the Greater London Authority has an agreement with London Municipal Archives to preserve its records of historical interest. LMA is the repository for the City of London Corporation and other entities. The Greater London Authority will transfer records when no longer needed as specified in its historical archiving policy, https://www.london.gov.uk/sites/default/files/records_management_policy_v3.3.pdf.
88. SAA Core Values Statement, https://www2.archivists.org/statements/saa-core-values-statement-and-code-of-ethics; Council on Library and Information Resources, The Societal Role of Archives, https://www.clir.org/pubs/reports/pub89/role/.
89. "The Archivist's Code," *American Archivist* 18 (4), 307–08 (1955), https://meridian.allenpress.com/american-archivist/issue/18/4.
90. Greenpeace evaluates data centers operated by cloud-based service providers with respect to their commitment to renewable energy, energy transparency, and environmental advocacy. G. Cook et al., *Clicking Clean: Who Is Winning the Race to Build a Green Internet?* (Washington, D.C.: Greenpeace, 2017), http://www.clickclean.org/usa/en/.

5

Information Access and Disclosure

Information access and information disclosure are related but not synonymous concepts. Information access is the act of obtaining or retrieving information, either electronically or physically, from the location or repository where is stored. The information may be viewed, printed, or copied. Access may be authorized by the owner or custodian of the information, or it may be unauthorized, as is the case with computer hacking. Some information is intended for access by interested parties with little or no restrictions. Examples include books and magazines in public libraries, certain public records maintained by government agencies, open access research journals, and much internet content. Alternatively, access may be restricted to persons with a verifiable need to know, such as employees who need information to do their jobs; members of defined groups, such as university students and faculty who need access to databases of scholarly research; or subscribers and others who are willing to pay for access to specific information. Access to personal information, an individual's financial data, or an individual's health records may be limited to the data subject or those authorized by the data subject.

With information disclosure, by contrast, an individual or organization that has custody of or access to information reveals or otherwise makes it available to another party who did not previously know it. This may be done by divulging the information verbally or in writing, by granting access to the location or repository where the information is stored, or by giving the receiving party data or documents that contain the information.[1] The receiving party may be an individual, group, or organization. The disclosing party may or may not be authorized to reveal the information, and the receiving party may or may not be authorized to view, print, or copy it. Information disclosure may be intentional or unintentional. Intentional disclosure may be based on the receiving party's demonstrated need to know the information for a specific purpose, as when a patient authorizes disclosure of his or her medical records to a health insurance provider, or it may be done with disruptive intent to achieve a specific political or societal objective, as when Daniel Ellsberg released the Pentagon Papers or Edward J. Snowden disclosed classified information about the National Security

Agency's global surveillance activities. Unintentional disclosure may be accidental, as when an email message with confidential content is mistakenly sent to the wrong party, or the result of malicious action, as when the perpetrator of a fraudulent email induces an unwary recipient to reveal bank account or credit card numbers.

LEGAL AND REGULATORY COMPLIANCE

Eight groups of laws and regulations specify compliance requirements for access to and disclosure of information:

- Freedom of information laws that mandate access for records maintained by government agencies and other public bodies
- Laws and regulations that give individuals access to information maintained about them by government agencies, companies, and nonprofit organizations
- Laws and regulations that give a corporation's shareholders the right to access information that is not available to the general public
- Laws and regulations that mandate proactive disclosure of information about certain matters or when specified events occur
- Laws and regulations that prohibit the disclosure of nonpublic personal information
- Laws and regulations that prohibit the disclosure of confidential nonpersonal information
- Laws and regulations that require the disclosure of information in response to a court order
- Laws and regulations that prohibit the disclosure of information that a person shares with certain professionals

These laws and regulations apply to a broad range of information maintained by organizations of all types and sizes. Every country has national and/or subnational legislation in at least one of the above groups. In some countries, all of them apply.

LAWS THAT MANDATE ACCESS TO GOVERNMENT INFORMATION

The United Nations views access to information as a fundamental human right and an integral component of freedom of expression, subject to reasonable limitations to protect individual rights and reputations, national security, public order, and public health.[2] In 2010, the Brisbane Declaration called on UN member states to enact laws guaranteeing the right to information with simple procedures for making requests and limited exclusions.[3] The United Nations General Assembly has established September 28 as the International Day for Access to Information.[4] At least half of the world's countries have some type of freedom of information legislation that grants a presumptive right to access information maintained by government agencies and other public bodies, subject to exclusions related to criminal law enforcement, national security, and foreign intelligence.[5]

In Sweden, where public access legislation dates from 1766, the public has a constitutional right to obtain non-secret information maintained by government agencies.[6] In Finland, freedom of information legislation dates from 1951.[7] The U.S. Freedom of Information Act (FOIA) was enacted in 1966.[8] It gives the public the right to request information maintained by federal government agencies. Exemptions and exclusions include classified information related to national defense, foreign relations, foreign intelligence, counterintelligence, and terrorism; personal, medical, and financial information about federal employees; certain information related to law enforcement; trade secrets and commercial information that is considered confidential; records protected by legal privilege; and certain geological and geophysical information, including maps. All fifty states have similar laws that give the public access to records maintained by state and local government agencies, subject to limitations that vary from state to state. Requests for access to specific government information may be made by individuals or organizations. Businesses and law firms account for more than half of Freedom of Information Act requests.[9]

Freedom of information laws in other countries contain similar provisions. In Canada, the Access to Information Act[10] gives individuals and corporations access to information maintained by federal government agencies, subject to exemptions related to national security, personal privacy, and certain confidential matters. Canadian provinces and territories have their own freedom of information laws. The Australian Freedom of Information Act 1982[11] gives the public access to the records of federal agencies and ministers, subject to exemptions for certain agencies and certain types of information. Every Australian state and territory has comparable legislation. In the United Kingdom, the Freedom of Information Act 2000[12] provides public access to information by requiring government agencies to publish certain information about their activities and allowing the public to request specific information from government departments and other public authorities. In China, the 2019 version of the Regulations on Open Government Information views access to public records as the norm, subject to exemptions for national security, public safety, and the lawful rights and interests of third parties.[13]

Compliance with freedom of information laws is an integral component of government's obligation to the public. Government agencies must inform the public about the times and locations where agency records are available for access, the persons to be contacted in order to request specific records, and fees for copies of requested records. Freedom of information laws typically specify the time frames for responses to information requests. In the United States, for example, federal government agencies must respond to FOIA requests within twenty business days from the date of receipt. Exceptions are limited to unusual circumstances such as the need to search for records from field facilities and requests that involve a voluminous quantity of separate and distinct records. Designated agency employees receive and evaluate requests, search for and process records, and respond to requesters. The agency's Freedom of Information Act officer is responsible for developing regulations and procedures for processing FOIA requests, allocating appropriate resources to request fulfillment, and reporting on the agency's FOIA activity. Noncompliance is not an option. A presumption of openness applies to all freedom of information requests. A request will only be denied if it is subject to exemption. There is an appeals process for denied requests, and requesters have the right to sue if denials are not satisfactorily resolved. The Office of Government Information Services periodically evaluates federal agencies for compliance.

LAWS THE MANDATE ACCESS TO PERSONAL INFORMATION

All freedom of information laws exempt personal information maintained by government agencies, apart from such publicly available information as the names of elected officials, names of agency employees that the public should contact about specific matters, names of property owners included in real estate records, and names that are mentioned in agency publications, press releases, and similar materials. Some freedom of information laws give individuals access to information that government agencies maintain about them. This is the case with the Canadian Access to Information Act and the Australian Freedom of Information Act 1982, for example. More often, however, the right of access to one's own personal information is mandated by personal data protection and privacy laws. These laws also allow data subjects to request changes if information maintained about them is inaccurate or incomplete.

According to article 15 and recital 63 of the General Data Protection Regulation (GDPR), the most widely cited data protection law, a data subject can request copies of personal information that an organization in an EU member state has collected about him or her along with information about the purpose of the collection, the source of personal information not collected from the data subject, and the recipients to whom the personal information was or will be disclosed. Where possible, the organization that control the data should provide the data subject with secure remote access to his or her personal information.[14] Paralleling the GDPR, article 43 of Directive EU 2016—the so-called Law Enforcement Directive—provides a comparable right of access to personal information collected for law enforcement purposes outside the scope of the GDPR.[15]

Many national data protection laws are modeled after EU Directive 95/46/EC, the GDPR's predecessor. Article 12 of that Directive affirms a data subject's right of access to his or her personal information.[16] As with the GDPR, exceptions are made for information related to national security, defense, public security, law enforcement, and the protection of the data subject or the rights and freedoms of others. In Canada, Fair Information Principle 9 of the Personal Information Protection and Electronic Documents Act (PIPEDA) gives data subjects the right to access personal information that an organization holds about them.[17] PIPEDA applies to most private-sector organizations that collect or use personal information for commercial purposes. Australian Privacy Principle 12 gives data subjects the right of access to their personal information held by organizations that are subject to the Privacy Act 1988.[18]

In the United States, which does not have omnibus data protection or privacy legislation, a right to access one's own personal information is a component of various federal and state laws. Compared to national data protection legislation, the U.S. laws that specify access rights apply to a narrower range of information and business activities. Examples, some of which predate European data protection laws, include the following:

- The Privacy Act of 1974 gives U.S. citizens and permanent resident aliens, or a third party designated by them, the right to access and obtain copies of their personal information maintained by federal government agencies, including executive departments, military departments, and independent regulatory agencies.[19] Exemptions are provided for classified information, investigative material compiled for law enforcement purposes, information that would reveal the identity of a confidential source, and certain other information. The Privacy Act does not apply to information maintained by the legislative branch of the U.S. government.
- The Family Educational Rights and Privacy Act (FERPA), which also dates from 1974, gives parents the right to review their children's student records maintained by schools, school districts, and postsecondary institutions that receive funding from any program administered by the U.S. Department of Education. This right of access transfers to the student when he or she reaches age eighteen or enrolls in a postsecondary institution.[20] FERPA does not apply to most private and religious elementary and secondary schools because such schools do not generally receive federal funding. FERPA's right of access is limited to current and formerly enrolled students. It does not extend to information collected by college and university admissions offices about applicants who were not admitted or did not enroll.
- The Children's Online Privacy Protection Act (COPPA) of 1998 gives parents the right to request a description of the specific types of personal information that a website operator has collected from their child under age thirteen.[21]
- The Fair Credit Reporting Act (FCRA), which was initially enacted in 1970, gives a consumer the right to request all information in his or her file maintained by a credit reporting agency, including the source of the information, the identification of each person that obtained a consumer report during a specified time period, information about any checks that caused an adverse characterization of the consumer, and a record of all inquiries in the previous one-year period related to a credit or insurance transaction not initiated by the consumer.[22]
- The California Consumer Privacy Act (CCPA) of 2018[23] gives California residents the right to request personal information maintained about

them by certain businesses. The Virginia Consumer Data Protection Act of 2021 and Colorado Privacy Act of 2021 gives Virginia and Colorado residents a similar right of access to personal information that businesses maintain about them.[24] Other states have similar legislation pending or in development. At the national level, the Fair Information Practice Principles developed by the Federal Trade Commission asserts consumers' right to access information that businesses collect and maintain about them, but the Principles are recommendations rather than legal mandates.

- The Health Information Portability and Accountability Act (HIPAA) of 1996 gives individuals access to medical and billing information that health-care providers and other covered entities maintain about them, subject to exceptions for psychotherapy notes and information compiled in anticipation of or use in legal proceedings.[25] State health-care information laws provide a similar right of access, subject to restrictions and exemptions. In New York State, for example, patients must be given an opportunity to inspect and obtain copies of information that health-care facilities and providers licensed by the Department of Health maintain about them, but a practitioner's personal notes and observations, information that a practitioner determines might substantially harm a patient, and certain other information is excluded.[26] Some state laws are identical to or preempted by HIPAA for covered entities. Others include additional provisions or rules for health-care entities not covered by HIPAA, such as certain counselors who do not maintain patient records in electronic form. In countries with omnibus data protection laws, medical information maintained by health-care providers is treated like other types of personal information. It is available to the data subject unless an exclusion applies. Some data protection laws provide an exclusion where a health-care entity reasonably believes that giving access would endanger the health of the data subject or where the record contains information that was given to the health-care entity with an obligation of confidentiality

To ensure compliance, many organization designate an official who will be responsible for developing, implementing, and monitoring policies and procedures for requests from data subjects for access to personal information maintained about them. According to articles 37 through 39 of the GDPR, government agencies and certain other organizations in EU member states must appoint a data protection officer who will receive comments and questions from data subjects regarding processing of their personal information. Where not required, the appointment of a data protection officer is recommended.[27]

Noncompliance with data protection laws that grant a right of access to one's personal information can have costly consequences. Administrative fines and penalties for noncompliance with the GDPR's right-of-access requirements, for example, are widely publicized and severe—up to twenty million EUR or 4 percent of worldwide annual turnover. Aggrieved data subjects can also pursue judicial remedies leading to compensation for material or nonmaterial damages resulting from noncompliance, as provided in GDPR articles 77 through 84. In Canada, PIPEDA violations may be prosecuted by the Department of Justice and can lead to substantial fines. Noncompliance with the Australian Privacy Act can result in multimillion-dollar fines.

Noncompliance with U.S. laws that provide for a right of access can result in significant civil penalties. Noncompliance with COPPA's provisions for parental access carries a maximum penalty of $40,000 per incident. At that rate, a violation involving information about five children could lead to a $200,000 fine. Willful noncompliance with HIPAA rules can result in fines exceeding $50,000 per incident. Violations can lead to criminal penalties in some cases. The Privacy Act also allows for criminal penalties in limited circumstances. At the state level, intentional violations of the California Consumer Privacy Act can result in fines up to $7,500 per incident.

SHAREHOLDER ACCESS LAWS

Business formation laws give individual shareholders of a corporation the right to access, inspect, and copy information beyond that which the corporation is obligated to disclose to all shareholders or to the general public. In some ways, these shareholder access laws are the corporate counterparts of freedom-of-information laws that provide access to government records—albeit, with a more limited scope. Shareholders wishing access to corporate records may assert a common law right based on the theory that shareholders are the beneficial owners of corporate assets. A shareholder's right of access applies to selected corporate records, which must be available to qualified requesters—typically, the owners of a company's stock or their authorized designees—during business hours at a designated location subject to restrictions and exclusions that vary from one political jurisdiction to another.

Shareholder access laws vary from country to country and, within federated countries, from one state or province to another. For example:

- In the United States, shareholder access is regulated at the state level. According to the Model Business Corporation Act (MCBA), which has been adopted by over thirty states, a shareholder of a corporation has a right of access to articles of incorporation, bylaws, lists of shareholders, notices and written communications to shareholders, names and businesses addresses of directors and officers, meeting minutes, resolutions taken without a meeting, and the corporation's financial statements and accounting records.[28] States that have not adopted the MCBA have laws with similar provisions. In most states, a shareholder must give written advance notice indicating the specific records to be inspected and the purpose for which access is required. Some state laws require the shareholder to state a proper purpose that is reasonably related to protection of the shareholder's interests. This is the case, for example, in Delaware, a state known for its corporation-friendly laws.[29]

- In Canada, shareholders have a right to inspect and make extracts from a corporation's by-laws, shareholder meeting minutes and resolutions, notices to shareholders, and a corporation's register of securities holders. The same access rights apply to a corporation's creditors. A corporation's shareholder lists are available to any interested party for a reasonable fee.[30] The Canada Business Corporation Act applies to corporations that conduct business nationwide. Shareholders of provincial and territorial corporations have comparable access rights.
- In the United Kingdom, the Companies Act 2006 gives shareholders the right to inspect lists of shareholders and minutes and resolutions of shareholder meetings. The statutory right of inspection does not include board minutes and accounting records, although a company's shareholder agreement may confer access to those records.[31]
- Shareholders in New Zealand have a right to inspect minutes of meetings and resolutions of shareholders, communications to shareholders for the preceding ten years, and the company's interests register. A company's certificate of incorporation, share register, and certain other information must be available for public inspection. [32]
- Australian law does not give shareholders a general right of access to corporate information, but Section 247A of the Corporations Act 2001 allows a shareholder to apply for a court order to inspect a company's books and records.[33] Broader access rights may be provided by shareholder agreements or internal governance rules.
- In Japan, shareholders can request access to and copies of articles of incorporation, minutes of shareholder and board meetings, financial statements, and business reports.[34]
- In China, a shareholder has the right to inspect and duplicate a company's articles of association, minutes of shareholder meetings, resolutions of the board of directors and board of supervisors, and financial and accounting reports. A shareholder may request access to a company's accounting records for a legitimate purpose.[35]

A shareholder's right to access information applies to both public and privately held corporations, although some countries limit the amount of information that privately held corporations must make available for shareholder inspection.[36] In some countries, the members of a limited liability company or partnership have access rights that are similar to those of corporate shareholders. In states that have enacted the Uniform Business Organizations Code, for example, partners and limited liability company members have the right to inspect and copy information during regular business hours without specifying a particular purpose. [37]

Noncompliance with shareholder access laws is punishable by fines and, in rare cases, criminal penalties, but a corporation can refuse requests for access that it believes are unreasonable or that would be harmful to the corporation's interests. In some jurisdictions, shareholders who believe that a request for access to corporate records was unjustly denied can seek judicial intervention to enforce compliance.

LAWS THAT MANDATE PROACTIVE INFORMATION DISCLOSURE

The information access laws discussed in the preceding sections require an organization to make specific information available for examination or copying in response to a request received from an authorized party or, in some cases, the general public. Many countries have laws that mandate proactive disclosure of certain information apart from a specific request. In the United States, the Freedom of Information Act requires federal government agencies to post frequently requested records and certain other information online in an electronic reading room.[38] At the state level, some freedom of information laws include similar requirements. In New York, for example, a centralized online portal provides access to electronic reading rooms of state agencies and public authorities.[39]

Other information access laws require individuals or companies to disclose certain information to the general public proactively. In many communities, for example, property owners, real estate developers, and others who are planning commercial or residential construction projects must publicly disclose information about the purpose, scope, and characteristics of proposed projects. EU Directive 2009/101/EC mandates proactive public disclosure of a company's incorporation documents, officers, registered office location, annual accounting documents that must be published in accordance with EU directives, and liquidation proceedings. In the United States, companies regulated by the Securities and Exchange Commission must comply with proactive disclosure requirements for descriptive information and financial statements specified in SEC regulations.[40] In Canada, information about a corporation's registered office and the names and addresses of its directors are available to the general public and searchable online.

Various laws and regulations require companies and government agencies to proactively disclose certain information to the general public or to designated individuals or organizations when specified events occur. For the most part, such legal requirements compel the disclosure of information related to suspected criminal activity or to potential threats to public health and safety. Examples include the following:

- Most countries have anti-money laundering, antiterrorism, or antidrug trafficking laws and regulations that require financial institutions to report suspicious transactions to financial regulators or law enforcement authorities. In the United States, which has a multidecade history of anti-money laundering legislation, any company that provides financial services must file a suspicious activity report with the Financial Crimes Enforcement Network (FinCEN) for large cash transactions or certain behavior that might indicate criminal activity.[41] The report must provide detailed information about the suspected business or person, the instruments or mechanisms used to facilitate the suspicious transaction, and the date, time, place, and nature of the suspicious activity. This proactive disclosure requirement applies to banks, credit unions, financial holding companies, brokers or dealers in securities, currency exchanges, insurance companies, casinos and card clubs, pawnbrokers, and other companies that receive money from or give money to customers.

- In some countries, regulatory authorities require publicly traded companies to proactively disclose nonpublic information that may affect investment decisions. In EU member states, regulated companies have a general obligation to disclose events that may affect the price of their stock.[42] In other countries, laws and regulations specify the situations in which information deemed relevant for investors must be disclosed. In addition to submitting annual and quarterly reports to the Securities and Exchange Commission, publicly traded companies in the United States must disclose the occurrence of specific developments that are considered significant by regulatory authorities, such as changes in control of the company, amendments of the company's charter or by-laws, election or resignation of directors, appointment or departure of a principal officer, creation of material financial obligations, changes in the company's certified financial accountants, changes in earnings guidance or a credit rating, and a conclusion that stockholders should no longer rely on a previously issued financial statement or audit report.[43] Japanese regulators provide a similar list of material events that trigger a disclosure obligation.[44]
- Laws in over two dozen countries require certain companies to disclose environmental, societal, and governance information.[45] In the European Union, the Non-Financial Reporting Directive requires companies listed on regulated exchanges, banks, insurers, and other large companies that are considered public-interest entities to disclose information about their handling of environmental issues, treatment of employees, respect for human rights, anti-corruption and bribery, and diversity on company boards.[46] The requirements apply to more than 11,700 companies in EU member states. In the United Kingdom, medium-size and larger companies must disclose greenhouse gas emissions in their annual reports.[47] In China, certain companies in highly polluting industries must report environmental issues that are likely to affect the price of their stock.[48] Other countries with laws requiring environmental or social disclosure include Australia, Canada, Chile, Peru, the Philippines, and South Africa.
- In many countries, pharmaceutical companies and clinical investigators must proactively disclose information to regulatory authorities about ad-

verse events that occur during clinical trials of investigational new drugs and biological products. An adverse event means any untoward medical occurrence associated with the use of a drug or biological product in humans. In the United States, the sponsor of a clinical trial must report serious or unexpected adverse events to the Food and Drug Administration as soon as possible.[49] Similar disclosure requirements apply in other countries. A pharmaceutical company's disclosure responsibilities do not end with clinical trials. For approved products, pharmacovigilance legislation requires pharmaceutical manufacturers to monitor and disclose adverse events, medication errors, product quality complaints, and other safety issues related to marketed drugs and therapeutic biologic products. Information about these matters must be reported to regulatory authorities in a timely manner.[50] Point of care reporting of adverse drug reactions is voluntary. In the United States, drug safety reports may also be submitted to pharmaceutical manufacturers by physicians, nurses, pharmacists, and other health-care professionals. Alternatively, health-care providers and consumers can submit reports of adverse drug experience directly to the Food and Drug Administration.

- Internal Health Regulations, which are legally binding in 196 countries, require health-care providers and clinical laboratories to disclose information related to cases of communicable diseases that may constitute a potential public health emergency.[51] Examples of diseases for which reporting is mandated include smallpox, polio, severe acute respiratory syndrome, and certain strains of influenza, but some national and subnational public health laws require dozens of diseases to be reported. In the United States, infectious diseases must be reported to the Centers for Disease Control and to state public health agencies. Similarly, public health laws in Canadian provinces and territories require health-care providers to report communicable diseases and infections. Medical practitioners and laboratories in England and Wales have a statutory obligation to report cases of certain diseases and causative agents to the UK Health Security Agency. The European Centre for Disease Prevention and Control collects reports of data on communicable diseases from all EU member states, as well as Norway and Iceland.[52]
- Many countries have laws that require professionals who have regular contact with children to report information about suspected maltreatment to a child protective services or law enforcement agency.[53] This may involve disclosure of information that a child or another party has shared with the mandated reporter. Some countries have a national child protection law that includes a proactive reporting mandate. In the United States, Canada, and other federated countries, reporting of suspected child abuse or neglect is mandated by state, provincial, or other subnational legislation. The list of mandatory reporters varies from one political jurisdiction to another but usually includes health-care providers, educators,

social workers, caregivers, daycare workers, and others who work with or provide services to children and families. In some jurisdiction, any family members or other persons who have reason to suspect child abuse are required to report it. Exceptions may be made for attorneys, clergy, and psychotherapists whose suspicions are based on privileged communications that they are prohibited from disclosing, as discussed later in this chapter. In some countries, mandatory reporting laws also apply to suspected mistreatment of elderly, disabled, or otherwise vulnerable persons.[54]

- Some countries have environmental right-to-know legislation that mandates disclosure of information about health hazards to which the public may be exposed.[55] In the United States, examples of federal right-to-know laws include the Emergency Planning and Community Right to Know Act,[56] which requires chemical manufacturing facilities to immediately notify the public about the accidental release of certain toxic substances, and the Safe Drinking Water Act,[57] which requires water utilities to notify customers when there is a problem with their drinking water. Canadian law similarly requires notification of any member of the public that might be affected by an environmental emergency, which is defined as an uncontrolled, unplanned, or accidental release of a harmful substance.[58] Workplace right-to-know laws require organizations to inform their employees about workplace hazards. In the United States, workplace right-to-know requirements are based on the Hazard Communication Standard issued by the Occupational Safety and Health Administration. Directive 89/391/EEC establishes the framework for workplace right-to-know requirements in EU member states. [59]

These proactive disclosure requirements differ from the periodic filings, reports, and other mandatory submissions discussed in chapter 2, but the consequences of noncompliance are comparable—monetary penalties, possible civil litigation, and, in extreme cases, criminal prosecution. Violations of financial disclosure regulations, which are closely associated with criminal activity, incur the largest penalties. In the United States, willful violation of disclosure requirements associated with anti-money laundering regulations is punishable by fines ranging from $57,000 to more than $299,000 per incident and up to ten years in prison. In 2021, eighty financial institutions were fined a total of $2.732 billion for noncompliance with U.S. anti-money laundering requirements, including failure to disclose suspicious transactions. In the preceding year, twenty-four institutions were fined a total of $3.225 million.[60] Penalties for noncompliance with non-financial disclosure requirements are lower but still significant. Fines for violations of the Emergency Planning and Community Right to Know Act, for example, can exceed $62,000 per incident. Some infractions, such as the failure to report child abuse when mandated by law, are misdemeanors—or, for repeat violations, felonies—that can lead to criminal prosecution in some jurisdictions.

LAWS THAT PROHIBIT DISCLOSURE OF NONPUBLIC PERSONAL INFORMATION

Nonpublic information is broadly defined as any information that is not intended for disclosure to the general public. Many countries have laws and regulations that prohibit disclosure of nonpublic information unless appropriate authorization is obtained or other conditions apply. Data protection and privacy laws, the most frequently cited examples of such legislation, prohibit the unauthorized disclosure of personal information maintained by companies, government agencies, and nonprofit entities:

- As previously discussed, the General Data Protection Regulation defines legal requirements and restrictions for processing of personal information by organizations that operate in EU member states, where processing is defined broadly to include disclosure of personal information verbally, in writing, by electronic transmission, or by any other means that make the information available. According to the GDPR, disclosure of personal information is generally prohibited unless it is expressly authorized by law or the data subject freely consents to the disclosure. The consent must be voluntary, informed, explicit, and unambiguous. The data subject must be aware of the types of information to be disclosed, the purpose of the disclosure, the parties to whom the information will be disclosed, the means of disclosure, and how the disclosed information will be used. The data subject retains the right to withdraw consent at any time. The GDPR places further restrictions on disclosure that involves cross-border transfer of personal information. Such disclosure is only permitted where the receiving country has appropriate data protection legislation in place or the receiving organization guarantees that the level of protection provided by the GDPR will not be compromised.[61]
- Similar restrictions on disclosure of personal information are included in national data protection laws that are modeled on the GDPR's predecessor, Directive 95/46/EC. Such data protection laws have been adopted by European countries that are not EU member states and by several dozen countries in Asia, the Middle East, Africa, and Latin America.
- In Canada, disclosure of personal information maintained by federal government agencies is regulated by the Privacy Act, which requires consent of the data subject except where disclosure is authorized by federal legislation, compelled by a court order, done for the clear benefit of the data subject, or where the public interest in the disclosure outweighs the right of privacy, such as an emergency situation where lives depend upon the

disclosure. Similar privacy laws regulate disclosure of personal information by Canadian provincial and territorial government agencies.

- Disclosure of personal information maintained by private sector organizations in Canada is regulated by the Personal Information Protection and Electronic Documents Act. It prohibits disclosure of personal information without the data subject's knowledge or consent. Exceptions are limited to disclosure to collect a debt, to comply with a court order, to respond to a request by a government institution in relation to national security or legal matters, or to communicate with the data subject's next of kin, authorized representative, or another person in the event of an emergency. Disclosure restrictions do not apply to information that is publicly available or information that is used for statistical or scholarly purposes, provided that confidentiality is assured and the data subject's consent cannot be obtained. Personal information that was created more than one hundred years ago or twenty years after the death of the data subject is also excluded. PIPEDA also applies to associations, charities, religious groups, advocacy groups, and other not-for-profit organizations to the extent that they engage in commercial activities, such as the sale of membership lists or donor lists. Some Canadian provinces have substantially similar data protection laws that take precedence over PIPEDA for disclosure of personal information within their jurisdictions.
- At the federal level, the Australian Privacy Act 1988, as previously cited, presents privacy principles that apply to commonwealth agencies, certain private sector companies, certain nonprofit organizations, and all private health-care providers. The law does not apply to government agencies in Australian states and territories, which have their own data protection legislation.[62]
- In New Zealand, the Privacy Act 2020 applies to all governmental and nongovernmental entities. Subject to limited exceptions, its core principles require authorization by the data subject for disclosure of personal information.[63]

In the United States, the same laws and regulations that give data subjects access to personal information that government agencies and nongovernmental entities maintain about them also prohibit the unauthorized disclosure of such information. The Privacy Act of 1974 limits disclosure of personal information by U.S. government agencies. Privacy laws with similar restrictions apply to personal information maintained by state and local government agencies.[64]

Various federal and state laws and regulations prohibit disclosure of specific categories of personal information. The HIPAA Privacy Rule, for example, restricts disclosure of individually identifiable health information maintained by health plans, health-care clearinghouses, health care providers, and their business associates.[65] The Family Educational Rights and Privacy Act requires written permission from students or parents of minor students to release information from educational records to a third party.[66] According to the Children's Online Privacy Protection Rule, website operators must obtain parental consent prior to disclosure of personal information about children under thirteen years of age.[67] The Internal Revenue Code prohibits unauthorized disclosure of taxpayer information and tax returns.[68] The Driver's Privacy Protection Act restricts the disclosure of personal information collected by state motor vehicle departments.[69] According to U.S. regulations, banks, credit unions, and other financial institutions have an "affirmative and continuing obligation" to protect the security and confidentiality of their customers' nonpublic personal information.[70]

A small but growing number of state laws give data subjects the right to prohibit sale of their personal information to third parties. In some states, personal information about library users can only be disclosed to the extent necessary for library operations, with consent of the data subject, or pursuant to a court order or statute.[71] Federal law prohibits the disclosure of personal information contained in motor vehicle records maintained by state governments without the consent of the data subject.[72]

As with other laws and regulations discussed in this chapter, unauthorized disclosure of personal information can lead to significant monetary penalties. The substantial fines imposed for GDPR violations were discussed in a preceding section. Fines up to $50,000 per incident may be imposed for willful violations of the HIPAA Privacy Rule. Educational institutions that violate FERPA provisions may lose federal funding. Organizations can be fined $10,000 NZ for violations of the New Zealand Privacy Act 2020, but an official complaint to the Human Rights Tribunal carries a maximum penalty of $230,000 NZ. In some countries, data subjects can also pursue judicial remedies for harm resulting from unauthorized disclosure of their personal information. In some cases, unauthorized disclosure of personal information is a criminal offense. In New York City, the District of Columbia, and other jurisdictions, for example, the disclosure of an intimate image of person without the consent of the depicted person is a misdemeanor punishable by fine and imprisonment. Civil remedies are also provided.[73]

LAWS THAT PROHIBIT DISCLOSURE OF CONFIDENTIAL NONPERSONAL INFORMATION

Confidential nonpersonal information is information that is not generally known, that does not relate to a readily identifiable person, that is identified as confidential by the person or organization who possesses it, that is intended for limited disclosure to a select group for a defined purpose, and that could have an adverse impact on a person or organization if it becomes more widely known. Various national and subnational laws prohibit the disclosure of confidential nonpersonal information to unauthorized persons or for an unauthorized purpose:

- Information that a government agency considers sensitive enough to prohibit unauthorized disclosure is designated as classified. In the United States, confidential information is the lowest of three categories of classified information. The other two levels are secret information and top secret information.[74] Other countries use similar designations. Classified status is typically reserved for information that must be protected from disclosure for reasons of national security. In the United States, federal law criminalizes the unauthorized disclosure of classified information.[75] That is also the case in Canada, Australia, the United Kingdom, and other countries.[76]
- Some countries have laws that prohibit the disclosure of trade secrets, which is confidential business information that derives its actual or potential economic value from not being generally known and which the owner of the information has implemented reasonable safeguards to protect from unauthorized disclosure. Trade secrets include, but are not necessarily limited to, product specifications and formulas, unpatented inventions, computer algorithms, business processes, manufacturing techniques, strategic plans, marketing plans, and customer lists. In the United States, unauthorized communication of trade secrets by any means is a federal crime.[77] Most states have adopted a version of the Uniform Trade Secrets Act, which prohibits misappropriation of trade secrets. Unauthorized disclosure is considered a misappropriation because public knowledge negates trade secret status.[78] Unauthorized disclosure of trade secrets is similarly unlawful in EU member states.[79] In some countries, like Australia and Canada, misappropriation of trade secrets is covered by common law rather than specific statutes.
- Inside information, sometimes termed insider information, is confidential information that is available to the officers, directors, and principal shareholders of a publicly traded company. Inside information is considered material if public disclosure could affect investment decisions about the company's stock. Examples include information about a company's plans to acquire or be acquired by another company, pending release of financial results that are different from public expectations, a pending change in the company's credit rating, a pending initiation or settlement of legal proceedings or regulatory actions, a pending product announcement, and the pending departure of a key executive. Laws and regulations in countries with major stock exchanges prohibit the disclosure of such material inside information.[80] This prohibition applies to company employees and any other person who may obtain inside information, including investment bankers, broker-dealers, and other financial service providers who may acquire nonpublic information about a company in the course of their work. Persons who obtain material inside information are prohibited from using it for investment decisions.

- Various laws and regulations prohibit the disclosure of information that endangers public safety or disrupts the enforcement of other laws. In the United States, for example, it is a federal crime to disclose any information pertaining to the manufacture or use of explosive, destructive devices in connection with a violent crime.[81] The unauthorized disclosure of suspicious activity reports filed by financial institutions is a violation of federal criminal law.[82] In some jurisdictions it is illegal to disclose that an indictment has been filed before the accused person has been served or is in custody.[83]
- As discussed in the preceding section, most data protection laws prohibit the transfer of personal information to countries that lack an adequate level of protection unless the data subject consents to the transfer. Some countries have laws that prohibit the cross-border transfer of specific types of nonpersonal information. These laws, which are collectively described as "blocking statutes," impede or prevent the collection of evidence for use in legal proceedings outside of the country where the information is sought. Among the best-known examples, the French blocking statute prohibits the disclosure of commercial, financial, or technical information for use in legal or administrative proceedings outside of France unless the disclosure is ordered by a French court.[84] Similar laws in other countries prohibit compliance with foreign discovery orders that may infringe national sovereignty or security. Examples include the UK Protection of Trading Interests Act 1980 and the Canadian Foreign Extraterritorial Measures Act.[85]

While violations of other information disclosure laws discussed in this chapter are punishable by monetary penalties and possible civil litigation, noncompliance with the disclosure prohibitions discussed above are criminal offenses that may lead to a prison term in addition to a fine. In the United States, unlawful disclosure of classified information related to national security is punishable by imprisonment for up to ten years. Criminal indictments for unauthorized disclosure of classified information to the press have been widely publicized.[86] The most extreme offense, disclosure of classified defense information to aid a foreign government, is punishable by multidecade or life imprisonment. Criminal indictments and prison terms for insider trading, the unauthorized use of inside information, have likewise been widely publicized.[87] Unauthorized disclosure of trade secrets generally results in monetary penalties, but criminal prosecution is also possible.

COURT-ORDERED DISCLOSURE

Legal prohibitions on the disclosure of personal or nonpersonal information can be overridden by a court order in the context of civil or criminal litigation. Data protection and privacy laws, which generally prohibit disclosure of personal information without a data subject's consent, allow such information to be released when ordered by a court of competent jurisdiction. This is the case, for example, in the United States with the Privacy Act of 1974 and Freedom of Information Act, in Canada with the Privacy Act and Access to Information Act, in Australia with the Privacy Act 1988, in the United Kingdom with the Data Protection Act 2018, and in EU member states with article 6 of the GDPR, which permits disclosure of personal information without a data subject's consent for compliance with a legal obligation.

In the United States, the HIPAA Privacy Rule allows covered entities to disclose protected health information in response to a court order provided that the disclosure is limited to information that is expressly covered by the court order. Similarly, federal regulations allow court-ordered disclosure of a patient's substance abuse treatment records where the court determines that a good cause exists, but the disclosure must be limited to essential parts of the patient's records. Courts can also order the disclosure of information about participants in clinical trials and other research studies that involve human subjects even if a confidentiality agreement is in effect.[88]

Courts have considerable discretion in ordering the disclosure of confidential nonpersonal information in civil litigation or criminal prosecution, but the owner of the information may seek to prevent or limit the order. In legal proceedings involving disclosure of data or documents that contain classified information, U.S. law allows the government to substitute an unclassified summary of the information or a statement admitting the relevant facts that the classified information would tend to prove. In either case, the party that receives the classified information is prohibited from disclosing it. An evidentiary rule known as the state secrets privilege allows the federal government to resist court-ordered disclosure of information during civil litigation if national security would be harmed.[89] The Classified Information Procedures Act serves the same purpose in criminal trials.[90] In litigation involving trade secrets, the owner of a trade secret may be required to disclose it in court. In such cases, the court records may be sealed or the courtroom may be closed during portions of a trial where trade secrets are disclosed.

A court order authorizing the disclosure of specific information is accompanied by a subpoena to compel compliance. Noncompliance without a valid defense can lead to harsh sanctions, including monetary penalties, a default judgment, and possibly a contempt citation.[91]

PROHIBITED PROFESSIONAL DISCLOSURES

In some jurisdictions, court-ordered disclosure is prohibited or limited by professional privilege laws that protect the confidentiality of information that a person shares with certain professionals. The protected information is said to be "privileged." Professional privilege laws are designed to encourage free and open discussion of confidential information in a professional context without fear that the information will be revealed to others. Depending on the law, the professional privilege to stop court-ordered disclosure may be asserted by the party who divulges the confidential information, the professional to whom it is divulged, or both:

- Attorney-client privilege—variously known as solicitor-client privilege, legal advice privilege, or legal professional privilege—preserves the confidentiality of information that a client shares with an attorney or other professional legal advisor in the context of providing legal assistance or advocacy. The privilege applies both to information that a client gives an attorney and to information that the attorney gives a client, provided that the information is given in confidence and in the context of obtaining or providing legal advice. Courts or other third parties cannot compel disclosure of such information unless the privilege is waived or a statutory exception applies, as would be the case with a client who seeks legal advice for purposes of committing a crime. In the United States, the principle of attorney-client privilege is a common law doctrine at the federal level and in all fifty states and the District of Columbia, although it may also be codified in statutes in some jurisdictions. An attorney-client privilege is also recognized, with some variations, in other countries, including Australia, Canada, England, and EU member states. In the United States, the privilege applies to information that is shared in confidence, either verbally or in writing, between attorney and client. In some other countries, the privilege is limited to written communications.
- In some countries, doctor-patient privilege laws prohibit court-ordered disclosure of personally identifiable information obtained by physicians and certain other health-care providers in their professional capacity without the prior consent of the patient.[92] In the United States, all states and the District of Columbia have laws that recognize the doctor-patient privilege for information that a patient shares with a physician for purposes of obtaining medical care. In some states, the privilege applies to a broad range of health-care providers, including dentists, podiatrists, chiropractors, and nurses.[93] Disclosure restrictions based on the doctor-patient privilege are narrower than other laws, such as the HIPAA Privacy Rule, which prohibit disclosure of a patient's health information. The doctor-patient privilege applies only to judicial proceedings and is further limited to information that the patient reveals with an expectation of privacy. Exceptions to the privilege may be made for information related to crimes, such as child abuse, and to diseases that public health laws require physicians to report.
- In some states, a psychotherapist-client privilege prohibits judicial disclosure of confidential information that a client communicates to a psychiatrist, clinical psychologist, or other mental health professional during a therapy session. Some state laws define psychotherapist broadly to include

school psychologists, clinical social workers, clinical counselors, marriage and family therapists, and registered nurses who are licensed to practice psychotherapy. The psychotherapist-client privilege is asserted by the client. Expressly modeled on attorney-client privilege, psychotherapist-client statutes are generally more protective of the client's confidential information than doctor-patient privilege laws. Unless a client waives the privilege, a psychotherapist cannot divulge any confidential information discussed in a therapy session, although an exception may be made for information related to child abuse.

- In the United States, the Internal Revenue Code extends common law protection of confidentiality to information that a taxpayer shares with a federally authorized tax practitioner (FATP).[94] This accountant-client privilege, also known as the FATP privilege, treats such confidential information as if it were shared between a taxpayer and an attorney, but the accountant-client privilege is narrower than the attorney-client privilege. It is limited to confidential tax advice. It does not apply to preparation of tax returns or to other business advice that an accountant might give, and it cannot be used to prevent court-ordered disclosure in criminal proceeding or in state court proceedings. It can only be asserted in noncriminal tax proceedings before the IRS or in federal court.
- All U.S. states and the District of Columbia have laws that prohibit the judicial disclosure of information that is revealed in confidence to members of the clergy by penitents, congregation members, or other persons.[95] Some other countries have similar laws that recognize this clergy privilege, which is variously known as a priest-penitent privilege, pastor-penitent privilege, confessional privilege, or clergyman-communicant privilege. The clergy privilege mirrors Catholic church law that forbids priests from disclosing confidential information heard in a penitent's confession, but it is not limited to priests or confessional disclosures. Depending on the law, the privilege may apply to confidential communications with a priest outside a formal confession, a minister of any denomination, a rabbi, an imam, a Christian Science practitioner, or other spiritual counselor affiliated with an established church, synagogue, mosque, or other place of worship. The privilege may be asserted by the penitent who revealed the confidential information, the clergy member, or both.

CONTRACTUAL COMPLIANCE

Consultants, vendors, and other contractors hired by government agencies, companies, and nonprofit organizations must have access to certain information in order to do their work. To protect an organization's information from unauthorized use, contracts typically limit the data or documents that a contractor 's employees can access. Certain information may be restricted to contractor personnel who have passed background investigations or obtained appropriate security clearances. Even then, a contractor may only access information that is absolutely necessary for the agreed-upon work.

A contract or other agreement may also include restrictions on disclosure of personal or nonpublic information that a contractor acquires in the course of its work. Contractor personnel are typically subject to the same data protection and privacy laws, regulations, and restrictions as an organization's own employees. In the United States, for example, the Privacy Act of 1974 applies to all federal government contractors who have access to systems of record that contain personal information.

A contract to protect confidential business information may take the form of a nondisclosure agreement (NDA), which is a legally enforceable contract that restricts the disclosure and use of specific nonpublic information that is divulged to the party that signs the agreement. The information might include strategic plans, competitive intelligence, financial information, customer information, product plans, pricing formulas, and other nonpublic business information that the disclosing organization will share with the receiving party, either verbally or by giving the receiving party access to documents or data that contain the information.[96] An NDA prevents the receiving party from disclosing the information covered by the agreement to unauthorized parties by any means. It also prevents unauthorized use of the nonpublic information for the receiving party's benefit.

An organization may use an NDA to maintain confidentiality of nonpublic information discussed during business interactions ranging from straightforward job interviews to complicated merger and acquisition negotiations. In some organizations, all employees, consultants, and contractors who are likely to gain knowledge of nonpublic information in the course of their work must sign an NDA or similar confidentiality agreement when they are hired. An NDA may also be used to maintain confidentiality about the terms and conditions of a legal settlement.

An NDA may be a unilateral or mutual agreement. A unilateral NDA obligates the receiving party to maintain the confidentiality of information revealed by the disclosing party. A mutual agreement is needed if all parties will disclose nonpublic information, as might be the case in discussions of mergers, acquisitions, or business partnerships. An NDA may be of limited or indefinite duration. It may be broadly written or limited to information that is specified in the agreement. An NDA may allow the receiving party to share nonpublic information with certain other parties, such as investors or lenders, for an agreed-upon purpose with the understanding that they will not further disclose the information. Because an NDA is a contract, noncompliance can lead to civil litigation and monetary penalties for disclosing information covered by the agreement, assuming that disclosure and the resulting damages can be proved.

Confidentiality agreements unrelated to nonpublic business information may be used to prevent disclosure in other situations. Hospitals, clinics, and other medical facilities routinely require employees, medical staff, medical students, and others who have access to medical records to sign an agreement prohibiting the unauthorized disclosure of confidential patient information. For research that is funded or conducted by the National Institutes of Health, a certificate of confidentiality protects the privacy of individuals who are the subjects of such research. A certificate of confidentiality is issued by the National Institutes of Health to an investigator or institution that receives federal funding. It prohibits the disclosure of personally identifiable information about human subjects that is collected or used during biomedical, clinical, behavioral, or other research projects.[97] Similarly, a school district may require administrators, counselors, teachers, and other employees to sign a confidentiality agreement prohibiting unauthorized disclosure of student information. A hotel may require employees to sign confidentiality agreements that prohibit disclosure of information about guests. In addition to restricting disclosure, these confidentiality agreements may also limit access to such information. Noncompliance with confidentiality agreements can lead to loss of employment and costly civil litigation.

STANDARDS AND INDUSTRY NORMS

There is no all-encompassing national or international standard that defines requirements for access to and disclosure of information. Several International standards address access to and disclosure of personal information in specific circumstances or work environments. Examples include ISO/TS 17975:2015, *Health informatics—Principles and data requirements for consent in the collection, use, or disclosure of personal information*; ISO/IEC 29184:2020, *Information technology—Online privacy notices and consent*; and ISO/IEC 15944-8:2012, *Information technology—Business operational view—Part 8: Identification of privacy protection requirements as external constraints on business transactions.* Most ISO standards, however, deal with disclosure in the context of information security, which is discussed in chapter 6.

Several international organizations have defined standards for access to and disclosure of personal information maintained by government agencies and nongovernmental entities. OECD Guidelines on the Protection of Privacy and Transborder Flows of Personal Data, issued by the Organization for Economic Cooperation and Development, do not have the force of law, but they have had a significant impact on national privacy and data protection legislation. OECD principles emphasize the need for safeguards to prevent unauthorized access to and disclosure of personal information, as well as the importance of a data subject's consent as a precondition for any disclosure that is not required by law.[98]

Data protection principles issued by Privacy International, a charity that promotes and defends the right to privacy, reflect the OECD guidelines and GDPR requirements for access to and disclosure of personal information.[99] According to the APEC Privacy Framework, which was endorsed by the twenty-one member countries of Asia-Pacific Economic Cooperation, a data subject's consent should be obtained for disclosure of personal information whenever possible. Like the OECD Guidelines, the APEC Framework is a statement of principles rather than a legal requirement; however, the APEC Cross-Border Privacy Rules require participating businesses to implement data protection policies that are consistent with the Framework.[100]

Ethical codes and other norms developed by professional associations parallel the requirements of privacy and data protection legislation in limiting the disclosure of confidential information that doctors, lawyers, and other professionals obtain in the course of their work. These professional norms have a broader scope than professional privilege laws, which are limited to disclosure of confidential information for judicial proceedings. In the United States, examples of professional norms that restrict disclosure include the following:

- Medical professionals have a widely recognized obligation to protect the confidentiality of information about their patients. The Hippocratic Oath includes a pledge of confidentiality regarding information that a physician obtains in the course of treatment.[101] According to the American Medical Association, patients are entitled to decide whether and to whom their personal health information is disclosed, but physicians do not require specific consent to disclose information to other health-care personnel for purposes of providing care, to appropriate authorities when required by law, or to prevent patients from harming themselves or others. In such situations, however, disclosure must be limited to the minimum information necessary for the intended purpose and the patient must be notified when feasible.[102] Similar guidance issued by the Canadian Medical Protective Association and General Medical Council addresses disclosure of patient information by physicians in Canada and the United Kingdom, respectively.[103]
- The American Psychological Association's code of ethics requires a client's consent for disclosure of confidential information. Exceptions are limited to disclosures mandated by law, disclosures to obtain professional consultations, disclosures to protect a client or others from harm, and disclosures necessary to obtain payment for services. Psychologists are prohibited from disclosing personally identifiable information about their clients in publications, lectures, or other presentations.[104] The code of ethics of the National Association of Social Workers contains similar requirements for disclosure of client information.[105] According to the code of ethics of the American Mental Health Counselors Association, the release of information without a client's consent can only take place in the most extreme circumstances, such as to protect life or prevent child abuse.[106]
- Other health-care professions impose restrictions on disclosure of confidential information obtained from patients or clients. According to the code of ethics of the American Speech-Language-Hearing Association, speech pathologists, audiologists, and scientists involved in speech, hearing, and

language research can only disclose confidential information about persons who receive professional services when required by law or when necessary to protect the welfare of the person or community. Similar provisions are included in the ethical codes of the American Physical Therapy Association, American Occupational Therapy Association, and Commission on Rehabilitation Counselor Certification.[107]

- According to the American Bar Association's Model Rules of Professional Conduct, a lawyer cannot disclose information relating to representation of a client without the client's informed consent unless it is necessary to prevent harm to the client or others, to comply with a law or court order, to resolve conflicts of interest in a way that will not harm the client, or to establish a claim or defense in a controversy with the client.[108]
- In some religions, clergy are prohibited from disclosing confidential information obtained in the performance of their pastoral duties. As an example, the common code of ethics for spiritual care professionals, which was developed by an interdenominational group of chaplains and pastoral care counselors, instructs clergy to respect the confidentiality of information entrusted to them by those who seek spiritual counseling, except when disclosure is necessary for pastoral care, the safety of any person, or when required by law.[109]
- Ethical codes issued by associations of accountants, financial planners, and financial service professionals resemble the legal profession's restrictions on disclosure of nonpublic client information. Members cannot disclose such information without a client's consent unless required by law. Examples include the ethical codes of the American Institute of Certified Public Accountants, the Society of Financial Service Professionals, and the CFP Board.[110]

Professional norms are intended as a standard of behavior. They do not have the force of law. Members of professional associations are expected to regulate their own practices for disclosure of confidential information and cannot condone violations. Members who possess nonprivileged information about suspected violations are expected to report it for investigation, which may lead to suspension of membership, expulsion, or other sanctions. Illegal disclosures of confidential information must be reported to appropriate law enforcement authorities and professional licensing bodies.

INTERNAL MANDATES

For the most part, the laws and regulations discussed at the beginning of this chapter mandate or limit access to an organization's information by the general public or by specific groups of nonemployees, such as litigants or shareholders. Rules for and restrictions on employee access to information are specified in an organization's internal policies. A government agency, company, or nonprofit organization cannot allow employees to have uncontrolled access to all nonpublic information that the organization collects, creates, or maintains in the course of business. An access control policy defines the conditions under which employees' access to information is permitted or restricted. It specifies which employees can have access to information associated with a particular business operation or activity and in what circumstances.[111] For purposes of access control, employee status may be defined broadly to include temporary workers, leased employees, paid and unpaid interns, and unpaid volunteers. The access privileges of contractors, who are nonemployees, are specified in contracts and agreements, as discussed in a preceding section.

Most access control policies are based on the need-to-know principle, which gives employees and other workforce members access to the least amount of information needed to their jobs. The principle applies to personal and nonpersonal information that is not available to the public. Need-to-know may be continuing or temporary. It is usually determined by an employee's job title or function, which presumably relates to duties that require access to specific information. A human resources department employee who is responsible for processing requests for medical leave or disability accommodations, for example, must have continuing access to confidential medical records that support such requests. Alternatively, need-to-know may be determined by the creator or custodian of the information for a defined purpose on a case-by-case basis. An employee who proposes the development of a new product may be given temporary access to proprietary market research or competitive intelligence information that may affect the proposed product's viability.

Access to specific confidential information may be limited to selected employees who are identified by name rather than job title or function. A company may maintain a list of employees who are authorized to access inside information that may affect investment decisions, for example. Selected inside information may also be accessible to designated employees of external parties, such as legal counsel or independent auditors, to the extent necessary to conduct business on the company's behalf.

To access certain information, additional requirements—such as a signed confidentiality agreement or a specific security clearance—may apply. Where a security clearance is involved, access will be limited to the minimum amount of information required for the employee's current job function regardless of the employee's level of security clearance. A need-to-know determination may be further limited to specific information. A university professor needs access to student records in order to provide academic advisement, but access may be limited to records of those advisees who are assigned to the professor.

An effective access control policy must be accompanied by a disclosure policy that specifies when and under what conditions an employee who has access to information can share it with others. An information disclosure policy has two objectives: (1) to ensure compliance with laws and regulations that mandate disclosure of information, and (2) to avoid the unauthorized disclosure of nonpublic information. The first objective may be the responsibility of a disclosure committee that monitors events or developments that trigger disclosure mandates, determines what information must be disclosed to satisfy legal and regulatory requirements, and ensures that the disclosure is completed in a timely, fully compliant manner. While not required by regulatory authorities, disclosure committees are common in publicly held companies. A corporate disclosure committee is usually chaired by a chief executive officer, chief financial officer, or other high-level company executive, with members drawn from departments that maintain business information that is subject to regulatory disclosure. To comply with disclosure requirements for public records, government agencies typically designate a freedom of information officer who may be supported by an advisory committee.

The second objective, safeguarding nonpublic information from unauthorized disclosure, is typically handled by a policy that prohibits employees from sharing strategic plans, competitive intelligence, financial information, customer information, product plans, pricing formulas, and other confidential business information with coworkers who are not authorized to access the information on a need-to-know basis as discussed above. The policy also specifies terms and conditions for sharing information with outside parties, including vendors, suppliers, strategic partners, legal counsel, auditors, lenders, underwriters, financial and professional advisors, counterparties in negotiations, and credit rating agencies. Where a signed nondisclosure agreement is a precondition for such sharing, disclosure of nonpublic business information is enforced by a contractual obligation rather than an internal policy.

As a further safeguard, a disclosure policy may prohibit discussion of nonpublic business matters or reading of confidential business documents in public places where they might be overheard or seen, as well as inclusion of such information in speeches and public presentations, news releases, reports, and other written materials without prior approval by a disclosure committee or a designated official. The disclosure policy may also prohibit participation in chat rooms, blogs, and other social media discussions, apart from employees who are specifically authorized to communicate with the public on such forums.

Disclosure of personally identifiable information is typically handled by a privacy policy that specifies how an organization will safeguard personal information it creates, collects, and maintains about its employees, clients, customers, suppliers, and others. In recent years, many organizations have revamped and strengthened their privacy policies to comply with disclosure requirements and restrictions specified in data protection legislation, especially the GDPR, which has a broader territorial reach than its predecessors. Most privacy policies severely limit disclosure of a data subject's personally identifiable information to third parties. Personal information will only be disclosed with the consent of the data subject, when required by law or court order, or when necessary to provide and obtain payment for services authorized by the data subject. An organization's privacy policy may also contain provisions that are not strictly related to disclosure. It may specify the types of personal information that the organization collects, how a data subject's personal information will be used, how long the information will be retained, the data subject's right to correction or removal of erroneous personal information, and provisions for continuation of privacy protection if ownership of the organization changes.

Because noncompliance with internal access control and disclosure policies exposes an organization to a variety of civil and criminal penalties, enforcement is critical. Employees who violate an organization's information access and disclosure mandates will be subject to disciplinary actions up to and including termination for cause and without notice. Legal violations will be reported to appropriate regulatory authorities and, where indicated, to law enforcement.

SOCIETAL COMPLIANCE

Many of the laws and regulations that specify information access and disclosure requirements originated in response to societal concerns. Freedom of information laws, for example, are an outgrowth of the open government doctrine, which views the citizen's right to access government information as essential to democratic processes, oversight of public administration, accountability of public officials, and scrutiny of government operations, activities, and initiatives.[112] Personal data protection legislation is based on the view that privacy is a human rights issue. According to the Universal Declaration of Human Rights of 1948, which is widely cited as a foundation for privacy and data protection concepts, a nation's laws must prevent arbitrary interference with an individual's right to privacy. The importance of privacy as a fundamental human right is also cited in the International Covenant on Civil and Political Rights, which was adopted by the United Nations General Assembly in 1966 and ratified by 173 countries, and by the European Convention on Human Rights, which was signed by forty-seven member states of the Council of Europe.[113] Mandatory reporter laws are designed to protect society's most vulnerable members. Right-to-know laws, which mandate disclosures about hazardous events, are designed to protect public health and the environment.

Increasingly, policy analysts, investors, environmentalists, political and social activists, and others have called for public disclosure of nonfinancial information related to business activities that impact the environment and society, including matters of sustainability, equity, and equality. As discussed earlier in this chapter, over two dozen countries have laws that require businesses to disclose environmental, societal, and governance information. The European Union has been a leader in requiring companies to disclose information on the way they manage social and environmental challenges. As previously cited, the Non-Financial Reporting Directive specifies disclosure requirements for non-financial and diversity information for companies listed on public exchanges, banks, insurers, and other public-interest companies with more than five hundred employees. The directive allows investors, policymakers, activists, and other stakeholders to evaluate a company's initiatives and encourage the development of a socially responsible approach to business.

Regulation (EU) 2019/2088, the Sustainable Financial Disclosure Regulation, took effect in 2021. It promotes transparency by requiring financial market participants and financial advisers to publish written policies on the integration of sustainability risk into their business and due diligence processes. The Regulation defines sustainability risk to include environmental, social, or governance events or conditions that could cause a negative material impact on the value of an investment.[114] The EU Corporate Sustainability Reporting Directive (CSRD), which is proposed as an amendment to the Nonfinancial Reporting Directive, will require large companies in EU member states to disclose targets and due diligence with regard to environmental matters, social and employee issues, respect for human rights, anticorruption and bribery, and diversity of their governing boards.[115]

These regulations focus on the impact of business activities on sustainability. They promote public awareness of corporate responsibility for and involvement in identifying and addressing environmental and societal risks. The target audience for sustainability disclosures is investors, investment advisors, industry analysts, and others who are concerned about ESG integration—that is, the inclusion of environmental, social, and governance factors in the analysis of investments. An emerging group of ESG reporting and guidance frameworks has been developed by concerned industry representatives and environmental groups. These frameworks specify compliance requirements for legally mandated and voluntary sustainability disclosures by companies and nonprofit organizations. For example:

- The Task Force on Climate-related Financial Disclosures (TFCD) has developed disclosure guidance that can be used by investors, lenders, and insurance underwriters to assess climate-related risks that are material for evaluation of a company's income statement and balance sheet. Climate-related disclosures should describe the company's strategy, processes, and metrics for identifying, assessing, and managing climate-related risks. They should also describe the role of executive management and board oversight in addressing those risks. The TFCD recommends that climate-related disclosures be incorporated into a publicly traded company's annual financial filings in accordance with national disclosure requirements. Climate-related disclosures that are incompatible with those requirements should be incorporated into other reports that are made available to investors and others.[116]
- The CDSB Framework, which was developed by the Climate Disclosure Standards Board, helps organizations present environmental and social information on climate, water, biodiversity, and social matters in reports they submit to regulatory authorities and the public. The CDSB Frame-

work, which was developed for the benefit of investors, connects an organization's sustainability performance to its current and future business strategy, financial condition, operational results, and prospects. The CDSB Framework is designed to produce disclosures that are clear, understandable, and verifiable. It is compatible with current and emerging regulations for sustainability disclosures, and it aligns with the recommendations of the Task Force on Climate-Related Financial Disclosures.[117]

- The IFRS Foundation, which oversees the International Accounting Standards Board, formed the International Sustainability Standards Board through consolidation of the Climate Disclosure Standards Board and the Value Reporting Foundation in late 2021. The Value Reporting Foundation, which was itself formed by a merger of the Sustainability Accounting Standards Board (SASB) and the International Integrated Reporting Council (IIRC), has developed standards to guide corporate disclosure of sustainability information that is financially material for investment decisions. The standards identify ESG issues that are relevant for financial performance in seventy-seven industries in eleven sectors, ranging from extractives and minerals processing to consumer goods.[118]
- Standards developed by Global Reporting Initiative (GRI) present global best practices for public disclosure of the environmental and social impact of an organization's activities. The disclosures are intended for policymakers, investors, and other stakeholders. The GRI standards specify the types of non-financial information to be disclosed about environmental and social matters. GRI's universal standards apply to a broad spectrum of organizations. Sector-specific standards have been developed for agriculture, aquaculture, fishing, oil, and other industries with a high environmental and social impact.[119]
- The CFA Institute, a nonprofit association of investment professionals, has developed standards, compliance requirements, and interpretive guidance for disclosures by investment managers related to the social and environmental impacts of listed equities, pooled funds, real estate, private debt, and other investment products. These standards and guidance support investment strategies and decisions based on sustainability factors.[120]
- CDP, a nonprofit charity, has implemented a global disclosure platform that collects information from companies and other entities about their business practices that impact the environment, including climate change, forests, and water security. The CDP platform provides online questionnaires that collect information about participants' policies, risks, strategies, targets, and other environmental matters. In addition to a general questionnaire, the CDP platform includes special questions for companies in sectors with a high environmental impact. The CDP platform includes reporting guidance to explain and clarify the questions.[121]

These ESG disclosure frameworks reflect the growing interest in and need for reliable information about the environmental and social impact of investments. While they are compatible with regulatory disclosure requirements, ESG disclosure frameworks do not have the force of law. Compliance is voluntary. As its principal benefit, compliance promotes trust by investors who are concerned about what companies are doing to combat climate charge, reduce carbon emissions, preserve air and water quality, hire a diverse workforce, and avoid corruption.[122] In particular, ESG disclosure frameworks counteract so-called greenwashing disclosures that exaggerate or otherwise misrepresent the ESG characteristics of investment products.[123]

SUMMARY OF MAJOR POINTS

- Information access and information disclosure are related but not synonymous concepts. Information access is the act of obtaining or retrieving information, either electronically or physically, from the location or repository where is stored. With information disclosure, an individual or organization who has custody of or access to information reveals or otherwise makes it available to another party who did not previously know it.
- At least half of the world's countries have some type of freedom-of-information legislation that grants a presumptive right to access information maintained by government agencies and other public bodies, subject to exclusions related to criminal law enforcement, national security, and foreign intelligence.
- At least half of the world's countries have data protection laws that grant data subjects the right of access to their own personal information. These laws also allow data subjects to request changes if information maintained about them is inaccurate or incomplete. In the United States, which does not have omnibus data protection or privacy legislation, a right to access one's own personal information is a component of various federal and state laws.
- Shareholder access laws give individual shareholders of a corporation the right to inspect and copy information that the corporation does not disclose to all shareholders or to the general public.
- Various laws and regulations require companies and government agencies to proactively disclose certain information related to suspected criminal activity or to potential threats to public health and safety.
- Data protection and privacy laws prohibit the disclosure of personal information unless it is expressly authorized by law or the data subject freely consents to the disclosure.
- Various national and subnational laws prohibit the disclosure of nonpersonal information that is not generally known, that is identified as confidential by the person or organization who possesses it, and that could have an adverse impact on a person or organization if it becomes more widely known.

- Legal prohibitions on the disclosure of personal or nonpersonal information can be overridden by a court order in the context of civil or criminal litigation.
- Professional privilege laws prevent the court-ordered disclosure of confidential information that a person shares with certain professionals, including attorneys, doctors, and psychotherapists.
- To protect an organization's information from unauthorized use, contracts typically limit the data or documents that a contractor's employees can access. A contract or other agreement may also include restrictions on disclosure of personal or nonpublic information that a contractor acquires in the course of its work.
- Ethical codes and other norms developed by professional associations parallel the requirements of privacy and data protection legislation in limiting the disclosure of confidential information that doctors, lawyers, and other professionals obtain in the course of their work.
- Rules for and restrictions on employee access to information are specified in an organization's internal policies. An access control policy defines the conditions under which employees' access to information is permitted or restricted. A disclosure policy specifies when and under what conditions an employee who has access to information can share it with others. A privacy policy specifies how an organization will safeguard the personal information it creates, collects, and maintains about its employees, clients, customers, suppliers, and others.
- Sustainability disclosures provide information about the financial impact of social and environmental concerns on listed equities, pooled funds, real estate, private debt, and other investment products.

NOTES

1. See 45 C.F.R. § 160.103, which defines disclosure as the release, transfer, provision of access to, or divulging any manner of information outside the entity holding the information, https://www.law.cornell.edu/cfr/text/45/160.103.
2. See, for example, the Universal Declaration of Human Rights, article 19, https://www.ohchr.org/en/human-rights/universal-declaration/translations/english; the International Covenant on Civil and Political Rights, article 19, https://www.ohchr.org/en/instruments-mechanisms/instruments/international-covenant-civil-and-political-rights.
3. Brisbane Declaration, May 3, 2010, http://www.unesco.org/new/en/unesco/events/prizes-and-celebrations/celebrations/international-days/world-press-freedom-day/previous-celebrations/2010/brisbane-declaration/. See also the Maputo Declaration, May 3, 2008, http://www.unesco.org/new/en/unesco/events/prizes-and-celebrations/celebrations/international-days/world-press-freedom-day/previous-celebrations/worldpressfreedomday2009001/maputo-declaration/.
4. 38C/Resolution 57, https://unesdoc.unesco.org/ark:/48223/pf0000243325.locale=en.

5. For a list, see http://www.freedominfo.org/?p=18223. See also J. Ackerman and I. Sandoval-Ballesteros, "The global explosion of freedom of information laws," *Administrative Law Review* 58 (1), 85–130 (2006), http://www.jstor.org/stable/40712005; P. Birkinshaw, *Freedom of Information: The Law, the Practice, and the Ideal* (Cambridge: Cambridge University Press, 2010); G. Michener, "FOI laws around the world," *Journal of Democracy* 22 (2), 145–59 (2011), https://doi.org/10.1353/jod.2011.0021.
6. SFS 2009:400, https://www.riksdagen.se/sv/dokument-lagar/dokument/svensk-forfattningssamling/offentlighets—och-sekretesslag-2009400_sfs-2009-400; Public Access to Information and Secrecy: the Legislation in Brief, https://www.government.se/4a72cf/contentassets/2ca7601373824c8395fc-1f38516e6e03/public-access-to-information-and-secrecy.pdf.
7. Act on the Openness of Government Activities, 21.5.1999/621, https://finlex.fi/fi/laki/ajantasa/1999/19990621, and its predecessor, 83/1951, https://finlex.fi/fi/laki/smur/1951/19510083.
8. 5 U.S.C. § 552—Public information; agency rules, opinions, orders, records, and proceedings, https://www.law.cornell.edu/uscode/text/5/552.
9. C. Schouten, "Who files the most FOIA requests? It's not who you think," *Columbia Journalism Review*, March 17, 2017, https://perma.cc/UTQ3-DCU4.
10. Access to Information Act (R.S.C., 1985, c. A-1), https://laws-lois.justice.gc.ca/eng/acts/A-1/index.html.
11. Freedom of Information Act 1982 (No. 3, 1982), https://www.legislation.gov.au/Details/C2022C00056.
12. Freedom of Information Act 2000, c. 36, https://www.legislation.gov.uk/ukpga/2000/36/contents.
13. Open Government Regulations of the People's Republic of China, https://perma.cc/CP3T-AR4H. See https://www.loc.gov/item/global-legal-monitor/2019-09-10/china-open-government-regulations-revised/.
14. See https://gdpr-info.eu/art-15-gdpr/.
15. Directive (EU) 2016/680 of April 27, 2016, On the protection of natural persons with regard to the processing of personal data by competent authorities for the purposes of the prevention, investigation, detection or prosecution of criminal offences or the execution of criminal penalties, and on the free movement of such data, https://eur-lex.europa.eu/legal-content/EN/TXT/PDF/?uri=CELEX-:32016L0680&from=EN.
16. See https://eur-lex.europa.eu/LexUriServ/LexUriServ.do?uri=CELEX-:31995L0046:EN:HTML.
17. See https://www.priv.gc.ca/en/privacy-topics/privacy-laws-in-canada/the-personal-information-protection-and-electronic-documents-act-pipeda/p_principle/principles/p_access/.
18. Australian Privacy Principles, Ch. 12, access to personal information, https://www.oaic.gov.au/privacy/australian-privacy-principles-guidelines/chapter-12-app-12-access-to-personal-information; Privacy Act 1988, https://www.legislation.gov.au/Details/C2021C00452.
19. 5 U.S.C. § 552a, https://www.law.cornell.edu/uscode/text/5/552a.
20. 20 U.S.C. § 1232g, https://www.law.cornell.edu/uscode/text/20/1232g; 34 C.F.R. Part 99, https://www.law.cornell.edu/cfr/text/34/part-99. Other countries have similar laws. In Canada, for example, Section 266(4)(b) of the Ontario Education

Act gives students and their parents the right to access their educational records and to request the correction or removal of inaccurate information.
21. 15 U.S.C. § 6502, https://www.law.cornell.edu/uscode/text/5/552a.
22. 15 U.S.C. § 1681g, https://www.law.cornell.edu/uscode/text/15/1681g.
23. Cal. Civ. Code, § 1798.100 et seq., https://leginfo.legislature.ca.gov/faces/codes_displayText.xhtml?division=3.&part=4.&lawCode=CIV&title=1.81.5.
24. Va. Code § 59.1-571 et seq., https://lis.virginia.gov/cgi-bin/legp604.exe?212+ful+CHAP0036+pdf; Colo. Rev. Stat. § 6-1-1301 et seq., https://leg.colorado.gov/sites/default/files/2021a_190_signed.pdf.
25. The HIPAA Privacy Rule, 45 C.F.R. § 164.524, https://www.law.cornell.edu/cfr/text/45/164.524.
26. New York Public Health Law, Section 18, https://www.nysenate.gov/legislation/laws/PBH/18.
27. Data Protection Working Party, Guidelines on Data Protection Officers, https://ec.europa.eu/newsroom/article29/items/612048.
28. American Bar Association, Model Business Corporation Act, 2016 revision, https://www.americanbar.org/content/dam/aba/administrative/business_law/corplaws/2016_mbca.authcheckdam.pdf; Corporate Laws Committee, ABA Business Section, "Changes in the Model Business Corporation Act—Proposed Amendments to Chapter 16," *Business Lawyer* 71 (2), 547-88 (2016), https://www.jstor.org/stable/26417570. See also, J. Velasco, "The fundamental rights of the shareholder," *UC Davis Law Review* 40 (2), 4-7-467 (2006), https://lawreview.law.ucdavis.edu/issues/40/2/articles/DavisVol40No2_Velasco.pdf; B. Jeffries, "Shareholder access to corporate books and records: the abrogation debate," *Drake Law Review* 59 (4), 108-64 (2011), https://lawreviewdrake.files.wordpress.com/2015/06/irvol59-4_jeffries-final.pdf.
29. Section 220 of Delaware's General Corporation Law, https://delcode.delaware.gov/title8/c001/sc07/index.html-220.
30. Canada Business Corporations Act, R.S.C., 1985 c. C-44, https://laws-lois.justice.gc.ca/eng/acts/c-44/fulltext.html. For examples of territorial corporation laws, see Ontario Business Corporations Act, R.S.O. 1990, C. B.16, https://www.ontario.ca/laws/statute/90b16-BK130, and British Columbia Corporations Act, SBC 2002, Ch, 57, https://www.bclaws.gov.bc.ca/civix/document/id/complete/statreg/02057_02-section46.
31. Companies Act 2006, c. 46, https://www.legislation.gov.uk/ukpga/2006/46/contents.
32. Companies Act 1993, https://www.legislation.govt.nz/act/public/1993/0105/latest/whole.html-DLM321137.
33. Corporations Act 2001, No. 50, 2001, https://www.legislation.gov.au/Details/C2018C00031.
34. Companies Act, No. 86 of July 26, 2005, https://wipolex-res.wipo.int/edocs/lexdocs/laws/en/jp/jp187en.pdf.
35. Companies Law of the People's Republic of China, October 27, 2005, article 34, https://www.ilo.org/dyn/natlex/docs/ELECTRONIC/92643/108008/F-186401967/CHN92643 Eng.pdf. For a discussion, see R. Huang, "Shareholder inspection right in China: an empirical inquiry," *Hastings International and Comparative Law Review* 44 (1), 3-37 (2021), https://repository.uchastings.edu/cgi/viewcontent.cgi?article=1855&context=hastings_international_comparative_law_review;

R. Huang and R. Thomas, "The Law and Practice of Shareholder Inspection Rights: A Comparative Analysis of China and U.S.," *Vanderbilt Journal of Transnational Law* 53 (3), 907-48 (2020), https://scholarship.law.vanderbilt.edu/cgi/viewcontent.cgi?article=1025&context=vjtl.
36. See, for example, D. Puchniak and S. Tang, *Limited Shareholder Inspection Rights in Singapore: Worrying Legal Gap or Unnecessary for Rankings?* ECGI Working Paper No. 608/2021 (Brussels: European Corporate Governance Institute, 2021), https://ecgi.global/sites/default/files/working_papers/documents/puchniaktangfinal.pdf.
37. https://www.uniformlaws.org/committees/community-home/librarydocuments/viewdocument?DocumentKey=92bf3cc8-8ef6-41aa-88d7-1871e5facbb8.
38. See, for example, https://vault.fbi.gov/reading-room-index-E, https://www.cia.gov/readingroom/home, https://www.archives.gov/foia/electronic-reading-room, https://www.nsa.gov/Helpful-Links/NSA-FOIA/Reading-Room/.
39. Open FOIL NY, ,https://www.ny.gov/programs/open-foil-ny-_blank.
40. See Regulation S-K (17 C.F.R. Part 229), https://www.law.cornell.edu/cfr/text/17/part-229; and Regulation S-X (17 C.F.R. Part 210), https://www.law.cornell.edu/cfr/text/17/part-210.
41. 31 C.F.R. Chapter X, https://www.law.cornell.edu/cfr/text/31/chapter-X; FinCEN Guidance on Preparing a Complete and Sufficient Suspicious Activity Report Narrative, https://www.fincen.gov/sites/default/files/shared/sarnarrcompletguidfinal_112003.pdf; M. Hall, "An emerging duty to report criminal conduct: banks, money laundering, and the suspicious activity report," *Kentucky Law Journal* 84 (3), 643-83 (1996), https://uknowledge.uky.edu/klj.
42. Directive 2004/109/EC on the harmonization of transparency requirements in relation to information about issuers whose securities are admitted to trading on a regulated market, https://eur-lex.europa.eu/legal-content/EN/TXT/?uri=celex%3A32004L0109.
43. Form 8K, Current Report pursuant to Section 13 or Section 15(d) of the Securities Exchange Act of 1934, https://www.sec.gov/files/form8-k.pdf.
44. Planning and Coordination Bureau, Financial Services Agency, Points to Note Regarding articles 27-36 of the Financial Instruments and Exchange Act (Fair Disclosure Rule Guidelines), April 2018, https://www.fsa.go.jp/en/laws_regulations/disclosure/20180206-2.pdf.
45. P. Krueger et al., *The Effects of Mandatory ESG Disclosure Around the World*, Finance Working Paper No. t54/2121 (Brussels: European Corporate Governance Institute, 2021), https://papers.ssrn.com/sol3/papers.cfm?abstract_id=3832745.
46. Directive 2014/95/EU amending Directive 2013/34/EU as regards disclosure of non-financial and diversity information by certain large undertakings and groups, https://eur-lex.europa.eu/legal-content/EN/TXT/?uri=CELEX%3A32014L0095.
47. The Companies Act 2006 (Strategic Report and Directors' Report) Regulations 2013, Part 7, https://www.legislation.gov.uk/ukdsi/2013/9780111540169.
48. H. Wang and D. Bernell, "Environmental disclosure in China: an examination of the green securities policy," *Journal of the Environment & Development* 22 (4), 339-69, https://doi.org/10.1177/1070496513506905; A. Wang, "Explaining environmental information disclosure in China," *Ecology Law Quarterly* 44 (4), 865-924 (2018), https://doi.org/10.15779/Z386688J63.

49. Guidance for Industry and Investigators: Safety Reporting Requirements for INDs and BA/BE Studies (Washington, DC: Food and Drug Administration, 2012), https://www.fda.gov/media/79394/download.
50. Post-marketing reporting of adverse drug experiences, 21 C.F.R. § 314.80, https://www.law.cornell.edu/cfr/text/21/314.80; in Canada, pharmaceutical manufacturers and hospitals must report adverse drug reactions and unusual efficacy failures to regulatory authorities. Food and Drug Regulations, C.R.C., C. 80m, Sections C.01.017 et seq, https://laws-lois.justice.gc.ca/eng/regulations/c.r.c.,_c._870/index.html; Good Pharmacovigilance Practices (GVP) Guidelines (GUI-0102), https://www.canada.ca/en/health-canada/services/drugs-health-products/compliance-enforcement/good-manufacturing-practices/guidance-documents/pharmacovigilance-guidelines-0102.html. In EU member states, manufacturers must submit adverse reaction reports to the European Medicines Agency. See M. Kaeding et al., *Pharmacovigilance in the European Union: Practical Implementation Across Member States* (Wiesbaden: Springer, 2017), https://library.oapen.org/bitstream/handle/20.500.12657/27845/1002159.pdf?sequence=1.
51. World Health Organization, *International Health Regulations* (Geneva: WHO Press, 2008). D. Fidler and L. Gostin, "The new International Health Regulations: an historic development for international law and public health," *Journal of Law, Medicine & Ethics* 34 (1), 85–94, https://doi.org/10.1111/j.1748-720X.2006.00011.x.
52. A. Janati et al., "Communicable disease reporting systems in the world: a systematic review article," *Iranian Journal of Public Health* 44 (11), 1453–65 (2015), https://www.ncbi.nlm.nih.gov/pmc/articles/PMC4703224/; W. Parmet, "Communicable disease law in the United States," in D. Orentlicher and T. Hervey, eds., *The Oxford Handbook of Comparative Health Law* (Oxford: Oxford University Press, 2021), 119–42; M. Frischhut and S. Greer, "EU public health law and policy—communicable diseases," in T. Hervey et al., *Research Handbook on EU Health Law and Policy* (Cheltenham, UK: Edward Elgar, 2017), 315–46.
53. B. Liu and M. Vaughan, "Legal and policy issues from the United States and internationally about mandatory reporting of child abuse," *International Journal of Law and Psychiatry* 64, 219–29 (2019), https://doi.org/10.1016/j.ijlp.2019.03.007; B. Mathews and M. Kenny, "Mandatory reporting legislation in the United States, Canada, and Australia: a cross-jurisdictional review of key features, differences, and issues," *Child Maltreatment* 13 (1), 50–63 (2008), https://doi.org/10.1177/1077559507310613; B. Mathews and D. Bross, eds., *Mandatory Reporting Laws and the Identification of Severe Child Abuse and Neglect* (Dordrecht: Springer 2015).
54. M. Rodriguez et al., "Mandatory reporting of elder abuse: between a rock and a hard place," *Annals of Family Medicine* 4 (5), 403–09 (2006), https://doi.org/10.1370/afm.575; P. Mixson, "Public policy, elder abuse, and adult protective services: the struggle for coherence," *Journal of Elder Abuse and Neglect* 22 (1–2), 16–36 (2010), https://doi.org/10.1080/08946560903436148.
55. M. Baram, "The right to know and the duty to disclose hazard information," *American Journal of Public Health* 74 (4), 385–90 (1984), https://ajph.aphapublications.org/doi/pdf/10.2105/AJPH.74.4.385; P. Sand, "The right to know: freedom of environmental information in comparative and international law," *Tulane Journal of International and Comparative Law* 20 (1), 4–30 (2011), https://www.academia.edu/15103396/The_Right_to_Know_Freedom_of_Environmental_Information_in_Comparative_and

_International_Law; T. Emerson, "Legal foundations of the right to know," *Washington University Law Quarterly* 1976, no. 1 (1976), 1–24, https://openscholarship.wustl.edu/cgi/viewcontent.cgi?article=2625&context=law_lawreview.
56. 42 U.S.C. § 11004, 42 U.S.C. § 11004; S. Wolf, "Fear and loathing about the public right to know: the surprising success of the Emergency Planning and Community Right-to-Know Act," *Journal of Land Use and Environmental Law* 11 (2), 218–313 (1996), https://ir.law.fsu.edu/cgi/viewcontent.cgi?article=1148&context=jluel.
57. 42 U.S.C. § 300f et seq., https://www.law.cornell.edu/uscode/text/42/chapter-6A/subchapter-XII.
58. Canadian Environmental Protection Act, 1999 (S.C. 1999, C. 33), https://laws-lois.justice.gc.ca/PDF/C-15.31.pdf.
59. Hazard Communication Standard, https://www.osha.gov/laws-regs/regulations/standardnumber/1910/1910.1200; Council Directive 89/391/EEC on the introduction of measures to encourage improvements in the safety and health of workers at work, https://eur-lex.europa.eu/legal-content/EN/ALL/?uri=celex%3A31989L0391. See also N. Ashford and C. Caldart, "The 'right to know': toxics information transfer in the workplace," *Annual Review of Public Health* 6, 383–401 (1985), https://www.annualreviews.org/doi/pdf/10.1146/annurev.pu.06.050185.002123; J. Millar, "The right to know in the workplace: the moral dimension," *Annals of the New York Academy of Sciences* 572, 113–21 (1989), https://doi.org/10.1111/j.1749-6632.1989.tb13584.x.
60. AML Fines 2021, https://www.kyckr.com/aml-fines-2021/.
61. General Data Protection Regulation, especially articles 5–7, 44–50 and recitals 32, 42–50, https://gdpr-info.eu/.
62. See B. Srinivas, *A Concise Guide to Various Australian Laws Related to Privacy and Cybersecurity Domains* (Bethesda, MD: SANS Institute, 2015), https://www.sans.org/reading-room/whitepapers/legal/concise-guide-australian-laws-related-privacy-cybersecurity-domains-36072; *Privacy Guide: A Guide to Compliance with Privacy Laws in Australia* (Melbourne: Justice Connect, 2017), https://www.nfplaw.org.au/sites/default/files/media/Privacy_Guide_Cth.pdf.
63. Public Act 2020, No. 31, https://www.legislation.govt.nz/act/public/2020/0031/latest/LMS23223.html.
64. For a survey of these privacy laws and regulations, see V. Jones, *Requirements for Personal Information Protection, Part 1: U.S. Federal Law* (Pittsburgh: ARMA International Educational Foundation, 2008), www.armaedfoundation.org/pdfs/FederalPrivacy.pdf; and V. Jones, *Requirements for Personal Information Protection, Part 2: U.S. State Laws* (Pittsburgh: ARMA International Educational Foundation, 2009), www.armaedfoundation.org/pdfs/Requirements_for_Personal_Information_US_States.pdf.
65. 45 C.F.R. Subpart E—Privacy of individually Identifiable Health Information, https://www.law.cornell.edu/cfr/text/45/part-164/subpart-E.
66. See J. Feder, *The Family Educational Rights and Privacy Act (FERPA): a Legal Overview* (Washington, DC: Congressional Research Service, 2013), https://www.higheredcompliance.org/wp-content/uploads/2018/10/CRS_FERPAOverview_2013_11_19.pdf; K. Surprenant et al., *IDEA and FERPA Confidentiality Provisions* (Washington, DC: U.S. Department of Education, 2014), https://www2.ed.gov/policy/gen/guid/ptac/pdf/idea-ferpa.pdf.
67. 16 C.F.R. § 312—Parental Consent, https://www.law.cornell.edu/cfr/text/16/312.5.

68. 26 U.S.C § 6103, https://www.law.cornell.edu/uscode/text/26/6103.
69. 18 U.S.C. § 2721, https://www.law.cornell.edu/uscode/text/18/2721.
70. 15 U.S.C. §§ 6801, https://www.law.cornell.edu/uscode/text/15/6801.
71. For links to applicable state laws on confidentiality of library records, see http://www.ala.org/advocacy/privacy/statelaws.
72. 18 U.S.C. § 2721, https://www.law.cornell.edu/uscode/text/18/2721.
73. New York City Administrative Code § 10-180, Unlawful disclosure of an intimate image, https://codelibrary.amlegal.com/codes/newyorkcity/latest/NYCadmin/0-0-0-6808; D.C. Code § 22-3052, Unlawful disclosure, https://code.dccouncil.us/us/dc/council/code/sections/22-3052.html; Uniform Law Commission, Civil Remedies for Unauthorized Disclosure of Intimate Images Act, https://www.uniformlaws.org/committees/community-home?CommunityKey=668f6afa-f7b5-444b-9f0a-6873fb617ebb.
74. A. Quist, *Security Classification of Information, Volume 2: Principles for Classification of Information* (Oak Ridge, TN: Oak Ridge National Laboratory, 1993), https://www.osti.gov/servlets/purl/6934153. See also *Government Security Classifications* (London: Cabinet Office 2018), https://assets.publishing.service.gov.uk/government/uploads/system/uploads/attachment_data/file/715778/May-2018_Government-Security-Classifications-2.pdf.
75. 18 U.S.C. § 798, https://www.law.cornell.edu/uscode/text/18/798; 18 U.S.C. § 1030, https://www.law.cornell.edu/uscode/text/18/1030; 18 U.S.C. § 794, https://www.law.cornell.edu/uscode/text/18/794.
76. Security of Information Act, R.S.C., 1985, c. 0-5, https://laws-lois.justice.gc.ca/eng/acts/o-5/fulltext.html; Criminal Code Act 1995, Part 5.6, https://www.legislation.gov.au/Details/C2022C00065; Official Secrets Act 1989, https://www.legislation.gov.uk/ukpga/1989/6/contents.
77. 18 U.S.C. § 1832, https://www.law.cornell.edu/uscode/text/18/1832.
78. Uniform Trade Secrets Act, https://www.uniformlaws.org/viewdocument/final-act-128?CommunityKey=3a2538fb-e030-4e2d-a9e2-90373dc05792&tab=librarydocuments.
79. Directive (EU) 2016/943 on the protection of undisclosed know-how and business information (trade secrets) against their unlawful acquisition, use and disclosure, https://eur-lex.europa.eu/legal-content/EN/TXT/?uri=CELEX:32016L0943.
80. 17 C.F.R. Part 243, https://www.law.cornell.edu/cfr/text/17/243.100; Financial Conduct Authority, Market Abuse Regulation 1.4, https://www.handbook.fca.org.uk/handbook/MAR/1/4.html; Regulation (EU) No 596 /2014 on market abuse, https://eur-lex.europa.eu/legal-content/EN/TXT/?uri=CELEX%3A02014R0596-20210101; J. Thompson, "A global comparison of insider trading regulations," *International Journal of Accounting and Finance* 3 (1), 1–23 (2013), https://doi.org/10.5296/ijafr.v3i1.3369.
81. 18 U.S.C. § 842, https://www.law.cornell.edu/uscode/text/18/842.
82. See https://www.fincen.gov/resources/statutes-regulations/guidance/unauthorized-disclosure-suspicious-activity-reports.
83. See, for example, Ariz. Crim. Code 13-2813, https://codes.findlaw.com/az/title-13-criminal-code/az-rev-st-sect-13-2813.html; N.Y. Penal Law 215.75, https://codes.findlaw.com/ny/penal-law/pen-sect-215-75.html.
84. Law No. 80-538, https://www.legifrance.gouv.fr/jorf/id/JORFTEXT000000515863/.

85. UK Protection of Trading Interests Act 1980, https://www.legislation.gov.uk/ukpga/1980/11; Canadian Foreign Extraterritorial Measures Act, R.S.C, 1985, c. F-29, https://laws-lois.justice.gc.ca/eng/acts/f-29/index.html. Publications that provide background information about blocking statutes include K. Alexander, *Economic Sanctions* (London: Palgrave MacMillan, 2009), esp. 224-57, https://link.springer.com/chapter/10.1057/9780230227286_9; K. Nakata, "The SEC and foreign blocking statutes: need for a balanced approach," *University of Pennsylvania Journal of International Business Law* 9, no. 3, 549-91, https://www.law.upenn.edu/journals/jil/articles/volume9/issue3/Nakata9U.Pa.J.Int%27l-Bus.L.549%281987%29.pdf; H. Dahl, "Forum non conveniens, Latin America and blocking statutes," *University of Miami Inter-American Law Review* 35, no. 1 (2004), 21-63, https://repository.law.miami.edu/cgi/viewcontent.cgi?referer=https://www.google.com/&httpsredir=1&article=1189&context=umialr; M. Hoda, "The Aerospatiale dilemma: why U.S. courts ignore blocking statutes and what foreign states can do about it," *California Law Review* 106, no. 1 (2018), 231-61, https://scholarship.law.berkeley.edu/cgi/viewcontent.cgi?article=4394&context=californialawreview; and V. Curran, "United States discovery and foreign blocking statutes," *Louisiana Law Review* 76, no. 4 (2016), 1142-49; https://digitalcommons.law.lsu.edu/cgi/viewcontent.cgi?article=6583&context=lalrev.
86. S. Mullgan and J. Elsea, *Criminal Prohibitions on Leaks and Other Disclosures of Classified Defense Information* (Washington, DC: Congressional Research Service, 2017), https://sgp.fas.org/crs/secrecy/R41404.pdf.
87. F. Sensenbrenner and M. Ryznar, "The law and economics of insider trading," *Wake Forest Law Review* 50 (5), 1155-79 (2015), https://scholarworks.iupui.edu/bitstream/handle/1805/11586/Ryznar_2015_law.pdf?sequence=1&isAllowed=y.
88. J. Ulatowski and R. Walker, "Missing in action: Exposing the moral failures of universities that desert researchers facing court-ordered disclosure of confidential information, *Educational Philosophy and Theory* 53 (5), 536-47 (2020), https://doi.org/10.1080/00131857.2020.1830061; L. Beskow et al., "Certificates of confidentiality and compelled disclosure of data," *Science* 322 (5904), 1054-55 (2008), https://doi.org/10.1126/science.1164100; L. Du et al., "Compelled disclosure of confidential information in patient safety research," *Journal of Patient Safety* 17 (3), 200-06 (2021), https://doi.org/10.1097/PTS.0000000000000293; K. Drake and R. Maundrell, "Researcher-participant privilege, confidentiality, and the jailhouse blues," *McGill Journal of Law and Health* 10 (2), 1-25 (2017), https://mjlh.mcgill.ca/publications/volume-10-issue-2-102-2017/researcher-participant-privilege-confidentiality-and-the-jailhouse-blues/.
89. T. Garvey and E. Liu, *The State Secrets Privilege: Preventing the Disclosure of Sensitive National Information During Civil Litigation* (Washington, DC: Congressional Research Service, 2011), https://www.ipmall.info/sites/default/files/hosted_resources/crs/R41741_110816.pdf.
90. 18a U.S.C. Compiled Act 96-456, https://www.law.cornell.edu/uscode/text/18a/compiledact-96-456.
91. See, for example, Rule 37, Federal Rules of Civil Procedure, https://www.law.cornell.edu/rules/frcp/rule_37.
92. D. Shuman, "The origins of the physician-patient privilege and professional secret," *Souuthwestern Law Journal* 39 (2-3), 661-87 (2016), https://scholar.smu.edu/cgi/viewcontent.cgi?article=3315&context=smulr; M. Wilkinson, "Codification

and the origins of physician-patient privilege," *Journal of Policy History* 32 (1), 78-102 (2020), https://doi.org/10.1017/S0898030619000289.
93. See, for example, Rules of the Board of Regents, 8 NYCRR 29.1, http://www.op.nysed.gov/title8/part29.htm. For a summary of selected state physician-privilege laws, see https://healthcare.uslegal.com/doctor-patient-confidentiality/select-state-disclosure-laws/.
94. 26 U.S.C. § 7525, https://www.law.cornell.edu/uscode/text/26/7525.
95. C. Bartholomew, "Exorcising the clergy privilege," *Virginia Law Review* 103 (6), 1015-77 (2017), https://digitalcommons.law.buffalo.edu/cgi/viewcontent.cgi?article=1036&context=journal_articles; A. al-Hibri, "The Muslim perspective on the clergy-penitent privilege," *Loyola of Los Angeles Law Review* 29 (4), 1723-32 (1996), https://scholarship.richmond.edu/cgi/viewcontent.cgi?article=1161&-context=law-faculty-publications.
96. For an overview of nondisclosure agreements, see C. Montville, "Reforming the law of proprietary information," *Duke Law Journal* 56 (4), 1159-200 (2007), https://scholarship.law.duke.edu/cgi/viewcontent.cgi?article=1316&context=dlj.
97. 42 U.S.C. § 241, https://www.law.cornell.edu/uscode/text/42/241.
98. OECD/Legal/0188, adopted in 1989, amended in 2013, https://legalinstruments.oecd.org/en/instruments/OECD-LEGAL-0188.
99. *The Keys to Data Protection: a Guide for Policy Engagement on Data Protection* (London: Privacy International, 2018), https://privacyinternational.org/report/2255/data-protection-guide-complete.
100. APEC Privacy Framework (Singapore: APEC Secretariat, 2005), https://www.apec.org/docs/default-source/publications/2005/12/apec-privacy-framework/05_ecsg_privacyframewk.pdf?sfvrsn=d3de361d_1; Cross Border Privacy Rules System, http://cbprs.org/documents/.
101. J. Moskop et al., "From Hippocrates to HIPAA: Privacy and confidentiality in emergency medicine—Part I: Conceptual, moral, and legal foundations," *Annals of Emergency Medicine* 45 (1), 53-59 (2004), https://doi.org/10.1016/j.annemergmed.2004.08.008.
102. Code of Medical Ethics, Opinion 3.2.1, https://www.ama-assn.org/delivering-care/ethics/confidentiality.
103. F. Riddick Jr., "The Code of medical ethics of the American Medical Association," *Ochsner Journal* 5 (2), 6-10 (2003), https://www.ncbi.nlm.nih.gov/pmc/articles/PMC3399321/; When to Disclose Confidential Information, https://www.cmpa-acpm.ca/en/advice-publications/browse-articles/2015/when-to-disclose-confidential-information; Confidentiality: Good Practice in Handling Medical Information, https://www.gmc-uk.org/-/media/documents/gmc-guidance-for-doctors—-confidentiality-good-practice-in-handling-patient-information——70080105.pdf.
104. Ethical Principles of Psychologists and Code of Conduct, Section 4, https://www.apa.org/ethics/code.
105. NASW Code of Ethics, Section 1.07, https://www.socialworkers.org/About/Ethics/Code-of-Ethics/Code-of-Ethics-English.
106. AMHCA Code of Ethics: Ethical Priorities for Clinical Mental Health Counseling, Section IA2c, https://www.amhca.org/HigherLogic/System/DownloadDocumentFile.ashx?DocumentFileKey=24a27502-196e-b763-ff57-490a12f7edb1&-forceDialog=0.

107. ASHA Code of Ethics, https://www.asha.org/code-of-ethics/; Code of Ethics for Physical Therapists, https://www.apta.org/siteassets/pdfs/policies/codeofethicshods06-20-28-25.pdf; Occupational Therapy Code of Ethics, https://research.aota.org/ajot/article/74/Supplement_3/7413410005p1/6691/AOTA-2020-Occupational-Therapy-Code-of-Ethics; CRCC Enforceable Standards of Ethical Practice, https://crccertification.com/wp-content/uploads/2021/03/CRC_CodeEthics_Eff2017-FinaLnewdiesign.pdf.
108. Model Rules of Professional Conduct, Rule 1.6, https://www.americanbar.org/groups/professional_responsibility/publications/model_rules_of_professional_conduct/rule_1_6_confidentiality_of_information/.
109. Common Code of Ethics for Chaplains, Pastoral Counselors, Pastoral Educators and Students, https://www.professionalchaplains.org/files/professional_standards/common_standards/common_code_ethics.pdf.
110. AICPA Code of Professional Conduct and Bylaws, https://us.aicpa.org/content/dam/aicpa/research/standards/codeofconduct/downloadabledocuments/2013june1codeofprofessionalconduct.pdf; CFB Board Code of Ethics and Standards of Conduct, https://www.cfp.net/ethics/code-of-ethics-and-standards-of-conduct; FSP Code of Professional Responsibility, https://societyoffsp.site-ym.com/page/FSPCode.
111. This is a paraphrase of the definition of access control policies used by the National Institute of Standards and Technology. See V. Hu et al., *Verification and Test Methods for Access Control Policies/Models*, NIST Special Publication 800-192, (Gaithersburg, MD: National Institute of Standards and Technology, 2017), https://nvlpubs.nist.gov/nistpubs/SpecialPublications/NIST.SP.800-192.pdf.
112. Examples of publications about open government include W. Parks, "The open government principle: applying the right to know under the Constitution," *George Washington Law Review* 26 (1), 1–77 (1957); D. Lathrop and L. Ruma, eds., *Open Government: Collaboration, Transparency, and Participation in Practice* (Sebastopol, Calif.: O'Reilly, 2010); R. Chapman and M. Hunt, eds., *Open Government in a Theoretical and Practical Context* (London: Routledge, 2006); A. McDonald and G. Terrill, eds., *Open Government: Freedom of Information and Privacy* (London: Macmillan, 1998); M. Gasco-Hernandez, *Open Government: Opportunities and Challenges for Public Governance* (New York: Springer, 2014); OECD, *Open Government and Way Forward* (Paris: OECD Publishing, 2016), https://doi.org/10.1787/9789264268104-en; K. Hansson et al., "Open government and democracy: a research review," *Social Science Computer Review* 33 (5), 540–55 (2014), https://doi.org/10.1177/0894439314560847.
113. United Nations Universal Declaration of Human Rights, https://www.un.org/sites/un2.un.org/files/udhr.pdf; the International Covenant on Civil and Political Rights, https://www.ohchr.org/en/instruments-mechanisms/instruments/international-covenant-civil-and-political-rights; European Convention on Human Rights, https://www.echr.coe.int/documents/convention_eng.pdf.
114. Regulation (EU) 2019/2088 on sustainability-related disclosures in the financial services sector, https://eur-lex.europa.eu/legal-content/EN/TXT/PDF/?uri=CELEX:32019R2088&from=EN.
115. Proposal for a directive amending Directive 2013/34/EU, Directive 2004/109/EC, Directive 2006/43/EC and Regulation (ED) No 537/2104, as regards cor-

porate sustainability reporting, https://eur-lex.europa.eu/legal-content/EN/TX-T/?uri=CELEX:52021PC0189.
116. Recommendations of the Task Force on Climate-related Disclosures, https://assets.bbhub.io/company/sites/60/2021/10/FINAL-2017-TCFD-Report.pdf.
117. CDSB Framework for Reporting Environmental & Social Information, https://www.cdsb.net/sites/default/files/cdsb_framework_2022.pdf.
118. SASB Standards, https://www.sasb.org/about/.
119. GRI Standards, https://www.globalreporting.org/how-to-use-the-gri-standards/gri-standards-english-language/.
120. Global ESG Disclosure Standards for Investment Products, https://www.cfainstitute.org/-/media/documents/ESG-standards/Global-ESG-Disclosure-Standards-for-Investment-Products.pdf.
121. See https://www.cdp.net/en.
122. P. Krueger et al., *The Effects of Mandatory ESG Disclosure around the World,* ECGI Working Paper No. 754/2021 (Brussels: European Corporate Governance Institute, 2021), https://papers.ssrn.com/sol3/papers.cfm?abstract_id=3832745; N. Raimo et al., "Extending the benefits of ESG disclosure: the effect on the cost of debt financing," *Corporate Social Responsibility and Environmental Management* 28 (4), 1412-21 (2021), https://doi.org/10.1002/csr.2134; J. Xie et al., "Do environmental, social and governance activities improve corporate financial performance?" *Business Strategy and the Environment* 28 (2), 286–300 (2019), https://doi.org/10.1002/bse.2224; El Yu et al., "Environmental, social and governance transparency and firm value," *Business Strategy and the Environment* 27 (7), 987-1004 (2018), https://doi.org/10.1002/bse.2047.
123. C. Ramus and I. Montiel, "When are corporate environmental policies a form of greenwashing?," *Business & Society* 44 (4), 377–414 (2005), https://doi.org/10.1177/0007650305278120; W.Laufer, "Social accountability and corporate greenwashing," *Journal of Business Ethics* 43 (3), 253-61 (2003), https://doi.org/10.1023/A:1022962719299; M. Delmas and V. Burbano, "The drivers of greenwashing," *California Management Review* 54 (1), 64-87 (2011), https://doi.org/10.1525/cmr.2011.54.1.64; C. Marquis et al., "Scrutiny, norms, and selective disclosure: a global study of greenwashing," *Organization Science* 27 (2), 483-504 (2016), https://doi.org/10.1287/orsc.2015.1039; J. Vos, "Actions speak louder than words: greenwashing in corporate America," *Notre Dame Journal of Legal Ethics and Public Policy* 23 (2), 673-97 (2009), https://scholarship.law.nd.edu/cgi/viewcontent.cgi?article=1111&context=ndjlepp.

6

Information Security and Protection

The preceding chapter discussed compliance requirements and controls for access to and disclosure of nonpublic information. The information security and protection requirements discussed in this chapter provide operational support for those access and disclosure requirements. Information security and protection encompasses administrative, technical, and physical measures that preserve the confidentiality, integrity, and availability of information—attributes that are termed the "CIA triad," a designation that has no relationship to the U.S. Central Intelligence Agency or any other entity that uses that abbreviation.[1] The compliance requirements discussed in this chapter apply to personal or business information that is not intended for disclosure to the general public. Information that is publicly available presumably requires no security safeguards.

As with other topics discussed in this book, compliance requirements for information security and protection are specified in laws and regulations, which are often referenced—along with other information security and protection obligations—in contracts and other legally binding agreements. Information security and protection requirements are also presented in international standards and in the internal policies of government agencies, companies, and nonprofit organizations. Societal compliance requirements address ethical issues associated with information security and protection, most notably in the context of cyberwarfare.

LEGAL AND REGULATORY COMPLIANCE

Three types of legislation specify compliance requirements for security and protection of nonpublic personal and business information maintained by government agencies, companies, and nonprofit entities:

- Laws and regulations that require government agencies and non-governmental organizations to develop and implement a security program for nonpublic information

- Laws and regulations that criminalize data breaches, theft of information, and other security violations that involve unauthorized access to or use of nonpublic information
- Laws and regulations that require organizations to report data breaches involving nonpublic information to designated supervisory authorities or, in the case of personal information, to the affected data subjects

As discussed in the following sections, most countries have national and/or subnational legislation in at least one of the above groups.

LAWS THAT MANDATE INFORMATION SECURITY

In the United States, the Federal Information Security Management Act (FISMA) establishes the foundation for information security in U.S. government agencies.[2] Signed into law in 2002 and amended in 2014, FISMA requires agency heads to develop, implement, and periodically evaluate policies and procedures to ensure the security of information and information systems that support agency operations and assets. OMB Circular A-130, which was first issued by the Office of Management and Budget in 1985 and subsequently revised, establishes minimum requirements for federal information security programs, including specific safeguards to protect information and information systems operated by federal agencies.[3] Agency security programs must comply with Federal Information Processing Standards (FIPS) for information and information systems that support executive agencies of the U.S. government, including FIPS PUB 199, which specifies security categorization requirements, and FIPS PUB 200, which specifies minimum security requirements.[4]

FISMA's information security requirements apply to information systems used or operated by contractors or others on a federal agency's behalf. OMB Circular A-130 specifies contractual and oversight requirements for federal information that is processed and stored on systems operated by nonfederal entities. In addition, federal regulations require defense contractors to provide adequate security for all unclassified information systems that process, store, or transmit military and space information that is subject to controls on access, use, reproduction, modification, performance, release, disclosure, or dissemination. Adequate security means protective measures commensurate with the consequences and probability of loss, misuse, or unauthorized access to or modification of information. Contractors are also subject to security requirements specified by the National Institute of Standards and Technology.[5]

Many states have laws or regulations that mandate security requirements for information and information systems that support state government operations. As an example, the California Government Code requires all state entities to establish an information security program that complies with policies, procedures, and requirements specified in the State Administrative Manual.[6] These security requirements apply to paper as well as electronic records. In most other states, information security laws focus on cybersecurity. The Florida State Cybersecurity Act is typical. It requires state agencies to implement a cybersecurity program based on the statewide cybersecurity strategic plan.[7] Similarly, Kansas law requires executive branch agencies to participate in the statewide cybersecurity program's initiatives and services.[8] Wyoming law requires every state agency to adopt and enforce a security program with administrative and physical safeguards for data that it collects and stores.[9] In North Dakota, the statewide cybersecurity strategy applies to local governments as well as state agencies.[10]

The United States does not have omnibus legislation that mandates the implementation and enforcement of information security policies and procedures by nongovernmental entities. A number of publications contend that information security policies and procedures are among the internal controls that publicly traded companies must implement for compliance with the Sarbanes-Oxley Act of 2002,[11] but information security is not mentioned in the act itself or in its implementing regulations. Various sector-specific laws and regulations do include information security requirements that are designed to protect personal information and serve the interests of regulatory authorities. Examples include the following:

- Among federal laws, the Health Insurance Portability and Accountability Act's Security Rule establishes nationwide standards for protecting patient information. The HIPAA Security Rule operationalizes the data protection provisions specified in the HIPAA Privacy Rule, which was discussed in chapter 5. It requires health-care providers, health plans, and health-care clearinghouses to implement appropriate administrative, technical, and physical safeguards to prevent unauthorized access to and use of patient information. A covered entity's security practices must be documented in written policies and procedures. The same security requirements apply to covered entities' business associates that perform certain functions or activities involving patient information on behalf of a covered entity. Unlike the HIPAA Privacy Rule, which protects patient information in all formats, the Security Rule is limited to electronic protected health information (ePHI), which is defined as any individually identifiable health information that is maintained or transmitted electronically by covered entitles and their business associates. The HIPAA Security Rule does not apply to paper health-care records or to individually identifiable patient information that is transmitted orally.[12]
- The Gramm-Leach-Bliley (GBL) Security Rule, which is a component of the federal Financial Services Modernization Act of 1999, requires certain financial service providers to develop and implement a security program that includes administrative, technical, and physical safeguards to protect customer information. The security program must be based on a

risk assessment that evaluates threats that could compromise customer information by unauthorized disclosure, misuse, alteration, or destruction. Customer information must be encrypted in transit and at rest. The GBL Security Rule, which is also known as FTC Safeguards Rule, applies to a covered entity's own employees and to any service providers that maintain customer information. Covered entities include all financial institutions over which the Federal Trade Commission has jurisdiction and that are not subject to the authority of another regulator. Examples of such financial institutions include mortgage lenders, payday lenders, finance companies, collection agencies, credit counselors, and tax preparation firms.[13]

- NERC CIP (Critical Infrastructure Protection) issued by the North American Electric Reliability Corporation defines a baseline set of cybersecurity requirements to manage the security of the Bulk Electric System in the United States and parts of Canada and Mexico. It requires utility companies to perform regular vulnerability assessments and implement IT controls with technical, operational, and procedural safeguards to protect information and information systems that impact the reliability of the Bulk Electric System. Utility companies must have a contingency and disaster recovery plan to respond to cybersecurity incidents and maintain business continuity. Personnel and contractors must receive periodic training to deal with cybersecurity threats and incidents. NERC CIP requirements have the force of federal regulations.
- About half of the states have laws that require companies to implement safeguards to protect personal information about state residents, but such laws do not necessarily mandate the implementation and enforcement of a comprehensive information security program. Among those that do, the California Security Breach Information Act, requires businesses that own or license information about a California resident to implement and maintain reasonable security procedures and practices to protect the information from unauthorized access, use, destruction, modification, or disclosure.[14] The Massachusetts Cybersecurity Law requires nongovernmental entities that own or license the personal data of state residents to implement an information security program with safeguards that are consistent with those of other laws to which the entity is subject. This requirement also applies to a nongovernmental entity's service providers.[15] In New York State, the Stop Hacks and Improve Electronic Data Security (SHIELD) Act requires companies to implement a cybersecurity program with administrative, technical, and physical safeguards to protect the security, confidentiality, and integrity of private personal information, which is defined broadly to include a data subject's biometric information, email addresses, and financial account numbers. The law has a broad territorial scope. It applies to businesses, regardless of location, that collect or have access to the personal data of New York State residents.[16]

- Connecticut, Ohio, and several other states have a "safe harbor" law that incentivizes the adoption of cybersecurity standards. Such laws allow business that have established and complied with a cybersecurity framework based on government or international standards to plead an affirmative defense to civil litigation related to failure to implement reasonable controls associated with a data breach involving personal information.[17] In New York State, the General Business Law lists criteria for a security program with reasonable administrative, technical, and physical safeguards for personal information. Such criteria include designating one or more employees to coordinate the security program, training employees, incorporating security safeguards into contracts with service providers, regularly testing and monitoring system controls and procedures, and protecting personal information against unauthorized access and use during collection, transport, and disposal. Organizations that comply with the HIPAA Security Rule or the Gramm-Leach-Bliley Security Rule are assumed to comply with New York State's requirements.[18]

Some states have adopted laws that require an information security program for business as well as personal information maintained by financial service providers. According to New York State Cybersecurity Requirements for Financial Services Companies, covered entities must maintain a cybersecurity program with written policies and controls for protection of nonpublic business and personal information, including information held by third-party service providers. The requirement applies to any companies that are licensed to operate under New York State's banking, insurance, and financial service laws.[19] More limited in scope, the Arkansas Fair Mortgage Lending Act requires mortgage bankers, mortgage brokers, and mortgage service providers to establish and implement cybersecurity and physical security policies and procedures to protect the confidentiality, integrity, and availability of information contained in electronic and non-electronic records.[20] Approximately 40 percent of the states have adopted versions the Insurance Data Security Model Law developed by the National Association of Insurance Commissioners. It requires insurers and other licensed entities to develop, implement, and maintain a program to protect the security of nonpublic information. It also gives insurance commissioners the authority to examine licensees for compliance and provide remedies for deficiencies.[21]

At the leading edge of a likely legislative trend, the California Internet of Things Cybersecurity Improvement Act of 2017 requires manufacturers to equip connected devices with reasonable security features to protect users' information from unauthorized access, destruction, use, modification, or disclosure.[22] At the federal level, the Internet of Things Cybersecurity Improvement Act of 2020 instructs the National Institute of Standards and Technology to develop security standards and guidelines for IoT devices used by U.S.

government agencies and federal contractors.[23] Addition IoT security legislation is likely in the future.

In Canada, the Personal Information Protection and Electronic Documents Act requires security safeguards to protect personal information against loss, theft, and unauthorized use. It provides a few examples of acceptable protection measures, including locked filing cabinets for paper records and the use of passwords and encryption for digital data.[24]

In other countries, Information security is a fundamental principle of national data protection legislation; but beyond asserting its importance, most data protection laws do not prescribe information security methods. In the GDPR, security is one of seven data protection principles. According to article 5, personal data must be processed in a manner that ensures "appropriate security . . . Including protection against unauthorized or unlawful processing and against accidental loss, destruction, or damage, using technical or organizational measures."[25] According to article 32, these measure must ensure the confidentiality, integrity, availability, and resilience of systems and services that process personal information, but neither the regulation nor its recitals specify what information security procedures an organization must implement to attain these objectives or how compliance is evaluated.[26] The GDPR's predecessor, Directive 95/46/EC, which has served as a model for the data protection laws of many other countries, similarly requires appropriate technical and organizational security measures without providing details.[27]

In Australia, the Privacy Act 1988 requires covered entities to take reasonable steps to protect personal information from unauthorized access, loss, or misuse.[28] In Israel, organizations must have written security procedures for databases that contain personal information.[29] In China, organizations must adopt necessary measures to safeguard the personal information they collect, process, and store.[30] In some countries, security requirements for personal information are also addressed in sector-specific laws. In the European Union, for example, the Digital Operational Resilience Act requires banks, investment firms, and other financial entities and third-party service providers in member states to implement policies and protocols to maintain the security, confidentiality, and integrity of information in storage and transit.[31]

Most of the regulations discussed in the section appear to assume that an information security program will include policies and procedures for the creation of backup copies of mission-critical information. Given the importance of data backup for information protection and recoverability, it is surprising that so few laws and regulations expressly require backup copies. The few that do are sector-specific. In the United States, for example, the HIPAA Security Rule requires covered entities and their business associates to develop and implement a data backup plan that creates and maintains retrievable exact copies of electronic protected health information.[32] According to regulations issued by the Food and Drug Administration, Good Manufacturing Practices for Finished

Pharmaceuticals require backup copies of data entered into master production and control records. FDA regulations similarly require backup copies of manufacturing records for medical devices.[33] Importers and exporters must maintain backup copies of all records required by U.S. customs regulations.[34] Minimum internal control requirements specified by the National Indian Gaming Commission for Class II gaming include data backup of critical systems with secure storage of backup copies.[35] In Saudi Arabia, payment service providers must create and maintain backup copies of their records.[36] The European Union Agency for Cybersecurity recommends the creation of multiple backup copies of important data, but that recommendation is not embodied in EU legislation.[37]

Noncompliance with the legal security mandates discussed in this section exposes an organization to fines or other sanctions and to possible civil litigation. Violations may be detected during a regulatory audit or in the context of a security breach involving unauthorized disclosure of nonpublic personal or business information. As discussed in the preceding chapter, fines for noncompliance with privacy and data protection laws can be substantial. GDPR violations can result in fines up to twenty million EUR, or 4 percent of the noncompliant entity's worldwide annual turnover. Fines up to $50,000 per incident and one-year imprisonment may be imposed for willful violations of the HIPAA Security Rule. New York State has imposed fines totaling millions of dollars for noncompliance with its Cybersecurity Requirements for Financial Services Companies. In China, operators of critical information infrastructure who fail to perform cybersecurity protection duties are subject to fines up to 1,000,000 RMB and directly responsible management personnel may be fined up to 100,000 RMB.

In addition to penalties, some laws that mandate information security requirements give a civil right of action to parties who are adversely affected by an organization's inadequate information security measures. Such litigation may involve a single plaintiff or a class action. It is typically based on the defendant's negligent failure to fulfill its duty of care by implementing and enforcing appropriate security safeguards to prevent reasonably foreseeable exposure of nonpublic information.[38] Plaintiffs may also charge breach of contract where there is a contractual obligation, either express or implied, to safeguard sensitive or confidential information.

LAWS THAT CRIMINALIZE DATA BREACHES

A data breach, also known as a data leak, is a security violation that involves access to or use of nonpublic personal or business information without the permission of the information's owner or custodian. A data breach may compromise the confidentiality, integrity, or accessibility of information by removing it from its custodian's possession, prohibiting access to the information by authorized parties, reproducing and distributing the information to unauthorized parties, altering or destroying all or parts of the information, or otherwise misusing the information.

A data breach may be intentional or accidental. An accidental data breach may occur when an employee or contractor obtains unauthorized access to confidential business or personal information incidental to the scope of employment,[39] when someone who is authorized to access nonpublic information mistakenly reveals it to an unauthorized party, or when paper documents, computer storage media, or personal computing devices that contain confidential information are lost or stolen. An intentional data breach may be perpetrated by an organization's own employees, contractors, or other internal threat agents or by external parties, such as criminals, activists, and state-sponsored actors with economic, political, social, or ideological motives.[40] Nonpublic business information may be breached when legitimate competitive intelligence gathering crosses the line, intentionally or unknowingly, into industrial espionage.[41] Employees involved in litigation with their employers have obtained unauthorized access to office files or computer databases to support their claims.[42]

In recent years, widely publicized data breaches have involved unauthorized access to computer systems, but information in any format may be breached. Document theft for political reasons, to support national intelligence objectives, to obtain strategic information for military operations, or for personal financial gain predates widespread computerization by centuries. In American history, infamous perpetrators of document theft have included Major John Andre who was arrested in possession of stolen papers obtained from Benedict Arnold; Julius Rosenberg, who gave the Soviet Union top-secret documents about nuclear weapons and other matters; Alger Hiss, a U.S. government official believed to be a Soviet spy who reportedly had his wife copy classified documents by retyping them; Aldrich Ames, a CIA officer turned Russian double agent who gave originals and copies of classified documents to his KGB handlers; Jonathan Pollard, a government intelligence analyst who delivered hundreds of classified documents to Mossad; Robert Hanssen, an FBI agent who sold thousands of classified documents to the KGB; and James McCord and others, who were arrested in an attempted burglary of the Democratic National Committee's Watergate offices.

Some laws discussed in the preceding section create a private right of action for data security breaches. In some circumstances, unauthorized access to or theft of information is a criminal offense comparable to theft of other forms of property. In the United States, for example, theft of federal government property, including agency records, is a crime, as is theft of federal court records with the intention of obstructing justice.[43] In Germany, it is a crime to obtain unauthorized access to correspondence or other papers that are protected by a sealed container.[44] In India, the Penal Code defines *theft* as taking removable property without the owner's consent with the intention of causing a wrongful gain or loss. While information itself is not movable property, a document or other information carrier is.[45]

In recent years, legislation has focused on cybersecurity breaches rather than document theft. According to the United Nations, most of the world's countries have enacted some form of cybercrime legislation, but provisions vary widely.[46] In Canada, for example, unauthorized access to or fraudulent use of a computer is a federal crime punishable by up to ten years in prison.[47] In Australia, unauthorized access to or impairment of computer-stored data is a federal crime subject to comparable punishment.[48] Australian state legislation contains similar provisions. Part 6 of the New South Wales Crimes Act 1900, for example, deals expressly with computer offenses, including unauthorized access to or modification of computer-stored information, which is punishable by imprisonment for two years.[49] In South Africa, cybersecurity legislation prohibits unauthorized access to computers, unlawful interception of data, and unlawful interference with a computer program or data.[50] Nigerian law enumerates and specifies punishments for a variety of computer-related crimes.[51]

Most European countries have laws that criminalize interference with computer operations. The Convention on Cybercrime, an international treaty commonly known as the Budapest Convention, calls for global harmonization of criminal laws dealing with computer-related offenses, including illegal access to computers and illegal interference with computer-stored information.[52] The Budapest Convention has been signed by one-third of the world's countries, including the United States, Canada, and Australia. The Convention's provisions are incorporated into Directive 2013/4/EU, which instructs EU member states to ensure that unauthorized access to information systems or damage to data by infringing cybersecurity measures is punishable as a criminal offense.[53]

According to the German criminal code, obtaining unauthorized access to computer stored data by circumventing security safeguards is punishable by a fine or imprisonment up to three years.[54] In Ireland, unlawful use of a computer for personal gain or to harm another is punishable by up ten years in prison.[55] In Finland, a person who obtains unauthorized access to a computer system protected by security measures with the intention of obtaining confidential business information is guilty of business espionage, which is punishable by a fine and imprisonment up to two years.[56] Among non-EU countries, the United Kingdom prohibits unauthorized access to computers or data.[57] In Norway, unauthorized access to a computer system by circumventing security measures is likewise punishable by a fine or prison term up to two years.[58]

The United States does not have an omnibus law that criminalizes information security breaches. As with privacy violations, cybersecurity violations are covered by multiple federal and state laws:

- At the federal level, the Computer Fraud and Abuse Act of 1986 prohibits unauthorized access to a computer containing national security information, a computer used in interstate or foreign commerce, and any nonpublic computer used by the federal government.[59] It also makes it a federal crime to knowingly access a protected computer with intent to defraud, damage the computer intentionally or recklessly, to traffic in passwords, or to transmit threats to damage a protected computer, to obtain information, or to compromise the confidentiality of information. Violations are punishable by a prison term from one to twenty years, depending on the nature of the offense. The law also provides for a civil cause of action where a violation results in physical injury, economic damage, or a threat to public health or safety.

- The Stored Communications Act, which is a component of the Electronic Communications Privacy Act of 1986, prohibits unauthorized access to a facility that provides electronic communication services, such as a remote computing service that stores or processes customer data, an email service provider, or an Internet service provider. It also prohibits obtaining, altering, or preventing authorized access to nonpublic electronic communications by someone who exceeds their authorized access.[60] Violations are punishable by a fine or imprisonment up to five years.
- The Economic Espionage Act of 1996 deals with information security breaches that involve trade secrets.[61] Unlike other U.S. cybercrime legislation, it applies to trade secrets that are recorded on either electronic or non-electronic media. As will be discussed more fully in the next chapter, a trade secret is broadly defined as proprietary business information that has actual or potential commercial value derived from the fact that it is not generally known. According to the Economic Espionage Act, the owner of a trade secret must implement reasonable physical or electronic security measures to prevent unauthorized access to it. Examples of reasonable security safeguards include locked doors and locked file rooms for paper records and password protection and network encryption for computer data. *Misappropriation*—defined as theft of, unauthorized access to, or possession of a trade secret by fraud, deception, or other improper means—requires an intentional breach of these security measures. Misappropriation of trade secrets with the intent to injure its owner or to benefit a foreign power is a federal crime punishable by up to fifteen years in prison or a fine up to $10 million, or three times the value of the misappropriated information.
- Various state laws similarly address computer crime. Alabama, Arizona, Colorado, Illinois, Nebraska, New Mexico, Utah, Vermont, and some other states have cybercrime or computer tampering laws that prohibit unauthorized access to computers, computer systems, or computer networks.[62] New York law prohibits unauthorized duplication of computer data.[63] In Maryland, an amendment to the criminal code prohibits the possession of ransomware with intent to impair the operation of state government, a utility company, a health-care facility, or a public school.[64] In California, Connecticut, and Wyoming, criminal penalties for extortion apply to the use of ransomware to restrict access to computers or data.[65] In most states, violations of these

computer crime laws are considered felonies that are punishable by fines or imprisonment for up to ten years.

DATA BREACH NOTIFICATION LAWS

Many countries have laws that require an organization to report the unauthorized release of nonpublic personal information to designated supervisory authorities and to notify the affected data subjects. In most countries, these notification requirements are incorporated into or aligned with national privacy and data protection laws.

As a widely cited example, article 4 of the GDPR defines a personal data breach as "a breach of security leading to the accidental or unlawful destruction, loss, alteration, unauthorized disclosure of, or access to, personal data transmitted, stored or otherwise processed." According to article 33, an organization that experiences a personal data breach that endangers the rights and freedoms of the affected data subjects must notify the competent supervisory authority in the appropriate EU member state. This must be done within seventy-two hours after the organization becomes aware of the breach, although notification can be made in phases where the full extent of the breach is not immediately known. The notification must describe the nature of the breach, including the categories and approximate number of data subjects affected and the approximate quantity of information involved. The notification must also state the likely consequences of the data breach and the measures proposed or taken to address the breach and mitigate its adverse effects.

According to article 34 of the GDPR, an organization must notify the affected data subjects without undue delay if a data breach is likely to result in a high risk to their rights and freedoms. GDPR recitals 75 and 85 list possible adverse effects of a data breach that might result in physical, material, or nonmaterial damage to data subjects, including identity theft or fraud, financial loss, and damage to reputation. According to GDPR recital 86, the notification should include recommendations for measures that a data subject can take to mitigate the potential adverse effects. Notification to the affected data subjects is not required if the organization has implemented security measures, such as encryption, that would render the breached data unintelligible to unauthorized parties; if the organization has taken subsequent measures to nullify risks to the affected data subjects; or if individual notification of data subjects would involve disproportionate effort, in which case a public communication might be substituted.[66] To enable supervisory authorities to determine compliance with GDPR notification requirements, an organization must fully document all personal data breaches, indicating the facts, effects, and remedial actions taken. Noncompliance is subject to the same penalties as other GDPR violations.

Other data protection laws specify similar notification requirements for breaches involving nonpublic personal information. In Canada, the Personal Information Protection and Electronic Documents Act states that personal data breaches that create a real risk of significant harm to an individual must be reported to the Office of the Privacy Commissioner and to the affected data subjects. Examples of significant harm include bodily injury, humiliation, damage to reputation or relationships, financial loss, loss of employment, identity theft, and loss of or damage to property. Affected data subjects must be notified by mail, email, phone, or another reasonable method as soon as feasible after a data breach is detected. Covered entitles are also responsible for compliance with notification requirements for data breaches involving personal information that they have transferred to a contractor of other third party for processing.[67] Data breach notification is similarly required by privacy and data protection legislation in Mexico,[68] the United Kingdom,[69] Australia,[70] New Zealand,[71] and South Africa, [72] among other countries. Switzerland[73] and China[74] have recently incorporated breach notification requirements into their personal data protection laws. The Chinese requirement is limited to security breaches that involve the personal data of one hundred thousand or more data subjects.

The United States does not have omnibus data breach notification legislation, but data breach notification requirements are increasingly incorporated into sector-specific federal laws and regulations. The Cyber Incident Reporting for Critical Infrastructure Act (CIRCIA) of 2022 applies to infrastructure sectors designated as critical in a 2013 Presidential Policy Directive.[75] The critical sectors include chemicals, communications, energy, financial services, food and agriculture, health care, transportation, and wastewater systems. Companies and other entities that operate in those sectors must report cybersecurity incidents that jeopardize the confidentiality, integrity, or availability of information to the Cybersecurity & Infrastructure Security Agency within seventy-two hours. Ransomware payments must be reported within twenty-four hours.

These data breach notification requirements overlap with other sector-specific regulations issued by federal agencies. As an example, a joint rule issued by the Federal Deposit Insurance Corporation, Office of the Controller of the Currency, and the Federal Reserve System requires banks and their service providers to notify their regulators within thirty-six hours about any security incident that threatens the confidentiality, integrity, or availability of the bank's information systems and disrupts or degrades the ability to carry out banking operations or deliver services to customers.[76] The notification requirement is not limited to breaches of personal information.

The Federal Communications Commission requires telecommunications carriers to notify the U.S. Secret Service and the Federal Bureau of Investigation within seven days about breaches of customer proprietary network information, which is defined as information about telephone calls, charges, and other matters related to a customer's use of a telecommunication service.[77] Customers must be informed about the breach after law enforcement is notified.

The HIPAA Breach Notification Rule requires covered entities and their business associates to report unauthorized disclosure of protected health information to the affected individuals by first-class mail or email and to the Secretary of Health and Human Services. Prominent media outlets must also be notified about breaches that involve more than five hundred residents of a state or jurisdiction.[78]

Legislation in every state and U.S. territory requires businesses, government agencies, and other organizations to notify data subjects in writing about security breaches involving unauthorized access to the personal information of state or territory residents.[79] Notification requirements aimed at businesses are often incorporated into or closely associated with consumer protection legislation. The California and Missouri notification requirements, for example, deal specifically with breaches of consumer information.[80]

Regardless of focus, state and territory breach notification laws share a common purpose and even use identical language to specify compliance requirements, but details differ. Some laws require a minimum number of affected data subjects—five hundred or more, for example—to trigger the notification requirement; others require notification for any breach of personal data. Some laws limit notification requirements to breaches that are likely to cause significant loss or injury, such as identity theft. Some laws specify a maximum time frame for notification; others simply require expedient notification without unreasonable delay. Some laws require written notification; others permit electronic notification, telephone notification or, in some cases, notification to media outlets or prominent posting on a website. Some laws also require notification of government officials, law enforcement authorities, or a consumer credit reporting agency.

Noncompliance with federal and state notification requirements for data breaches are punishable by monetary penalties. Federal fines for violations of health-care and financial services regulations can be substantial. HIPAA violations, for example, can result in fines up to $50,000 per incident. Some state laws specify even greater penalties. Noncompliance with Alabama's breach notification law can result in fines of $5,000 per day up to a total of $500,000. In Arizona, fines can range from $10,000 to $500,000. In Florida, fines start at $1,000 per day for the first thirty days but increase to $50,000 for each thirty-day period thereafter. In South Dakota, fines can equal $10,000 per day. In Oklahoma, violations are punishable by fines up to $150,000 per breach.[81] Civil litigation initiated by affected data subjects is also possible.

CONTRACTUAL COMPLIANCE

Many companies, government agencies, and nonprofit organizations outsource certain business functions that involve information storage, access, processing, and disclosure to cloud service providers, professional service firms, third-party administrators, commercial record storage companies, and other contractors or agents. In the course of its work for a given organization, a contractor may have access to or take possession of personal or business information of a confidential, sensitive, or proprietary nature. Such nonpublic information requires appropriate security safeguards to prevent unauthorized disclosure or use. A contractor may be authorized to access nonpublic information on a client's own servers. Alternatively, a client may transfer the information to servers operated by the contractor. In either case, outsourcing arrangements raise concerns about the confidentiality, integrity, and availability of a client's nonpublic information.[82]

Some of the legal and regulatory security requirements discussed in the preceding sections apply to an organization's contractors. The HIPAA Security Rule, for example, applies to the business associates of health-care providers, hospitals, and other covered entities. Requirements for security of protected health information must be included in business associate contracts and in any agreements with subcontractors that a business associate may enter into in connection with work performed for a covered entity.[83] Similarly, defense contractors are subject to the same regulations as federal agencies regarding security requirements for military and space information. Certain state laws, like the California Consumer Protection Act, require contracts to specify restrictions on the use of nonpublic personal information that a contractor may access in the course of its work. In Canada, companies subject to the Personal Information Protection and Electronic Documents Act are responsible for data breach notifications involving information that they send to third parties for processing.

Laws and regulations aside, many contracts and agreements include clauses that specify a contractor's security and protection obligations for nonpublic personal and business information that the contractor processes and stores for a client. Such contracts and agreements typically include some combination of the following compliance requirements:

- The contractor must comply with all applicable laws and regulations for handling of the client's nonpublic information. A contract may include a list of such laws and regulations. HIPAA business associate agreements, for example, specifically reference the HIPAA Privacy Rule and HIPAA Security Rule for protected health information. A contract may also specify compliance with one or more of the information security standards and industry norms discussed in the next section.
- The contractor is only authorized to access, store, use, disclose, and reproduce the client's nonpublic information to the extent necessary to perform obligations under the contract.
- The contractor must implement administrative, technical, and physical safeguards to protect the confidentiality, integrity, and availability of nonpublic information that it obtains from the client or that it creates, processes, or stores on the client's behalf. These safeguards must be embodied in written policies and procedures. Safeguards to prevent unauthorized

access to and use of the client's nonpublic information must be applied at all stages of the information's life cycle. The contractor's security measures must be at least as stringent as the client's internal security safeguards.

- Some contracts require the contractor to store a client's nonpublic information on a dedicated server or in a dedicated physical space. If this is not possible, the client's nonpublic information must be isolated from unrelated information.
- The contractor must employ risk assessment processes and procedures to regularly evaluate threats to the client's nonpublic information, identify vulnerabilities associated with the contractor's information systems or facilities that a threat agent can exploit, and implement countermeasures to mitigate the risk of unauthorized access, destruction, alteration, disclosure, or other misuse of the client's nonpublic information.
- Some contracts specify detailed requirements for specific security precautions, such as firewalls, virus and malware detection measures, network security testing, passwords used to access the client's nonpublic information, data encryption, and controlled access to storage rooms or office areas where nonpublic information may be exposed to viewing or theft by unauthorized persons.
- The contractor's employees must have limited access to a client's nonpublic information on a demonstrable need-to-know basis. Employees must be authorized to view, print, reproduce, or otherwise use the least amount of nonpublic information needed to perform assigned duties related to a contract. Some clients require contractors to identify the employees, by name or job title, who will perform work requiring access to the client's nonpublic information. Some contracts require the contractor to conduct background checks to the extent permitted by law for all employees who will have access to the client's nonpublic information.
- An employee's access to a client's nonpublic information must be stopped immediately and completely upon termination of employment, when there is a change in the employee's assigned duties for which the client's nonpublic information is no longer required, or upon termination of the contract, whichever occurs first.
- The contractor must provide employees with training regarding security requirements and restrictions for access to and use of a client's nonpublic information. The training must emphasize procedures for secure handling of nonpublic information and restrictions on disclosure of the information, including precautions to prevent accidental disclosure. The training must be tailored to a given employee's information-handling responsibilities. The contractor's training program must include a testing component. Refresher training must be provided annually or whenever there is a significant change in security requirements or procedures related to the client's nonpublic information.

- The contractor must closely supervise employees who have access to the client's nonpublic information. The contractor must have written procedures for monitoring employee compliance with security requirements and restrictions pertaining to use of a client's nonpublic information. The contractor must respond in a timely manner to actual or suspected security violations.
- The contractor must allow the client or the client's authorized representative to conduct periodic onsite assessments, examinations, or audits of the contractor's information security program, practices, and facilities related to the client's nonpublic information in order to confirm compliance with laws, regulations, and contractual terms. The contract may limit the frequency of such assessments, examinations, or audits—once or twice per year, for example, unless a data breach occurs or a credible security complaint or allegation of a security violation is made.
- A contract must specify the contractor's responsibility for response and remediation, including notification requirements and costs, following a data breach that involves a client's nonpublic information. The contractor must notify the client immediately when such a data breach occurs.
- Most contracts specify that the client organization will determine if data breach notification is legally required in a specific instance and will control the timing and content of all public communications relating to the breach. An exception is typically made for notifications to government authorities or law enforcement that the contractor must make immediately.
- The contractor must investigate the cause of a data breach, including a breach that does not rise to the level that requires notification, as soon as feasible and exert its best efforts to prevent future breaches.
- The contractor must be given explicit instructions for disposition of the client's nonpublic information in its possession when the contract terminates or the information is no longer needed to satisfy contractual obligations. Depending on the circumstances, the contractor may be required to return nonpublic information to the client by a specified date, transfer the information to another party designated by the client, or destroy the information in a timeframe and manner approved by the client.
- Return, transfer, or destruction of the client's nonpublic information upon termination of the contract must include all copies in the contractor's possession, but a contractor may be allowed to defer destruction of backup copies that are stored in remote locations or that contain the client's nonpublic information comingled with unrelated information that the contractor needs to retain for an additional brief period of time for disaster recovery purposes. In that case, a reasonably short extension will be allowed for destruction of the backup copies and the contractor must agree not to use the client's nonpublic information for any purpose in the interim.

- The contract must specify that any subcontractor agreements with affiliated or nonaffiliated entities and individuals must include all of the security requirements that apply to the prime contractor. Some contracts state that any subcontractors who will have access to a client's nonpublic information must be identified and the subcontracting agreements approved in advance by the client. The prime contractor must be responsible for monitoring and ensuring each subcontractor's compliance with the client's security requirements for nonpublic information.
- The contractor and any subcontractors may be required to purchase cybersecurity insurance, also known as cyber liability insurance, with specified levels of coverage for data breach response, including breach notifications required by law. Cybersecurity insurance may also be required for data recovery as well as credit monitoring and identity recovery protection for data subjects affected by a security breach. The contractor must be aware, however, that cybersecurity insurance is not a substitute for compliance with diligent security measures specified by the client.

A contractor's failure to comply with security requirements for a client's nonpublic information may result in termination of the contract with or without warning. Noncompliance also exposes a contractor to civil litigation based on breach of contract or, in the case of data breach or other security incident that harms the client, negligence.

STANDARDS AND INDUSTRY NORMS

As noted in the preceding section, a contract or agreement may mandate compliance with information security and protection standards and industry norms. These standards and norms are important because they are widely accepted as reflective of best practices for information security policies and procedures. Rather than citing specific standards, some contracts and agreements state that a contractor will adopt best practices for information security, in which case applicable standards and industry norms provide a benchmark for compliance assessment. Contracts aside, an organization may require compliance with standards and norms to satisfy regulatory authorities or internal policies requiring adherence to best practices for security of nonpublic personal or business information.

The following sections survey widely adopted examples of information security standards and norms. The survey is not comprehensive. It emphasizes standards and norms that specify concepts and requirements that are relevant for the development, implementation, and enforcement of information security programs. Standards that deal with specific technical topics, such as encryption algorithms or data transmission, are excluded. As with other topics discussed in this book, compliance with information security standards and norms is voluntary except in the context of a contractual obligation.

ISO/IEC 27000 SERIES

The ISO/IEC 27000 series is a family of interrelated security standards published jointly by the International Standardization Organization and the International Electrotechnical Commission.[84] At the time this chapter was written, the 27000 series consisted of sixty published and planned international standards that deal with specific aspects of information security management. Like all international standards, the 27000 series titles are subject to regular review and revision. Five of the standards are broadly applicable to all types of organizations:

- As its title suggests, ISO/IEC 27000:2018, *Information technology—Security techniques—Information security management systems—Overview and vocabulary* is an introductory standard. It defines key terminology and discusses the importance of an information security management system (ISMS) as a critical component of an organization's information management strategy.
- ISO/IEC 27001:2013, *Information technology—Security techniques—Information security management systems—Requirements* presents general requirements for establishing, implementing, maintaining, and continually improving an ISMS tailored to the needs of an organization. ISO/IEC 27001 is the most widely cited information security standard. Most of the other 27000 series standards assume familiarity with ISO/IEC 27001.
- ISO/IEC 27002:2022, *Information security, cybersecurity and privacy protection—Information security controls* provides guidance for assessing and implementing commonly accepted administrative, physical, and technological controls to manage information security risks.
- ISO/IEC 27003:2017, *Information technology—Security techniques—Information security management systems—Guidance* provides recommendations for implementing the requirements presented in ISO/IEC 27001.
- ISO/IEC 27004:2016, *Information technology—Security techniques—Information security management systems—Monitoring, measurement, analysis, and evaluation* provides guidelines for evaluating the effectiveness of an information security management system.
- ISO/IEC 27005:2018, *Information technology—Security techniques—Information security management systems—Information security risk management* takes a methodology-independent risk management approach to implementing the requirements presented in ISO/IEC 27001.

Other titles in the 27000 series deal with specific aspects of information security management. ISO/IEC 27701:2019, *Security techniques—Extension to ISO/IEC 27001 and ISO/IEC 27002 for privacy information management—Requirements and guidelines* deals with security measures for ensuring the privacy of personal information. ISO/IEC 27017:2015, *Security techniques—Code of practice for information security controls based on ISO/IEC 27002 for cloud services* is intended for cloud service providers and organizations that contract with cloud providers for services involving nonpublic personal or business information. ISO/IEC 27018:2019, *Security techniques—Code of practice for protection of personally identifiable information (PII) in public clouds acting as PII processors* applies the security controls presented in ISO/IEC 27002 to public cloud service providers. ISO/IEC 27040:2015, *Information technology—Security techniques—Storage security techniques* deals with the security of information storage devices, media, and networks.

The 27000 series standards that deal with sector-specific information security issues include ISO/IEC 27799:2016, *Health informatics—Information security management in health using ISO/IEC 27002*; *Information technology—Security techniques—Code of practice for information security controls based on ISO/IEC 27002 for telecommunications organizations*; and ISO/IEC 27019:2017, *Information technology—Security techniques—Information security controls for the energy utility industry.*

Third-party certification bodies, also known as conformity assessment bodies, will evaluate and certify an organization's information security management system for compliance with the ISO/IEC 27001 standard. A company, government agency, or nonprofit entity may want ISO/IEC 27001 certification to satisfy internal governance or external audit requirements. Some contractors, cloud services, and other providers of information-related services advertise that their information security management systems are ISO/IEC 27001-certified. Certification presumably increases customer confidence that a contractor or service provider will be able to maintain confidentiality, integrity, and availability of nonpublic personal and business information. ISO/IEC 27001 series certification bodies are evaluated by accreditation agencies like the ANSI National Accreditation Board (ANAB), a subsidiary of the American National Standards Institute. ISO/IEC 27006:2015, *Information technology—Security techniques—Requirements for bodies providing audit and certification of information security management systems* specifies competence and reliability requirements for accreditation of ISO/IEC 27001 certification bodies.

OTHER STANDARDS

While they are not as well known or broadly applicable as the ISO/IEC 27000 series, other standards provide requirements and guidance for specific aspects of information security. For example:

- ETSI, the European Telecommunications Standards Institute, develops standards for information and communications technologies (ICT). ETSI standards are intended for transposition into national standards in EU member states and elsewhere. ETSI's technical committee on cybersecurity (TC CYBER) establishes base standards and guidance to maintain and enhance the security of nonpublic personal and business information. The ETSI GS ISI series identifies, defines, describes, and categorizes information security incidents (intrusions and external attacks, malfunctions, and internal deviant behaviors) and vulnerabilities (behavioral, software, configuration, technical, and organizational) and provides guidelines for detecting security events.[85] TC CYBER standards support Directive (EU) 2016/1148, the EU cybersecurity directive, which requires member states to adopt and implement a national cybersecurity strategy, and its proposed successor.[86]

- The IEC/TS 62443 series issued by the International Electrotechnical Commission provides information security standards and guidance for industrial communication networks, supervisory control systems, and data acquisition systems in electricity transmission and distribution networks, gas and water distribution networks, oil and gas production operations, gas and liquid transmission pipelines, and other industries.[87] IEC /TS 62443 conformity assessment and certification is offered by accredited testing and inspection companies.
- ISO/SAE 21434:2021, *Road vehicles—Cybersecurity engineering* specifies information security requirements for electric and electronic systems in cars, trucks, and other vehicles intended for transporting passengers, goods, or animals by road. The standard addresses security issues involved in developing, producing, operating, maintaining, and decommissioning cellular communication systems, Bluetooth connections, geolocation sensors, and other mobile connectivity components intended for installation and use in vehicles.
- The Payment Card Industry Security Standards Council develops and administers standards for merchants, financial institutions, service providers, and other entities that store, process, or transmit data related to credit card holders and credit card transactions. The PCI Data Security Standard (PCI DSS), which applies to merchants worldwide, specifies detailed requirements for system and network security, storage and encryption of cardholder data, access to card holder data, and regular monitoring and testing to protect cardholder and transaction data.[88] PCI DSS compliance is mandated by major credit card brands. Depending on the volume of transactions, compliance is verified by self-assessment or by certified internal or external assessors. The Payment Card Industry Security Standards Council has issued two other payment card standards, PCI PTS and PCI PA-DSS, which apply to companies that manufacture credit card entry devices and companies that develop software for payment applications, respectively.
- UL 2900-1 is a series of interrelated standards developed by UL, a safety testing and certification company formerly known as Underwriters Laboratories. It presents cybersecurity requirements and guidelines for eval-

uation, testing, and implementation of security risk control software in network-connectable products. Published and planned standards in the UL 2900 series present requirements for networked-connectable components in medical devices and accessories, invitro diagnostic devices, wellness devices, and other health-care systems; process control systems, data acquisition systems, and other industrial control systems; and intrusion detection devices, alarm control units, smoke detectors, and other security and life safety signaling systems. UL offers a cybersecurity certification program for evaluating network-connectable products and systems.

NIST CYBERSECURITY FRAMEWORK

The standards discussed in the preceding sections define models or norms for information security based on acknowledged best practices. An information security framework provides a structure for adopting best practices. It defines principles and processes for the development and implementation of policies and procedures to assess risks, address vulnerabilities, safeguard an organization's nonpublic personal and business information, and comply with laws and regulations that require an organization to have an effective information security program.

In the United States, the National Institute of Standards and Technology (NIST), a unit of the U.S. Department of Commerce, develops guidelines for a broad range of operations and activities, including the security of information and information systems. The Cybersecurity Enhancement Act of 2014 made NIST responsible for developing a cybersecurity risk framework for voluntary use by owners and operators of critical infrastructure, defined as systems and assets that are so vital to United States that their incapacity or destruction would have a debilitating impact on national security, economic security, public health, or safety. Critical infrastructure sectors include information technology, telecommunications, chemicals, transportation systems, emergency services, and postal and shipping.[89]

NIST introduced its Cybersecurity Framework in 2014 in response to Executive Order 13636, which directed NIST to work with government and industry stakeholders to develop a voluntary framework for reduction of cyber risks to critical infrastructure.[90] The NIST Cybersecurity Framework is intended for government agencies and nongovernmental organization. The framework's core is a structured set of cybersecurity measures and outcomes for identifying critical information assets, assessing threats and vulnerabilities, implementing information security processes and procedures, and detecting, responding to, and recovering from cybersecurity events. In addition to categorizing and explaining cybersecurity measures and outcomes, the NIST framework references applicable standards, including the ISO/IEC 27000 series. It also references other information security frameworks discussed below.

The NIST Cybersecurity Framework is supported by NIST's SP-800 series of special publications, which deal with computer security:

- NIST SP 800-53 provides a catalog of security controls for information systems. The controls are grouped into categories that address key aspects of information security, including system access, audit and accountability, awareness and training, configuration management, contingency planning, user identification and authentication, media protection, physical and environmental protection, risk and security assessment, and system protection and integrity.[91]
- NIST SP 800-53B, a companion publication, presents security control baselines and guidance for security threats with low, medium, and high impact levels.[92]
- NIST SP 800-171 presents basic security requirements for nonfederal systems that store unclassified nonpublic information that is important for the missions and functions of federal agencies and that requires dissemination controls to preserve confidentiality.[93] NIST SP 800-172, a companion publication, presents enhanced security requirements for such information.[94]
- Other special publications in the NIST 800 series present standards and guidance for specific aspects of information security, including Internet of Things (IoT) devices (SP 800-213), cloud systems (SP 800-144 and SP 800-210), storage infrastructure (SP 800-209), access control systems (SP 800-205), email (SP 800-177), and mobile applications (SP 800-164).[95] The NIST 1800 series of special publications includes cybersecurity guidance on such sector-specific topics as industrial control systems (SP 1800-10), telehealth rebote patient monitoring (SP 1800-30), property management systems (SP 1800-27), energy sector assets (SP 1800-23), and health-care imaging systems (SP 1800-24).[96]

Compared to information security standards, which are typically written at a relatively high level of abstraction, the requirements, guidelines, and recommended practices presented in NIST special publications are more detailed. They have been adopted by federal government agencies and have influenced the information security policies and practices of state and local governments, companies, and nonprofit organizations. NIST special publications are frequently referenced in contracts, agreements, requests for proposals, and other procurement documents.

COBIT AND COSO FRAMEWORKS

Some information security frameworks were specifically developed to address cyber risks; the NIST Cybersecurity Framework discussed above is one example. Others are based on frameworks developed for other purposes. Two of the best-known examples, the COBIT and COSO frameworks, predate the NIST framework. The COBIT and COSO frameworks are highly respected and widely implemented by companies, government agencies, and nonprofit organizations. They are often cited as useful benchmarks for information security program:

- COBIT, an acronym for Control Objectives for Information and Related Technologies, is an IT governance framework developed in 1996 by ISACA, a nonprofit association of information control and systems audit professionals with regional chapters throughout the world. COBIT grew out of guidance for auditing data processing operations, but ISACA subsequently expanded its scope to incorporate requirements and best practices for IT governance, quality assurance, risk management, and information security. COBIT has been updated regularly since its introduction to include new IT developments and address emerging business requirements. COBIT 2019, the latest version available at the time this chapter was written, is often considered an information security standard, but it is more accurately described as an information security framework. It specifies four domains for information security: Plan and Organize, Acquire and Implement, Deliver and Support, and Monitor and Evaluate. COBIT 2019 specifies requirements for each of these domains, and the domains can be mapped to guidance specified in ISO/IEC 27001 and other 27000 series standards.[97]
- COSO, the Committee of Sponsoring Organizations of the Treadway Commission, was formed in 1985 by a group of professional accounting and auditing associations to address the problem of fraudulent financial reporting. Since that time, COSO has issued a number of guidance documents that deal with effective internal controls to support an organization's business operations and reporting objectives, with particular emphasis on meeting the requirements of laws and regulations.[98] The COSO Enterprise Risk Management (ERM) Framework was introduced in 2004 to align risk-related initiatives with an organization's governance, business objectives, and stakeholder interests. COSO updated the Framework in 2017 to address cyber security risks with reference to the following components: Governance and Culture to heighten organizational awareness of cybersecurity risks with special emphasis on the risk oversight responsibilities of an entity's governing body and top executives; Strategy and Objective-Setting to integrate information security risk management into an organization's strategic objectives; Performance to identify, evaluate, and prioritize cyberthreats, organizational vulnerabilities, and risk mitigation options; Review and Revision to assess and revise the organization's cyber risk management practices in the light of changing threats, vulnerabilities, and objectives; and Information, Communication, and Reporting to share information that stakeholders need for effective cyber risk management.

The COBIT and COSO frameworks are similar in approach but differ in their scope. While COBIT is specifically intended for IT operations, the COSO ERM Framework grew out of financial and accountability concerns. It emphasizes the integration of information security with organizational governance and oversight. In recent years, both frameworks have gained prominence as resources for achieving compliance with Section 404 of the Sarbanes-Oxley Act of 2002, which requires a public company's executive management to affirm the effectiveness of internal controls that ensure the accuracy of the company's financial reporting.

COBIT 2019 and the COSO Enterprise Risk Management Framework are compatible with the NIST Cybersecurity Framework and with requirements and guidance presented in NIST special publications. Compared to NIST publications, however, COBIT 2019 and the COSO ERM Framework emphasize concepts that lay the foundation for an effective information security program rather than detailed operational guidance that addresses specific information security issues and problems. Like its NIST counterpart, the COBIT and COSO frameworks are intended to address an organizations cybersecurity requirements and concerns, but they are also relevant for security of nonelectronic information.

OTHER INFORMATION SECURITY FRAMEWORKS

While they are not as well known as the NIST, COBIT, and COSO frameworks, other nonprofit organizations have developed useful frameworks for planning, implementing, and evaluating security programs for nonpublic information. Examples include the following:

- Like COSO and COBIT, the Information Technology Infrastructure Library (ITIL) predates the NIST framework and widespread concerns about cybersecurity. ITIL is a collection of best practices for the development and management of IT services that are aligned with an organization's business needs.[99] ITIL was initially developed by the British government in the twentieth century, but it has been updated and expanded over time. ITIL 4, the latest version, includes an information security management framework with five components: control to develop an information security policy and defined responsibilities; plan to understand the organization's security requirements and recommend solutions that are appropriate to the organization's budget and corporate culture; implement to put the plan into effect; evaluate to monitor the plan's effectiveness; and maintain to update the plan as necessary to address changing requirements. While it is not as well known in the United States as the COBIT and COSO frameworks, ITIL 4 and its predecessors have been adopted by government agencies and companies in other parts of the world. ITIL 4 certification is available at multiple skill levels.
- The HITRUST CSF (Common Security Framework) is an information security and privacy framework developed by the HITRUST Alliance, a non-

profit entity formed in 2007 by a consortium of health-care organizations and service providers. Designed for regulatory compliance and risk management, the HITRUST CSF supports HIPAA requirements for security of protected health information and has been widely adopted by health-care organizations, but the latest version is not limited to health-care compliance. It is used in manufacturing, finance, education, and other sectors. HITRUST CSF is compatible with ISO/IEC 27000 series standards and with other security and privacy regulations and industry norms covering a broad range of information types and activities. Organizations can have their information security programs validated by an authorized HITRUST Assessor, which will submit its findings to HITRUST for their approval and official certification. HIPAA covered entities may require their internal IT operations and business associates to obtain HITRUST validation or certification to ensure compliance with privacy requirements for protected health information.[100]

- CIS Controls and CIS Benchmarks issued by the Center for Internet Security, a nonprofit organization formed to address cybersecurity issues, provide a framework of best practices and recommended actions for securing information and information systems.[101] CIS Controls specifies cybersecurity requirements and safeguards for IT activities and operations, including inventory and control of enterprise and software assets, access control management, continuous vulnerability management, email and browser protections, malware defenses, network infrastructure management and defense, security awareness and skills training, penetration testing, incident response management, and data recovery. CIS Controls are mapped to ISO 27000 series, PCI DSS, and other Information security standards and to NIST, ITIL, COBIT, and other information security frameworks. CIS Benchmarks provide cybersecurity guidelines that enable an organization to compare its information security measures to widely accepted best practices.
- AICPA System and Organization Controls (SOC) is a cybersecurity framework developed by the American Institute of Certified Public Accountants.[102] Designed for multidisciplinary IT audit teams led by certified public accounting firms, it produces assessment reports for an organization's governing body, executive management, external regulators, and other interested parties. The reports reliably describe and evaluate an organization's cybersecurity risk assessment initiatives and the effectiveness of its cybersecurity policies and controls, including awareness and oversight of cybersecurity measures by the organization's directors and senior management. The AICPA framework includes criteria that evaluate an organization's communications about internal cybersecurity controls and its ability to respond to, recover from, and prevent the recurrence of cybersecurity incidents. The AICPA framework is compatible with the NIST Cybersecurity Framework.

INTERNAL MANDATES

As discussed above, contracts and agreements often specify information security and protection requirements that obligate an organization's external vendors, suppliers, and other providers of goods and services. Internal information security policies define compliance requirements for an organization's employees and other workforce members, including trainees, interns, temporary workers, volunteers, and others. Designed to complement or supplement the internal privacy and access control requirements discussed in chapter 5, these information security policies define workforce members' responsibilities for safeguarding the confidentiality, integrity, and availability of nonpublic personal and business information that they create, receive, process, or otherwise handle in the course of their assigned duties.

An information security policy may be issued as a separate directive or integrated into an organization's code of conduct. It is often developed by a committee or working group headed by a chief information security officer or other high-level executive with membership drawn from key departments or business functions that have nonpublic information. The broadest policies specify security requirements for nonpublic information of all types in all locations and all formats—databases maintained on an organization's servers, computer files saved on shared drives or mobile devices, paper records stored in office files, video recordings created by surveillance systems, and so on. Alternatively, a narrowly focused IT security policy may be limited to information that is maintained on an organization's computer systems and network-connected devices. Given concerns about cybersecurity threats and the high likelihood that an organization's most valuable and sensitive nonpublic information will be maintained electronically, prioritization of IT security is understandable, but some organizations also have confidential paper records that require security safeguards.

Regardless of scope, internal information security policies typically include some combination of the following compliance mandates:

- Information security is an organization-wide responsibility. Individual departments or other business units must be accountable for implementing administrative, technical, and physical measures to safeguard nonpublic information in their custody or under their supervisory control. Each department or other business unit must designate at least one employee at an appropriate level of authority who will have primary responsibility for the business unit's information security practices and initiatives. That employee will be in charge of local implementation and enforcement of information security policies and will serve as a liaison with officials, committees, working groups, and taskforces who are responsible for information security at the enterprise level. The responsible business unit employee may delegate specific information security tasks as appropriate.

- Individual departments or other business units must maintain an up-to-date inventory of computer systems, office files, and other repositories that contain nonpublic personal and business information. The inventory must identify threats and vulnerabilities that place the repositories at risk as well as security safeguards that are currently in place or need to be implemented.
- Individual departments or other business units must provide security training for their workforce members. The training must heighten awareness of threats to the organization's nonpublic information and emphasize the importance of security procedures to reduce the organization's vulnerabilities and mitigate the adverse impact of data breaches or other security incidents. All workforce members must be trained to formulate secure passwords and protect them from unauthorized disclosure, to recognize suspicious email, to challenges unauthorized persons in work areas where nonpublic information is stored, and to identify and report suspected security problems. Other training topics must be appropriate to the needs of specific users or business units. Training for IT workers will require more technical content than training for managers or clerical staff. Training must be repeated periodically to reinforce its message and address new security issues.
- Employment practices must be modified to reflect information security requirements. Responsibilities for information security must be included in job descriptions and advertisements for open positions. To the extent permitted by law, onboarding procedures must include background checks for workforce members who will have access to nonpublic information and critical information systems. New workforce members must receive security awareness training during orientation and job-specific security training at an appropriate level of detail before they are allowed to access nonpublic information.
- IT management must implement technical and administrative safeguards to counteract malware, denial of service attacks, eavesdropping, intrusion attempts, and other cyberthreats to nonpublic information stored on network servers, network-connected devices, and mobile devices, including devices installed in home offices or other remote work sites.
- Departments and other business units must define and enforce entry control and site supervision requirements for areas where information is stored and used. IT administration must implement physical safeguards to prevent unauthorized access to data centers, server rooms, media vaults, and other locations that house nonpublic information or critical information systems. Records management must have similar responsibility for physical security of storage facilities that house paper records or photographic media with nonpublic content.
- Workforce members must prevent unintended exposure of nonpublic data, documents, or images. Nonpublic information displayed on computer

workstations must be protected from viewing by unauthorized persons when in use, and such displays must be suppressed when the workstations are unattended. Workforce members who use mobile devices in public spaces must conceal nonpublic information from unauthorized viewing. Desks or other work surfaces must be cleared of paper records and photographic media that contain nonpublic information at the end of each day or whenever work areas will be left unsupervised.

- Remote workers must be responsible and accountable for information security in their home offices or other locations. Downloading of nonpublic information from network servers for local storage should be prohibited to the extent possible. Where downloading is necessary, nonpublic information must be stored on computers that are not used for other purposes. Paper records that contain nonpublic information and printing of electronic records with nonpublic content must be prohibited in home offices and other remote work sites.
- Backup copies must be created and updated as necessary for nonpublic information that supports mission-critical operations or activities. IT administration will be responsible for backing up information stored on servers that it operates.
- Certain types of nonpublic information will require encryption for storage on network servers or personal computers, transmission over public or private networks, or use with mobile devices. The need for encryption must be determined by the department or business unit that is responsible for nonpublic information in consultation with other stakeholders. IT administration will configure and support encryption when it is needed. Encryption must be limited to mechanisms approved by IT administration. Implementation of encryption measures by individual departments, business units, or workforce members is prohibited.

Some of these internal mandates rely on technical measures, but many managers recognize that the behavior of workforce members is a significant threat to information security. Organizational psychologists and other researchers suggest a variety of reasons for this and recommend corrective actions based on motivational or social science theories.[103] Most organizations use a combination of prevention, through training of workforce members, and deterrence, through sanctions to punish noncompliance. Depending on severity of the infraction, noncompliance with internal information security mandates may be punishable by an informal warning, a written warning, mandatory security training or retraining, an adverse performance evaluation, restrictions on the use of nonpublic information, or, for the worst offenses, demotion or termination of employment. Noncompliant business units may be required to bear the cost of corrective actions or regulatory fines.

SOCIETAL COMPLIANCE

While most discussions of information security compliance focus on regulatory requirements or the adverse economic consequences of data breaches or other security incidents, the societal significance of information security must not be overlooked. Failure to protect the confidentiality, integrity, and availability of nonpublic information can have an adverse impact on an individual's well-being, as well as devastating consequences for society as whole. Failure to prevent unauthorized access to classified government information can imperil national security, while damage to or unauthorized alteration of information processed by state and local government agencies can disrupt essential social services and put vulnerable communities at risk. Failure to protect nonpublic academic and administrative information maintained by schools can have an adverse impact on students, parents, and teachers. Failure to safeguard nonpublic business information can damage a company's reputation, erode its competitive position, and lead to loss of customers, reduced revenue, and employee layoffs. Failure to prevent unauthorized disclosure of a person's bank account numbers or credit card information can lead to financial losses from identity theft and other fraudulent acts. Failure to prevent unauthorized disclosure of protected health information can undermine the patient-physician trust that is essential to medical care and have a negative effect on an individual's relationships with family, friends, employers, and others. Failure to prevent security breaches that disrupt the operation of health-care information systems can endanger patients' lives.

From an ethical perspective, the implementation and enforcement of effective information security safeguards is a moral duty.[104] The custodian of nonpublic personal or business information has an ethical obligation to prevent harm from unlawful or unauthorized access, use, disclosure, reproduction, alteration, or destruction. Unfortunately, the complicated nature of this ethical obligation raises issues that prevent the formulation of definitive compliance requirements. While the importance of information security is universally acknowledged, the well-being of individuals or organizations may require the violation of information security measures implemented by others. Such violations may themselves be motivated by a sense of moral duty. For example:

- Nations have a right and responsibility to defend themselves and their populations. To obtain nonpublic military and defense information about possible threats to a country's sovereignty and security, national intelligence agencies depends on document theft, computer intrusion, interception of electronic communications, and other measures that are certainly unauthorized by custodians of the information and often violate the laws of other nations. In some cases, a nation's own security objectives cause it to attack another nation's cybersecurity defenses to destroy information, as in the case of the Stuxnet virus that was reportedly used by the United States and Israel to damage Iran's ability to develop nuclear weapons. Some observers defend such cyberattacks as a morally justifiable form of active cyberdefense.[105] The International Code of Conduct for Information Security, which was adopted by the United Nations General Assembly in 2012 and revised in 2015, prohibits uses of information and communications technologies that threaten international peace, but the Code does not have the force of an international treaty.[106]

- Information security measures are indifferent to morality. They may protect a confidential medical report that a physician sends to a patient or a text message that a drug dealer sends to a customer. Some organizations purposefully violate information security safeguards to achieve objectives that they believe supports a greater good. To identify possible terrorist activity, a law enforcement agency may circumvent security measures that protect the privacy of phone calls, texts, and email of many innocent people. Similarly, a company can detect unauthorized disclosure of trade secrets, confidential business plans, insider information that may affect stock prices, and other nonpublic information by monitoring the email of all employees without their knowledge, possibly exposing personal information of a private nature in the process.
- Political and social activists, advocating freedom of expression or motivated by other factors, have circumvented security measures that block access to information that government chooses not to disclose to the public. Such activists often believe that they have a moral duty to reveal confidential information that the public has a right to know, even though their security violations are illegal. Well-known perpetrators of information theft motivated by political activism include Daniel Ellsberg, whose photocopies of the so-called Pentagon Papers were subsequently published by the *New York Times*; Edward J. Snowden, who copied and leaked classified information about the National Security Agency's global surveillance activities; and Julian P. Assange, whose WikiLeaks organization published classified documents about the Iraq war and other matters.

Cyberattacks on the information networks of government agencies, financial institutions, utility companies, and strategic business enterprises by political activists and state-sponsored actors are increasingly common. In a one-month period in 2022, Russian-sponsored hackers reportedly attacked Lithuanian government agencies and transportation systems, Chinese-sponsored hackers reportedly attacked American telecommunication networks, Iranian-sponsored hackers reportedly penetrated the email of Israeli officials and military personnel, an activist group of hackers halted production at three Iranian steel companies, and a disinformation campaign linked to China targeted an Australian mining company.[107]

These cyberattacks are a form of undeclared warfare and information security safeguards are the cyber counterparts of military defensive measures. Consequently, the International Humanitarian Law (IHL)—also known as the law of armed conflict or, colloquially, the rules of war—presents principles that are relevant for information security. The International Committee of the Red Cross affirms that the IHL applies to and restricts cyber operations.[108] In particular, the international humanitarian law's principles of necessity, distinction, proportionality, and humanity have implications for societal compliance:

- According to the necessity principle, an organization's information security measures must not be applied indiscriminately. They must be needed to protect the confidentiality, integrity, and availability of nonpublic personal or business information. Security requirements must not be used as a justification to suppress information that is essential to the well-being of a nation's citizens, an organization's employees, a corporation's shareholders, a physician's patients, or others who have a legitimate interest in the information.
- According to the distinction principle, the benefits of information security safeguards must outweigh any restrictions they impose on access to or disclosure of the information. Security measures often require additional time and effort to identify authorized users and verify their access privileges. The additional time and effort must not unnecessarily discourage authorized access to information, and it must not impede immediate access to information that is urgently needed—as would be the case with an emergency room physician who requires access to the medical history of a severely injured patient in order to provide care or a firefighter who requires access to floor plans before entering a burning building.
- According to the proportionality principle, an organization's information security safeguards must not be excessive in relation to the anticipated objectives. All security implementations involve trade-offs. Some information-related privileges—retrieval of information by employees who have a reasonable but not essential need to access the information, for example—must be sacrificed to achieve security, but the anticipated benefits must justify the sacrifice.
- According to the humanity principle, an organization's information security measures must be implemented in a manner that limits unnecessary harm to persons who are not involved in security violations in the same manner that the rules of armed conflict seek to protect noncombatants. This principle raises concerns about mass surveillance of private communications to identify the terrorist or criminal intent of a few wrongdoers.

An additional ethical concern relates to security vulnerabilities or defects that an organization discovers in its own information systems and that might be exploited by a threat agent to obtain access to nonpublic personal or business information. In such situations, a risk assessment is required to determine whether specific information-related operations must be modified or discontinued until the vulnerability is addressed or the defect is corrected. If and when the vulnerability or defect leads to a data breach, the organization may have a legal obligation to notify the affected parties individually or via a public announcement, as discussed in a preceding section. If no data breach has been detected, the organization has an ethical obligation to notify customers, contractors, vendors, suppliers, and other stakeholders if the vulnerability or defect could compromise the confidentiality, integrity, or availability of their nonpublic information. Such notification should indicate the risks associated with the vulnerability or defect, the corrective measures to be implemented, and the anticipated timeframe for resolution of the problem.

SUMMARY OF MAJOR POINTS

- Information security and protection encompasses administrative, technical, and physical measures that protect the confidentiality, integrity, and availability of nonpublic personal or business information.
- Many countries have laws and regulations that require government agencies and, in some cases, nongovernmental entities to develop, implement, and enforce security programs to prevent unauthorized access to or misuse of nonpublic information. In the United States, various sector-specific laws and regulations include information security requirements that are designed to protect personal information and serve the interests of regulatory authorities.
- In some countries, unauthorized access to or use of documents that contain nonpublic information is a crime, a form of theft. In recent years, legislation has focused on data breaches rather than document theft as the dominant type of information security crime.
- Many countries have laws that require an organization to report the unauthorized release of nonpublic personal information to designated supervisory authorities and to notify the affected data subjects. In most countries, these notification requirements are incorporated into or aligned with national privacy and data protection laws.
- Many contracts and agreements include clauses that specify a contractor's security obligations for nonpublic personal and business information that the contractor processes and stores for a client. Failure to comply may result in termination of the contract or civil litigation for breach of contract.
- Information security standards and norms are important because they are widely accepted as reflective of best practices. Some contracts and agreements require adoption practices for information security and protection, in which case applicable standards and industry norms provide a benchmark for compliance assessment. Contracts aside, an organization may require compliance with standards and norms to satisfy regulatory authorities or

internal policies requiring adherence to best practices for security of nonpublic personal or business information.

- Internal information security policies define compliance requirements for an organization's employees and other workforce members. These information security policies define workforce members' responsibilities for safeguarding the confidentiality, integrity, and availability of nonpublic personal and business information that they create, receive, process, or otherwise handle in the course of their assigned duties. Most organizations use a combination of prevention, through training of workforce members, and deterrence, through sanctions to punish noncompliance.
- Failure to safeguard the confidentiality, integrity, and availability of nonpublic information can have an adverse impact on an individual's well-being, as well as devastating consequences for society as whole. The custodian of nonpublic personal or business information has an ethical obligation to prevent harm from unlawful or unauthorized access, use, disclosure, reproduction, alteration, or destruction, but the complicated nature of this ethical obligation prevents the formulation of definitive compliance requirements.

NOTES

1. The three components of information security were introduced in the so-called Anderson report on computer security planning, which was prepared for the Air Force in 1972, but they were not termed a triad until the early 1980s. For a historical review of the CIA triad, see S. Samonas and D. Coss, "The CIA strikes back: redefining confidentiality, integrity and availability in security," *Journal of Information System Security* 10 (3), 21–45 (2014), https://www.proso.com/dl/Samonas.pdf.
2. 44 U.S.C. Subchapter II-Information Security, https://www.law.cornell.edu/uscode/text/44/chapter-35/subchapter-II.
3. Circular No. A-130, Appendix I: Responsibilities for Protecting and Managing Federal Information Resources, https://obamawhitehouse.archives.gov/sites/default/files/omb/assets/OMB/circulars/a130/a130revised.pdf.
4. FIPS PUB 100, Standards for Security Categorization of Federal Information and Information Systems (Gaithersburg, MD: National Institute of Standards and Technology, 2004), https://nvlpubs.nist.gov/nistpubs/fips/nist.fips.199.pdf; FIPS PUB 200, Federal Information Processing Standard Publication, *Minimum Security Requirements for Federal Information and Information Systems* (Gaithersburg, MD: National Institute of Standards and Technology, 2006), https://nvlpubs.nist.gov/nistpubs/fips/nist.fips.200.pdf.
5. 48 CFR 252.204-7012, Safeguarding covered defense information and cyber incident reporting, https://www.law.cornell.edu/cfr/text/48/252.204-7012.
6. Calif. Gov. Code 11549.3, https://leginfo.legislature.ca.gov/faces/codes_displayText.xhtml?lawCode=GOV&division=3.&title=2.&part=1.&chapter=5.7.&article=1; Calif. Gov. Code 8592.35, https://leginfo.legislature.ca.gov/faces/codes_displayText.xhtml?lawCode=GOV&division=1.&title=2.&part=&chapter=7.&article=6.4; State Administrative Manual, Section 5300, https://www.dgs.ca.gov/Resources/SAM/TOC/5300.

7. Fla. Stat. 282.318, http://www.leg.state.fl.us/statutes/index.cfm?App_mode=Display_Statute&Search_String=&URL=0200-0299/0282/Sections/0282.318.html.
8. Kan. Stat. 75-7240, http://www.kslegislature.org/li_2020/b2019_20/statute/075_000_0000_chapter/075_072_0000_article/075_072_0040_section/075_072_0040_k/.
9. Wyo. Stat. 9-21-101, https://codes.findlaw.com/wy/title-9-administration-of-the-government/wy-st-sect-9-21-101.html.
10. N.D. Century Code 54-59-05 et seq., https://www.ndlegis.gov/cencode/t54c59.pdf.
11. See, for example, M. Qiu and C. Wright, "The role of information security in Sarbanes-Oxley compliance," *Issues in Information Systems* 6 (2), 124–30 (2005), https://doi.org/10.48009/2_iis_2005_124-130; L. Wallace et al., "Information security and Sarbanes-Oxley compliance: an exploratory study," *Journal of Information Systems* 25 (1), 185–211 (2011), https://doi.org/10.2308/jis.2011.25.1.185; S. Anand, "Information security implications of Sarbanes-Oxley," *Information Security Journal: a Global Perspective* 17 (2), 75–79 (2008), https://doi.org/10.1080/19393550801953372; B. Nearon et al., "Life after Sarbanes-Oxley: the merger of information security and accountability," *Jurimetrics* 45 (4), 379–412 (2005), https://www.jstor.org/stable/29762906.
12. The HIPAA Security Rule is presented in 45 CFR Part 160—General Administrative Requirements, https://www.law.cornell.edu/cfr/text/45/part-160; and 45 CFR Part 164, Subparts A and C, https://www.law.cornell.edu/cfr/text/45/part-164.
13. 16 CFR Part 314-Standards for safeguarding customer information, https://www.law.cornell.edu/cfr/text/16/part-314.
14. Calif. Civil Code 1798.81.5, https://leginfo.legislature.ca.gov/faces/codes_displaySection.xhtml?lawCode=CIV&sectionNum=1798.81.5.
15. 21 CMR 17.00, Standards for the protection of personal information of the residents of the Commonwealth, https://www.mass.gov/doc/201-cmr-17-standards-for-the-protection-of-personal-information-of-residents-of-the/download.
16. SHIELD Act, SB 5575B, https://legislation.nysenate.gov/pdf/bills/2019/s5575b.
17. Public Act No. 21-119, https://www.cga.ct.gov/2021/act/Pa/pdf/2021PA-00119-R00HB-06607-PA.PDF; Ohio Rev. Code 1354.02, https://codes.ohio.gov/ohio-revised-code/section-1354.02.
18. General Business Law, 899-bb, https://www.nysenate.gov/legislation/laws/GBS/899-BB.
19. 23 NYCRR 500, https://www.governor.ny.gov/sites/default/files/atoms/files/Cybersecurity_Requirements_Financial_Services_23NYCRR500.pdf.
20. AR S.B. 149, https://custom.statenet.com/public/resources.cgi?id=ID:bill:AR2021000S149&ciq=ncsl&client_md=f9b9a5094309a22915b1352f099c821f&mode=current_text.
21. NAIC Insurance Data Security Model Law, https://content.naic.org/sites/default/files/inline-files/MDL-668.pdf.
22. Calif. Civil Code 1798.91.04, https://codes.findlaw.com/ca/civil-code/civ-sect-1798-91-04.html.
23. 15 U.S.C. 278g-3b—Security standards and guidelines for agencies on use and management of Internet of Things devices, https://www.law.cornell.edu

/uscode/text/15/278g-3b; M. Fagan et al., *IoT Device Cybersecurity Guidance for the Federal Government: Establishing IoT Device Cybersecurity Requirement*, NIST Special Publication 800213 (Gaithersburg, MD: National Institute of Standards and Technology, 2021), https://nvlpubs.nist.gov/nistpubs/SpecialPublications/NIST.SP.800-213.pdf; M. Fagan et al., *IoT Device Cybersecurity Guidance for the Federal Government: IoT Device Cybersecurity Requirement Catalog*, NIST Special Publication 800213A (Gaithersburg, MD: National Institute of Standards and Technology, 2021), https://csrc.nist.gov/publications/detail/sp/800-213a/final.

24. Personal Information Protection and Electronic Documents Act, Clause 4.7, Schedule I, https://laws-lois.justice.gc.ca/eng/acts/P-8.6/FullText.html.
25. See https://gdpr-info.eu/art-5-gdpr/.
26. See https://gdpr-info.eu/.
27. Directive 95/46/EC, Artlcle 17, https://eur-lex.europa.eu/legal-content/EN/TXT/?uri=celex%3A31995L0046.
28. Australian Privacy Principle 11—Security of personal information, https://www.legislation.gov.au/Details/C2014C00076.
29. Protection of Privacy Regulations (Data Security) 5777-2017, https://www.gov.il/BlobFolder/legalinfo/data_security_regulation/en/PROTECTION OF PRIVACY REGULATIONS.pdf.
30. Personal Information Protection Law of the People's Republic of China, articles 9, 42, https://digichina.stanford.edu/work/translation-personal-information-protection-law-of-the-peoples-republic-of-china-effective-nov-1-2021/.
31. See https://eur-lex.europa.eu/legal-content/EN/TXT/?uri=CELEX-%3A52020PC0595.
32. 45 C.F.R. 164.308, https://www.law.cornell.edu/cfr/text/45/164.308'.
33. 21 CFR 211.68, https://www.accessdata.fda.gov/scripts/cdrh/cfdocs/cfcfr/cfrsearch.cfm?fr=211.68; 21 C.F.R. 820.180, https://www.accessdata.fda.gov/scripts/cdrh/cfdocs/cfcfr/CFRSearch.cfm?fr=820.180.
34. 19 C.F.R. 163.5, https://www.law.cornell.edu/cfr/text/19/163.5.
35. 25 C.F.R 543.20, https://www.law.cornell.edu/cfr/text/25/543.20.
36. Saudi Arabian Monetary Authority, Payment Services Provider Regulations, Section 15.3, https://www.sama.gov.sa/en-US/RulesInstructions/Documents/PSPs Regulations 111.pdf.
37. See https://www.enisa.europa.eu/securesme/cyber-tips/strengthen-technical-measures/secure-backups.
38. M. de Villiers, "Reasonable foreseeability in information security law: a forensic analysis," *Hastings Communications and Entertainment Law Journal* 30 (3), 420–78 (2008), https://repository.uchastings.edu/cgi/viewcontent.cgi?article=1658&-context=hastings_comm_ent_law_journal. See also M. Rustad and T. Koenig, "The tort of negligent enablement of cybercrime," *Berkeley Technology Law Journal* 20 (4), 1553–611 (2005), https://btlj.org/data/articles2015/vol20/20_4/20-berkeley-tech-l-j-1553-1612.pdf; S. Romanosky et al., "Empirical analysis of data breach litigation," *Journal of Empirical Legal Studies* 11 (1), 74–104 (2014), https://doi.org/10.1111/jels.12035.
39. According to 38 C.F.R 75.122, such incidental access is not considered a data breach, https://www.law.cornell.edu/cfr/text/38/75.112.

40. L. Ablon, *Data Thieves: The Motivations of Cyber Threat Actors and their Use and Monetization of Stolen Data*. Testimony presented before the House Financial Services Committee (Santa Monica, CA: RAND Corporation, 2018), https://www.rand.org/content/dam/rand/pubs/testimonies/CT400/CT490/RAND_CT490.pdf; B. Arief et al., "Understanding cybercrime from its stakeholders' perspectives: Part 1—Attackers," *IEEE Security & Privacy* 13 (1), 71-76 (2015), https://doi.org/10.1109/MSP.2015.19; R. Sabillon et al., "Cybercrime and cybercriminals: a comprehensive study," *International Journal of Computer Networks and Communications Security* 4 (6), 165-76 (2016), http://openaccess.uoc.edu/webapps/o2/handle/10609/78507.
41. A. Crane, "In the company of spies: When competitive intelligence gathering becomes industrial espionage," *Business Horizons* 48 (3), 233-40 (2005), https://doi.org/10.1016/j.bushor.2004.11.005; P. Wright and G. Roy, "Industrial espionage and competitive intelligence: one you do; one you do not," *Journal of Workplace Learning* 11 (2), 53-59 (1999), https://doi.org/10.1108/13665629910260743; T. Hemphill, "Oracle vs. Microsoft: Corporate espionage of competitive intelligence?" *Business and Society Review* 107 (4), 501-11 (2002), https://doi.org/10.1111/1467-8594.00149; D. Jameson, "The rhetoric of industrial espionage: the case of *Starwood v. Hilton*," *Business Communication Quarterly* 74 (3), 289-98 (2011), https://doi.org/10.1177/1080569911413811; T. Toriola, *Industrial Espionage of Competitive Intelligence*, CERIAS Tech Report 2011-10 (Purdue, IN: Purdue University, Center for Education and Research, information Assurance and Security, 2011), https://www.cerias.purdue.edu/assets/pdf/bibtex_archive/2011-10.pdf; and T. Hou and V. Wang, "Industrial espionage—a systematic literature review (SLR)," *Computers & Security* 98, 1-11 (2020), https://doi.org/10.1016/j.bushor.2004.11.005.
42. In *O'Day v. McDonnell Douglas Helicopter Co.*, 79 F.3d 756 (9th Cir. 1996), for example, the plaintiff, having been denied a promotion, entered his supervisor's office after hours and copied documents that he thought might be useful for his discrimination claim, https://caselaw.findlaw.com/az-supreme-court/1006795.html. In *Vannoy v. Celanese Corp.*, No. 09-1118, 2011 DOLSOX LEXIS 68 (ARB Sept. 28, 2011), an employee removed confidential and sensitive documents to support a disclosure under the IRS Whistleblower Rewards Program, https://www.employment-lawgroup.com/wp-content/pdf/09_118.SOXP_.pdf. In *Quinlan v. Curtiss-Wright Corp.*, 204 N.J. 239 (N.J. Dec. 2, 2010), the plaintiff was fired for copying hundreds of documents to support her claim of widespread sex discrimination, https://www.courtlistener.com/opinion/2556532/quinlan-v-curtiss-wright-corp/.
43. 18 U.S.C. 641, https://codes.findlaw.com/us/title-18-crimes-and-criminal-procedure/18-usc-sect-641.html; 18 U.S.C. 1506, https://www.law.cornell.edu/uscode/text/18/1506; 18 U.S.C. 2071, https://www.law.cornell.edu/uscode/text/18/2071.
44. German Criminal Code, articles 202-202a, https://www.gesetze-im-internet.de/englisch_stgb/englisch_stgb.html-p1868.
45. Indian Penal Code, Section 378, https://www.indiacode.nic.in/show-data?actid=AC_CEN_5_23_00037_186045_1523266765688&sectionId=46161&sectionno=378&orderno=435.
46. United Nations Conference on Trade and Development, Cybercrime Legislation Worldwide.

47. Criminal Code (R.S.C., 1985, c. C-46) 342.1, https://laws-lois.justice.gc.ca/eng/acts/C-46/section-342.1.html.
48. Criminal Code Act 1995, Section 477 et seq., https://www.legislation.gov.au/Details/C2021C00183/Html/Volume_2-_Toc69803762.
49. Crimes Act 1900, no. 40, Section 308 et seq., https://legislation.nsw.gov.au/view/html/inforce/current/act-1900-040-pt.6.
50. CyberCrimes Act of 2020, https://www.gov.za/sites/default/files/gcis_document/202106/44651gon324.pdf.
51. Cybercrimes (Prohibition, Prevention, Etc.) Act, 2015, https://www.cert.gov.ng/ngcert/resources/CyberCrime__Prohibition_Prevention_etc__Act__2015.pdf.
52. Convention on Cybercrime, Budapest 23.XI.2001, https://rm.coe.int/1680081561. For a discussion of the Budapest Convention, see E. Wennerstrom, *EU-Legislation and Cybercrime: a Decade of European Legal Developments* (Stockholm: Stockholm Institute for Scandinavian Law, 2004), https://scandinavianlaw.se/pdf/47-21.pdf.
53. Directive 2013/40/EU of August 12, 2013 on attacks against information systems, articles 3-5, https://eur-lex.europa.eu/LexUriServ/LexUriServ.do?uri=OJ:L:2013:218:0008:0014:EN:PDF.
54. German Criminal Code, articles 202-202a, https://www.gesetze-im-internet.de/englisch_stgb/englisch_stgb.html-p1868.
55. Criminal Justice (Theft and Fraud Offenses) Act 2001, Section 9, https://www.irishstatutebook.ie/eli/2001/act/50/enacted/en/html.
56. Criminal Code of Finland, Ch. 30, Section 4, https://finlex.fi/en/laki/kaannokset/1889/en18890039.pdf.
57. Computer Misuse Act 1990, https://www.legislation.gov.uk/ukpga/1990/18/data.pdf.
58. Penal Code, Section 204, https://lovdata.no/dokument/NLE/lov/2005-05-20-28.
59. 18 U.S.C. 1030, https://www.law.cornell.edu/uscode/text/18/1030.
60. 18 USC 2701 et seq., https://www.law.cornell.edu/uscode/text/18/2701.
61. 18 U.S.C. 183 et seq., https://www.law.cornell.edu/uscode/text/18/1831.
62. Ala. Code 13A-8-112, https://codes.findlaw.com/al/title-13a-criminal-code/al-code-sect-13a-8-112.html; Ariz. Rev. Stat. 13-2316, https://codes.findlaw.com/az/title-13-criminal-code/az-rev-st-sect-13-2316.html; C.R.S. 18-5.5-102, https://codes.findlaw.com/co/title-18-criminal-code/co-rev-st-sect-18-5-5-102.html; 720 ILCS 5/17-50, https://codes.findlaw.com/il/chapter-720-criminal-offenses/il-st-sect-720-5-17-50.html; Neb. Rev. Stat. 28-1345, https://nebraskalegislature.gov/laws/statutes.php?statute=28-1345; New Mex. Stat. 30-45-1, https://codes.findlaw.com/nm/chapter-30-criminal-offenses/nm-st-sect-30-45-1.html; Utah Code 76-6-702, https://le.utah.gov/xcode/Title76/Chapter6/76-6-S703.html; Vt. Stat. Ann. tit. 13, 4101 et seq., https://legislature.vermont.gov/statutes/chapter/13/087.
63. New York, Penal Law, 156.30, https://www.nysenate.gov/legislation/laws/PEN/156.30.
64. MD Criminal Law Code Ann., 7-302, https://custom.statenet.com/public/resources.cgi?id=ID:bill:MD2021000H425&ciq=ncsl&client_md=6ebb72a2de132e45add586c50b6403d3&mode=current_text.

65. Calif. Penal Code 523, https://leginfo.legislature.ca.gov/faces/codes_displaySection.xhtml?lawCode=PEN&sectionNum=523; Conn. Gen. Stat. 53a-262, https://www.cga.ct.gov/current/pub/chap_952.htm-sec_53a-262; Wyo. Stat. 6-3-507, https://codes.findlaw.com/wy/title-6-crimes-and-offenses/wy-st-sect-6-3-507.html.
66. GDPR, sections 4, 33, and 34; recitals 75, 85, and 86, https://gdpr-info.eu/; the European Data Protection Board has issued a guideline with examples to facilitate compliance with data breach notification requirements, https://edpb.europa.eu/sites/default/files/consultation/edpb_guidelines_202101_databreachnotificationexamples_v1_en.pdf.
67. Breach of Security Safeguards Regulations: SOR/2018-64, https://canadagazette.gc.ca/rp-pr/p2/2018/2018-04-18/html/sor-dors64-eng.html.
68. Regulations to the Federal Law on the Protection of Personal Data in the Possession of Private Parties, articles 63 et seq., https://www.diputados.gob.mx/LeyesBiblio/regley/Reg_LFPDPPP.pdf.
69. Data Protection Act 2018, article 7, https://www.legislation.gov.uk/ukpga/2018/12/part/3/chapter/4/crossheading/obligations-relating-to-personal-data-breaches/enacted.
70. Privacy Amendment (Notifiable Data Breaches) Act 2017, https://canadagazette.gc.ca/rp-pr/p2/2018/2018-04-18/html/sor-dors64-eng.html.
71. Privacy Act 2020, Part 6, https://www.legislation.govt.nz/act/public/2020/0031/latest/LMS23223.html.
72. Protection of Personal Information Act, 2013, article 22, https://www.gov.za/sites/default/files/gcis_document/201409/3706726-11act4of2013protectionofpersonalinforcorrect.pdf.
73. Federal Act on Data Protection (Revised), 2020, https://www.parlament.ch/centers/eparl/curia/2017/20170059/Schluzssabstimmungstext 3 NS D.pdf.
74. Regulations on the Management of Online Data Security (Draft), article 11, https://www.chinalawtranslate.com/en/data-security-management-draft/.
75. Cyber Incident Reporting for Critical Infrastructure Act of 2022, https://www.cisa.gov/sites/default/files/publications/Cyber-Incident-Reporting-ForCriticalInfrastructure-Act-o-f2022_508.pdf; Presidential Policy Directive/PPD-21—Critical Infrastructure Security and Resilience, https://obamawhitehouse.archives.gov/the-press-office/2013/02/12/presidential-policy-directive-critical-infrastructure-security-and-resil.
76. 12 C.F.R. Subpart C, https://www.law.cornell.edu/cfr/text/12/part-304/subpart-C. See also https://www.fdic.gov/news/board-matters/2021/2021-11-17-notational-fr.pdf.
77. 47 C.F.R. 64.2011, https://www.law.cornell.edu/cfr/text/47/64.2011.
78. 45 C.F.R. Subpart D, https://www.law.cornell.edu/cfr/text/45/part-164/subpart-D.
79. The National Conference of State Legislatures provides links to the full texts of enacted laws and proposed legislation. See https://www.ncsl.org/research/telecommunications-and-information-technology/overview-security-breaches.aspx
80. Cal. Civil Code, 1798.2; Mo. Rev. Stat. 407.1500, https://revisor.mo.gov/main/OneSection.aspx?section=407.1500&bid=23329&hl=.

81. Ala. Code 8-32-2, http://alisondb.legislature.state.al.us/alison/CodeOfAlabama/1975/8-38-2.htm; Ariz. Rev. Stat. 18-551 et seq., https://www.azleg.gov/viewdocument/?docName=https://www.azleg.gov/ars/18/00551.htm; Fla. Stat. 501.171, http://www.leg.state.fl.us/statutes/index.cfm?App_mode=Display_Statute&Search_String=&URL=0500-0599/0501/Sections/0501.171.html; S.D. Cod.Laws 20-40-19 et seq., https://sdlegislature.gov/Statutes/Codified_Laws/2047702; 24 Okla. Stat. 165., https://casetext.com/statute/oklahoma-statutes/title-24-debtor-and-creditor/chapter-8-credit-services-organization-act/security-breach-notification-act/section-165-enforcement-authority-to-bring-action.
82. Examples of the many publications on the security risks in outsourcing information-related business operations include G. Dhillon et al., "Information security concerns in IT outsourcing: identifying (in)congruence between clients and vendors," *Information & Management* 54 (4), 452–64 (2017), https://doi.org/10.1016/j.im.2016.10.002; J. Bronfman, "The undercover detective looks at data breach contract clauses: who should be responsible under contract for costs of cover," *South Carolina Law Review* 67 (3), 536–60 (2016), https://scholarcommons.sc.edu/sclr/vol67/iss3/3/?utm_source=scholarcommons.sc.edu%2Fsclr%2Fvol67%2Fiss3%2F3&utm_medium=PDF&utm_campaign=PDFCoverPages; Z. Khalfan, "Information security considerations in IS/IT outsourcing projects: a descriptive case study of two sectors," *International Journal of Information Management* 24 (1), 29–42 (2004), https://doi.org/10.1016/j.ijinfomgt.2003.12.001; B. Bhatti et al., "Information security risk management in IT outsourcing: a quarter-century systematic literature review," *Journal of Global Information Technology Management* 24 (4), 259–98 (2021), https://doi.org/10.1080/1097198X.2021.1993725.
83. See guidelines for business associate agreements issued by the Department of Health and Human Services, https://www.hhs.gov/hipaa/for-professionals/covered-entities/sample-business-associate-agreement-provisions/index.html.
84. ISO/IEC 27000 standards are discussed in many publications. See, for example, A. Gillies, "Improving the quality of information security management systems with ISO 27000," *TQyM Journal* 23 (4), 367–76 (2011), https://doi.org/10.1108/17542731111139455; G. Disterer, "ISO/IEC 27000, 27001, and 27002 for information security management," *Journal of Information Security* 4 (2), 92–100 (2013), http://dx.doi.org/10.4236/jis.2013.42011; I. Akinyema et al., "SWOT analysis of information security management system ISO 27001," *International Journal of Service Operations and Information Management* 10 (4), 305–29 (2020), https://doi.org/10.1504/IJSOI.2020.111297; R. Alexander and S. Panguluri, "Cybersecurity terminology and frameworks," in R. Clark and S. Hakim, eds., *Cyber-Physical Security: Protecting Critical Infrastructure, Vol. 3* (Cham, Switzerland: Springer, 2017), 19–47, https://doi.org/10.1007/978-3-319-32824-9_2.
85. For online access to TC CYBER standards, see https://www.etsi.org/cyber-security/tc-cyber-roadmap.
86. Directive (EU) 2016/1148 concerning measures for a high common level of security of network and information across the Union, https://eur-lex.europa.eu/legal-content/EN/TXT/PDF/?uri=CELEX:32016L1148&rid=1; on the proposed successor, see https://ec.europa.eu/transparency/documents-register/detail?ref=SWD(2020)345&lang=en.

87. For a list of 62443 series titles, see https://webstore.iec.ch/publication/7029.
88. For an informative introduction, see PCI DSS Quick Reference Guide, https://listings.pcisecuritystandards.org/documents/PCI_DSS-QRG-v3_2_1.pdf. Examples of the many publications on PCI DSS requirements and compliance include E. Morse and V. Raval, "PCI DSS: Payment card industry data security standards in context," *Computer Law & Security Review* 24 (6), 540–54 (2008), https://doi.org/10.1016/j.clsr.2008.07.001; G. Ataya, "PCI DSS audit and compliance," *Information Security Technical Report* 15 (4), 138–44 (2010), https://doi.org/10.1016/j.istr.2011.02.004; K. Razikin and A. Widodo, "General cybersecurity maturity model: best practice to achieve Payment Card Industry-Data Security Standard (PCI-DSS) compliance," *CommIT (Communications and Information Technology* 15 (2), 91–104 (2021), https://doi.org/10.21512/commit.v15i2.6931.
89. The Cybersecurity Enhancement Act of 2014 is codified at 15 U.S.C. § 272(e), https://www.law.cornell.edu/uscode/text/15/272. Critical infrastructure is defined in Committee on National Security Systems (CNSS) Glossary, CNSSI 4009 (Ft. Meade, MD: Committee on National Security Systems, 2015), https://rmf.org/wp-content/uploads/2017/10/CNSSI-4009.pdf.
90. Executive Order—Improving Critical Infrastructure Cybersecurity, February 12, 2013, https://obamawhitehouse.archives.gov/the-press-office/2013/02/12/executive-order-improving-critical-infrastructure-cybersecurity. See also Framework for Improving Critical Infrastructure Cybersecurity (Gaithersburg, MD: National Institute of Standards and Technology, 2018), https://nvlpubs.nist.gov/nistpubs/CSWP/NIST.CSWP.04162018.pdf.
91. *Security and Privacy Controls for Information Systems and Organizations*, Special Publication 800-53, Rev. 5 (Gaithersburg, MD: National Institute of Standards and Technology, 2020), https://csrc.nist.gov/publications/detail/sp/800-53/rev-5/final-pubs-documentation.
92. *Control Baselines for Information Systems and Organizations*, Special Publication 800-53B (Gaithersburg, MD: National Institute of Standards and Technology, 2020), https://csrc.nist.gov/publications/detail/sp/800-53b/final.
93. *Protecting Controlled Unclassified Information in Nonfederal Systems and Organizations*, Special Publication 800-171, Rev. 2 (Gaithersburg, MD: National Institute of Standards and Technology, 2021), https://csrc.nist.gov/publications/detail/sp/800-171/rev-2/final.
94. *Enhanced Security Requirements for Protecting Controlled Unclassified Information: A Supplement to NIS Special Publication 800-171*, Special Publication 800-172 https://csrc.nist.gov/publications/detail/sp/800-172/final.
95. For a full listing of SP 800 series titles with links to the publications themselves, see https://csrc.nist.gov/publications/sp800.
96. For a catalog of SP 1800 series titles, see https://pages.nist.gov/NIST-Tech-Pubs/SP1800.html.
97. See, for example, M. Wolden et al., "The effectiveness of COBIT 5 information security framework for reducing cyber attacks on supply chain management system," IFAC Papers OnLine 48 (3), 1846–52 (2015), https://doi.org/10.1016/j.ifacol.2015.06.355; K. Nistrina and H. Bin Bon, "Information security for hospital information system using Cobit 5 framework," *Proceedings of the International Conference on Industrial Engineering and Operations Management*

(Southfield, MI: IEOM Society International, 2019), 3369–73, http://ieomsociety.org/ieom2019/papers/767.pdf.

98. The COSO sponsoring organizations are the American Accounting Association, the Association of International Certified Professional Accountants, Financial Executives International, the Institute of Management Accountants, and the Institute of Internal Auditors. Summaries of COSO guidance documents are collected at https://www.coso.org/SitePages/Guidance.aspx?web=1.
99. N. Ahmad and Z. Shamsudin, "Systematic approach to successful implementation of ITIL," *Procedia Computer Science* 17, 237–44 (2013), https://doi.org/10.1016/j.procs.2013.05.032; R. Anand, "Benefits of adopting Information Technology Infrastructure Library (ITIL), *Journal of Management Research* 14 (3), 159–68 (2014), https://indianjournals.com/ijor.aspx?target=ijor:jmr&volume=14&issue=3&article=002; T. Elkebrokk and J. Iden, "Enabling a culture of IT services; the role of the IT infrastructure library," *International Journal of Information Technology and Management* 15 (1), 14–40 (2016), https://doi.org/10.1504/IJITM.2016.073911; S. Ali and T. Soomro, "Integration of information security essential controls into Information Technology Infrastructure Library," *International Journal of Applied Science and Technology* 4 (1), 95–100 (2014), https://www.academia.edu/22721536/Integration_of_Information_Security_Essential_Controls_into_Information_Technology_Infrastructure_Library_A_Proposed_Framework.
100. J. Ahlstrom, "Healthcare cyber security and HIPAA assurance with business associates," *Cyber Security* 3 (2), 145–58 (2019–2020), https://www.ingentaconnect.com/content/hsp/jcs/2019/00000003/00000002/art00006.
101. S. Gros, "A critical view on CIS Controls," in M. Antonic and J. Babic, eds, 2021 Sixteenth International Conference on Telecommunications (ConTEL) (Zagreb, Croatia: University of Zagreb, Faculty of Electrical Engineering and Computing, 2021), 122–28, https://doi.org/10.23919/ConTEL52528.2021.9495982; V. Viegas and O. Kuyucu, *Information Security Frameworks* (New York: Apress, 2022), 67–102, https://doi.org/10.1007/978-1-4842-7799-7_3.
102. A. Al-Moshaigeh et al., "Cybersecurity risks and controls: Is the AICPA's SOC for cybersecurity a solution," *CPA Journal* 89 (6), 36–41 (2019), https://www.cpajournal.com/2019/07/08/cybersecurity-risks-and-controls/; T. Eaton et al., "Accounting and cybersecurity risk management," *Current Issues in Auditing* 13 (2), C1-C9 (2019), https://doi.org/10.2308/ciia-52419; S. Kahyaoglu and K. Caliyurt, "Cyber security assurance process from the internal audit perspective," *Managerial Auditing Journal* 33 (4), 360–76 (2018), https://doi.org/10.1108/MAJ-02-2018-1804.
103. N. Safa et al., "Information security policy compliance model in organizations," *Computers & Security* 56 (1), 70–82 (2016), https://doi.org/10.1016/j.cose.2015.10.006; M. Siponen et al., "Compliance with information security policies: an empirical investigation," *Computer* 43 (2), 64–71 (2010), https://doi.org/10.1109/MC.2010.35; L. Myyry et al., "What levels of moral reasoning and values explains adherence to information security rules? An empirical study," *European Journal of Information Systems* 18 (2), 126–39 (2009), https://doi.org/10.1057/ejis.2009.10.
104. On information security and ethics, see S. Vallor and W. Rewak, *An Introduction to Cybersecurity Ethics*, an ethics module for cybersecurity-related courses issued

by the Markkula Center for Applied Ethics at Santa Clara University, https://www.scu.edu/ethics/focus-areas/technology-ethics/resources/an-introduction-to-cybersecurity-ethics/; K. Macnish and J. van der Ham, "Ethical approaches to cybersecurity," in C. Veliz, ed., *Oxford Handbook of Digital Ethics* (Oxford: Oxford University Press, 2022), available online in advance of print publication, https://doi.org/10.1093/oxfordhb/9780198857815.013.28; M. Manjikian, *Cybersecurity Ethics: an Introduction* (London: Routledge, 2018); B. Stahl et al., "Critical theory as an approach to the ethics of information security," *Science and Engineering Ethics* 20 (3), 675-99 (2014), https://doi.org/10.1007/s11948-013-9496-6l; H. Nemati, *Information Security and Ethics: Concepts, Methodologies, Tools, and Applications* (Hershey, PA: Information Science Reference, 2008); M. Quigley, ed., *Encyclopedia of Information Ethics and Security* (Hershey, PA: Information Science Reference, 2007); M. Quigley, ed., *Information Security and Ethics: Social and Organizational Issues* (Hershey, PA: IRM Press, 2005).

105. D. Denning and B. Strawser, "Active cyber defense: Applying air defense to the cyber domain," in G. Perkovich and A. Levite, eds., *Understanding Cyber Conflict: Fourteen Analogies* (Washington, DC: Georgetown University Press, 2017), 193–210, https://carnegieendowment.org/2017/10/16/active-cyber-defence-applying-air-defence-to-cyber-domain-pub-73416; S. Stevens, "A framework for ethical cyber-defense for companies," in M. Christen et al., eds., *The Ethics of Cybersecurity* (Cham, Switzerland: Springer Nature, 2020), 317–30, https://doi.org.10.1007/978-3-030-29053-5.
106. The code originated in a proposal from the Russian Federation, China, Tajikistan, and Uzbekistan, see http://www.pircenter.org/media/content/files/9/13512404110.pdf. See P. Meyer, "Norms of responsible state behaviour in cyberspace," in M. Christen et al., eds., *The Ethics of Cybersecurity* (Cham, Switzerland: Springer Nature, 2020), 347–60, https://doi.org.10.1007/978-3-030-29053-5.
107. The Center for Strategic & International Studies (CSIS), a nonprofit policy research organization, maintains a timeline of significant cyber incidents involving government agencies, strategic companies, and economic crimes since 2006. See https://www.csis.org/programs/strategic-technologies-program/significant-cyber-incidents.
108. International Committee of the Red Cross, "Weapons: Statement of the ICRC to the United Nations, 2017," https://www.icrc.org/en/document/weapons-statement-icrc-united-nations-unag-2017. Examples of the many articles on the application of the IHL to cybersecurity include J. Kelsey, "Hacking into International Humanitarian Law: the principles of distinction and neutrality in the age of cyber warfare," *Michigan Law Review* 106 (7), 1427–51 (2008), https://www.jstor.org/stable/40041623; C. Droege, "Get off my cloud: cyber warfare, international humanitarian law, and the protection of civilians," *International Review of the Red Cross* 94 (886), 533–78 (2012), https://doi.org/10.1017/S1816383113000246; D. Wallace, *Cyber Weapon Reviews under International Humanitarian Law: a Critical Analysis* (Talinn, Estonia: NATO Cooperative Cyber Defense Centre of Excellence, 2018), https://ccdcoe.org/uploads/2018/10/TP-11_2018.pdf; E.

Diamond, *Applying International Humanitarian Law to Cyber Warfare* (Tel Aviv, Israel: Institute for National Security Studies, 2014), http://www.jstor.com/stable/resrep08957.8; T. Ramlucken, "International humanitarian law and its applicability to the South African cyber environment," *Journal of information Warfare* 19 (3), 102–17 (2020), https://www.jstor.org/stable/27033635; S. Kleeman, "Cyber warfare and the 'humanization' of international humanitarian law," *International Journal of Cyber Warfare and Terrorism* 11 (2), 1011 (2021), https://doi.org/10.4018/IJCWT.2021040101; and A. Cassimitas, "International humanitarian law, international human rights law, and fragmentation of international law," *International Comparative Law Quarterly* 56 (3), 623–39 (2007), https://doi.org/10.1093/iclq/lei185.

7

Ownership of Information

According to the *Collins Dictionary of Law*, the concept of ownership is either so simple that it needs no explanation or so elusive that it defies definition. Nonetheless, the Dictionary provides a succinct definition of ownership as "the full and complete right of dominion over property."[1] Citing examples dating from the sixteenth century, the *Oxford English Dictionary* defines ownership as the legal right of possession of a thing and the owner as the person who possesses it.[2] Similarly, Black's Law Dictionary defines ownership as the complete dominion, title, or propriety right in a thing or claim and the *owner* as the person in whom such right is vested.[3]

In these definitions, *ownership* is the legal right to possession and control of property. The earliest conceptions of ownership were limited to tangible property—real estate, for example, or objects, such as factory equipment or farm implements—but that limitation no longer applies. Since the late nineteenth century, the concept of property has been de-physicalized.[4] The *Encyclopedia Britannica*, which was itself de-physicalized in 2012, defines *ownership* as the legal relation between an individual, group, corporation, or government and an object, noting that the object may be corporeal or a purely legal creation, such as a patent or a copyright.[5]

The compliance requirements discussed in this chapter treat information as property, a view that is supported by a 1984 decision of the U.S. Supreme Court that recognized trade secrets as property.[6] Like other forms of property, information may be owned by an individual, a group, a business, a nonprofit entity, or, in the case of government records, the public. The owner may be the information's creator or another party who acquired it from its creator. There is general agreement in legal literature that ownership confers a bundle of rights related to the possession, control, use, modification, and disposition of property.[7] These ownership rights apply to information as a type of property. Specifically, the owner of information has the exclusive right to use it, reproduce it, alter it, disclose it, transfer it to another party, sell it, donate it, exchange it, bequeath it, destroy it, earn income from it, or use it as collateral for financing. Depending on the circumstances and type of information involved, these ownership rights may remain in effect for a brief period of time or for many decades.

As discussed in the following sections, ownership of certain types of information is regulated by laws and contractual obligations. Compliance requirements for information ownership may also be defined in industry norms and rules of professional conduct, as well as in an organization's internal policies. The chapter closes with a discussion of societal concerns about the relationship between information ownership and the public welfare.

LEGAL AND REGULATORY COMPLIANCE

Most countries have laws that determine who can properly claim ownership of information and control its use, disclosure, transfer, and disposal for economic gain, to maintain personal privacy, to protect the welfare of individuals or the general public, or to achieve other objectives. As discussed in the next sections, the following types of legislation are relevant for compliance with information ownership requirements in specific situations:

- Intellectual property laws that define rights and privileges that govern the ownership and exploitation of written works, artistic works, inventions, symbols, and images
- Laws that protect trade secrets and other confidential business information
- Archival legislation related to ownership of government records
- Laws that address the ownership of medical records

INTELLECTUAL PROPERTY LAWS: COPYRIGHT

Intellectual property laws have the dual purpose of encouraging writing, research, invention, artistic expression, and other activities that create information while allowing the information's owner to control and profit from it. According to the World Intellectual Property Organization (WIPO), a self-funding agency of the United Nations, *intellectual property* refers to "creations of the mind, such as inventions, literary and artistic works, designs, and symbols, names, and images used in commerce."[8] WIPO divides intellectual property laws into two categories: (1) copyright laws that protect an organization's literary and artistic works, and (2) laws that protect an organization's industrial property. The latter includes patents, trademarks, and trade secrets, which will be discussed in subsequent sections. National laws in both categories specify permissible uses and restrictions for intellectual property as well as penalties for noncompliance.

Intellectual property laws pose significant compliance challenges. Because intellectual property is an intangible asset with anticipated benefits, infringement of protected works can degrade an organization's financial performance, damage its reputation, and harm its competitive position. Consequently, an organization must be vigilant about the infringement of its intellectual property rights. It also must be concerned about the possibility that its own business operations and the activities of its employees will infringe upon the intellectual property rights of others. Given the long periods of protection provided by intellectual property laws, there is ample time for these noncompliant events to occur.

Copyright gives authors and artists exclusive rights over their original written or artistic works. In the 181 countries that are parties to the Convention for the Protection of Literary and Artistic Works, the so-called Berne Convention, copyright laws protect the intellectual property rights of writers, translators, musicians, painters, photographers, cinematographers, and other creators of literary, artistic, and scientific content, subject to limited exclusions.[9] The copyright holder, the party whose intellectual property rights are protected, may be the author, composer, artist, or other creator of a work. It may also be the creator's employer in the case of work performed as part of assigned job duties or another party, such as a publisher, to whom copyright ownership is assigned. Copyright protection does not depend on a work's literary or artistic merits. It applies equally to a scholarly publication that required years of painstaking research and to a business document or email message that took a few minutes to write.

Where a work is protected by copyright law, the copyright holder has the exclusive right to reproduce, publish, translate, display, recite, sell, or distribute it. Other parties must obtain the copyright holder's permission to perform any of these actions. The Berne Convention also gives the copyright holder a moral right to object to any mutilation, deformation, or other derogatory modifications of a protected work, although there are variations in the national implementation of this provision. In the United States, for example, moral rights are limited to works of visual art, while copyright laws in Canada and the European Union extend moral rights to all protected works. U.S. copyright law also limits a copyright holder's distribution rights. According to the first sale doctrine, copyright holders have exclusive control over distribution of their work up until the time of first sale. The purchasers can then sell, rent, or lend a copyright-protected work as they see fit. Exceptions are limited to software and audio recordings of musical works, which cannot be rented to the public.[10]

The scope of copyright protection varies from country to country. In the United States, for example, the Copyright Act of 1976 applies to any original work that is fixed in a tangible medium of expression—that is, the work must be recorded on a physical medium that allows it to be communicated to others by visual or audio means.[11] Examples of information that satisfies this requirement include, but are not limited to, written works, paintings, drawings, artistic print, sculptural works, architectural designs, sound recordings, photographs, motion pictures, and video recordings. In Canada, copyright protection applies to original literary, dramatic, musical, and artistic works, including such incomplete creations as proposals and treatments, as well as to sound recordings, performances, and broadcast communication signals.[12] Broadcasts by air, cable, and satellite are likewise protected by copyright law in the European Union.[13] In most countries, copyright laws also encompass related or neighboring rights, which protect the rights of performers and producers of a creative work independent of the author's rights.[14]

Perpetual copyright applies to a small number of works in certain countries. The most frequently cited example, the King James Bible, is protected by Crown Copyright in the United Kingdom. In most cases, however, the duration of copyright is limited but longer than the protection provided for other forms of intellectual property discussed in this chapter. According to the Berne Convention, copyright laws must protect a work for at least fifty years after the author's death. For anonymous and pseudonymous works, the required duration of protection is fifty years after the work is made public. An audiovisual work must be protected for at least fifty years from its release to the public or, if that does not occur, fifty years from its creation. These Berne Convention requirements have been adopted in Canada, China, and many other countries, with some exceptions and exclusions, but some national copyright laws provide a longer period of protection for certain works.

In the United States, the duration of copyright protection is seventy years after the death of the author for works created after January 1, 1978. Older copyright legislation with different provisions applies to works created before 1978. For anonymous or pseudonymous works, copyright protection remains in effect for ninety-five years after first publication or 120 years from creation, whichever is shorter. The same period of protection applies to works made for hire; in the United States, content created by an employee as part of their assigned duties is the intellectual property of the employer, a concept that does not exist in some other countries. In the European Union, copyrighted works are protected for seventy years after the death of the author or, for films and other audiovisual works, the death of the principal director, screenwriter, and composer of music specifically created for the work. All parties to the Berne Convention agree to honor the copyright protection granted in the country where a work originated, even if a national copyright law provides a shorter term of protection than the country of origin.

Copyright protection is automatic and absolute. It begins as soon as a written or artistic work is fixed in tangible form. It does not require any special action on the creator's part. It does not depend on the purpose of the work or the circumstances in which it is created. A book is protected by copyright when it is published. A business document is protected by copyright the moment it is recorded on paper or a digital medium. Registration of the work is not required, but some countries provide a formal copyright registration mechanism that is entirely voluntary. Copyright registration provides *prima facie* evidence of facts related to the ownership of a copyrighted work. It can help resolve legal disputes about the authorship and ownership of literary and artistic works.

The United States does not require registration or even a copyright notice for protection. Registration is necessary, however, if the copyright holder wishes to initiate litigation for infringement in a federal court, although many foreign works are exempt from this requirement. The U.S. Copyright Office registers over 450,000 copyright claims annually, but the vast majority of eligible works are never registered.[15]

Noncompliance with copyright law is common and, given the wide range of circumstances in which it can occur, difficult to detect. In the United States, the fair use exception allows copyrighted images or text to be reproduced on a limited basis for research, education, literary criticism, or other nonprofit purposes.[16] Copyright laws in Canada, Australia, the United Kingdom, and some other countries have similar provisions with a more limited range of exceptions. Apart from that exception, infringement occurs when a substantial part of a copyrighted work is reproduced, distributed, performed, exhibited, translated, adapted, or otherwise used without the permission of the copyright holder.

Infringement may be intentional, to obtain financial or commercial advantages, or unintentional, due to lack of knowledge or understanding of copyright restrictions, which are complicated and unfamiliar to most people. An employee who freely photocopied or printed copyright-protected publications in a high school or college library may not be aware that such reproduction is only legally permissible in the context of a fair use exception. Copyright violations involving digital images and text are an especially pervasive problem. Reportedly, as many as 85 percent of images on websites and social media are reproduced without the copyright holder's knowledge or permission.[17] During the first half of 2021, over seven hundred million copyright infringement claims were submitted to YouTube alone.[18] Recognizing the prevalence of noncompliance with copyright protection for digital information, the European Union has issued guidance to online content-sharing service providers instructing them to obtain authorization from copyright holders for content uploaded to their websites and to avoid unauthorized uploads.[19] In the United States, a copyright holder can file a notice under the Digital Millennium Copyright Act to compel a website to remove or block access to infringing content.[20]

National laws protect copyrighted works, but copyright holders are responsible for enforcing their rights. A copyright holder can initiate legal action to stop and possibly punish an infringer. Various civil remedies are possible. An injunction may be issued to restrain or prevent the infringement. Illegal copies or other infringing items may be impounded and ultimately destroyed. A monetary award may be granted, based on the copyright holder's actual damages and the infringer's profits plus the copyright holder's legal fees and court costs. Alternatively, a fine may be imposed with the greatest penalties for willful noncompliance, but civil litigation, arbitration, mediation, or other legal proceedings to enforce copyright compliance can be time-consuming and costly, especially in complicated cases that involve multiple infringements or foreign political jurisdictions. Criminal prosecution leading to fines or imprisonment is possible if the copyright infringement was to obtain financial gain.

To avoid the aggravation of holding infringers accountable for noncompliance, some copyright holders expressly relinquish copyright protection after a period of time or simply ignore noncompliance, effectively allowing their work to enter the public domain, which is the ultimate fate of copyrighted works when the period of protection elapses. Open access, which is principally used for online publishing of scientific research and other scholarly work, eliminates most copyright restrictions, but it forfeits the commercial benefits of copyright protection.

INTELLECTUAL PROPERTY LAW: TRADEMARKS

A *trademark* is a word, phrase, or symbol that identifies and distinguishes a particular product. If a trademark identifies a service, it is termed a service mark. Other attributes that identify a product, such as a distinctive package or color shade, are termed *trade dress*. National trademark laws, which vary from country to country, confer the exclusive right to use trademarks, service marks, and trade dress. In some countries, an organization can obtain trademark protection by being the first to use a mark for commercial purposes. Alternatively and more commonly, a trademark's owner can register it with a national or regional trademark authority. While trademark registration is not required, it provides public notice and creates a legal presumption of an ownership claim. In the United States, registration is required for civil actions concerning trademark infringement in federal court.

Trademark protection is territorial. It is limited to the countries in which a trademark is registered. The World Intellectual Property Organization provides a mechanism for registration of trademarks in multiple countries with a single application. Unlike copyrights, trademark protection does not necessarily expire. Trademark registration is initially valid for ten years, with unlimited renewals possible at prescribed intervals. Protection will be lost, however, if a trademark does not remain in continuous use for commercial purposes or if the owner abandons it.

Trademark infringement is the unauthorized use of a valid trademark or one that is similar enough to confuse a consumer. Trademark dilution is the use of a similar mark that diminishes the distinctiveness and commercial value of a valid trademark or tarnishes its image by associating it with something objectionable, even if a consumer is unlikely to be confused by the similarity. In many countries, trademark infringement connected to the sale or importing of counterfeit goods is a crime.[21] In the United States, for example, it is a felony offense under the Trademark Counterfeiting Act of 1984 and the Anticounterfeiting Consumer Protection Act of 1996. More often, trademark infringement or dilution leads to civil litigation. Trademark owners must enforce their intellectual property rights to main the validity of their trademarks. Possible remedies include an injunction to stop the infringing activities, forfeiture or destruction of infringing products, monetary compensation for damages to the trademark owner, and payment of the trademark owner's attorneys' fees and court costs.

INTELLECTUAL PROPERTY LAW: PATENTS

Just as copyright law protects original written and artistic works, patent law protects *original inventions*, which the World Intellectual Property Organization defines as products or processes that provide "a new way of doing something."[22] A patent does not authorize the production or sale of an invention. It gives a patent holder a time-limited right to stop others from making, using, distributing, importing, selling, or otherwise commercially exploiting an invention without permission. The patent owner may be the inventor, an employer to whom the invention rights have been assigned by an employment agreement or other contractual obligation, or another party to whom the patent rights have been transferred.

Unlike copyright protection, which is automatic, patents are awarded by national patent offices or regional patent authorities through an application process that involves a thorough examination of the invention's characteristics and an evaluation of its patentability. To qualify for a patent, an invention must be novel, useful in the real world at the present time, and not an obvious variation of what is already known. A patent only protects an invention in the country in which it is issued. The Patent Cooperation Treaty provides an international application process that allows an inventor to seek patent protection in multiple countries, but the application must be individually approved by each country. A unitary patent issued by the European Patent Office is valid in all EU member states.

Under the Agreement on Trade-Related Aspects of Intellectual Property Rights (TRIPS), which applies to the 159 countries that are members of the World Trade Organization, a utility patent, which is based on the way an invention works, must remain in force for at least twenty years, but no starting date is specified for the period of protection. In the United States, Canada, EU member states, Australia, China, and most other countries, utility patents remain in force for twenty years from the date the patent application was filed, but an extension may be allowed in some circumstances. For an industrial design patent, which is based on an item's distinctive appearance rather than its functional characteristics, the period of protection varies from country to country. In the United States, design patents remain in force for fifteen years from the date of issue. In Canada, an industrial design is protected for ten years after registration or fifteen years after the filing date, whichever is later. In the European Union, designs are protected for an initial term of five years, which can be renewed up to a maximum of twenty-five years. In Australia, the term of a design patent is ten years from the filing date.

Patent infringement is the unauthorized production, sale, distribution, or other use of a patented invention for commercial purposes while patent protection is in effect. Design infringement involves a comparable violation involving the visual appearance of a protected industrial design. As with copyright, patent infringement is common and difficult to detect. In the United States, three to four thousand infringement proceeding are initiated each year, but they are thought to represent a fraction of undetected patent infringements. The more general and broadly useful the scope of a patent or industrial design, the greater the number of potential infringements, many of them unintentional. In the absence of a diligent patent search, an organization's product development, design, or manufacturing operations can inadvertently infringe a patent of which it is not aware.

In some countries, patent infringement is a criminal offense that is punishable by a fine or imprisonment. In Norway, for example, patent infringement is punishable by imprisonment for up to one year or, if aggravating circumstances exist, three years.[23] In the Netherlands, prison terms for patent infringement range from six months to four years.[24] In Germany, infringement for commercial gain is punishable by up to five years in prison.[25] In the United States, patent infringement is a civil offense. Litigation in federal court is necessary to enforce an organization's patent rights.[26] Damage awards are the penalty for noncompliance with patent laws, but willful infringement, which results in the highest awards, can be difficult to prove. Most patent litigation is settled by payment of reasonable royalties to the patent owner.

TRADE SECRETS

As discussed above, patent protection requires public disclosure of an invention. Infringement of a patent can be avoided by keeping the invention a trade secret rather than filing an application for protection. As defined in the preceding chapter, a trade secret is business information that it is not generally known and that has actual or potential commercial value to those who are not authorized to know it. To be considered a trade secret, business information cannot be readily ascertainable, and it must be protected by reasonable security measures to prevent unauthorized access. Unlike other types of intellectual property, which are subject to a registration and approval process, protection of a trade secret takes effect immediately and remains in effect unless and until the secret is exposed.

Examples of trade secrets include unpatented inventions, product formulations, undisclosed industrial designs, proprietary research methods or manufacturing processes, computer code, technical data, and proprietary sales or distribution methods. Trade secrets may also include commercial information, such as customer lists, proprietary information about customer requirements, pricing information, marketing plans, and confidential supplier agreements. Even information gained through unsuccessful initiatives, such as a failed scientific experiment or an unfavorable outcome of a market test for a new product, can be considered a trade secret if knowledge of the negative results would be advantageous to a competitor.

A trade secret is usually recorded in tangible form on paper or electronic media, but this is not a requirement. Trade secrets are sometimes equated with "know-how," which is practical knowledge a person acquires through experience. In the European Union, know-how is considered intellectual property provided that it is secret, substantial, and identifiable as such.[27] In other countries, know-how is widely recognized as an economic asset, but it is not necessarily protected by intellectual property rights.

Acquisition of a trade secret by improper means—such as espionage, misrepresentation, or bribery—is termed *misappropriation*, a form of information theft. In the United States, misappropriation of trade secrets is prohibited by the following intellectual property laws:

- The Uniform Trade Secrets Act, first issued by the Uniform Law Commission in 1976 and amended in 1985, has been adopted, with variations, by most U.S. states and territories.[28] The Act codifies the basic principles of common law protection for the rights of a trade secret's owner and provides uniform definitions of trade secrets and misappropriation. It prohibits trade secret acquisition, disclosure, or use by improper means while acknowledging the possibility of discovering a trade secret by legal means, such as independent invention, parallel research and development, reverse engineering, or under a valid license arrangement. In such cases, multiple parties may hold property rights to the same trade secret, although they would not know it unless the secret is revealed by one of the parties. The Uniform Trade Secrets Act specifies a statute of limitations for civil litigation related to misappropriation and provides remedies, including injunctive relief and payment of damages.
- At the federal level, the Economic Espionage Act (EEA) of 1996, which was discussed in chapter 6, criminalizes the misappropriation of a trade secret with the intent to benefit a foreign government or any agency or organization controlled by a foreign government.[29] The intended benefit may be economic, strategic, tactical, or reputational. More broadly, the EEA prohibits any type of misappropriation of trade secrets regardless of beneficiary where an economic benefit is anticipated, the misappropriation is intended to harm the owner of the trade secret, and the secret is related to a product involved in interstate or foreign commerce. Violators are subject to forfeiture of the proceeds of misappropriation plus a multimillion-dollar fine and imprisonment up to fifteen years, depending on the circumstances of the misappropriation.
- The Defend Trade Secrets Act of 2016 provides an alternative to state courts for trade secret owners seeking redress for misappropriation. It

amends Title 18 of the U.S. Code to provide a private right of civil action in federal court for unauthorized acquisition or disclosure of a trade secret involved in interstate or foreign commerce.[30] It provides a maximum penalty of $5 million for misappropriation and adds trade secret theft to the list of offenses that constitute racketeering.

Global protection of trade secrets is important for organizations with multinational research, development, design, and manufacturing operations. There are no international laws that specifically address trade secrets and no global standards for protection. Historically, some European countries have included trade secret protection in their industrial property codes, and a general duty of confidentiality for an organization's employees is widely assumed in most countries. Designed to harmonize protection across member states, the EU Trade Secrets Directive, which took effect in 2018, prohibits the unauthorized acquisition, use, or disclosure of trade secrets.[31] It requires the owner of a trade secret to implement reasonable contractual, technical, and administrative measures to prevent misappropriation. Possible remedies for misappropriation include injunctions and recall or destruction of infringing goods. Member states can exceed baseline requirements specified in their national implementations of the Directive.

Elsewhere trade secret protection varies from country to country. In Canada, there is no federal law dealing exclusively with trade secrets. To comply with the United States-Mexico-Canada Agreement, which replaced NAFTA in 2020, the Canadian Criminal Code was amended to prohibit misappropriation of trade secrets.[32] For civil litigation, misappropriation is treated as a tort claim in provincial courts. Under Australian law, trade secrets are treated as a form of confidential business information. The Corporations Act of 2001 prohibits the improper use of such information by officers or employees of a corporation to gain an advantage for themselves or others or to harm the corporation.[33] In South Korea, the Unfair Competition Prevention and Trade Secrets Protection Act defines trade secrets, prohibits misappropriation, and provides court-ordered remedies, including injunctive relief and award of damages.[34] Criminal prosecution is also possible. Korean entities that commit trade secret appropriation overseas are subject to criminal proceedings in Korea if the country where the misappropriation occurred does not provide criminal penalties. China does not have legislation that deals specifically with trade secrets, but some measure of protection is provided by the Anti-Unfair Competition Law and other Chinese laws and regulations.[35]

Compliance with trade secret laws is problematic because trade secrets are difficult to protect and misappropriation is easy to commit, often inadvertently. Employees may not understand trade secret concepts and may not know which information in their custody or under their supervisory control is considered a trade secret. Business partners, contractors, suppliers, and others who gain knowledge of an organization's trade secrets may not limit access to their own employees or properly inform their employees about restrictions on disclosure. According to the legal doctrine of "inevitable disclosure," a former employee or contractor who takes a job with a competitor cannot help but rely on the former company's trade secrets when making decisions about competing products developed by a new employer.[36]

OWNERSHIP OF GOVERNMENT RECORDS

Ownership of government records is established by archival legislation. In the United States, archival statutes and regulations affirm public ownership of records created by federal, state, and local government. At the national level, the Federal Records Act and the Presidential Records Act establish ownership of the records of the U.S. government. The Federal Records Act of 1950 defines *government records* to include all recorded information, regardless of form or characteristics, made or received by a federal agency under federal law or in connection with the transaction of public business.[37]

The Federal Records Act does not apply to records created and received by the president and the vice president. Such records were initially considered private property. The Presidential Records Act of 1978 established the federal government's ownership, possession, and control of the official records of the president and vice president created or received after January 20, 1981.[38] The Act also applies to records created by certain entities, such as the National Security Council and the Council of Economic Advisors, that advice and assist the president. Both the Federal Records Act and the Presidential Records Act provide for the ultimate transfer of government records to the legal custody of the archivist of the United States. For records covered by the Presidential Records Act, the transfer must happen as soon as a president leaves office.

Many state and local archival laws are modeled on the Federal Records Act. They define *state and local government records* to include information in any format—in some cases, paraphrasing the language of the federal statute—and they require agencies to transfer records of enduring value to a state or local archives. Public ownership of government records is implied in most of these laws, but there are notable exceptions. The Illinois State Records Act contains an explicit assertion that all records created or received in the course of a State agency's public duties "are the property of the State."[39] The Utah Public Records Management Act contains the same statement.[40] North Carolina law affirms that all records of state government are "the property of the people."[41] Texas law takes an expansive view of state records, noting that they include recorded information from periods when the state was a province, colony, or republic.[42] Some state archival laws apply to legislative and court records. The National Archives is responsible for official records of federal courts, but the Federal Records Act does not apply to the records of Congress or the Supreme Court.

Other countries have archival laws that cover records created and received by national and, where they exist, subnational governments. While these laws may not explicitly state that government records are public property, they give archival agencies possession of and control over government records to an extent typically associated with legal ownership. Archival laws in some eastern European and Asian countries carry the concept of information as public property a step further, claiming public ownership of culturally significant records maintained by private companies, religious bodies, nonprofit organizations, and other nongovernmental entities. These laws reflect the concept of a national archive first articulated in V. I. Lenin's archival decree of 1918.[43] In some countries, organizations that maintain private archives are required to turn them over to a state-operated archival agency after a prescribed period of time. Private archives cannot be sold or transferred out of the country without the approval of archival authorities. The same prohibition applies to public records.[44]

In most countries, government records are inalienable. The archival laws discussed in this section prohibit the private possession of public records and allow the replevin of government records that are in private hands.[45] Noncompliance may involve government employees who take records out of an agency office or from government computers, former employees who took records with them when they left government service, contractors who took possession of government records in the course of their work, and private parties who come into possession of government records by some means. Penalties for noncompliance typically involve some combination of fines and imprisonment. Minor violations of the Federal Records Act, for example, are punishable by a fine or imprisonment for up to one year, but the most serious offenses can result in greater penalties.[46] In Indonesia, a person who knowingly possesses public records is subject to a fine and imprisonment for up to five years.[47]

OWNERSHIP OF MEDICAL RECORDS

As discussed later in this chapter, the idea that personal information should be considered the property of the data subject has been much discussed and is often applauded, but such property rights are not recognized by laws or regulations in any country.[48] As discussed in previous chapters, data protection and privacy laws give individuals some measure of control over the content, processing, disclosure, transfer, and retention of information that organizations collect and maintain about them, but data subjects do not have a "full and complete right of dominion" over their personal information, which is an essential characteristic of ownership as defined at the beginning of this chapter. By the same token, data protection and privacy laws limit the ownership rights of government agencies, companies, and other entities that collect and maintain personal information.

Medical information maintained by a health-care provider is a type of personal information. Medical records contain information about an individual patient's medical history, care, and treatment. The health-care provider may be a medical doctor, osteopathic physician, podiatrist, optometrist, dentist, chiropractor, nurse practitioner, clinical psychologist, clinical social worker, or another trained professional who is licensed or otherwise authorized to provide health-care services.[49] The information included in medical records may be obtained during clinical encounters or from external sources, such as medical laboratories and pharmacies. Medical records may be kept in paper files or in electronic databases that reside on in-house computers or cloud-based services.

Ownership of medical records is variously claimed by the health-care practitioners who created them; by the group practices, hospitals, and other health-care facilities that employ the health-care practitioners; and by patients who are the subjects of the medical and personal information the records contain. Ownership of medical information created by health-care practitioners who work for health-care facilities or group practices—an issue that may arise when a practitioner leaves a practice—is typically specified in employment contracts. Patients' ownership of medical information that is created and maintained about them by health-care providers and health-care facilities is often discussed in the broader context of patient empowerment. It has been widely supported by patient advocates, legal scholars interested in health care, and even some health-care practitioners, but patients' ownership of their medical information is poorly understood from a legal perspective.[50]

In the United States, there is a widely held view that health-care providers own the medical records they create and maintain, while patients own the medical information contained in their records,[51] but that view has no legal basis. The United States does not have federal laws that address ownership of either medical records or the information they contain. The HIPAA Privacy Rule, which was discussed in previous chapters, gives patients the right to inspect, review, and obtain copies of medical records maintained about them by health-care providers, but it does not state or imply that patients own those records. As with retention of medical records, ownership is regulated by state law:

- New Hampshire is the only state where a patient's property right to medical information is specifically affirmed by law. According to the Patients' Bill of Rights, information contained in medical records maintained by certain licensed health-care facilities are "the property of the patient," but property does not appear to have the meaning discussed in the introduction to this chapter.[52] The law does not give the patient exclusive possession or control of the information. It merely states the patients shall have a right to obtain copies of their medical records on request. The New Hampshire law is further limited to medical information maintained about patients by hospitals, health services operated by educational institutions, home health-care providers, medical laboratories, outpatient rehabilitation and surgery facilities, dialysis facilities, emergency medical care facilities, residential care facilities, and adult daycare services. Medical records maintained in physicians' offices and other health-care settings are specifically exempt.

- Laws and regulations in twenty-one states affirm that medical records are owned by health-care providers. As an example, Georgia law categorically states that a patient's medical records "are owned by and are the property of the provider."[53] According to Florida health-care regulations, the "records owner" is the health-care practitioner who generates a medical record.[54] In Wyoming, patients can request access to their medical records, but "the paper, microfilm, or data storage unit upon which the patient's information is maintained belongs to the physician and/or health facility." Patients "do not have a right to possess the physical means by which the information is stored."[55] The South Carolina Physicians' Patient Records Act states that "the physician is the owner of medical records in his possession that were made in treating a patient," but the physician's property right is not absolute. Patients have the right to take possession of their medical records if the physician's practice is sold to another health-care provider.[56] The scope of some of these state laws is limited to medical records maintained by hospitals and other health-care facilities.[57] Records related to patient care provided by a hospital are owned by the hospital. The same property rights may be accorded to medical records related to care provided by ambulatory surgery centers and similar outpatient facilities, but this may not be explicitly stated.
- The remaining twenty-eight states and the District of Columbia do not have laws or regulations that address the ownership of medical records. Patients' rights in those states are limited to accessing and obtaining copies of their records, subject to some exceptions. Where property rights to medical records are not covered by legislation, ownership disputes may be decided in court cases based on common law. In this respect, legal treatment of medical records is similar to legal treatment of property rights for client records maintained by attorneys and accountants. For the most part, ownership of those records is addressed in practice rules issued by professional associations at the national, state, or local levels, and in ownership disputes that are adjudicated in court.[58]

Few other countries provide specific legal guidance about ownership of medical information. There are some notable exceptions. A Canadian Supreme Court ruling in a 1992 case affirmed that medical records belong to health-care providers, although patients have a right to see the content of their records.[59] In Indonesia, the Law on Health Workers makes it clear that medical records belong to health-care facilities.[60] In Japan, medical records are owned by health-care providers, and patients have no legal right to access them.[61]

The laws discussed in this section do not impose any particular compliance obligations related to the ownership of medical records. Noncompliance issues involve the information access and disclosure requirements discussed in other chapters. In this respect, data protection and privacy laws constrain the property rights of owners of medical information as they do with other types of personal information.

CONTRACTUAL COMPLIANCE

Companies and other organizations often use contracts and agreements to assert and protect their ownership rights to specific information. This section reviews compliance requirements related to information ownership in the following commonly encountered types of contracts:

- Contracts for services that involve the protected intellectual property of the client organization or another party
- Contracts for cloud computing services
- Employment contracts that address ownership of work for hire
- Non-disclosure agreements that protect an organization's ownership of trade secrets and other nonpublic business information
- Agreements that transfer ownership of information or intellectual property rights from one party to another

CONTRACTS FOR SERVICES

Most contracts and agreements include clauses that address ownership issues and property rights for information that an organization provides to contractors and that contractors may create or collect in the course of their work for a client organization. Such clauses typically include some combination of the following compliance requirements and assertions that the contractor must acknowledge:

- The client organization retains all property rights and interests in data, documents, or other information provided to and created or collected by the contractor in fulfillment of the contract, subject to specified exclusions. The contractor must acknowledge that it has no ownership rights to such information, subject to exceptions and exclusions that may be specified in the contract itself.
- Where contract provisions designate the contractor as the owner of specific data, documents, or other information to be used in fulfillment of the contract, the client organization reserves the right to inspect, copy, or audit the information.
- The contractor must comply fully with intellectual property laws that apply to information provided by the client organization or collected by the contractor in the course of its work. The contractor must avoid any actions that endanger or invalidate the client organization's intellectual property rights.
- The contractor must limit the use of the client organization's trademarks to situations that are approved in advance by the client organization.

- To preserve ownership of the client organization's trade secrets, the contractor must implement reasonable physical, technical, and administrative security measures that will prevent unauthorized access and ensure compliance with national laws that require such measures.
- The contractor must agree to assign to the client organization all intellectual property rights to any original written works and inventions it creates in fulfillment of the contract. The contractor must agree that it will not sue the client organization for intellectual property violations relating to information it creates in fulfillment of the contract.
- The contractor must alert the client organization immediately if infringement of its intellectual property rights, by the contractor itself or another party, is detected or suspected.
- The contractor must not violate copyright, patent, trademark, or trade secret laws by using protected information without an appropriate license or other authorization obtained from the owner of the intellectual property rights.
- The contractor must indemnify the client organization against claims related to alleged violations of intellectual property rights or other ownership rights relating to information it creates in fulfillment of the contract.
- Where deliverables created by a contractor contain information that is properly considered the contractor's intellectual property, contracts and agreements should include a clause that grants the client organization that commissioned the work a perpetual, royalty-free license to use such information in connection with the deliverables.
- The contract must specify what ownership rights will apply to information upon termination of the contract.
- All the above contract clauses must apply to any subcontractors, business partners, and affiliated entities that will have access to the client organization's information.

As with other contractual obligations discussed in this book, a contractor's failure to comply with these compliance requirements may result in termination of the contract with or without warning. Noncompliance also exposes a contractor to civil litigation based on breach of contract or infringement of intellectual property rights.

CLOUD COMPUTING CONTRACTS

A cloud computing service provides online access to computer resources for processing, retrieval, publication, distribution, retention, or other use of digital content, which is stored on servers operated by the cloud service provider. Cloud services offer an alternative or supplement to an organization's in-house computing capabilities. They may be operated by global cloud providers, such as Amazon and Microsoft, or by various regional and special-purpose providers, including those that offer cloud-based email, office productivity software, and backup services.

Cloud computing poses challenges for ownership and control of an organization's information. Ownership rights to cloud content are determined by intellectual property laws and contract provisions. Cloud service providers disavow ownership of digital content that is uploaded to their computing platforms or created by customers using their online applications, but their terms of service may authorize certain actions that are customarily associated with ownership. Cloud computing contracts typically require customers to grant them a license to host, store, use, and reproduce their intellectual property for purposes of providing services, which are rarely specified in detail. Some cloud computing contracts also require a worldwide license that allows them to modify, publish, or create derivative works, such as translations and adaptations, from a customer's intellectual property. In some cases, the license to use the customer's intellectual property remains in effect after the cloud computing contract terminates.

A cloud service provider can delete or deny an organization access to its own intellectual property when an account is delinquent, when a customer is suspected of infringing or misappropriating another organization's intellectual property, or for any other breach of the provider's terms of service.

WORK FOR HIRE

A work made for hire is a written or artistic work prepared by an employee within the scope of his or her employment.[62] As a legal concept, the work-for-hire doctrine addresses ownership of information in the context of copyright, but it may have implications for other situations, such as ownership of trade secrets or other confidential information that may come up during work performed by an independent contractor but that are unrelated to that work.[63] The work-for-hire doctrine does not apply to patents. An employer has no rights to an employee's invention except through a written assignment of intellectual property rights or where the employee was specifically hired to create an invention.

Employment contracts must address the concept of work for hire and its relationship to an employer's ownership of information:

- Employment contracts must specify that any data, documents, or other information that employees create in the course of their assigned duties will be considered work for hire and that all copyright, patent, or other intellectual property rights to the information will be vested in the employer.
- Contract clauses related to ownership of work made for hire should also apply to agreements involving leased employees, temporary employees, part-time employees, paid interns, and other contingent workers.

- Volunteers, student interns, and other unpaid workers should be asked to sign a statement that relinquishes any claim to intellectual property rights for any data, documents, or other information that they create or collect in the course of assigned tasks.

Legislative treatment of work for hire varies from country to country. In the United States, the work-for-hire doctrine is an aspect of copyright law. The United Kingdom, Ireland, the Netherlands, Japan, Australia, and some other countries have adopted similar pro-employer ownership rules, subject to some exceptions. In some countries, however, the work-for-hire doctrine is either nonexistent or limited in scope. In Germany, Italy, Belgium, Denmark, Spain, Portugal, and Greece, for example, the employee who creates a work is considered its author and owner unless copyright is transferred by an employment contract or other written agreement to the employer or organization that commissioned the work.[64]

In the United States, the work-for-hire doctrine also applies to certain written or artistic work that is specially ordered or commissioned by an organization, subject to express agreement by the parties involved. Commissioned works are created by independent contractors rather than employees. To be considered a work for hire under U.S. Copyright Law, a commissioned work must fall into one of the following categories: a contribution to a collective work, a part of a motion picture or other audio-visual work, a translation, a supplemental work, a compilation, an instructional text, a test, answer material for a test, or an atlas. Contracts and agreements with independent contractors should include a clause stating that any data, documents, or other information created as deliverables under the contract or agreement are the property of the organization that commissioned the work. The clause should further state that all intellectual property rights to the deliverables are vested in the organization that commissioned the work, excluding any information that is properly considered the intellectual property of the independent contractor or another party. The independent contractor must acknowledge these clauses in writing before beginning the commissioned work.

NONDISCLOSURE AGREEMENTS

As discussed in a preceding section, owners of trade secrets and other information that is not generally known must implement reasonable measures to preserve their intellectual property rights and prevent misappropriation. Failure to do so endangers ownership of the information. To avoid this, employment contracts should include clauses that prohibit unauthorized disclosure of an employer's trade secrets and other proprietary or confidential information that employees learn about in the course of their work, either by direct means or through secondhand communication. Employees who do not have written contracts should be asked to sign a separate nondisclosure agreement (NDA).

When sharing trade secrets and other nonpublic business information with contractors, consultants, suppliers, business partners, job applicants, and other nonemployees, organizations typically rely on nondisclosure agreements that prohibit them from revealing the information to unauthorized parties except in circumstances permitted by the agreement, such as a court-ordered disclosure.

A unilateral nondisclosure agreement is a written contract between the party who will disclose the nonpublic information and one or more parties who will receive the information. With bilateral and multilateral agreements, all participating parties will disclose nonpublic information that must not be shared with others. A nondisclosure agreement typically requires the receiving parties to exert reasonable efforts to keep the information secure.

Nondisclosure agreements may be nonterminating, time-limited, or a combination of durations. An agreement may be perpetual for trade secrets, for example, but limited to one or two years for other nonpublic information. Time-limited nondisclosure agreements may be renewed annually or at other predetermined intervals. Enforceability of an indefinite agreement may be limited by law in some national or subnational jurisdictions. In any case, a nondisclosure agreement ends if the trade secret or confidential business information it is designed to protect becomes public knowledge. A nondisclosure agreement may be invalidated if the owner of a trade secret or other nonpublic information fails to implement reasonable security measures to maintain confidentiality, as required by trade secret laws.

Nondisclosure agreements are legally binding. Failure to comply with disclosure restrictions exposes the noncompliant party to litigation for breach of contract or violation of trade secret laws, but a court may be reluctant to enforce restrictions that are too broad, vague, or unreasonable.[65] Some laws prevent legal proceedings against whistleblowers who disclose trade secrets that are related to suspected illegal acts or regulatory violations. A nondisclosure agreement only applies to specific information obtained from a disclosing party in the context covered by the agreement. It does not prohibit disclosure of nonpublic information if the information is obtained from a source that is not a party to the agreement or in circumstances not covered by the agreement.

TRANSFER OF INFORMATION OWNERSHIP

In some situations, contracts and agreements are used to transfer ownership of information or intellectual property rights from one party to another. For example:

- Copyrights, patents, industrial designs, and trademarks are sometimes sold by their rights holders. An intellectual property purchase agreement is used for the sale of intellectual property rights and supporting technology and documentation. It provides for an irrevocable transfer to the buyer of all ownership rights, title, and interest in specified intellectual property.

The agreement must also specify that the seller's rights to the intellectual property are undisputed and that the sale does not infringe the intellectual property rights of another entity or person.

- Ownership of copyrights, patents, trademarks, and trade secrets is an important concern in mergers and acquisitions, especially in industries such as pharmaceuticals and information technology where intellectual property is a critical asset and, in some cases, a motivating factor for a merger or acquisition. Ownership of intellectual property must be addressed in merger and acquisition agreements. When two companies or other entities merge, their assets—including all intellectual property as well as business records, databases, and other information assets—generally become the property of the new legal entity, subject to any exceptions or exclusions that may be specified in the merger agreement. Similarly, when one company is acquired by another, ownership of the acquired company's intellectual property and other information assets is transferred to the acquiring company. To get to the point where ownership is transferred, however, significant due diligence and negotiation is required to resolve issues related to valuation of intellectual property and other matters.
- A deed of gift is an agreement that transfers ownership of data, documents, or other information to an archives, library, historical society, or other research repository. It describes the specific information involved in the transfer of ownership and may establish terms and conditions for care, use, reproduction, and preservation of the information. In most cases, the agreement encompasses transfer of the donor's intellectual property rights, although others may own the intellectual property rights to publications, sound recordings, or other some other information covered by a deed of gift. If scholarly materials or intellectual property rights are sold to an archives or other research repository, a deed of gift may be accompanied or replaced by a purchase agreement.

STANDARDS AND INDUSTRY NORMS

Unlike the topics discussed in other chapters, international standards do not play a significant role in establishing compliance requirements for information ownership. No international standards specify guidelines or best practices for ownership of information in general. A few international standards address specific aspects of information ownership. As an example, ISO 56000:2020, *Innovation management—Fundamentals and vocabulary* defines terms related to intellectual property. ISO 56005:2020, *Innovation management—Tools and methods for intellectual property management—Guidance* presents a framework for management of intellectual property rights and discusses their role in the innovation process. Treating a specialized aspect of intellectual property, ISO/IEC TS 23078-1:2020, *information technology—Specification of DRM technology for digital publications—Part 1: Overview of copyright protection technologies in use in the publishing industry* describes technologies that inhibit the unauthorized redistribution and use of copyrighted digital content. For compliance requirements, however, organizations concerned about information ownership must look to industry norms and rules of professional conduct rather than international standards.

INTELLECTUAL PROPERTY

Compliance with intellectual property laws is a component of many ethical codes issued by professional associations, particularly those whose membership consists of information workers. Among the many examples that might be cited:

- The American Library Association's code of ethics requires members to respect intellectual property rights and advocates a balance between the interests of rights holders and information users. Copyright is the most important type of intellectual property for libraries, which purchase, circulate, and reproduce copyright-protected materials within parameters defined by the fair use exception and the first sale doctrine discussed in a preceding section.[66]
- The code of ethics of the International Federation of Library Associations and Institutions (IFLA) similarly recognizes the intellectual property rights of authors and other creators. Libraries and information associations must negotiate the most favorable terms to ensure that access is not unnecessarily restricted by the administration of intellectual property laws and that licenses do not override exceptions for libraries in national legislation.[67]
- The Association of Independent Information Professionals (AIIP) requires members who provide fee-based information services to recognize intellectual property rights, respect licensing agreements, and advise clients about the compliant use of copyright-protected materials.[68]
- The ethical code of the International Society for Medical Publication Professionals (ISMPP) requires members to recognize, respect, and protect intellectual property rights. It advocates the sharing of information within the limits of intellectual property protection.[69]
- According to the code of ethics of the Association for Computing Machinery (ACM), computer professionals are obligated to protect the integrity of intellectual property and not take credit for the work of others, even when the work is not protected by copyrights or patents. The ACM code of ethics for software engineering requires that developers inform their employers or clients if a project may violate intellectual property law.[70]
- The International Web Association (IWA) requires members to protect the intellectual property of others to ensure that originators realize all the benefits of their work.[71]

- Members of the Association of Registrars and Collections Specialists and the Collections Stewardship Professional Network of the American Alliance of Museums (AAM) must maintain accurate records of intellectual property and traditional knowledge rights associated with collection objects.[72]

Even professional associations with no clear connection to information work require their members to avoid knowingly infringing intellectual property rights. This obligation is included in ethical codes of groups as different as the International Right of Way Association, UFI—the Global Association of the Exhibition Industry, and the Public Relations Society of America.[73]

OWNERSHIP OF CLIENT RECORDS

Some ethical codes and professional practice rules address issues related to ownership of client records. For example:

- According to the Code of Ethics of the National Society of Professional Engineers (NSPE), an engineer's designs, data, records, and notes referring exclusively to an employer's work are the employer's property. Before undertaking work involving improvements, plans, inventions, or other records that may justify copyrights or patents, an engineer should enter into a positive agreement regarding ownership.[74]
- According to the Code of Professional Conduct of the American Institute of Certified Public Accountants (AICPA), a CPA must return, transfer, or otherwise provide clients with any records obtained from them during an engagement and any CPA-prepared records related to completed and issued work products for which the client has paid. Working papers, on the other hand, are the property of the CPA unless a state or local law or a contractual obligation states that a client is entitled to them.[75]
- In the United Kingdom, the Chartered Institute of Management Accountants (CIMA) advises members that tax files, financial statements, and final versions of other documents prepared for a client belong to the client, but working copies, drafts, and correspondence with third parties belong to the accountant.[76]
- The American Bar Association's model rules do not define the papers and property that a client is entitled to when representation ends, although there is general agreement that any data or documents that an attorney receives directly from a client is the client's property and must be returned upon termination of representation. According to ABA Formal Opinion 471, clients are not entitled to papers and property that attorneys prepare or collect for their own purposes when working on client matters. State and local bar association rules provide varying opinions about ownership of

client files. In New York City, for example, a client has a presumptive right to an attorney's entire file related to a representation.[77]

- In Canada, provincial law societies issue practice guidelines regarding ownership of client files. These guidelines are based on court decisions. Clients own any documents that predate a retainer agreement with an attorney plus any documents the attorney prepares for the client's benefit and for which the client has paid. Such documents include legal opinions, documents created for use in court, and witness statements. In the absence of a contractual arrangement, an attorney owns working notes and other documents that are prepared for the attorney's benefit and at the attorney's expense.[78]
- Canadian guidance is based on English rules issued by the Law Society.[79] Australian ownership rules are similar. Guidelines issued by the Office of the Legal Services Commissioner in New South Wales, for example, indicate that most documents in a client file belong to the client, but lawyers own any documents that were prepared for their own use and benefit.[80] According to the Law Institute of Victoria, documents created for a client's benefit belong to the client, while those created for the lawyer's benefit belong to the lawyer.[81]

INTERNAL MANDATES

As discussed above, contracts and agreements typically include clauses that address ownership issues and property rights for information that an organization provides to contractors and that contractors may create or collect in the course of their work for a client organization. Internal mandates define information ownership rights and compliance requirements for an organization's employees and other workforce members, including trainees, paid and unpaid interns, temporary workers, volunteers, and others. These mandates may be specified in an information ownership policy or integrated into an organization's code of conduct that also includes requirements for information retention, storage, access, and disclosure as discussed in previous chapters. In either case, internal mandates related to information ownership typically include some combination of the following compliance requirements:

- All data, documents, audio recordings, video recordings, and other information that is created, collected, received, or maintained by workforce members in relation to their assigned duties and the organization's mission, goals, objectives, or operations are the property of organization. This ownership policy applies to original information and to copies in all formats and media.
- No workforce member has, by virtue of his or her position, any property right to or property interest in data, documents, or other information re-

lated to work performed for the organization, even though he or she may be named as the creator, recipient, or custodian of them.

- All data, documents, and other information owned by the organization must be stored in the organization's offices, on computers that are owned and operated by the organization, by commercial storage providers and cloud-based services operating under contract to the organization, or in other approved locations. Storage of the organization's information in employees' homes or on employee-owned computers or mobile devices is prohibited.
- Data, documents, or other information owned by the organization may be kept in other locations or on employee-owned devices while they are in the process of being created, collected, or revised, but they must be transferred to a location approved by the organization as soon as the work is completed. Any locally saved copies must be deleted at that time.
- Workforce members must not take any data, documents, or other information owned by the organization, or copies of such information, when they retire, resign, or otherwise terminate employment.
- The written policy must affirm the work-for-hire doctrine in countries where it applies. Intellectual property rights associated with information created by workforce members in the course of their assigned duties will be vested in the employer to the extent permitted by law.
- Any exceptions to the work-for-hire doctrine must be clearly stated. Universities, for example, often exempt the academic writings and artistic creations of faculty members, even though they are required to prepare such work to qualify for tenure and promotion. A church or synagogue may exempt sermons, prayers, or other devotional writings prepared by clergy, even though they may be expected to present such material at religious services as a condition of employment.
- Workforce members must avoid improper usage or other actions that endanger the organization's intellectual property rights for copyrights, patents, and trademarks.
- Department managers must be responsible for ensuring that their employees understand protection measures necessary to preserve the organization's ownership of trade secrets and confidential business information contained in data or documents.
- Workforce members must respect the intellectual property rights of other organizations. Unlicensed use of copyright-protected material, patented inventions, and registered trademarks is prohibited.

Noncompliance with these internal mandates endangers an organization's ownership of information. Depending on the severity of the infraction, noncompliance may be punishable by an informal warning, a written warning, or an adverse performance evaluation.

Actions that endanger an organization's intellectual property rights, or that expose the organization to civil litigation for infringing the intellectual property rights of others, may be cause for demotion or termination of employment. Removal of data or documents from an organization's facilities or computer systems may be prosecuted as criminal offenses, just like the theft of other forms of an organization's property.

SOCIETAL COMPLIANCE

The principal societal issues related to ownership of information involve societal benefits and possible harms posed by intellectual property rights and the status of personal information as the intellectual property of the individuals to whom the information pertains.

INTELLECTUAL PROPERTY RIGHTS

In most countries, intellectual property rights are considered a public good that encourages creativity and innovation not merely for rights holders, but for the benefit of society as a whole. Article 1 section 8 of the U.S. Constitution recognizes this. It provides copyright and patent protection to "promote the progress of science and useful arts" by granting authors and inventors exclusive rights to their "respective writings and discoveries." In England, the Statute of Anne, widely cited as the world's first copyright law, was specifically intended for the "encouragement of learning."[82] Since creating literary and artistic works or developing scientific and technical innovations are costly activities, authors and inventors must have the prospect of sufficient return on their investments through a time-limited monopolistic right to exploit the work they produce for society's benefit as well as their own.

That is the more or less official view, but the role of intellectual property rights as a social good is not undisputed. It has been debated for more than a century by public policy analysts, economists, social activists, and others who argue there is no empirical evidence that copyright and patent protection increase creativity and innovation. On the contrary, intellectual property laws are often criticized for impeding the free flow of information. They protect the work of authors, artists, and inventors to an extent that harms rather than helps society. As one commentator noted, if James Joyce had had to negotiate with Homer's heirs over the use of material from *The Odyssey*, it would have taken him longer to write *Ulysses*, assuming he had been able to write it at all.[83] The same observation applies to the Coen brothers' 2000 film, *O Brother, Where Art Thou?*, which acknowledges *The Odyssey* as its source.[84]

Far from supporting the public good, critics argue, intellectual property rights sometimes work against the public interest by allowing state-enforced monopolies that unduly benefit rights holders to the ultimate detriment of society. These critics claim that intellectual property laws stifle competition, increase prices for creative and innovative works, and enable excessive profit-taking. As a notable exception, however, the societal benefits of trademark legislation, which prevents infringers from misleading the public by masquerading as established providers of goods and services, is rarely disputed. There is general agreement that trademark protection benefits both the rights holder and society as a whole. The same cannot be said of copyright and patent laws. Even those who support their role in encouraging the progress of knowledge concede that from a societal perspective, they are, at best, a necessary evil, an imperfect attempt to balance the interests of rights holders and the public good.

Abuses of patent law are often cited to support this view. On the one hand, patent protection gives inventors an exclusive opportunity to profit from their innovations for a specified amount of time, but rather than being exploited to manufacture new products, some patents are used as legal weapons to stop innovation by threatening potential competitors with costly litigation. Among the earliest examples, the Wright Brothers tried to block other early aviation companies by suing them for infringements that went well beyond the scope of their patents, a practice that is now characterized as patent trolling.[85] The early automotive industry was similarly beset by anticompetitive uses of patent litigation, the most notorious case involving George B. Selden, who sued the Ford Motor Company for infringement, claiming he held a patent that applied to every gasoline-powered automobile in America.[86] More recently, critics of intellectual property rights cite abuses of the patent system that keep drug prices high and block the development of lower-cost generic and biosimilar versions of lifesaving medicines. In particular, they cite the anticompetitive practice of extending the period of protection by obtaining overlapping patents for minor variations of a single drug. Recognizing the threat posed by the abuse of intellectual property rights, the World Trade Organization allows member countries to authorize the use of patents without the consent of the rights holder when necessary to protect public health.[87]

Some well-respected economists view copyright and patent protection as unnecessary. They challenge the historical justification that intellectual property laws are needed to encourage innovation investments and preserve profitability that is the principal incentive for creativity and innovation. Even if copyright and patent protection were abolished, they argue, writers, artists, and inventors would still enjoy the significant competitive advantage of being the first to market a new product. They further point out that much creativity and invention originates in universities and government-sponsored laboratories where the profit motive is not a factor. Many scholarly and scientific studies are created by academics who do not expect to profit from their research; in fact, some scholarly and scientific journals expect authors to pay a fee to cover the cost of publishing their work. Economists who question the value of patent protection also note that intellectual property laws are not the only method of protecting the return on investment in innovations. Rather than applying for patents, some organizations prefer to maintain their innovative ideas as trade secrets and rely on security measures and non-disclosure agreements to prevent their exploitation by unauthorized persons.

While intellectual property laws may not be necessary to ensure the progress of knowledge and may actually work against it by impeding the free exchange of ideas, the outright abolition of copyright and patent protection—an extreme solution advocated by some free market libertarians, info-anarchists, and other fringe thinkers—is unlikely. As a more realistic alternative, various sources have proposed measures to reform certain aspects of copyright and patent laws to better realize the societal benefits of creativity and innovation. Some of these measures would require legislative action that might be strongly opposed by rights holders; others can be put into effect by individuals without legislative involvement. While a complete discussion of copyright and patent reform is beyond the scope of this book, the following examples of copyright and patent changes promote compliance with the public interest:

- Some critics of intellectual property law advocate shortening the term of copyright in countries like the United States, where protection exceeds the requirements of the Berne Convention. They contend that copyright protection should last long enough to encourage creativity but not so long as to stifle the dissemination and use of information. As a significant complication, however, shortening the copyright term would negate existing intellectual property rights for previously published works with a resulting adverse impact on authors and their heirs. While the economic value of written works typically diminishes with age, some older works remain valuable properties, and forgotten works from the past occasionally experience an unanticipated surge in popularity when mentioned by politicians, celebrities, or news media. In the United States, a revocation of existing copyrights would appear to violate the prohibition on uncompensated seizure of private property provided in the takings clause of the Fifth Amendment to the Constitution.[88]
- Copyright laws could require registration to minimize the number of works that are protected by copyright. At present, as discussed in an earlier section, copyright protection is automatic, and many countries do not provide a registration mechanism. As a more practical measure that does not require legislative action, copyright holders could be encouraged to relinquish protection by deliberately contributing their work to the public domain, either immediately or after a period of time before protection elapses.
- Less radical alternatives are available for copyright holders who advocate sharing of information but prefer to retain some control over their work. Subject to variations, these alternatives allow copyright holders to license their work with some rights reserved. A Creative Commons license allows copyright holders to authorize use of their work with varying degrees of re-

striction ranging from unlimited commercial or noncommercial use as long as the copyright holder receives attribution to non-commercial use with some restrictions on modification and redistribution. A copyleft license, which is used for software as well as written and artistic works, similarly allows copyright-protected works to be used with varying degrees of restriction. The most permissive license allows copyright-protected works to be modified and shared as long as any derived works are released under a compatible license.

- Patent reform initiatives have a long history in the United States and elsewhere. Some economists and attorneys have advocated selectively reducing the term of patent protection, which is currently twenty years regardless of the industry in which innovation occurs. Some economists contend that a decade of patent protection is sufficient to encourage innovation investments. Others suggest that the length of a patent term should be tied to the cost of innovation, with industries that have high innovation costs—pharmaceuticals being a prime example—eligible for a longer period of patent protection than industries such as software development that have lower innovation costs and rapidly superseded products.[89]
- Critics of the patent system advocate the elimination of statutory provisions that allow patent extensions. In particular, reforms are needed to address the pharmaceutical industry's use of evergreening, the monopoly-extending process of obtaining new patent protections by making minor modifications to an existing drug. In most cases, the modifications do not constitute significant medical improvements. According to a 2018 study, evergreening tactics have extended the average period of protection for twelve bestselling drugs to thirty-eight years.[90]
- In the United States, various legislative solutions have been proposed to make litigation more difficult and expensive in cases that involve patent trolling. These include prohibiting vague allegations of infringement, requiring a plaintiff to post a bond sufficient to cover the defendant's legal costs at the beginning of a case, and requiring the plaintiff to reveal all parties who will financially benefit from litigation.

OWNERSHIP OF PERSONAL INFORMATION

The status of personal information as intellectual property has increasingly emerged as a societal concern in the context of individual privacy and personal data protection. The GDPR and other data protection laws and regulations are sometimes viewed as giving individuals ownership right to the personal information that organizations maintain about them, but that interpretation is open to debate.[91] As discussed in preceding chapters, data protection laws do give data subjects certain rights that are often associated with ownership—the right to determine who can access their personal information and the right to have it deleted when no longer needed for its original purpose, for example—but they do not expressly confer property rights. A 2005 draft dealing with protection of personal information in the People's Republic of China declared that personal information is a citizen's intangible property, but that provision was never officially adopted.[92]

At present, no intellectual property laws encompass personal information, and there is general agreement that national legal systems do not currently provide a sufficient basis for ownership of personal information.[93] A 2017 report by the British Academy and Royal Society noted that the idea of individual ownership of personal information makes "compelling soundbites" but dismissed it as a simplified notion that confuses intellectual property with identity.[94] In the United States, legal scholarship highlights the complexities associated with treatment of personal information as a data subject's intellectual property.[95] It often cites the analogy, presented in a much-discussed property law case, between wild animals and personal information. Just as wild animals belong to no one until they are captured, personal information does not have an owner until it is collected; then it belongs to the collector.[96] If the personal information is incorporated into a database, report, or other written work created by the collector, it would presumably be protected by copyright as discussed earlier in this chapter, and the collector, not the data subject, would be the rights holder.

Counterarguments for personal information as the intellectual property of the data subject are variously based on moral or economic concepts. These arguments are still at a formative stage of development, but their basic concepts can be summarized as follows:

- From a moral perspective, social activists, academics, and others view individual ownership of personal information as a fundamental human right. Acknowledging that existing data protection and privacy laws do not formally recognize that right, they contend that ownership of personal information is essential for individual data sovereignty and informational self-determination. Data subjects should have the ability to determine how their personal information will be used and how it will affect their lives.[97] Those who argue that ownership of personal information is a human rights issue cite article 12 of the United Nations' Universal Declaration of Human Rights, article 8 of the Council of Europe's Convention for the Protection of Human Rights and Fundamental Freedoms, and article 8 of the European Convention on Human Rights, all of which deal with respect for an individual's private life, to support their views.[98] Those documents do not specifically address property rights to personal information, but they do imply that an individual's rights to personal information are inalienable and incompatible with their ownership by others.[99]

- The economic argument recognizes the commercial value of personal information and asserts a data subject's right to transfer his or her information to others for monetary compensation. This argument, which appears to raise personal information to the status of intellectual property, assumes that the recipient of personal information will exploit it for commercial advantage, which the data subject is entitled to share. In his 2019 State of the State speech, California governor Gavin Newsom proposed that a mechanism be developed to enable data subjects to share in financial gains associated with the use of their personal information.[100] In the 2020 democratic primary campaign, one candidate, Andrew Yang, similarly suggested that personal information should be treated as the property of the data subject and that data subjects should be compensated for its use by others.[101] Several working groups have since been formed to promote further development of this "data dividend" concept and to explore issues related to valuation, collection, and compensation methods associated with the sale of personal information by data subjects. Some of these groups set personal data ownership within the broader context of economic inequality and social reform.[102]

SUMMARY OF MAJOR POINTS

- The owner of information has the exclusive right to use it, reproduce it, alter it, disclose it, transfer it to another party, sell it, donate it, exchange it, bequeath it, destroy it, earn income from it, or use it as collateral for financing. Like other forms of property, information may be owned by an individual, a group, a business, a nonprofit entity, or, in the case of government records, the public.
- Most countries have laws that determine who can properly claim ownership of information and control its use, disclosure, transfer, and disposal for economic gain, to maintain personal privacy, to protect the welfare of individuals or the general public, or to achieve other objectives.
- Intellectual property laws have the dual purpose of encouraging writing, research, invention, artistic expression, and other activities that create information while allowing the information's owner to control and profit from it.
- An organization must be vigilant about infringement of its intellectual property rights. It also must be concerned about the possibility that its own business operations and the activities of its employees will infringe the intellectual property rights of others. Given the long periods of protection provided by intellectual property laws, there is ample time for these noncompliant events to occur.
- Copyright infringement occurs when a substantial part of a copyrighted work is reproduced, distributed, performed, exhibited, translated, adapted, or otherwise used without the permission of the copyright holder. Non-

compliance with copyright law is common and, given the wide range of circumstances in which it can occur, difficult to detect.

- Trademark infringement is the unauthorized use of a valid trademark or one that is similar enough to confuse a consumer. In some circumstances, trademark infringement can lead to criminal prosecution. More often, trademark infringement or dilution leads to civil litigation.
- As with copyright, patent infringement is common and difficult to detect. The more general and broadly useful the scope of a patent or industrial design, the greater the number of potential infringements, many of them unintentional. In some countries, patent infringement is a criminal offense that is punishable by a fine or imprisonment. More often, infringement is the subject of civil litigation.
- Infringement of a patent can be avoided by keeping an invention a trade secret rather than filing an application for patent protection. Legal protection of a trade secret remains in effect unless and until the secret is exposed. Misappropriation of trade secrets is a form of information theft.
- Ownership of government records is established by laws that give archival agencies possession of and control over government records to an extent typically associated with legal ownership. Archival laws in some eastern European and Asian countries carry the concept of information as public property a step further, claiming public ownership of culturally significant records maintained by private companies, religious bodies, nonprofit organizations, and other nongovernmental entities.
- Ownership of medical records is variously claimed by the health-care practitioners who created them; by the group practices, hospitals, and other health-care facilities that employ the health-care practitioners; and by patients, who are the subjects of the medical and personal information the records contain. In the United States, ownership is regulated by some state laws. Few other countries provide specific legal guidance about ownership of medical information.
- Most contracts and agreements include clauses that address ownership issues and property rights for information that an organization provides to contractors and that contractors may create or collect in the course of their work for a client organization.
- Cloud computing poses challenges for ownership and control of an organization's information. Cloud computing contracts typically require customers to grant them a license to host, store, use, and reproduce their intellectual property.
- Employment contracts must specify that any data, documents, or other information that employees create in the course of their assigned duties will be considered work for hire and that all copyright, patent, or other intellectual property rights to the information will be vested in the employer.
- When sharing trade secrets and other nonpublic business information with contractors, consultants, suppliers, business partners, job applicants, and

other non-employees, organizations typically rely on non-disclosure agreements that prohibit them from revealing the information to unauthorized parties.

- Contracts and agreements may be used to transfer ownership of information or intellectual property rights from one party to another, as in the case of mergers and acquisitions or information that is donated to an archives or other research repository.
- Compliance with intellectual property laws is a component of many ethical codes issued by professional associations, particularly those whose membership consists of information workers. Some ethical codes and professional practice rules also address issues related to ownership of client records in service industries.
- Internal mandates define information ownership rights and compliance requirements for an organization's employees and other workforce members, including trainees, paid and unpaid interns, temporary workers, volunteers, and others. These mandates may be specified in an information ownership policy or integrated into an organization's code of conduct.
- In most countries, intellectual property rights are considered a public good that encourages creativity and innovation, not merely for rights holders but for the benefit of society as a whole, but intellectual property rights are sometimes criticized for allowing state-enforced monopolies that unduly benefit rights holders to the ultimate detriment of society.
- Arguments for individual ownership personal information are variously based on moral or economic concepts. From a moral perspective, social activists, academics, and others view individual ownership of personal information as a fundamental human right. The economic argument recognizes the commercial value of personal information, which data subjects are entitled to share.

NOTES

1. *Collins Dictionary of Law, Third Edition* (Glasgow: Collins, 2006), quoted at https://legal-dictionary.thefreedictionary.com/ownership.
2. "Owner, n." *OED Online* (Oxford: Oxford University Press, 2013; updated 2022), https://www.oed.com/view/Entry/135516.
3. *Black's Law Dictionary, Sixth Edition* (St. Paul, MN: Thomson Reuters, 2021). The second edition is quoted at https://thelawdictionary.org/ownership/.
4. K. Vandervelde, "The new property of the nineteenth century: the development of the modern concept of property," *Buffalo Law Review* 29 (2), 325–67 (1980), https://digitalcommons.law.buffalo.edu/buffalolawreview/vol29/iss2/2.
5. *Encyclopedia Britannica* online, https://www.britannica.com/topic/ownership.
6. *Ruckelshaus v. Monsanto Co.*, 467 U.S. 986 (1984), https://supreme.justia.com/cases/federal/us/467/986/.
7. Example of publications that discuss the bundle of rights theory of property ownership include D. Johnson, "Reflections on the bundle of rights," *Vermont Law*

Review 32 (1), 247-79 (2007), https://lawreview.vermontlaw.edu/wp-content/uploads/2012/02/johnson2.pdf; J. Penner, "The bundle of rights picture of property," *UCLA Law Review* 43 (3), 711-820 (1996), http://hdl.handle.net/10822/528833; J. Baron, "Rescuing the bundle-of-rights metaphor in property law," *University of Cincinnati Law Review* 82 (1), 58-101 (2014), https://scholarship.law.uc.edu/cgi/viewcontent.cgi?referer=&httpsredir=1&article=1164&context=uclr; and H. Smith, "Property is not just a bundle of rights," *Econ Journal Watch* 8 (3), 279-91 (2011), https://econjwatch.org/articles/property-is-not-just-a-bundle-of-rights.

8. "What Is Intellectual Property?" https://www.wipo.int/about-ip/en/. See also *Understanding Industrial Property, Second Edition, WIPO Publication No. 895E* (Geneva: World Intellectual Property Organization, 2016), https://www.wipo.int/edocs/pubdocs/en/wipo_pub_895_2016.pdf.
9. The text of the Berne Convention is online at https://www.law.cornell.edu/treaties/berne/. On its history and development, see S. Ricketson and J. Ginsburg, *International Copyright and Neighboring Rights: the Berne Convention and Beyond, Third Edition* (Oxford: Oxford University Press, 2022), https://doi.org/10.1093/oso/9780198801986.001.0001.
10. The first sale doctrine is codified in 17 U.S.C. 109, https://www.law.cornell.edu/uscode/text/17/109. Examples of the many articles on the first sale doctrine include A. Katz, "The first sale doctrine and the economics of post-sale restraints," *Brigham Young University Law Review* 55 (1), 55-142 (2014), https://digitalcommons.law.byu.edu/cgi/viewcontent.cgi?article=2912&context=lawreview; H. Hovenkamp, "Post-sale restraints and competitive harm: the first sale doctrine in perspective," *NYU Annual Survey of American Law* 66 (2), 487-547 (2011), https://annualsurveyofamericanlaw.org/wp-content/uploads/2015/01/66-3_hovenkamp.pdf; L. Graham and S. McJohn, "Intellectual property's first sale doctrine and the policy against restraints on alienation," *Texas A&M Law Review* 7 (3), 497-541 (2020), https://scholarship.law.tamu.edu/cgi/viewcontent.cgi?article=1198&context=lawreview; R. Geist, "A 'license to read': the effect of e-books on publishers, libraries, and the first sale doctrine," *IDEA—The Intellectual Property Law Review* 52 (1), 63-100 (2012), https://ipmall.law.unh.edu/sites/default/files/hosted_resources/IDEA/idea-vol52-no1-geist.pdf; M. Rachman and J. Podolnick, "ReDigi and the application of the first sale doctrine to digital works," *NYSBA Bright Ideas* 28 (1), 9-12 (2019), https://www.dglaw.com/wp-content/uploads/2021/09/Bright_Ideas_Journal_ReDigi.pdf.
11. *Circular 92: Copyright Law of the United States and Related Laws Contained in Title 17 of the United States Code*, May 2021, https://copyright.gov/title17/.
12. Copyright Act, R.S.C., 1985, c. C-42, https://laws-lois.justice.gc.ca/eng/acts/c-42/.
13. Directive 2001/29/EC on the Harmonization of Certain Aspects of Copyright and Related Rights in the Information Society, https://eur-lex.europa.eu/legal-content/EN/TXT/?uri=CELEX%3A02001L0029-20190606.
14. See G. Bodenhausen, "Protection of 'neighboring rights'," *Law and Contemporary Problems*, 19, no. 2 (1954), 156-71, https://www.jstor.org/stable/1190485; H. Jehoram, "The nature of neighboring rights of performing artists, phonogram producers and broadcasting organizations," *Columbia-VLA Journal of Law & the Arts* 15, no. 1 (1991), 75-92, https://heinonline.org/HOL/LandingPage?handle=hein.journals/cjla15&div=18&id=&page=; R. Towse, "The singer or the song? Developments in

performers' rights from the perspective of a cultural economist," *Review of Law and Economics* 3, no. 3 (2007), 745-66, https://doi.org/10.2202/1555-5879.1158.
15. United States Copyright Office Annual Report, FY 2021, https://www.copyright.gov/reports/annual/2021/ar2021.pdf.
16. Examples of the many scholarly articles on fair use include P. Leval, "Toward a fair use standard," *Harvard Law Review* 103 (5), 1105-36 (1990), https://doi.org/10.2307/1341457; B. Beebe, "An empirical study of U.S. copyright fair use opinions," *University of Pennsylvania Law Review* 156 (3), 549-624 (2008), https://www.jstor.org/stable/40041357; L. Patterson, "Understanding fair use," *Law and Contemporary Problems* 55 (2), 249-66 (1992), https://doi.org/10.2307/1191784; and W. Fisher III, "Reconstructing the fair use doctrine," *Harvard Law Review* 101 (8), 1659-795 (1988), https://doi.org/10.2307/1341435.
17. *Copytrack Global Infringement Report 2019: International Image Theft in Comparison* (Berlin: Copytrack GmbH, 2019), https://www.copytrack.com/wp-content/uploads/2019/03/Global_Infringement_Report_2019_EN.pdf.
18. Status of automatically detected copyright claims to YouTube H1 2021, https://www.statista.com/statistics/1281165/automatic-copyright-claims-youtube-by-status/.
19. Guidance on article 17 of Directive 2019/790 on Copyright in the Digital Single Market, https://eur-lex.europa.eu/legal-content/EN/TXT/?qid=1625142238402&uri=CELEX%3A52021DC0288.
20. Public Law 105-304, Digital Millennium Copyright Act, https://www.congress.gov/105/plaws/publ304/PLAW-105publ304.pdf; Digital Millennium Copyright Act of 1998, U.S. Copyright Office Summary, December 1998, https://www.copyright.gov/legislation/dmca.pdf.
21. For a survey of national laws, see *Criminal Liability for Trademark Infringement: a Collaborative International Study*, prepared by Merchant & Gould, January 2021, https://www.vda.pt/xms/files/05_Publicacoes/2021/Criminal_Liability_ForTrademark_Infringement_STP_Chapter_VAN_JCA_CGR_01.2021.pdf.
22. "What is a patent?" https://www.wipo.int/patents/en/.
23. Norwegian Patents Act, Section 57, https://www.patentstyret.no/en/norwegian-patents-act.
24. Dutch Patents Act, article 79, https://english.rvo.nl/sites/default/files/2013/12/ROW95_ENG_niet_officiele_vertaling_0.pdf.
25. German Patents Act, Section 142, https://www.gesetze-im-internet.de/englisch_patg/englisch_patg.html.
26. On the criminal aspects of patent infringement, see J. Sherkow, "Patent infringement as criminal conduct," *Michigan Telecommunications and Technology Review* 19 (1), 2-41 (2012), https://repository.law.umich.edu/mttlr/vol19/iss1/1.
27. EC Regulation No 316/2014, https://eur-lex.europa.eu/legal-content/EN/TXT/PDF/?uri=CELEX:32014R0316&from=EN.
28. Uniform Trade Secrets Act with 1985 Amendments, https://www.uniformlaws.org/viewdocument/final-act-128?CommunityKey=3a2538fb-e030-4e2d-a9e2-90373dc05792&tab=librarydocuments.
29. 18 U.S.C. §§ 1831-1832, https://www.law.cornell.edu/uscode/text/18/part-I/chapter-90.
30. Public Law No. 114-153, https://www.congress.gov/bill/114th-congress/senate-bill/1890; 18 U.S.C. § 1836, https://www.law.cornell.edu/uscode/text/18/1836.

31. Directive (EU) 2016/943 on the protection of undisclosed know-how and business information (trade secrets) against their unlawful acquisition, use, and disclosure, https://eur-lex.europa.eu/eli/dir/2016/943/oj. See also *The Baseline of Trade Secrets Litigation in the EU Member States* (Alicante, Spain: European Union Intellectual Property Office, 2018), https://op.europa.eu/en/publication-detail/-/publication/25fe67c7-bc82-11e8-99ee-01aa75ed71a1/language-en.
32. Criminal Code, R.S.C., 1985, c. C-46, Section 391, https://laws-lois.justice.gc.ca/eng/acts/c-46/page-53.html-docCont.
33. No. 50, 2001 as amended, https://www.legislation.gov.au/Details/C2022C00215.
34. Act No. 9537, https://www.kipo.go.kr/upload/en/download/UnfairAct.pdf.
35. Anti-Unfair Competition Law, as amended, https://www.hongfanglaw.com/wp-content/uploads/2019/10/Anti-Unfair-Competition-Law-of-the-Peoples-Republic-of-China-2019-AmendmentEnglish.pdf.
36. Examples of the many publications on the inevitable disclosure doctrine include S. Lowry, "Inevitable disclosure trade secret disputes: dissolutions of concurrent property interests," *Stanford Law Review* 40, no. 2 (1988), 519–44, https://www.jstor.org/stable/1228823; J. Edelstein, "Intellectual slavery?: The doctrine of inevitable disclosure of trade secrets," *Golden Gate University Law Review* 26, no. 3 (1996), 717–36, https://digitalcommons.law.ggu.edu/cgi/viewcontent.cgi?article=1686&context=ggulrev; J. Saulino, "Locating inevitable disclosure's place in trade secret analysis," *Michigan Law Review* 100, no. 5 (2002), 1184–214, https://repository.law.umich.edu/cgi/viewcontent.cgi?article=1901&context=mlr; E. Rowe, "When trade secrets become shackles: fairness and the inevitable disclosure doctrine," *Tulane Journal of Technology and Intellectual Property Law* 7, no. 2 (2005), 169–226, https://scholarship.law.ufl.edu/cgi/viewcontent.cgi?article=1065&context=facultypub; R. Wiesner, "A state-by-state analysis of inevitable disclosure: a need for uniformity and a workable standard," *Intellectual Property Law Review* 16, no. 1 (2012), 211–29, http://scholarship.law.marquette.edu/cgi/viewcontent.cgi?article=1187&context=iplr; M. Reder and C. O'Brien, "Managing the risk of trade secret loss due to job mobility in an innovation economy with the theory of inevitable disclosure," *Journal of High Technology Law* 12, no. 2 (2012), 373–449, http://hdl.handle.net/2345/2632; M. Flowers, "Facing the inevitable: the inevitable disclosure doctrine and the Defend Trade Secrets Act of 2016," *Washington and Lee Law Review* 75, no. 4 (2019), 2207–63, https://scholarlycommons.law.wlu.edu/cgi/viewcontent.cgi?article=4631&context=wlulr.
37. 44 U.S.C. 3301, https://www.law.cornell.edu/uscode/text/44/3301. See also W. Ginsberg, *Common Questions about Federal Records and Related Agency Requirements* (Washington, D.C.: Congressional Research Service, 2015), https://sgp.fas.org/crs/secrecy/R43072.pdf.
38. 44 U.S.C. Chapter 22, https://www.law.cornell.edu/uscode/text/44/chapter-22.
39. 5 ILCS 160/3, https://www.ilga.gov/legislation/ilcs/ilcs3.asp?ActID=86&ChapterID=2.
40. Utah Code 63A-12-105, https://le.utah.gov/xcode/Title63A/Chapter12/C63A-12-S105_1800010118000101.pdf.
41. N.C. Gen. Stats., 132-1, https://www.ncleg.net/enactedlegislation/statutes/html/bysection/chapter_132/gs_132-1.html.

42. Tex. Govt. Code, 441-180, https://www.tsl.texas.gov/slrm/pubs/bulletin4 - s441181.
43. P. Grimsted, "Lenin's archival decree of 1918: the Bolshevik legacy for Soviet archival theory and practice," *American Archivist* 45 (4), 429-43 (1982), https://doi.org/10.17723/aarc.45.4.tjn581l686q4u0r1.
44. See, for example, the Law on Archives of the People's Republic of China, especially articles 16-17, https://sgp.fas.org/prcarch.html.
45. For a more detailed discussion of the inalienability of archival records, see E. Ketelaar, *Archival and Records Management Legislation and Regulations: a RAMP Study with Guidelines* (Paris: UNESCO, 1985), https://unesdoc.unesco.org/ark:/48223/pf0000064948.
46. 18 U.S.C. 641, https://www.law.cornell.edu/uscode/text/18/641; 18 U.S.C. 2071, https://www.law.cornell.edu/uscode/text/18/2071; 36 C.F.R. 1230.12.
47. Law No. 43 of 2009 on Records and Archives Administration, article 81, https://jdih.anri.go.id/peraturan/Law Of The Republic Of Indonesia Number 43 Of 2009.pdf.
48. A 2019 bill, the Own Your Own Data Act (S.806), that addressed ownership of data posed on social media was introduced in the U.S. Senate. It was referred to committee. See https://www.congress.gov/bill/116th-congress/senate-bill/806?q=%7B"search"%3A%5B"own+your+data+act"%5D%7D&s=1&r=1.
49. This definition is adapted from 29 C.F.R. 825.125, which is part of the regulations for the Family and Medical Leave Act. See https://www.law.cornell.edu/cfr/text/29/part-825/subpart-A.
50. On the complexity of patient ownership of medical information, see J. Contreras, "The false promise of health data ownership," *New York University Law Review* 94 (4), 624-61 (2019), https://dc.law.utah.edu/cgi/viewcontent.cgi?article=1263&-context=scholarship; M. Hall and K. Schulman, "Ownership of medical information," *JAMA* 301 (12), 1282-84 (2009), https://doi.org/10.1001/jama.2009.389; K. Liddell et al., "Patient data ownership: who owns your health?" *Journal of Law and Biosciences* 8 (2), lsab023, (2021), https://doi.org/10.1093/jlb/lsab023; J. Koskinen et al., "The concept of Datenherrschaft of patient information from a Lockean perspective," *Journal of Information Communication and Ethics in Society* 14 (1), 70-86 (2016), https://doi.org/10.1108/JICES-06-2014-0029; L. Smith et al., "Health information ownership: legal theories and policy implications," *Vanderbilt Journal of Entertainment & Technology Law* 9 (2), 207-41 (2016), https://scholarship.law.vanderbilt.edu/cgi/viewcontent.cgi?article=1117&context=jetlaw. On patient empowerment and medical records, see L. Kish and E. Topol, "Unpatients—why patients should own their medical data," *Nature Biotechnology* 33 (9), 921-24 (2015), https://doi.org/10.1038/nbt.3340; S. Ross and C. Lin, "The effects of promoting patient access to medical records: a review," *Journal of the American Medical Informatics Association* 10 (2), 129-38 (2003), https://doi.org/10.1136/jamia.2003.294; M Anshari, "Redefining electronic health records (EHR) and electronic medical records (EMR) to promote patient empowerment," *International Journal of Informatics for Development* 8 (1), 35-39 (2019), https://doi.org/10.14421/ijid.2019.08106; T. Rising et al., "Evaluating patient empowerment in association with eHealth technology," *Journal of Medical Internet Research* 19 (9), e329, https://doi.org/10.2196/jmir.7809; T. Giardina et al., "Patient access to medical records and healthcare outcomes: a systematic review," *Journal of the American*

Medical Informatics Association 21 (4), 737–41 (2014), https://doi.org/10.1136/amiajnl-2013-002239.

51. See, for example, https://www.jucm.com/owns-patient-medical-records/, which states that "historically, individuals own their own medical information."
52. N.H. Rev. Stat. Ann. 151.21, http://www.gencourt.state.nh.us/rsa/html/xi/151/151-mrg.htm.
53. Ga. Code, 31-33-3, https://codes.findlaw.com/ga/title-31-health/ga-code-sect-31-33-3.html.
54. Fla. Stat. Ann. 456.057, https://www.flsenate.gov/laws/statutes/2011/456.057.
55. Wyo. Code R. 024-052-003, https://rules.wyo.gov/Search.aspx?mode=7.
56. S.C. Code Ann., 44-115-10 et seq., https://www.scstatehouse.gov/code/t44c115.php.
57. See, for example, Cal. Code Regs., tit. 22, 70751, https://www.law.cornell.edu/regulations/california/22-CCR-70751; 7 AAC 12.770, https://www.law.cornell.edu/regulations/alaska/7-AAC-12.770; Md. Code Regs. 10.01.16.04, https://www.law.cornell.edu/regulations/maryland/COMAR-10-01-16-04; and Kan. Admin. Regs. 28-34-9a, https://www.law.cornell.edu/regulations/kansas/K-A-R-28-34-9a.
58. In the best known of these cases, a Texas court ruled that the entire contents of an attorney's client file belongs to the client. Resolution Trust Corp. v. H_____, P.C., 128 F.R.D. 647 (N.D. Tex. 1989), https://casetext.com/case/resolution-trust-corp-v-h____-pc. Similarly, a New Mexico court found that, as a general principle of law, client files belong to the client. Grand Jury Proceedings, 727 F.2d 941 (10th Cir. 1984), https://casetext.com/case/in-re-grand-jury-proceedings-26. Some countries have legislation that addresses ownership of client records. In Germany, for example, Section 50 of the Federal Code for Lawyers states that attorneys must hand over to clients any documents they have received from them or on their behalf. See https://www.gesetze-im-internet.de/englisch_brao/englisch_brao.html.
59. *McInerney v. MacDonald*, 126 NBR (2d) 271, June 11, 1992, https://ca.vlex.com/vid/mcinerney-v-macdonald-680659877.
60. Law No. 36 of 2014, Section 71, https://www.ilo.org/dyn/natlex/natlex4.detail?p_lang=en&p_isn=98589. See also A. Erawati and H. Iswandari, "Ownership of medical records in Indonesia: discourse on legal certainty and justice," *Udayana Journal of Law and Culture* 6 (2), 184–203 (2022), https://doi.org/10.24843/UJLC.2022.v06.i02.p04.
61. M. Nakamura, "Current status of electronic medical recording in Japan," *JMAJ* 49 (2), 70–80 (2006), https://www.med.or.jp/english/pdf/2006_02/070_080.pdf; S. Nagaoka, "The disclosure of medical records to patients: the Japanese experience," *Journal of Philosophy and Ethics in Health Care and Medicine* 6, 39–61 (2012), https://itetsu.jp/main/wp-content/uploads/2012/11/6-3NAGAOKA.pdf; H. Hattori et al., "The patient's right to information in Japan—legal rules and doctor's opinions," *Social Science & Medicine* 32 (9), 1007–16 (1991), https://doi.org/10.1016/0277-9536(91)90158-9.
62. 17 U.S.C. § 101, https://codes.findlaw.com/us/title-17-copyrights/17-usc-sect-101.html; I. Hardy, "An economic understanding of copyright law's work-made-for-hire doctrine," *Columbia-VLA Journal of Law & the Arts* 12 (1), 181–227 (1988), https://scholarship.law.wm.edu/cgi/viewcontent.cgi?article=2120&context=facpubs.

63. R. Saka, "Confidential ideas and independent contractors: trade secret ownership in the age of the hired gun," *Hastings Business Law Journal* 10, no. 1 (2014), 245-69, https://repository.uchastings.edu/cgi/viewcontent.cgi?article=1044&context=hastings_business_law_journal; S. MacDougall and D. Hurst, "Identifying tangible costs, benefits and risks of an investment in intellectual capital," *Journal of Intellectual Capital* 6, no. 1 (2005). 53-71, https://doi.org/10.1108/14691930510574663 notes the risks associated with exposing contingent workers to confidential competitive information.
64. On European copyright provisions, see R. Jacobs, "Work-for-hire and the moral right dilemma in the European Community: a U.S. perspective," *Boston College International and Comparative Law Review* 16, no. 1 (1993), 29-79, https://lawdigitalcommons.bc.edu/cgi/viewcontent.cgi?article=1318&context=iclr.
65. D. Almeling et al., "A statistical analysis of trade secret litigation in federal courts," *Gonzaga Law Review* 45 (2), 291-334 (2010), https://www.tradesecretsandemployeemobility.com/files/2014/05/Statistical-Analysis-of-Trade-Secret-Litigation-in.pdf; D. Almeling et al., "A statistical analysis of trade secret litigation in state courts," *Gonzaga Law Review* 46 (1), 57-101 (2010), https://www.tradesecretslaw.com/wp-content/uploads/sites/232/uploads/file/Statistical Analysis of Trade Secret Litigation in State Courts.pdf; C. Bast, "At what price silence: are confidentiality agreements enforceable?" *William Mitchell Law Review* 25 (2), 627-714 (1999), https://open.mitchellhamline.edu/cgi/viewcontent.cgi?article=1914&context=wmlr.
66. ALA Code of Ethics, https://www.ala.org/tools/ethics.
67. IFLA Code of Ethics for Librarians and other Information Workers, https://www.ifla.org/publications/ifla-code-of-ethics-for-librarians-and-other-information-workers-full-version/.
68. AIIP Code of Ethical Business Practice, https://www.aiip.org/about/professional-standards.
69. ISMPP Code of Ethics for Medical Research Publication: Principles for Publication Professionals, https://www.ismpp.org/ethics.
70. ACM Code of Ethics and Professional Conduct, https://ethics.acm.org/code-of-ethics/previous-versions/1992-acm-code/; Software Engineering Code of Ethics and Professional Practice, https://ethics.acm.org/code-of-ethics/software-engineering-code/.
71. IWA Code of Ethics, https://iwanet.org/about/code-of-ethics/.
72. Code of Ethics and Professional Practices for Collections Professionals, https://www.aam-us.org/wp-content/uploads/2021/03/Code_Ethics_Collections_Professionals_2021_02_24.pdf.
73. IRWA Code of Ethics, https://www.irwaonline.org/about-us/code-of-ethics/; UFI Code of Ethics, https://www.ufi.org/industry-resources/intellectual-property-rights/ufi-code-of-ethics/; PRSA Code of Ethics, https://www.prsa.org/about/ethics/prsa-code-of-ethics.
74. NSPE Code of Ethics, https://www.nspe.org/resources/ethics/code-ethics.
75. AICPA Code of Professional Conduct, https://pub.aicpa.org/codeofconduct/Ethics.aspx.
76. CIMA, Ownership and Withholding of Client Documents, https://www.cimaglobal.com/Documents/Members handbook/Guidance on withheld documents.pdf.

77. ABA Formal Opinion 471, https://www.ycrlaw.com/wp-content/uploads/aba-formal-opinion-471-07012015-pdf-daf0.pdf; New York City Bar, Formal Opinion 2008-01, https://www.nycbar.org/member-and-career-services/committees/reports-listing/reports/detail/formal-opinion-2008-01-a-lawyers-ethical-obligations-to-retain-and-to-provide-a-client-with-electronic-documents-relating-to-a-representation. See also NYC Bar, Formal Opinion 1986-4, https://www.nycbar.org/member-and-career-services/committees/reports-listing/reports/detail/formal-opinion-1986-4.
78. See, for example, Practice Resource: Ownership of Documents in a Client's File, prepared by the Law Society of British Columbia, https://www.lawsociety.bc.ca/Website/media/Shared/docs/practice/resources/ClientFiles-ownership.pdf; see also Guide to Retention and Destruction of Client Files for Lawyers, Appendix 2, issued by the Law Society of Ontario, https://lso.ca/lawyers/practice-supports-and-resources/topics/managing-files/file-retention-and-destruction.
79. The Law Society, Ownership of Documents, https://www.lawsociety.org.uk/topics/client-care/ownership-of-documents.
80. Fact Sheet 14, File Ownership and Handling, https://www.olsc.nsw.gov.au/Documents/Fact Sheet 14 File Ownership July2015 AC.pdf.
81. File Ownership, Retention and Destruction Guidelines, https://www.liv.asn.au/download.aspx?DocumentVersionKey=73dcb2c9-df65-41b1-8dc7-8ef86840a5bf.
82. On the relationship between the Statute of Anne and American copyright law, see O. Bracha, "The Statute of Anne: an American mythology," *Houston Law Review* 47 (4), 877-918, https://houstonlawreview.org/article/4176-the-statute-of-anne-an-american-mythology; O. Bracha, "The adventures of the Statute of Anne in the land of unlimited possibilities: the life of a legal transplant," *Berkeley Technology Law Journal* 25 (3), 1427–73 (2010), https://www.jstor.org/stable/24119471.
83. R. Posner, "The law & economics of intellectual property," *Daedalus* 131 (2), 5-12 (2002), https://www.jstor.org/stable/20027754.
84. For a discussion, see J. Siegel, "The Coens' *O Brother, Where Art Thou?* and Homer's *Odyssey*," *Mouseion: Journal of the Classical Association of Canada* 7 (3), 213-45 (2007), https://doi.org/10.1353/mou.0.0029; M. Toscano, "Homer meets the Coen brothers: memory as artistic pastiche in *O Brother, Where Art Thou?*" *Film & History* 39 (2), 49–62 (2009), https://doi.org/10.1353/flm.0.0125.
85. H. Johnson, "The Wright patent wars and early American aviation," *Journal of Air Law and Commerce* 69 (1), 21-63 (2004), https://scholar.smu.edu/jalc/vol69/iss1/3; D. Lea, "From the Wright brothers to Microsoft: issues in the moral grounding of intellectual property rights," *Business Ethics Quarterly* 16 (4), 579–98 (2006), https://doi.org/10.5840/beq200616450.
86. C. Welsh, "Patents and competition in the automobile industry," *Law and Contemporary Problems* 13 (2), 260–77 (1948), https://www.jstor.org/stable/1189998.
87. M. Avery, "Continuing abuse of the Hatch-Waxman Act by pharmaceutical patent holders and the failure of the 2003 amendments," *Hastings Law Journal* 60 (1), 171-200 (2008), https://repository.uchastings.edu/hastings_law_journal/vol60/iss1/6; D. Matthews and O. Gurgula, "Patent strategies and competition law in the pharmaceutical sector: implications for access to medicines," *European Intellectual Property Review* 38 (11), 661-67 (2016), http://qmro.qmul.ac.uk/xmlui/handle/123456789/13672.

88. Note, "Copyright reform and the takings clause," *Harvard Law Review* 128 (3), 973-94 (2015), https://harvardlawreview.org/2015/01/copyright-reform-and-the-takings-clause/.
89. S. Lester and H. Zhu, "Rethinking the length of patent terms," *American University International Law Review* 34 (4), 788-806 (2019), https://digitalcommons.wcl.american.edu/auilr/vol34/iss4/4; L. Ouellette and H. Williams, *Reforming the Patent System* (Washington, D.C.: The Hamilton Project, Brookings Institution, 2020), https://www.hamiltonproject.org/assets/files/Ouellette_Williams_LO_6.16_FINAL.pdf.
90. E. Lin, *Recommendations for Statutory Reform of the Patent Term Extension System to Increase Public Accountability and Fight Soaring Drug Prices* (New York: New York University School of Law, Engelbert Center on Innovation Law & Policy, 2021), https://www.law.nyu.edu/sites/default/files/recommendations-for-statutor-reform-of-the-patent-term-extension-system-2021-03.pdf.
91. H. Pearce, "Personality, property, and other provocations: exploring the conceptual muddle of data protection rights under EU law," *European Data Protection Law Review* 4 (2), 190-208 (2018), https://doi.org/10.21552/edpl/2018/2/8; J. Victor, "The EU General Data Protection Regulation: toward a property regime for protecting data privacy," *Yale Law Journal* 123 (2), 513-28 (2013), https://www.yalelawjournal.org/comment/the-eu-general-data-protection-regulation-toward-a-property-regime-for-protecting-data-privacy; N. Purtova, "The illusion of personal data as no one's property," *Law, Innovation and Technology* 7 (1), 83-111 (2015), https://doi.org/10.1080/17579961.2015.1052646.
92. Cited in D. Glancy, "Personal information as intellectual property," https://www.law.berkeley.edu/files/bclt_IPSC2010_Glancy2.pdf.
93. S. Attar and F. Parvin, "The EU law and the challenge of data ownership in the era of the digital economy," *International Law Review* 38 (65), 281-304 (2021), https://doi.org/10.22066/CILAMAG.2021.245186.
94. *Data Management and Use: Governance in the 21st Century: A Joint Report by the British Academy and the Royal Society* (London: Royal Society, 2017), https://royalsociety.org/-/media/policy/projects/data-governance/data-management-governance.pdf.
95. See, for example, S. Black, "Who owns your data?" *Indiana Law Review* 54 (2), 305-39 (2021), https://papers.ssrn.com/sol3/papers.cfm?abstract_id=3987369; V. Bergelson, "It's personal but is it mine? Toward property rights in personal information," *UC Davis Law Review* 37 (2), 379-451 (2003), https://doi.org/10.7282/00000015.
96. The wild animals theory is based on the much-discussed court decision in *Pierson v. Post* (3 Cai R. 175). A. Fernandez, "The lost record of *Pierson v. Post*, the famous fox case," *Law and History Review* 27 (1), 149-78 (2009), https://doi.org/10.1017/S0738248000001693; D. Dharmapala and R. Pitchford, "An economic analysis of 'riding to the hounds': *Pierson v. Post* revisited," *Journal of Law, Economics, and Organization* 18 (1), 39-66 (2002), https://doi.org/10.1093/jleo/18.1.39.
97. P. Hummel et al., "Own data? Ethical reflections on data ownership," *Philosophy & Technology* 34 (3), 545-72 (2021), https://do i.org/10.1007/s13347-020-00404-9; *Big Data and Health—Data Sovereignty as the Shaping of Informational Freedom* (Berlin: German Ethics Council, 2017), https://www.ethikrat.org/en/publications/publication-details/?tx_wwt3shop_detail%5Bproduct%5D=4&tx_wwt3shop_

detail%5Baction%5D=index&tx_wwt3shop_detail%5Bcontroller%5D=Products&cHash=7bb9aadb656b877f9dbd49a61e39df2f; P. Hummel et al., "Data sovereignty: a review," *Big Data & Society* 8 (1), online open access, https://doi.org/10.1177/2053951720982012.

98. Universal Declaration of Human Rights, https://www.un.org/en/about-us/universal-declaration-of-human-rights; Convention for the Protection of Human Rights and Fundamental Freedoms, https://www.unhcr.org/4d93501a9.pdf; European Convention on Human Rights, https://www.echr.coe.int/documents/convention_eng.pdf.
99. N. Purtova, "Property in personal data: a European perspective on the instrumentalist theory of propertisation," 2 (3), 193–208 (2010), https://ejls.eui.eu/wp-content/uploads/sites/32/pdfs/The_Future_of_Autumn_Winter_2010/A_EUROPEAN_PERSPECTIVE_ON_THE_INSTRUMENTALIST_ PROPERTY_IN_PERSONAL_DATA_.pdf.
100. "Governor Newsom delivers State of State address," February 12, 2019, https://www.gov.ca.gov/2019/02/12/state-of-the-state-address/; Newsom's State of the State, annotated, https://calmatters.org/politics/2019/02/newsom-state-of-the-state-annotated/.
101. "Op Ed: Andrew Yang: Make tech companies pay for your data," *Los Angeles Times*, June 23, 2020, https://www.latimes.com/opinion/story/2020-06-23/andrew-yang-data-dividend-tech-privacy.
102. Y. Feygin et al., *A Data Dividend That Works: Steps Toward Building an Equitable Data Economy* (Los Angeles: Berggruen Institute, 2021), https://www.berggruen.org/ideas/articles/a-data-dividend-that-works-steps-toward-building-an-equitable-data-economy/; J. Muldoon, "Data-owning democracy or digital socialism," *Critical Review of International Social and Political Philosophy*, September 2022, open access, https://doi.org/10.1080/13698230.2022.2120737; A. Collis et al., *Information Frictions and Heterogeneity in Valuations of Personal Data*, November 2021, https://papers.ssrn.com/sol3/papers.cfm?abstract_id=3974826.

Index

About the Author

William Saffady is an independent records management and information governance consultant and researcher based in New York City. He is the author of over three dozen books and many articles on records management, record retention, document storage and retrieval technologies, and other information management topics. His latest books are *Managing Information Risks: Threats, Vulnerabilities, and Responses*, which was published by Rowman & Littlefield in 2020, and *Records and Information Management: Fundamentals of Professional Practice, Fourth Edition*, which was published by Rowman & Littlefield in 2021. He received his BA degree from Central Michigan University and his MS, PhD, and MSLS degrees from Wayne State University. Before establishing his full-time consulting practice, he was a professor of library and information science at the State University of New York at Albany, Long Island University, Pratt Institute, and Vanderbilt University. He is a fellow of ARMA International and is profiled in the *Encyclopedia of Archival Writers, 1515–2015*, a reference work published by Rowman & Littlefield in 2019.

www.ingramcontent.com/pod-product-compliance
Ingram Content Group UK Ltd.
Pitfield, Milton Keynes, MK11 3LW, UK
UKHW012043150926
475560UK00001B/157

9 781538 167663